A SHIP'S LOG BOOK II

by

CAPTAIN FRANK F. FARRAR

Being a chronicle of some of his voyages, together with

his thoughts and viewpoints pertaining thereto.

Published by
The Sextant Press
P.O. Box 51-0131
Melbourne Beach, FL 32951

The Sextant Press
P.O.Box 51-0131.
Melbourne Beach, FL 32951

©1992 by Frank F. Farrar

Library of Congress Catalog Card Number 88-081968

ISBN: 0-8200-1036-7

Photo credits

CONTENTS

CONTENTS (CONTINUED)

FOREWORD

The largest gap which we have in our knowledge of America's merchant marine is for the period which encompasses the early years of steam-driven cargo ships; that is, the years from 1860 up to and including World War II. Records of the trade routings of the earlier days, the ships, and of the men who sailed them are disappointingly lacking. The later World War II is no exception to this sparsity.

Custom House statistics disclose that at the outbreak of the Civil War, 66.5% of our foreign commerce was carried in American bottoms. Then followed the so-called "flight from the flag," a result of high insurance rates brought about by the threat of Confederate raiders. By 1870, American bottoms carried only 33% of our foreign trade, a complete reversal of the proud position our merchant fleet had held before the war. By 1890, American shipping accounted for less than 13% of exports and imports.

When we mobilized for the war with Spain in 1898, we suffered the humiliation of having to send a large part of our troops to Cuba and Puerto Rico on ships purchased from British companies. We learned then that a nation surrounded by the sea was ill-fitted to wage war upon foreign shores without a merchant fleet suited for troop lift and resupply. With peace, the lesson was soon neglected, and we allowed our merchant marine to again degenerate into a coastal transport system.

By 1915, U.S. shipping company participation in our carriage of foreign trade was back to the dismal point where it had been in 1890. In an attempt to alleviate that disparity and to prepare us for war should we become directly involved, the Congress passed the Shipping Act of 1916. Its preamble read:

"To establish a United States Shipping Board for the purpose of encouraging, developing and creating a naval auxiliary and naval reserve and a merchant marine to meet the requirements of the commerce of the United States within its territories and possessions and with foreign countries..."

This time, better prepared than in 1898, we entered the World War in 1917. By the time the conflict ended, we had a merchant fleet which rivaled that of the major maritime powers. But our shipping position at 43 % in foreign trade by 1920, still did not meet the parity it should have had. By 1928, the volume of trade carried in our own ships had dropped to 34 %. Congress hoped that the Jones-White Act would provide a cure by funneling federal subsidies (in the form of mail contracts) to those ship owners engaged in the Atlantic trade. But before the effect of that assistance could be realized, along came the world depression and most of the hopes evaporated.

In 1931, over 4,500,000 Americans were out of work. No solution was in sight to alleviate the unemployment. Shipping, as is usually the case in such a time, was one of the first industries to feel the pinch. During that same year, Japan chose to march into Manchuria, a direct violation of the Kellogg-Briand Pact which had as its purpose the outlawing of war. Japan, a signatory to the Pact, had by its invasion of another-stepped across that threshold which would lead the world again to war.

It was also during that year (1931) that Frank Farrar entered the maritime industry when, as a 16-year old, he walked up the gangway of his first ship.

His subsequent career from deck boy to master would include the Great Depression, World War II, and the immediate years that followed. He was destined to witness, during that time, an ascendancy of America's shipping industry to the point in 1945 when, as a nation, we boasted the largest tonnage of any merchant fleet in history. He was sad witness to that fleet's postwar decline, back to the level of a third rate maritime power.

Farrar's experiences, told here in essay form, speak not only of the years of peace and war, but they also relate to the change in one man's attitudes as he progresses from focsle to master's cabin. In a low key style that reflects the writer's professionalism as a mariner, he episodically describes the experiences
he best remembers.

Captain Farrar goes a long way in filling a void in the literature of the seaman's occupation. His work is invaluable in aiding us to understand the human element of that era which has regrettably been so neglected by technical historians.

Charles Dana Gibson

PREFACE

The writer begs the forgiveness of the reader for any inaccuracies of dates, places, and the characters, all of whom were real.

One's memory can play tricks, and some of the events took place upwards of fifty years ago.

It has been most difficult to stick to the truth. It has been tempting to exaggerate, but to the best of my recollection, all the happenings took place as I have described them.

Captain Frank F. Farrar

DEDICATION

For some time I have pondered who to dedicate these stories to. There is no one that I can thank, because I wrote them all alone.

Then it came to me. I'll dedicate them to the men and ships that they came from.

So these stories are in memory of my many shipmates and the ships that we sailed.

"Fools walk in where angels fear to tread. "
Alexander Page

-1-

EASTBOUND TO THE BALTIC

(STUCK IN THE ICE)

The log book of a deepwater vessel is like a skeleton. Dry bones—a framework of terse phrases. The body, the flesh and blood, are hidden between the lines, concealed by the stilted, abbreviated notations. To the initiated, though, there are stories of high adventure to be found in those tattered, salt-stained chronicles. One accustomed to reading between the lines may come upon deeds of heroism, of danger, suffering and misery. Death, too is often present, peering over the shoulder of some tired, forgotten deck officer as he makes his brief entries by the fitful light of a swaying lamp.

I am a shipmaster who has *swallowed* the anchor, a term used by seafarers for one who has left the sea and come ashore. Tonight, as I sit before the fireplace, safe and warm on dry land, the urge to reminisce is strong. In the bookcase beside me are several old log books of my voyages. Taking one at random, I idly turn the pages. As my eyes skim over the entries made so long ago, I am no longer aware of the fire and the warmth. I am again, a young Captain, worried, tired, and more than a little apprehensive. My gaze centered on an entry made one cold winter day.

S.S. THEODORE PARKER, FEB. 5TH,
NOON POSITION-LAT. 58-41, NORTH.
LONG. 9-23, West.   SEA.   SLIGHT.
COURSE 089 DEGREES, TRUE.
SPEED, 10.3 KNOTS.   APPROACHING
PENTLAND FIRTH. 4.00 P.M. ON SOU-
NDINGS, 150 FATHOMS.   SIGHTED
THE FLANNEN LIGHT, BEARING 173
DEGREES, TRUE. RADIO DIRECTION
FINDER BEARING OF THE BUTT OF
LEWIS, 100 DEGREES, TRUE. SOUND-
INGS, 75 FATHOMS, INDICATE VES-
SEL TWO MILES INSIDE OF COURSE.
CHANGED COURSE TO 087, TRUE.

In my mind's eye, I am once more on the bridge of that rusty tramp,

1

loaded to her marks with coal, bound from Norfolk to Copenhagen. At the onset of the voyage, I had made my decision to proceed by way of Pentland Firth, a narrow, desolate strip of water separating the Northern tip of Scotland from the Orkney Islands, rather than go by way of the South of England and the English Channel. Pentland Firth is one of the world's worst places to navigate, but my destination was a day's run shorter by this route. I was young and ambitious, and anxious to show my owners that they had chosen wisely when they placed me in command. Now I was not so sure. The *Sailing Directions*, which I had been studying all the way up the Great Circle route, had nothing encouraging to say. The Firth was not to be taken lightly. Heavy fog prevailed most of the time. The passage was very narrow and obstructed by two rocky islands. No anchorages were available in the locality. But these were minor compared to the fearful tides for which the Firth was noted. Twice in every twenty-four hours the tidal flow from the North Sea rushes through this bottleneck on its way to and from the Atlantic Ocean, amassing, in the Firth, the incredible rate of ten knots. The *Sailing Directions* explained very clearly that when this tremendous flow of water passing over a shallow bottom, met with winds in the opposite direction, even slight winds, a sea was swept up which had swamped and capsized many vessels. Throughout, caution and prudence were emphasized. But, the die had been cast. The Flannens, a group of islands lying off the Northwest coast of Scotland, were in sight and the Firth itself, only twelve hours over the horizon.

My glance lifted from the page. The fire burned steadily. Another log would be superfluous. This was living! Night coming on: February, a winter's night. A heaving deck underfoot. All snug below decks and all secured topside. The day watch would be coming off watch to a brightly lighted messroom and a hot supper. The young Skipper on his black, windswept bridge had no regrets. No thoughts of lights and warmth and home crept into his mind. Rather, a feeling of elation, born partly of fear, buoyed him and made him disdain the Mate's suggestion that he slip below for a bite. Those feelings that he had could be compared to those of a craftsman's fierce pride in his creation; of a job well done. Work for work's sake? Maybe, but this man was experiencing pride and satisfaction a bit prematurely. The job was yet to be done. And was it such a feat? Ships traversed this passage daily. Why should he, standing there, feel that this was such a challenge? Probably because it was his first time. I don't know, because it was I that stood there. I only knew that I felt good. I would do something that was quite commonplace, that was expected of me, that I was paid to do. Yet, knowing this, I still had wished and hoped all my life for the chance of being Master of my own ship. *Well, here it was. What do you do next, smart guy?*

Again my gaze lifted, and as I thought back, I wondered. Were those feelings as strong as they seemed in remembrance? Sitting by the fire, I could still feel them as though it were tonight. The Mate had thoughtfully taken the chair from his stateroom, lengthened the legs, and had it installed on the bridge for my comfort. (Oddly enough, I had done the same thing when I was Mate.)

Settled in the chair, I took stock. The night was dark but clear. The sea was slight with a moderate ground swell. Plans must be made, I reminded myself. But they had all been made. Daily, during the voyage I had charted the courses through the Firth, and committed them to memory, because once a vessel started through, there would be no time to go into the chart room and mess around with parallel rulers and dividers. Sharp turns abounded and there would be no time for reflection and indecision. The whole night was before me, and inaction makes one restless. *Go over everything again. Make sure.* On my knees was a small chart of the area. All the courses, bearings, and distances had been carefully inked in. Tide Tables were at hand. Another peek at them, with the Mate holding a flashlight, verified what I had known for a week. A fair tide, just commencing, and therefore of small strength, would occur at six A.M. the next morning. An ideal time to transit the Firth. Just conn her through like an automobile on a curving stretch of road. Nothing to it, I reassured myself. All this occupied ten minutes. Still a long night ahead.

Summoning the Chief Engineer, a discussion was held on speed, propeller revolutions per minute, and the stupidity of engineers as compared to the super-intelligence of all deck officers. He tramped off the bridge muttering something about what would *they* do without engines. Feeling better about the whole thing, I sent for the Chief Steward and complained bitterly about the way eggs were being fried on this ship. *Not fit for a dog, Steward.*

Quietness settled in. Also, the best part of an hour had passed. Somewhat mollified by this unnecessary display of authority, I decided that a sandwich or two would be in order. The Steward will never believe that it wasn't spite, because, unthinkingly, I ordered a couple of fried egg sandwiches.

> *9:20 P.M.   SIGHTED CAPE WRATH.*
> *CROSS BEARINGS OF THE CAPE AND*
> *THE BUTT OF LEWIS INDICATES VES-*
> *SEL ONE MILE OUTSIDE OF COURSE.*
> *SPEED ELEVEN KNOTS.*

Cape Wrath, one of the bleakest spots to be found on this earth. Here, against its headlands beats the whole Western Ocean. Gales, originating in Labrador and Newfoundland, sweep Eastward, skirting the Southern tip of Greenland, gaining in force and piling huge seas before them. Nothing obstructs them until they reach Cape Wrath. It has been written that the seas pounding on the Northwest coast of Scotland have sent spray a hundred feet into the air with the spume carried over a mile inland. No wonder that wool sheared from

3

sheep raised on the Outer Hebrides Islands is considered the finest. Those sheep have to be super animals to withstand such weather. The Cape, in the moonlight, looked as if it had been subjected to such treatment for thousands of years, which indeed it had. Black and foreboding, it reached Westward, daring the seas to destroy it.

> *3:30, A.M., SIGHTED DUNNET HEAD*
> *LIGHT, THE WESTERN ENTRANCE TO*
> *PENTLAND FIRTH. SPEED REDUCED*
> *TO REACH THE HEAD AT 6:15, A.M.,*
> *THE BEGINNING OF THE FAIR TIDE.*

The night was passing. The Chief Mate had been relieved by the Third Mate, who had in turn been relieved by the Second Mate. Four o'clock was approaching, time for the Chief Mate to return for his morning watch. He would be most welcome because he would bring his own coffee percolator to the bridge, and, as it had always been my habit at sea to take early morning star sights, I had become quite accustomed to his strong, black, 4:30 A.M. brew. He heaved himself up the ladder, grunting at the chill and darkness. He and the Second Mate hurriedly went through the time honored business of changing the watch. *The course was so and so. Such and such had been sighted, or was in sight.* Nodding in my direction, *The Old Man has the bridge,* he mumbled good night and went below to write up his log. The Mate busied himself checking the compasses, running lights, and saw to it that the bow lookout was properly posted. Then his pot was set to boil and soon the fragrance of brewing coffee made me stretch and get out of my chair.

"Mister," I said as we leaned against the wind dodger warming our hands on the steaming mugs,

"Not that I anticipate any untoward incidents this morning, but it wouldn't do any harm if you broke out the ship's carpenter and had the anchors cleared away. Then, on the off chance that we got into difficulty, those insurance people couldn't say that every precaution hadn't been taken."

Chips, the carpenter, shortly reported to the bridge, and he and the Mate went forward to the focsle head where they removed the devil's claws and hawse pipe stoppers. (Strange words, here, tonight). Left alone on the bridge except for the man at the wheel, I paced back and forth, mentally anticipating the next couple of hours. As I completed a turn of the bridge, my foot stumbled against the engine room telegraph. Guiltily, I brought up short. It was perfectly normal to stumble in such pitch darkness, but I remembered other ships when I had been the helmsman. The most minute move of the Old Man was always observed, *Is the ship OK? Does he know what he's doing? Is he worried?* With deadly accuracy, the Old Man's thoughts, attitude, and

4

capability were deduced by the man at the wheel, and like wildfire, were transmitted below deck. No cause for nervousness. Everything anticipated, planned for. Just another voyage. I resumed my pacing, but with slow deliberate steps. I observed, oh so very carefully to the helmsman, that by the feel of the morning, the day should break clear and fine. His answering grunt was noncommittal and therefore reassuring. His apparent lack of interest was sure proof that he felt, and hence the entire ship's company, that things were as they should be.

5:30 A.M., TOR NESS BEARING 066, TRUE. 6 A.M. RESUMED FULL SPEED.

DUNNET HEAD BEARING 119, TRUE. VESSEL IS 3/4 MILE OUTSIDE OF COURSE AND 5 1/2 miles WEST OF DUNNET HEAD. 6:20, A.M., DUNNET HEAD ABEAM. ENTERED PENTLAND FIRTH WITH STROMA AND THE SKER-RIES ON RANGE BEARING 093, TRUE.

Strange Scottish names: Stroma, Tor Ness, Swilkie Point, Tarf's Tail. Now there was no time except for doing. We entered the Firth at 6:20 on course 093. At 6:45, with Swona bearing 065, course was changed to 065. Nine minutes later, with Stroma abeam, course was changed to 090. At 7:02, Tarf's Tail was abeam and the course was changed to 125. At 7:10, Swilkie Point bore 226. Course changed to 146. At 7:45, Duncansby Head bore 302. Course again changed to 099, and we were clear of Pentland Firth, all squared away nine degrees South of East for our next landfall, the Norwegian coast.

6:20 entered the Firth. 7:45, all clear. One hour and twenty-five minutes. There had been anxious moments. A deep laden tramp with old engines doesn't respond to the helm as you would wish. The log book states:

WHEN VESSEL ENTERED THE FIRTH STROMA AND THE SKERRIES ON RANGE BEARING 093.

Stroma is a rocky, uninhabited island smack in the middle of Pentland Firth. Some miles beyond it, there is a lighthouse on another rocky, wave swept reef, the Skerries. The idea is to line them up on a bearing of 093, and then steer that course. In other words, you head directly for the island, Stroma. This course must be held until another island, Swona, just to the left of Stroma, bears 065. Then hard aport on course 065, and head straight for it. All this is

5

being done in very close quarters. You hold the vessel on course, right for an unfriendly shore, where any ship would surely be lost, until the last minute. Then, quick, up with the helm and hope she answers in time. In the early morning light, the land seems far too close, especially after two weeks of open sea.

After a surreptitious glance at the helmsman to see if he was listening, I very casually shouted to the Mate on the bow to secure the anchors. When he returned to the bridge, I managed to appear slightly bored. (An air that all Skippers are expected to assume).

"Well, Mister, she's all yours. I believe that I'll slip below for a bit of breakfast."

Once I reached the comparative privacy of the chart room, I gave myself over to a brief session of self-satisfaction. I had done it! And without a hitch, nor with the slightest sign of nerves or muddle. Little did I know, as I swung down the companionway to the saloon and breakfast, that within two days we would be confronted with something that all seafarers dread—ICE!

We wallowed along in the peculiar North Sea swell all that day and the next night. The next morning the Southwestern coast of Norway reared up over the horizon. The Log Book merely states:

10:50, A.M.   SIGHTED LAND THREE
POINTS ON THE PORT BOW.   SOUNDI-
NGS, 81 FATHOMS.

Yet the great painters of history would have sought in vain among the tubes on their palettes if they tried to duplicate the color and grandeur. Authors, famed for their descriptive passages would have lacked the words to describe the mountains as they looked from seaward on a clear wintry day. When first seen, we were at least forty miles away. Despite the distance, the snow caps could be plainly seen in sharp contrast to the deep purple of the rock. As the ship drew nearer, the purple color, which is a visionary illusion caused by great distances, gradually changed. The sun reflected from the snow on the ridges making the ravines, or fjords, assume all the colors of the spectrum. It was a breath-taking sight. As a rule, most seamen are a phlegmatic lot. The wonder and the beauty of the seven seas almost invariably elicits, at the most, a bored shrug, a cursory glance, or nothing. On this morning, though, something about this spectacle, now broad on the port bow, seemed to affect the entire crew. I was amazed to look aft from the flying bridge and see sailors, firemen, even those whose watch it was below, all peering at this wondrous sight. Even the cook was at the rail. His thin cotton singlet showed white against his blue skin, and his apron flapped wildly in the winter wind. Yet they all continued to watch the ever changing colors. It was obvious that they, like myself, were fascinated.

6

The cold and the wind told their common sense that this was crazy. *Go below where it's warm. But wait, look there! Never saw anything like it. Aw, it's only a bunch of mountains.*

For many years I was a sailor, too. I know of the pride a seaman takes in never exhibiting any feelings of surprise, fear, or any other emotion. Don't ask me why. I don't know, nor do I especially condone it. Nevertheless, it is very real. I, too, on the bridge, was doing the same thing. Deliberate steps—Twelve steps to Port, sniff the wind, look briefly at the coastline—twelve paces to Starboard. To any bystander I might have been waiting for a street car. This never to be forgotten scene, though, was vividly imprinted on my mind. It had to be, or how could I remember it so many years later? I don't think that I have ever consciously thought of that voyage until tonight, when I opened my log book. It was the first time that I had reread the entries since they were made. Maybe memory tricks one, magnifies. In retrospect, possibly everything is more important, bigger, more moving. I don't know. I only know that tonight, here at home, I am just as much at a loss for words as I was on that February day so long ago. I wish that I could adequately describe a few mountains. Unfortunately, I am just a shipmaster who has swallowed the anchor. I wonder if the Vikings, those stalwart Norsemen, returning home from their voyages, saw what I saw? And did their imagination run wild, and did they exaggerate because it was home? They had ventured half way around the world in their frail cockleshells. After months of hardships and privation, did this same scene confront them? What must have been their comments?

All afternoon we steamed along the Southern coast of Norway, maintaining a distance off of about seven miles.

4:20, P.M. RADIO REPORT INDICATES
SERIOUS ICE CONDITIONS IN THE
KATTEGAT.

After several years at sea, I was finally to meet that arch enemy of shipping. Tall tales are told in focsles about vessels being caught in the ice. Some were fast for days and weeks. Some were lost. Sparks tuned in on the local Norwegian and Danish frequencies. The air was full of reports that verified my fears. The flow ice was solid all the way from the Skaw South to beyond Copenhagen. Sparks handed me a message which he had just received from a Danish ice breaker.

LOW POWERED STEAMERS MAY EX-
PECT DIFFICULTY NAVIGATING IN
ICE. NO IMMEDIATE POSSIBILITY OF
ICE BREAKER ASSISTANCE DUE TO

COMMITMENTS IN THE KATTEGAT AND COPENHAGEN HARBOR. RECOMMEND TAKING A PILOT AT THE SKAW.

Directly South of Norway, and separated by an Eastern arm of the North Sea, is the coast of Jutland, a part of Denmark. This body of water is called the Skagerrak. The Northeastern tip of Jutland is called the Skaw. The Skaw is the entrance to the body of water called the Kattegat. It extends North and South. It is bordered on the East by Sweden, and on the West by Denmark. Just before reaching Copenhagen, the Kattegat narrows to a ten mile wide stretch of water known as the Oresund. On the Danish side, Kronborg Castle, where Shakespeare had Hamlet deliver his famous soliloquy, is still there, and can be seen by passing ships. South of Kronborg, the Kattegat again widens, and the seafarer has only to pass Hven Island before making the approach to the harbor of Copenhagen.

At this point I am tempted to skip the rest of this voyage and pass on to a subsequent one made in the summer months. We steamed a thousand miles up the coast of Norway to the port of Narvik, above the Arctic Circle. The midnight sun shone twenty-four hours a day. The weather was fine, and the two hundred mile approach to Narvik, up the Vestfjord unforgettable. The ice, and the worry, which now lay heavy upon me, even now makes me uneasy. A reassuring glance at the now low burning fire helps to dispel the anxiety that has crept into my mind despite the passing of so many years. How vividly one's memory recreates events which were once so moving to a young shipmaster.

Sparks handed me another radiogram, this time from the Danish pilot vessel which was normally stationed off Skagen Light. She had been driven Westward by the ice. The message informed me that if I desired a pilot, she would meet us at a little fishing village, Hirtshalls, in Jutland. I hurriedly consulted the chart and told Sparks to arrange the rendezvous. A new course was laid out from the ship's dead reckoning position to Hirtshalls. As soon as we had hauled around on the new course, I tried to take stock of the new situation. Unfortunately, we didn't have a large scale chart of Hirtshalls. The only chart available was a coastal chart. Most of the detail necessary to make a landfall had been omitted. The *Sailing Directions* were equally vague, Hirtshalls being only a fishing hamlet. The coastal chart did, though, show something that concerned me, sunken wrecks left untouched since World War II. Our approach would be made in darkness, therefore, any landmarks would be useless. What looked to be a safe anchorage was pricked off on the chart, and bearings laid off to the one light on the harbor mole, and to the one lighthouse in the vicinity. Just as all this was completed, the Second Mate stuck his head in the chart room and informed me that he had sighted Hirtshalls Light. Returning to the bridge, I was gratified to see that the night, although bitterly cold, was clear and fine. On a Slow Ahead bell, cross bearings indicated that we were in position. The Starboard anchor was let go, and the Mate bellowed that she had *fetched up,* meaning that the ship had settled to her mooring and was safely at anchor.

Not knowing just when the pilot vessel would arrive, we relaxed for awhile. The anchor watch was set. There was no wind and consequently no swell. A blessing when laying at anchor on an unprotected shore. Had there been a typical North Sea winter blizzard, things would have been quite different. Thankful for the brief respite, the Mate and I draped ourselves comfortably over the chart room table. His never empty coffee pot bubbled softly as we talked the night into dawn.

As I look back, the thought strikes me. *When did I sleep?* To be truthful, I didn't, much. To people on shore, accustomed to regular hours of sleep and work, it is unbelievable that seamen can so abuse themselves. Actually, it is surprising how little sleep the body requires. We slept, whenever possible, like hunting hounds. Short naps, a few winks, most of the time in our clothes. Sounds uncivilized, I know, to say that we thrived on such fare. We did, though. I once made a winter crossing from Charleston, South Carolina to Le Havre, France. For eleven days I never took my shoes off. That may sound like an endurance contest of some kind. It wasn't. High seas, constant gales, and a badly overloaded ship called for constant attention. I obtained rest in small measure, but enough to remain alert, and without any permanent after effects.

It was early afternoon before the Second Mate informed me that what looked to be a pilot vessel was heading in. I followed him up the ladder to the bridge. A quick look through the glasses was enough to identify a typical North Sea pilot boat. Sort of a European schooner rig. Black, rakish, but oh so seaworthy. The Chief Mate had already been called, and was on the focsle head with Chips, ready to heave in the anchor. The small vessel came up on our lee quarter. There was a brief flapping of sails, and the growl of her powerful Diesel. In a moment, she was fast alongside. Smart work. Those Danes are fine sailormen. The pilot clambered up the ladder to the main deck. As soon as he reached the deck, his vessel cast off. Her sails filled rapidly, and aided by a quick from her engine, she sheered off. The pilot joined me on the bridge. He was a fairly young Dane. Blonde, with a ruddy complexion, he had an air about him of knowing his business. As soon as we had introduced ourselves, I asked him about the ice. He said that it was bad enough, but if the wind remained light, we had a good chance of getting through. It was now up to me to decide. Should I radio our owners? Under the terms of our Charter Party, the ship was not required to navigate in ice. Her Master could, at his discretion, nominate another port of discharge, the nearest one that was ice free. On the other hand, this would put the Charterer to great expense. What should I do? No good seaman knowingly takes his ship into danger. I weighed everything as carefully as I could and finally resolved to proceed to my original destination, ice or no ice.

The anchor was hove up and the engines put on Full Ahead, as we squared away for the Skaw, the Kattegat, and the ice.

It was a brilliant sunny afternoon. We were steaming Eastward, consequently the late afternoon sun was astern of us. Shortly before five o'clock, I thought that I saw a bright streak on the horizon, dead ahead. Picking up the glasses, I looked again. I felt that old familiar feeling in the pit of my stomach. You know, the one that you get in an elevator when it drops quickly? As far as the eye could see, there stretched an unbroken sea of ice. I jumped for the engine room telegraph and rang down, Slow Ahead. The pilot quickly came over to me and said that we must not slow down. We would need every bit of our speed and power to maintain headway through the ice.

"But pilot, we can't just go bashing full speed through that solid ice,"

He smiled and asked me if this was my first encounter with ice. Many times before we finally made port, I was to be thankful for his good judgement and advice. With many misgivings, I ordered the engines to be put back on Full Ahead. The Chief Engineer was instructed that from now on, everything was to be cracked on, and no monkey business about holding reserve power up his sleeve.

We were rapidly approaching the ice, and the nearer we got, the more concerned I became. It seemed as though we were steaming full speed right for a solid wall. I paced back and forth, forgetting, this time, to be deliberate. I was worried and didn't care if the helmsman did know it. My hand itched to ring the engines down again. We had over nine thousand tons of coal in our holds. The ship herself weighed another three thousand tons, and here we were, all twelve thousand tons, helling along at eleven knots. In a matter of minutes, we were up to the ice. The bows crunched through the first of it. The ship shuddered and slowed, and then the powerful propeller took up its beat again. We were in ice about five inches thick. The noise of it grinding against the hull was deafening. We had to shout to make ourselves heard. We were making knots, though, for by ten o'clock that night we had raised the Swedish coastline. Vinga Light was abeam and we were proceeding. Slowly, to be sure, and with enough noise to awaken all the good sailors who had been sleeping in Davey Jone's Locker since the beginning of time.

7:42, A.M. FAST IN HEAVY ICE.

A brief entry in the log book. An ignominious situation, to say the least, with no mention of the dire straits in which we now found ourselves. On our port hand, and not too far away, lay the rocky coast of Sweden. There was a slight breeze blowing onshore. The pilot didn't make me feel a bit better when he told story after story of ships being lost when the wind blew hard enough to move the ice shoreward, carrying ships with it until their bottoms were ripped out on the rocks. In some instances, after a vessel had impaled herself on the rocks, the ice literally buried her, the wind forcing the ice against her sides, and up and over the decks until she disappeared forever.

The Chief Engineer was summoned to the bridge, again, and a conference held. This time with no sarcasm. First, it was apparent that no immediate assistance could be expected from an ice breaker. Second, we were in no danger as long as the wind remained light. The question to be answered was: *How do we get out of this mess?* The ice was too thick for our engines to cope. The Chief said that in his opinion, we had reason enough to *break the seals*. All ships' boilers are regularly inspected by government inspectors. They decide what the maximum boiler pressure shall be, and the safety relief valves are set to that pressure. They are then sealed with official seals. The engineer who breaks them, or the Captain who orders them broken, are subject to investigation and possible loss of his license, should he not be able to show the grave necessity for such a step.

Not wanting to involve the Chief and me in lengthy investigations and hearings upon our return to the States, I decided that before breaking the seals, we would have one more try at breaking free from the ice.

"Get your ass below, Chief, and give it all she's got."

Full Astern! Everything on the ship was flapping and vibrating from the thrust of the engines. The funnel just behind me was trying to shake itself down. The shrouds on the masts were quivering like giant fiddle strings. Water boiled under the stern and poured up over the ice. We never moved an inch.

Full Ahead, and give it to her, Chief.

Still no movement. Leaving the engines on Full Ahead, I picked out an ice hummock alongside and fastened my eye on it. It moved! Nope. It must have been my imagination being stimulated by hope.

I'll count to twenty, I said to myself. *Then we'll call it quits. After that, we'll just have to pray that an ice breaker can reach us before the weather worsens.* Slowly, I counted. When I reached twenty, I sneaked another look at the ice hummock. No change. *Oh, well, I meant that I would count to twenty by fives. One, two, three, four, five,-one. One, two, three, four, five,—two.* (Used to do that when I was a kid.) All this while I was leaning over the bridge rail with what I hoped was a proper Skipper look. Unconcerned, a bit bored, and with confidence oozing out all over me. Actually, cold sweat was oozing, and I was scared. The bridge telephone jangled and interrupted my counting. It was the sailor on the bow, and he was shouting so loudly that we could hear him without picking up the receiver. *We're moving!* To say that I was relieved was a masterpiece of understatement. Slowly but surely, we were crunching our way through the ice.

This business of getting underway, getting stuck again, backing and

Alongside, Copenhagen, 1946 or 47

Another view, Copenhagen

The author on
the bridge

Tom Poole, a <u>good</u>
Second Mate

**Tied up, safe in harbor, after a rough
winter passage of the Western Ocean**

Copenhagen again

Winter in the North Atlantic, 1943

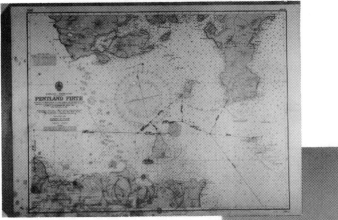

A bad place to take an old, slow ship. Coffee mug stains bear mute evidence

Heavy ice in the Oresund

filling to free ourselves, went on for days. One entry in the Log was typical:

PROCEEDING IN HEAVY ICE. BACK-
ING AND FILLING WITH ENGINES TO
BREAK VESSEL FREE. DISTANCE
MADE GOOD THIS DAY, ONE MILE.

One mile after twenty-four hours of struggling! Finally, there came a time when we could move no more. The ice was piled up four feet high in places. It was hopeless to try any more. An urgent radio message was sent requesting the assistance of an icebreaker.

That night about midnight, the Mate on watch reported a ship approaching at high speed. I was in the chart room at the time, and when the Mate told me this I growled,

"Nonsense. Can't you recognize a low flying plane when you see one? What vessel is proceeding at all, let alone at high speed?"

Just as I spoke, the running lights of a ship flashed by the chart room port hole. Astounded, I bounded out onto the bridge. There was a Danish icebreaker rounding our stern. He proceeded completely around us, breaking the ice loose. Then he swung alongside, and a rope ladder was dropped onto his deck. Her Skipper mounted the ladder and stepped aboard. A veritable giant of a man he was, dressed in a great fur coat, fur hat, and skin boots.

"Hello, Captain," he boomed. "Having trouble?"

We repaired to my quarters for coffee, spiked with Aquavit, a fiery Danish drink which he had thoughtfully brought with him. What he proposed to do was crazy. He was going to take us in tow. Imagine—twelve thousand odd tons and his vessel less than half the size of ours. We were not to use our engines, just leave everything to him. The man was mad. However, he was such a commanding figure and so full of confidence that I was partly convinced.

After all, what could we lose? Certain signals were agreed upon and he returned to his ship. The Mate broke out the watch and went forward where they took aboard the towing bridle from the icebreaker. It was made fast and the Dane went slowly ahead. Just as the cable came taut, her Skipper roared back,

"Captain, I'll tow you right into Copenhagen and average four knots. A pound of tobacco on it."

Believe it or not, but he did. He towed us all the way to Copenhagen, into the harbor, alongside the dock, and averaged four knots. I would never have believed it possible. And we never used our engines, once.

Once we were tied up, he came aboard again. He held an empty pipe in his enormous hand, and apologetically said that he meant what he said about the tobacco. Good pipe tobacco was scarce in Denmark. We had a couple of quick snorts of his Aquavit, after which he left with two cases of Prince Albert tobacco. Our heartfelt thanks went with him.

What a man he was. And such a superb seaman. What he did for us was commonplace to him, an every day occurrence during the ice season. Still, he was a rare figure by today's standards. Nothing was impossible to him and he proved it.

And so we made port. Just another Eastbound passage of the Western Ocean. Troubles and difficulties beset us. They were all there in the log book, between the lines. Indeed, the initiated can glean a lot from those terse, abbreviated phrases.

A log had just fallen through the andirons. Red sparks shot up the chimney. The house was very still. I realized with a start that I could no longer see to read. The firelight was nothing but a red glow. I was loath to return to the present, yet the predicament of being caught in the ice was not one that I remembered with any great joy. Seagoing habits, acquired from years at sea are part of me. Going to the door, I sniffed the weather. Clear and dry with an earthy smell of spring in the air. The day would break fine. But why should I care? Safe on land——Let it blow and howl. I returned to my chair and my thoughts went back to that cold February up in the Baltic. Let's see—We had just made fast to the dock in Copenhagen. It was after midnight and I had gone to my cabin for a long sleep, the first for many a night. Nothing on my mind. The ship was safe and I could sleep.

Sprawled in my chair, I mused on the homeward bound voyage from Copenhagen. My thoughts were interrupted by that smell of earth coming to life. Spring was in the air. It smelled just like a jungle river that I once sailed up, in British Guiana. Monkeys chattered and green birds screeched in the trees that formed a solid canopy over the ship as we glided through the water. That voyage, too, almost ended in disaster.

My log book of that voyage was also conveniently at hand in the book case. But as I opened the pages, I thought, *I can't leave that other ship in Copenhagen. She has to get home, and I must tell about the howling blizzard that struck us when we reached the Skaw, and how, after a week of bucking the ice, it was now impossible to disembark the pilot because no pilot boat could live in such a gale. And of how we took the pilot with us, and refused to put him off in a Dutch port. Instead, we took him all the way to England, where we hoodwinked a British pilot vessel into thinking that we had a British pilot aboard.* When the Dane stepped off the ladder into their boat, I immediately rang up, Full Ahead. I can still hear the curses flung at us when they found out that they had a Dane on their hands. Faintly, though, because we were homeward bound.

I must leave that ship, however, safe in Copenhagen. The smell of that jungle river is too strong.

Drive her, Johnny, drive her.
                Old Sea Chanty

-2-

A COUPLE OF CLOSE CALLS

On that voyage we were bound from Savannah, Georgia, down to Port McKenzie, in British Guiana, there to load a full cargo of aluminum ore consigned to Port Alfred, Canada.

The Chief Engineer and I were standing on the boat deck idly plying tooth picks in an endeavor to dislodge pieces of undercooked breakfast bacon, when the Agent's runner came up the gangway. He requested that I come to the office as soon as it was convenient. The vessel's next assignment had been received from our owners in Boston. This was welcome news. We had been laying at a dock in Savannah for several days, enduring the Georgia heat. Inactivity had began to pall.

After a quick shower and a change into shore clothes, I emerged from the semi-darkness of the dock shed onto a waterfront street. The soaring temperature influenced me to indulge in the luxury of a taxi. My Owners, being Bostonians, were naturally conservative and looked with high favor at voyage expense accounts that itemized *trolley carfare,* and *bus ticket* instead of *taxi.* During the short ride to the office, I mused on our next assignment. I made a mental wager that it would be Southward. It always seemed to be my misfortune to be in Northern waters during the winter months, half frozen and miserable. Then, when the fine weather arrived, away we'd go bound down South for the Equator, where the bugs and prickly heat rash lay in wait.

Sure enough, a hot weather trip. I glanced through our sailing orders from the Marine Superintendent, put away for later, the Traffic Department's instructions in connection with the Charter Party, and bade the Agent so long. On the way back to the ship I bemoaned the fact that at this time of year, the North Atlantic trade routes were enjoying fine, settled weather and all the Skippers up there were sleeping in their bunks all night instead of battling hurricanes down in the Caribbean, where we were bound.

Once back on board, a conference was held with the Chief Engineer, the Mate, and the Chief Steward. Our Owners had instructed us to proceed, forthwith, when, *in all respects, ready for sea.* This meant just as soon as possible. The Chief reported his engines ready to go, no stores needed. The Steward began his stores list and the Mate reported a full crew, no stores needed, with all hatches battened down and the deck gear secured for sea. Only one matter remained to be settled——bunkers. In order to ascertain fuel oil requirements, the distance between ports had to be known. The Chief followed me up to the chart room. I searched in vain for Port McKenzie. It was not to be found on any chart, and we were fully equipped. Puzzled, I sent the Second Mate ashore to phone the Agent. Maybe a mistake in copying our owners' teletyped orders had been made. He returned. Port McKenzie it was. The Chief drummed his fingers on the table and sucked his teeth. Obviously, he had a nincompoop Skipper who if he couldn't even locate the port on the charts, was assuredly incapable of sailing a ship there. He had that typical Engineer's look spread all over his silly face. At last, I located Port McKenzie in an Atlas. It was so far up the Demarrera River in British Guiana, that the chart makers had omitted it. Turning to the Chief, I gave him the distances involved and requested that he check his tanks and report his requirements.

"That is," I observed, *"if you can read."*

Oh, me. When Kipling wrote, *East is East and West is West, and never the twain shall meet,* he must have been thinking of Engineers and deck officers in the Merchant Service.

The Chief went off to sound his tanks while I sat down in my day room to write a letter to my son. He was in school in New Hampshire and it was now a year and a half since I had seen him. Such are the vagaries of a tramp steamer.

At dinner, the Chief and I compared notes and agreed that sufficient bunkers were on board to take us from Savannah to Port McKenzie, and from there round to Trinidad, where we were to complete loading. Trinidad, being a major fueling port, we could bunker there for the voyage to Canada much cheaper than at Savannah.

I remember, very vividly, a conversation that then took place. I would like to think that I started it off. However, if I stick to the truth, it was the Chief. The talk ranged far afield, but the essence of it was that ever since engines were introduced into ships, Engineers and Captains had been bickering and arguing. There was mutual distrust, jealousy, and misunderstanding existing between the two departments, both of whom had the same interest, the ship. In a burst of magnanimity, it was resolved that on this ship it would cease. We would become one happy family. One purpose, one goal, the furtherance of our owner's interests. We would all be brothers, striving in the same vineyard. *Woe is me,* as the Bible says. We had the best of intentions, but later events were to prove how spurious all our high sounding promises would be.

I would like to think that we were all, completely sincere. We weren't, though, because we both had reservations. Sort of an armed truce. Both sides adopted the attitude, *I'll go along with this insane alliance as long as* **he** *doesn't get out of line.* Getting ahead of my story, all this background has been necessary because later in the voyage the ship was almost lost, twice, because of engineers and the lack of complete cooperation and trust between them and the deck.

15

All that afternoon the Second Mate and I studied the charts, laid off courses, and planned our voyage. All hands were readying the ship for sea. As we were in ballast, and therefore light, everything must be battened down and secured. A light ship caught in a tropical hurricane will roll and pitch pretty badly.

All in all, a busy day. The die had been cast, but what our destiny would be, as charted by the Master Navigator, was not divulged to us. Knowing what I do now, it was just as well. The only log book entry recording all this read,

> *S.S. AUGUSTUS P. LORING, AUGUST*
> *5TH. THIS DAY RECEIVED ORDERS*
> *AND CHARTER PARTY TO PROCEED*
> *WHEN IN ALL RESPECTS READY FOR*
> *SEA TO PORT McKENZIE BRITISH*
> *GUIANA, THERE TO LOAD FOR PORT*
> *ALFRED, CANADA. VESSEL BEING*
> *MADE READY FOR SEA.*

That evening, our last in Savannah, was spent in desultory conversation while sprawled in canvas deck chairs under a bright Georgia moon. The general theme was our new-formed pact between engine room and deck, and of how, henceforth, we would be one happy family. Turning in for the night, my misgivings on the matter were heightened by the unpleasant discovery that some stupid engineer had turned the wrong valve in the engine room. My radiators were smoking hot and the room like a furnace. This, with the outside temperature hovering around a hundred degrees. I dragged my mattress out into the wheel house and prepared for an uncomfortable night. As I drowsily swatted mosquitoes, I remembered something my grandfather said after a lifetime in sail. *Steamboats are fine, but look what they spawned,* meaning engineers.

The next morning I went ashore to clear the ship at the Customs House, after which a last visit was paid to the Agent. The Shipping Commissioner returned to the ship with me to sign the crew on Articles. This was accomplished by noon, and it was time to go. Leaving the saloon after a quick dinner, I heard the Mate's familiar order,

"Bosun, fore and aft. All hands."

The sailing of a cargo ship is a run of the mill affair, nothing like the glamorous passenger ships with their parties, streamers, and bunting, and crowds of friends waving from the pier. The lines were cast off, a tow boat swung us down river, and we were away. As we were passing the center of the city and drawing abreast of our Agent's office building, I did give three mournful blasts of farewell on the ship's whistle. He had been kind and helpful

16

Southbound for British Guiana

during our stay in Savannah and only the Lord knew when we might return again.

The pilot got off at the river's mouth and our official departure was taken from the Savannah Light Vessel. At sea again. A comfortable, old shoe feeling in spite of the midsummer sun which was making a griddle out of our steel decks.

The days passed pleasantly. We were making our Southing and Easting, passing well to the Eastward of Cuba and the Bahamas. We steamed through the Mona Passage and were now in the Caribbean. The island of Puerto Rico lay just over the horizon on our port hand, and, although out of sight, was used to excellent advantage for radio bearings which verified our celestial observations. We were making a fine passage right on course. The weather remained perfect and the sea was like blue glass. All hands, including myself, were down to shorts. The tropical sun blazed down every day, turning every one a dark brown. That is, every one except the Second Mate. He was an old salt who had spent a lifetime at sea. His face and hands were the color of old, polished mahogany, but the rest of his body looked like the thin, blue-white skimmed milk that farmers fed to their pigs. Being Second Mate, he stood the noon to four PM bridge watch. His shirt would be tightly buttoned at neck and wrists, and he remained under cover in the wheel house, coming out only when necessary to take an azimuth or shoot the sun with his sextant, after which he would scurry back into the shade for all the world like an old mole. I used to spend the afternoons on the bridge taking advantage of the beautiful weather, and as my hide blackened and my hair bleached, he would mutter predictions of sun stroke, skin cancer, and what he called, *a frying of a man's brains.*

In a few days we were off the mouth of the Demarrara River in British Guiana. A little brown skinned pilot boarded us and guided the ship to just inside the mouth. The anchor was dropped off the port of Georgetown, famous for its rum, which is as potent as lightning, yet slips down the throat of the unwary as smoothly as Vermont maple syrup. There, the formalities of Customs and Immigration were gone through, and an exchange of pilots was made. This time there were two of them. Whereas our first pilot had been sort of a light brown fellow, these two were as black as ebony. It would seem that as one's Latitude grows less towards the Equator, the color of the inhabitants grew darker. They padded up to the bridge in their bare feet. Splayed toes, spread out like fingers, did not indicate any close acquaintance with shoes. Their speech, though, was delightful. A cultured British accent rolled out with beautiful resonance, softly slurred by negro idioms. The British Empire is, indeed, far reaching.

When I inquired why we needed two pilots for the up river passage, their explanation was anything but reassuring. They proposed to do their own

17

steering. I was most reluctant to agree to any such arrangement, pointing out that our quartermasters were familiar with the feel of our ship and knew just how much wheel was needed to execute a steering order. They in turn, presented logical arguments that finally persuaded me. The river abounded in sudden turns and shoals. The tide rushing up on the flood and then streaming down on the ebb, created hazards, and they were doing this daily on different ships that all had their steering peculiarities. Accordingly, one stationed himself at the wheel, while the other politely asked me to have the Mate heave up the anchor, if it was convenient.

The trip up this jungle river was a memorable one. The heat and oppressive humidity excepted, it was like one of those National Geographic accounts. The virgin jungle came right down to the edge of the water. It was so lush and impenetrable that nothing could be seen more than a couple of feet inland. However, the ears were assailed by a cacophony of noise that indicated a teeming life engaged in an unceasing struggle for survival. This noise seemed to reach a crescendo at dusk with the buzzing and humming of myriads of insects, punctuated by the hoarse coughs and grunts of alligators. The screams and snarls of unseen animals, and the screeching and crying of thousands of birds made conversation well nigh impossible.

We had reached a shallow part of the river and it became necessary to anchor to await the arrival of the flood tide. One of the pilots explained that even though our ship, being in ballast, and therefore not drawing much water, could safely proceed at any stage of the tide, he would rather wait for more water. I heartily agreed and dispatched the long suffering Mate forward to drop the hook. He had spent the entire day in the cargo holds with the crew, readying them to receive our cargo. And on that hangs a tale which I'll come to in a moment, because something happened down in number five lower hold which, weeks later, almost caused the ship to founder on her way up to Canada with a full load of ore.

Darkness descended like a black mantle. The trees at the water's edge were so overgrown with creepers and vines and their roots were so undermined by the river that they leaned so as to form a living roof over the ship. I was fearful of snakes dropping down on us in the night time but the pilots seemed to make light of it.

After supper I joined the Mate on the bridge where he was standing anchor watch. We discussed his progress down in the cargo holds. He was a bit concerned at finding a small amount of water in the bilges of number five lower hold. The ore that we were to load had to be delivered dry or claims would result. The water was obviously only condensation that had collected on the ship's steel sides and run down into the bilges. He had sent word to the engine room to put a suction on number five. However, nothing had happened. The big bilge pump had labored mightily but the water had remained. One of the engineers had gone into the hold with the Mate to see at first hand what the trouble was. The strainers were all free so the engine force decided that the valve, located in the bilge, was either out of order or plugged. Even now, as we passed the time away on the bridge, one of the assistant engineers was down in number five, dismantling the valve. Shortly before midnight he reported that he had found the trouble, reassembled the valve, and pumped out the water. Fine, we were already to load. I think now, looking back, that had I known what had been done down in that hold by that careless man, violence would have been done that night.

The reader has probably by now gotten the impression that I have a low opinion of all engineers. Such is not the case. I have sailed with dozens of fine, capable engineers. It just so happens that some of the stories being told here have to do with engineers that I differed with, and in whom I had little confidence. Do not construe my remarks about those few to include that great group of men who, day after day, and year after year, keep the propellers churning the waters of the seven seas. (I hope that I've made my peace with all you good Chiefs, Firsts, and Seconds.)

The next morning at dawn we were underway again. Dawn in the tropics is an experience to a seaman. Out on the open sea daybreak is a gradual thing. Little by little the horizon becomes perceptible. To the Eastward, a faint glow shows itself. A deep red, shading off to purple. The sky brightens. Clouds can be seen massed on the Western horizon. I always used to liken these black clouds setting in the West to the passing of the night. Night sank over the Western horizon just as day broke over the Eastern rim of the sea. At sea, all this seemed to be a gradual process. There was plenty of time to observe all the beautiful changing details of the coming of a new day. Here, in a jungle river, it was quite different. There was no far flung horizon towards which one could watch and wait and hope. There were only trees and creepers; vines and mosses, almost meeting overhead. The transition from night to day was instantaneous. So quickly did day come that I found myself squinting, the same as you do upon stepping out of a movie house into the afternoon glare.

All day we steamed up the river. Mile after mile of monotonous repetition. Here and there a few clearings. Log canoes pulled up on the mud banks gave indications that people were hereabouts. How did they live? And on what? And for what in this steaming jungle? Maybe they were happier and more content than the residents of Park Avenue with all their wealth and power. Being only a sailor instead of a philosopher I can't say.

By late afternoon we were close to our destination. The pilots explained that it would be necessary to turn the ship around so that when loading was completed, it would only be necessary to cast off. The river was quite narrow and the current fairly strong. I asked them how they proposed to turn the ship. Just as I spoke, the ship rounded a bend and we had arrived. As I remember it, the pilots never answered my question. There was no time. First, it was, **Hard Right.** Then, **Full Astern. Wheel Amidships.** The vessel answered beautifully. We seemed to spin around like a big floating top. Maybe they never wore shoes. Maybe they hadn't much schooling, but By God, those pilots could handle a ship. We tied up to a new, efficient looking wharf that ran parallel to the river bank. All sorts of conveyors, tracks and overhead structural steel made one think of the inroads made by the twentieth century. Deserts, jungles, mountains, rivers, they have all fallen before technology. Man and knowledge have truly just about conquered the world, even to its most remote corners.

Aluminum ore is called Bauxite. It is very valuable and very necessary to the welfare of the world. To a sailor, it is also the most devilish stuff ever loaded into a ship. It can penetrate into the most minute cracks and crevices. As it is also an excellent abrasive, it damages any machinery with which it comes in contact. All night long thousands of tons were dumped into the holds. There was no sleeping. The heat was stifling and the dust choking. By daylight, everything was covered with dust. But though it looked like pink snow, it didn't melt. Breakfast was eggs with Bauxite. The gritting sensation when chewing made food nauseating. Every stateroom was powdered with the stuff, notwithstanding the fact that every door and porthole had been dogged fast.

Shortly before noon, our cargo was aboard. Such was the loading schedule at the port that a ship arrived and departed simultaneously from the time that the ice went out of the Saint Lawrence River in Canada to freeze up time. This schedule had to be maintained day and night, seven days a week, come hell or high water, otherwise the big sprawling aluminum plant in Canada might grind to a halt at a time when aluminum, or the lack of it, could mean the difference between a free world, and slavery and oppression.

Off down the river. The same trip in reverse. The ship was only about three quarters loaded, the reason being that there was a mud bank off the mouth of the river that had defied dredging. Therefore, it was necessary for deep water vessels such as ours, to go 'round to Chageramus on the island of Trinidad, and there load the remainder of our Bauxite, which had been brought around by small intercoastal steamers, and stock piled.

We dropped swiftly down the river and before I knew it we were again anchored off Georgetown. Again, the usual formalities were gone through. Crew lists, manifests, carbon copies to everyone including the Lord himself. At the last minute a large launch came alongside with twelve passengers for Port of Spain. They were all British or Canadian families bound on leave. As we were not due to leave until the next morning, all the passengers, the Chief and myself congregated in the saloon and got acquainted. Several couples had children with them who were soon tucked in their bunks. Fortunately for us, these people were experienced travelers, and came plentifully supplied with

Georgetown's famous rum. The Steward rounded up sufficient glasses. Ice cubes were pilfered from the crew's mess, and, in a manner of speaking, the ice was broken.

It's a peculiar thing about women aboard a ship. Seamen are not exactly savages. Most of us are fairly normal, have an average education, and know good manners. Yet a ship, being a community of males, exclusively, no matter how plain she may be, any woman, once on board, looks devastating. By the same token, I think that to any woman on a ship, the officers and crew take on an aura of adventure and glamour that we don't at all deserve. However, this phenomena, together with the insidious effect of the rum, produced a delightful evening for all of us. All, that is, except the husbands, who were thoroughly disgusted with the gay talk and dancing indulged in by their otherwise devoted and sensible spouses. We, on our part, felt that we were the gay dogs who could have been more charming had not those doltish husbands been present. Wasn't it Puck who said, *What fools these mortals be.* If the truth must be said, the phonograph was silenced, and all hands abed before midnight.

The next morning the brown pilot replaced the black ones and the anchor hove up. While getting underway, the pilot explained to me the method of getting over the river bar. I was astounded. I was also very annoyed at the Charterers for not having explained the situation to me prior to loading. Briefly, this is it. The ship was drawing about four more of water than there was over the bar. He said that it was only soft mud, and that it was imperative to maintain maximum speed, and under no conditions, was the speed to be reduced while dragging over the bar. Should the vessel lose her headway, it would be impossible to get her moving again, and the falling tide would leave her hanging on the hump, possibly with a broken back. A fine kettle of fish. There was no turning back, though. The Chief Engineer was told of the situation, and I impressed on him the importance of maintaining speed. He went off to instruct the Engineer on watch. This man was a native of Poland. He spoke very broken English, and when exited, lapsed immediately into Polish, a failing that was shortly to almost prove our undoing.

We passed out of the river mouth and headed for the bar. I telephoned the engine room and instructed the Pole to *'hook her up,'* a seagoing expression that means what, *cracking on,'* meant in the days of the big wind ships. In other words, *Give her the works.'* In many ways the next few minutes were the same as when we first entered the ice up in the Baltic. We hit the mud bank at full speed but in the distance of hardly a ship's length, we had slowed to a crawl. Unconsciously, I leaned forward, urging her on. Suddenly the engines stopped. The Pilot yelled, and I jumped for the telegraph. It was still on Full Ahead. Savagely, I yanked the handle back and forth and slammed it back on, Full Ahead. Grabbing the telephone, I spun the crank. A flood of Polish

21

poured out, then a click. He had hung up. All this while the pilot was yelling,
"Please, Captain, you must get the engines going. We have only a short time before the tide leaves us."

The bridge phone jangled. Picking up the receiver, I snarled my opinion of all engineers. The Chief's voice interrupted my cursing. It seemed that the Pole had not fully understood the Chief's explanation of how we were to pass over the bar. So when we hit the mud he assumed that the ship had run aground. Without any orders from the bridge, he, on his own initiative, had stopped the engines. To do this was unthinkable, but he had done it. Now, to really foul things up, he told me that because we had lost headway, the main condenser was plugged with mud and he couldn't give us any revolutions just at present. My remarks of the next couple of minutes destroyed for all time my chances of passing through the Pearly Gates. Fortunately for all of us, he hung up on me and went to work. I paced back and forth like a wild man, helpless to do anything. The pilot cowered in the wing of the bridge and avoided me. I had just glanced at my watch for the hundredth time when I heard the telegraph jingle. The handles swung from Full Ahead, around to Full Astern, and the then back to Full Ahead. Those bells were sweet music. They meant that the propeller was churning again. But was it too late? Maybe the tide had fallen too much for us to ever get underway again. Would this would be an ignoble end to my career? *Lost his ship on a mud bank within sight of the shore. No fog or storm, just stupidity.* Would that be what they'd be saying? As the beat of the propeller increased, I anxiously watched the bearing of a landmark, nearby. *Please change.* It did. By God, we were moving! Slowly the ship inched herself along. She gave a final lurch and we were in deep water. *Whew!* The past hour had put years on my life. Such experiences become part of a man and remain woven in the fiber of him for the rest of his life. I can feel the rage and the fear now, just as vividly I did then.

The pilot's little launch appeared up ahead and we stopped to let him off. I know that he was glad to go. Our course was shaped for the island of Tobago, a beautiful spot in the Southeastern Caribbean. We were to make a left turn at Tobago, passing between it and Trinidad. Our course from the pilot station off the mouth of the Demarrara River would expose us to the strength of the South Equatorial Current. This current is one of the major currents of the world, and corresponds in many ways to the Gulf Stream in that, although its direction and limits are fairly constant, its velocity varies considerably, according to the wind. The Chief Mate and I hovered long over the chart room table estimating the effect of the current on our speed and course. We finally set the course and estimated our time of arrival off Tobago. About suppertime a haze settled down. Not quite so thick as fog but still bad. Darkness closed in. The haze was confusing for we were not sure how much visibility there was. At times we had the feeling that we could see for miles if there was anything to be seen. At others, we felt hemmed in by thick fog. There was only one Radio Direction Finder station in the locality which we took advantage of, but because of its direction, aft on our port quarter, it was not of too much help. We steamed along, blowing the fog whistle occasionally and peering into the murk. Suddenly the Chief Mate remarked,

"It's clearing up, Skipper. There's a star just over the foremast."

"Fine, Mister, because we should be up to Tobago within the hour and we've got to pick up the lighthouse."

Idly, I watched the star as the foremast swung in answer to the ship's roll.

"Full Astern. That star is flashing. Stop, Engines."

What we had mistaken for a star was the lighthouse high up on the cliffs of Tobago. We were right under it. The current had fooled us.

"That was close, Mister. Lucky for us that the haze cleared when it did. And all those little kids down below in their bunks. Supposing we had gone bashing into those cliffs?"

I shuddered in the darkness. Another experience filed in memory. Maybe to return and haunt, jeering, *poor judgement. Sure, you were lucky, nothing happened. No damage. Still, poor judgement.* It is not allowed to have many mistakes in judgement at sea. The gods that rule on such matters are never lenient. They have never heard the phrase, *one more chance.* I guess that maybe they had recessed for a few moments when we raised Tobago.

We rounded the North coast of Trinidad and headed down toward Port of Spain, the island's capital and principal port. Soon we were at anchor off the city. Once more the business of Quarantine, Customs, and Immigration. All our new friends, the passengers left in a flurry of farewells. Then we upped anchor and steamed over to the port of Chageramus, about ten miles away. It was a duplicate of Port McKenzie. Another Bauxite pier. And once more there was no sleep through the night. When morning came, the ship was low in the water. She was loaded to her Tropical Marks, which is fully laden, with only enough reserve buoyancy to keep her afloat. For the last time the lines were cast off. Slowly, we swung away from the pier. The ship was very sluggish and slow to answer the helm. Finally she was headed around and clear of the harbor. Our departure was taken from Trinidad and the course laid off for the voyage North to Canada.

Our course took us near the beautiful Windward and Leeward Islands of Grenada, Santa Lucia, Saint Vincent, Barbados, Guadaloupe, Antigua. As I noted them on the chart, I thought of the days of the Buccaneers, Captain Kidd, Blackbeard, pieces of eight, fifteen men on a dead man's chest. Those were the days! High adventure, gold, beautiful captives who whiled away the hours with the victors. Boyhood memories, long since dispelled by reality. In this case, a rust bucket full of ore waddling her way up the sixtieth meridian of

West Longitude towards Sable Island, the graveyard of the Atlantic.

Someday I would like to visit the islands of the Caribbean as a tourist. I I would like to walk on Tobago's cliffs and remember Robinson Crusoe, for it is generally accepted that Tobago was the island about which Defoe wrote. I can just picture Crusoe and his man Friday chasing the wild goats over the high cliffs. And Barbados. Ah, there's an island for you. Crawling with pirates. Surely some of their ghosts can still be heard on some lonely beach roaring. *Yo, ho, ho, and a bottle of rum,* as they buried their chests of gold and jewels. Then 'way over to the Northwest lies Hispaniola, Treasure Island. I'll bet that old Long John Silver's peg legged footprints can still be found in the sand. Is the ghost of Ben Gum catching up with him? He surely will, some night. I'd like to be there and watch Ben even the score.

Day after day we steamed up the sixtieth meridian averaging ten knots. Again, we were enjoying perfect weather. It was on one of those mornings that an incident took place that snapped all of us out of the lethargy into which we had fallen. I think that we were five or six days out of Trinidad. The Third Mate had the morning watch, and I was on the bridge with him enjoying the weather. Chips, the carpenter, came up to report his bilge soundings. I listened, idly, as the Third rang up the engine room and instructed them to put a suction on number five lower hold. It is customary to pump a bilge whenever the soundings exceeded five or six inches. and so far this voyage all the holds had remained practically dry, showing only an inch or two. Evidently condensation was increasing as we approached cooler waters. Soon, through the engine room skylight, I could hear the big pump thumping away. After a bit, it stopped and the engineer phoned up to the Third Mate and asked if he had pumped long enough. The Third blew his whistle for Chips and sent him aft to sound number five again. Pretty soon Chips came flying back up to the bridge, shouting,

"There is something wrong. She's showing two feet now."

I grabbed Chip's sounding rod and ran aft to sound the bilge myself. Sure enough, there were twenty-five inches of water down in the Bauxite! Returning to the bridge, I summoned the Chief Mate and the Chief Engineer and told them what had happened. It was decided to try again. The Mate stationed himself aft with the sounding rod and the Chief went below to his pump. Once more the signal to pump was given. A half hour later the Mate reported that there was no change. If anything, the water level had gone down an inch or two. In the light of later events, it hadn't. It was coming in fast, and permeating the Bauxite. We decided to leave the pump on. At four-thirty in the afternoon, Chips made his customary rounds. Again, he came flying up to the bridge where the Mate and I were arguing the respective merits of reciprocating engines versus turbines. Chips was shouting from the lower bridge ladder,

"Five feet, Captain, five feet in number five."

24

I immediately ordered the pump stopped. Now what? A ship loaded as deeply as we were wouldn't need much water in her to sink her. I mentally tried to calculate the weight of five feet of water in a hold the size of number five. The result wasn't reassuring. A little more and we would all slip beneath the waves. In view of the seriousness of the situation, I ordered all the life boats swung out and additional provisions stowed in them. All hands were alerted and told to remain dressed and ready to abandon ship. Another conference was held. Had we sprung a leak? Struck a submerged derelict? What was it? All at once a peculiar fact became apparent to me. The only time that water came in was when the pump was operating. The Chief scoffed at the thought, and pressed for pumping again. Something made me veto his idea. Instead, a man was stationed at the number five sounding pipe with orders to sound the hold every fifteen minutes. This was continued, all day and night, until we arrived at Port Alfred. No more water came in and no further attempts were made to pump any out. The solution to the mystery appeared after the ship was discharged, about which, more later in its proper place. In the meantime, we were fast approaching Sable Island, off the coast of Cape Breton.

Sable Island; a lighthouse, shifting sands, gales, fog, and a few wild horses, surviving God only knows how. Two days South of Sable we ran into the usual pea soup fog that prevails most of the time. With good reason, Sable has an excellent Radio Direction Finder station, and I had opportunity to take full advantage of it. This was in the days before Radar. However, we had a first class radio and a modern fathometer. To this day, it pleases me to remember how, with the radio and depth indicator, we proceeded right up to the island, passed it a half mile on our port hand. Then, with the radio indicating that we were clear, put the helm hard left and headed Northwest for Cabot Strait and the Gulf of Saint Lawrence. And all this while the fog was so thick that the bow was invisible from the bridge. I felt that it was a fair piece of seamanship. It was times like this that paid me my wages. I know, now, that I would have gone to sea for no wages, just for the chance of doing things like this.

Through the Cabot Strait and across the Gulf of Saint Lawrence we sailed, never seeing a thing. Bird Island lay close to on the Starboard hand. We knew that we were on course, thanks to our fathometer. The hundred fathom curve is a direct course line, clear of land. We had only to stay on it and keep the fog horn going. I was getting pretty weary, though. Three days of cold, Newfoundland fog had penetrated my bones and I felt stiff and cold. According to our dead reckoning, Anticosti Island was now just off our Starboard bow. It would soon be time to turn and head up the Saint Lawrence River. At last, just before dawn, the fog lifted. And about time, too. Several shore lights and beacons were clearly visible, and a quick check showed us on course. One more look around to make sure that it had cleared before dragging my weary bones down the ladder to my room.

25

As I dropped my boots, tired as I was, I couldn't help wondering, *How did that water get into number five?* It was an uneasy sleep that finally claimed me, for even now the water just might be gaining.

By the time I awakened, we had passed Cape Chat and were steaming up the broad Saint Lawrence, heading for Father Point, the pilot station. The fog had cleared completely, and the air was so clear that it seemed to sparkle. We were shortly to be treated to one of the rare sights of the sea. A short distance ahead of us was an old British tramp steamer, also heading for the pilot station. She looked to be four or five miles ahead of us. I remember noting the details of her poop without the aid of my binoculars. I had never been up here before, so once more *The Sailing Directions* were consulted, and I read that the Quarantine, Immigration officials, and the pilot would board us while the ship remained underway on a slow bell. In other words, we would not come to anchor. Returning to the bridge, I reasoned that the Britisher just ahead would arrive just a few minutes before us and would be occupied the best part of an hour. Meanwhile, we would be forced to maneuver about until he was finished. I figured that it would be much more sensible to slow down so as to arrive an hour or so after he had left. In that way, he would be finished and out of the way, leaving us plenty of room to steam about. I put the engines on half speed. An hour or so later, the buildings and dock at Father Point could be clearly seen up ahead on the left bank. Oddly enough, though, the Britisher hadn't pulled away from us at all. He was still just ahead. I rang the engines down to Slow Ahead. Pretty soon, we saw our friend up ahead veer to the left, heading in for the Point. The pilot boat could be seen getting underway. The two vessels closed and we saw the Canadian officials climbing up the Jacob's ladder. Not wanting to crowd in, I put the engines on stop. After awhile the officials could be seen climbing down the ladder into their boat. The Britisher pulled back out into the river and I rang up, Full Ahead. Believe it or not, but we steamed for the next two hours at ten knots and still weren't up to the Point. After we had gotten the pilot aboard, he told us that on very rare occasions, especially after an unusually thick fog, something happened to the air on the river. Something to do with refraction of light, dryness, temperature. Anyway, it increased visibility to unheard of distances. He said that sometimes one could clearly distinguish landmarks forty miles away! I believed him for that British steamer was probably between twenty and thirty miles ahead of us, yet I would have sworn that she was only four miles off, at the most. This was one of those things like water spouts, Saint Elmo's Fire, and sea serpents that you hear about in focsles but usually never encounter in a lifetime at sea.

We were now in for a rare treat. Port Alfred, our destination is located 'way up the Saguenay River, a tributary of the Saint Lawrence River into which it empties a short distance above Father Point, It is a bit confusing to use the word above, because, although the traveler is steaming **up** the Saint Lawrence, he is heading almost due South. The Saguenay angles off in a general Northwest direction up into the province of Quebec. The Saguenay is considered to be one of the most scenic trips in the world, and during the summer months, excursion steamers leave Montreal, daily, for the overnight trip down the Saint Lawrence, up the Saguenay to Port Alfred where they remain overnight, returning to Montreal the next day.

Our pilot was a small, cheerful French Canadian who, as we steamed along, explained the highlights of the renowned river. He told us that it is incredibly deep, being in places, six hundred feet deep! Imagine a river a hundred fathoms deep. It had been cut through the mountains thousands and thousands of years ago by a glacier. I like to think of that glacier as a gigantic ship; a ship with a razor sharp keel which, as the glacier meandered Southward, sliced this crack now known as the Saguenay. It was, indeed, a beautiful trip between the high cliffs, some barren and rocky, others covered with spruce, hemlock, and pine.

Just before sunset the little pilot said that we were approaching 'The Shrine.' When pressed for details, he told the following story. Many years ago a wealthy traveler was crossing the river on the ice. Upon reaching midstream, the ice went out, pitching him and his horse among the grinding floes. He had only one chance in a million of ever surviving. Hope dies hard, though, and as he struggled for his life in the swift running icy water, he made a vow that if the Lord would spare him, he would erect a statue of the Virgin Mary on the river bank. Miraculously, he found himself washed ashore, still alive. True to his word, he caused to be built a mammoth figure which now appeared around the bend. The pilot said that it was the custom for all ships to pull over, close to the cliffs, and blow three long blasts on the whistle, all the while saying a silent prayer. Also, most travelers threw coins into the river for luck. A quaint custom but it appealed to me. I nodded to the helmsman who had been listening intently, and we swung left. When we were abreast of the statue, I leaned on the whistle cord. The mournful blasts echoed and re-echoed between the cliffs. Going to the rail, I dropped a few coins in the water. Looking up at the silent figure, I silently breathed my own silent prayer. *Please, God, no fog!* With six hundred feet under us, there could be no question of anchoring, and with no room to maneuver, would surely slam into the cliffs and lose the ship. Was it my imagination or did I detect the ghost of a smile as a bend in the river hid the statue from view? I chose to think that she smiled for didn't we not only arrive at Port Alfred in good weather, but came back down the river as well. I remember when we again drew abeam of her on our way down. I circled my forefinger and thumb and waved in the manner of fellow conspirators.

Well, there we were at Port Alfred. Another Bauxite pier. We had no sooner tied up when giant grabs commenced digging us out.

Now to solve the mystery of the water in number five. The big clam shell grab soon struck water soaked Bauxite. What a mess. An analysis verified what we already suspected. The water was salt water. All the ore that was wet had to be kept apart from the remainder of the cargo. It was later dried and used, but as several hundred tons were involved, my owners eventually paid a substantial claim.

At last the lower hold was empty. The Chief Mate and I went down the ladders. Upon reaching the bottom, we immediately went to the bilge boxes. Lifting up the covers, we looked in. Everything seemed to be in order. The Mate straightened up and for no particular reason, swung his flashlight around. Light glinted from a small metal object resting on one of the frames just above the bilges. I think that we both realized, at the same instant, what had happened. Remember the night down in the jungle river? The night that one of the assistant engineers had repaired the bilge valve? When he reassembled the valve, he had forgotten to replace what is known as a non-returnable blank. These blanks act in a valve so that water can only pass in one direction through the valve. In this case, instead of water being pumped from the bilge, through the manifold in the engine room, and overboard, the reverse had taken place. We had been pumping the Atlantic Ocean into the ship. A few more hours of pumping and Lloyds of London would have tolled the bell for us as they do for every casualty of the sea that results in a ship being lost.

For those in peril on the sea.
Old Sailor's Hymn

-3-

ORDERS TO ASSUME COMMAND

When I received my first letter from the Marine Superintendent, Captain Litchfield, to assume command my feelings were indescribable. Elation, pride, overwhelming pride, gratefulness. Words cannot describe what I felt. It was the culmination of all that had gone on before. All that I had dreamed of, worked for, yearned for. When I opened that letter, all my dreams had literally come true. I had finally made it.

I had sailed as Chief Mate long enough. Maybe, too long. I stayed on one ship that slogged the North Atlantic in convoy, back and forth. On another, we got stuck for several months in the Mediterranean. Then I did a long stint during the Normandy invasion. Three or four other ships for voyages of two or three months each. It was time that I sat for my Master's ticket, so I paid off and went home to study.

And study I did, day and night. The living room floor was strewn with papers, books, navigational tables. The examination for Master was unlike the previous ones for Third Mate and Chief Mate. The list of subjects was so long that I wondered how it could all be crammed into my head. On top of this, two other obstacles faced me. The first was the time limit, five days. Unfortunately, I am a slow writer. I'm left handed, and in my early school years, the teachers attempted to switch me over to being a righty. They were only partially successful. As a result, I print with my right hand, which slows me up considerably. The other obstacle was equally frustrating. Before the War, celestial navigation was a tedious business. The task of solving a spherical triangle involved trigonometry. This meant using the Logarithm Tables of the Trigonometric functions, which were carried out to five decimal points. A poor Second Mate, rousted out of his bunk after only a couple of hours sleep, found himself struggling with the Cosecant of this added to the Sine of that. The whole subtracted from the Cotangent of something or other. It was slow work, and the margin for error was considerable. Then, early in the War, marvelous books appeared in chart rooms all over the seas. *Dreisenstock's H.O. 208, H.O. 211, and finally, H.O. 214.* These books did all the Trigonometric functions for you. Also, about this time, the *Air Almanac* made its appearance. It was far superior to the old *Nautical Almanac.* Equipped with a set of *H.O.214, the Air Almanac,* and accurate Chronometer time, thanks to radio ticks from NSS, navigation was a cinch. Shoot the sun with your sextant, note the chronometer

29

time, enter the Tables for a couple of simple, quick calculations, and presto, there was a fine LOP. (Line of Position.) The trouble was, though, that in those days the Examiners wouldn't let you use these wonderful new books. You had to use the Logarithm Tables and the old *Nautical Almanac,* and we had all become rusty.

The Coast Guard had taken over the duties of the Steamboat Inspection Service, administered by the Commerce Department. They did it by putting the civilian Steamboat Inspectors into Coast Guard uniforms. These ex-civil servants were not unlike Supreme Court judges, in that change of any kind evolved very slowly. They were not yet ready to accept the new tables.

So it was back to the Bowditch for me. I still have the list of required subjects. It looked endless.

> *LATITUDE BY POLARIS*
> *EX-MERIDIAN*
> *LONGITUDE BY CHRONOMETER (SUN,*
> *MOON, Star)*
> *GREAT CIRCLE SAILING*
> *FUEL CONSUMPTION*
> *STABILITY AND HULL CONSTRUC-*
> *TION*
> *OCEAN WINDS, WEATHER, CURRENTS*
> *NAVIGATION LAWS*
> *SEAMANSHIP*

On and on it went. And those are just the highlights. The very last on the list was the most ominous, **Miscellaneous.** How do you study for that one?

Day after day, night after night, I struggled and memorized until my head was about to burst. At last I could go no further. I was as ready as I'd ever be.

The next morning I took the bus to Boston and offered myself up to the examiners, promptly at eight, A.M. I was directed to a room that looked just like a school room; rows of desks facing the examiner. He motioned me forward. He looked so forbidding and grim. He just nodded as I presented my discharges. He went over them very carefully, to make sure that I had served as Chief Mate the required time. By this time there were several men in the room, all writing furiously, or gazing off into space with their faces all screwed up with the effort of recalling an illusive answer.

There were four card index boxes on the examiner's desk, labeled Third Mate, Second Mate, Chief Mate, and Master. He selected a card from the Master's box and handed it to me, together with two sheets of paper.

"Write your answer on one sheet. Use the other for scratch. When you finish, bring me both sheets. You may work at your own pace. However, if you haven't finished by four P.M. Friday, you will have failed. Good Luck!"

This was Monday morning. I wrote and wrote. All that I had memorized spilled out on those lined sheets. As soon as I finished one card, it was taken from me and another was silently given me. At noon I would dash down stairs and up the street to a cafeteria for a bowl of soup. I had left two notebooks with the cashier. One contained my notes, the other was blank. During the morning I could tell from the way the cards were running what the next subject would be, so I'd skim over the notes. In the other note book I scribbled all the questions that I could remember. I had done the same thing when I had sat for my Chief Mate's ticket. I had an idea in the back of my head that if shipping got tough, I'd maybe start a little navigation school for men seeking to upgrade their tickets.

The week dragged on. Every night I would study until late at night, going over and over the subjects that were yet to come. Then, the next day, I'd write and compute. My nerves were getting tighter and tighter. When Thursday rolled around, I figured that I would finish that afternoon. In spite of my slow handwriting, I'd been sailing along at a pretty good clip. When I went up for my last card for the day, I asked the examiner if I was ahead or behind schedule.

"Mmm," says he. "Same time tomorrow, eight, A.M."

Friday, the last day. Would I make it? I was so nervous that the first two cards seemed almost impossible to answer. I sort of got my second wind, though, and was stepping up the pace. No going for soup today. I stayed right at it. I could tell from the cards that I was coming down the home stretch. The last few cards had to do with Navigational Laws. At about two-thirty, I walked up to his Lordship's desk and handed in a card and my answer.

"That will be all. Please return to your seat."

My God! I was finished.

"What about Miscellaneous?", I stuttered.

"Mister, I give out cards at my discretion. On any given subject I might give two, four, or any amount until your answers satisfy me that you have, or have not, grasped the subject. If you want more cards, I'll be quite happy to oblige, up to four o'clock."

"Oh, no Sir, I..."

"Well, just go and sit down. It has been a tiring week."

I hadn't realized it but he had been correcting my papers as fast as I turned them in. It wasn't ten minutes later that he pointed a bony finger at me and barked,

"You, come here."

I marched up to his desk, trying in vain to stop my legs from shaking. They were trembling so badly that my pants were flapping as if a half gale was blowing. He was scribbling on a card.

"Take this to the next office. They will process your new ticket."

I walked out of the room forty feet tall. *Master! You will address me as Captain, damn your eyes!* An enlisted man made out my ticket, had it signed by the Commander, Officer in charge of Marine Inspection, slipped it into a manila envelope. and handed it to me.

"There you are, Cap."

"Captain," I shot back.

Monday morning, right on the stroke of nine, the phone rang.

"Captain Farrar?"

Captain? How did who ever it was, know?

"This is Captain Litchfield's secretary. The Captain would like to see you in an hour if you can make it. Bye."

Make it? Nobody **ever** keeps Captain Litchfield waiting. I was out the door in five minutes, plowing through the snow to the bus stop. I arrived at 40 Central Street with five minutes to spare. Speeding up in the elevator, the operator said,

"Cold morning, Captain, right?"

Entering the office, the switchboard girl flung me a *High, Captain. What in the hell is going on?* I entered Captain Litchfield's outer office. His secretary invited me to be seated.

"The Captain will see you shortly, Captain."

The whole damned city of Boston seemed to know something that I didn't. A man didn't rate being called Captain until he had a command, even if he did have the ticket.

She answered the Captain's buzzer and bounced back out.

"Captain Litchfield is on long distance, but he thought that you would like to read this while you wait."

I opened the envelope and unfolded a letter to "Captain" Frank F. Farrar. Typed in capital letters at the head of it were the words, **ORDERS TO ASSUME COMMAND.** Usually, I am pretty stoic. Not this time. I choked up and my eyes got all blurred. The secretary, a very kind, gray haired soul, came over with a small paper cup.

"Congratulations, Captain. You,re not the first one to feel that way, you know. A few have come before you."

I downed the water. Water, hell. It was very good Scotch whiskey.

"The Captain, poor dear, has been working twelve hours a day all through the War, and sometimes, at night, on his way home, he'll stop for a little sip. Oh, there he is, buzzing for you now. Go straight in, please."

Captain Litchfield was one of the finest, most able men that I have ever known. He had been one of Eastern's crack skippers on the overnight, New York-Boston run., a killer if there ever was one. Those ships sailed from the North River at five P.M. They went down around the Battery, through Hell's

Gate, up the East River with its traffic and currents to Long Island Sound, Buzzard's Bay, and through the Cape Cod Canal to Boston. Gales, fog and more fog, never stopped him. And a thousand passengers weighing him down. Then, when World War II came, and the Company took on dozens of Liberty and Victory ships, he took on the almost impossible job of crewing them, storing them, repairing them, and dispatching them. But, by God, he was equal to it.

Now, as always, he was pressed for time. His remarks to me made me glow.

"You have been a good Chief Mate. You will also be a good Master. If you need me, write or call. The very best to you in your first command. Now, be off. If you hurry, you can catch the seven P.M. train out of the South Station for Charleston, South Carolina."

A quick handshake, a walloping thump on my back, and I was out the door. What a great guy. I vowed, then and there, that I would never let him down.

Back home on the bus again. It was snowing like blazes, and we already had a foot on the ground from the last storm. The bus slithered to a stop and back up the hill I trudged, kicking the snow gleefully. Walking on the clouds, I was.

In no time I had my suitcase and seabag packed. My boy was at school. I got the principal to bring him to the phone. I said so long to him, and asked him to pick up his sled at the bottom of the hill. I flung my suitcase and seabag on the sled, buttoned my overcoat, and was off down the hill again, sextant box in one hand, the other pulling the sled.

As Litchfield knew I would, I made the seven o'clock Southbound train. I checked my seabag and suitcase through on the baggage car and fought through to a coach seat, no berths being available.

There was little sleep on the train that night. Service men were prowling the aisles drinking out of bottles in brown paper bags. I placed my sextant box on my lap and carefully smoothed out my precious letter. I gloated over it; drooled over it. It was for real! Let's see, now. I was to proceed with all possible dispatch to Charleston, there to assume command of the S.S. Augustus P. Loring, presently loading for Brest, France. Upon arriving, I was to go directly to the Customs House and sign the ship's Register. That little exercise would make me officially and legally her Master.

The next morning I staggered off the train, stiff and sore from a sleepless night in the coach. Clutching my sextant, I went to claim my baggage. It couldn't be found, nor was it ever found for two years. Then it turned up in Boston, moldy and worthless. Well, there I was, facing a winter crossing of the North Atlantic with nothing but the old brown suit and topcoat to my name. Some of the euphoria started to leak out. Oh, well, I still had my sextant, didn't I?

33

First, I went to the Customs House to sign the ship's Register. Then on to the Agent's office. To my horror, they told me that were scheduled to sail that same night just as soon as the last of the cargo was loaded. The ship had been stored and bunkered. The previous Skipper was waiting on board to turn the ship over to me. I had time for a quick sandwich, then back to the Customs House to clear the ship. As the Agent and I parted, I told him to order me a tow boat for eleven P.M.

Back on board, I had a quick session with the old Skipper. I signed for his inventory and he was off for the railroad station. Then a series of meetings, first with the Chief Engineer. More than enough bunkers. Then with the Chief Steward. The ship was stored for three months. Finally with the Chief Mate. I was well impressed with him. A Harvard graduate, and a real proper Bostonian, indeed. We went to the chart room where he showed me the course laid out by the previous Captain. He had been ultra conservative. Southeast to Latitude 33, North, off Bermuda. Then East, along 33, then North to the Azores. Then to Brest. I changed that. We would stick our snout Northerly, all the way up to a point just South of Newfoundland and then follow a Great Circle course Eastward. This meant a winter crossing of the Western Ocean with all its gales and raging storms. I was young and brave in those days, but not foolhardy, I hope.

I impressed on the Mate the necessity of battening down, especially the life boats. By the time we finished, supper was over, so we both went ashore for a bite. I was worn out for the lack of sleep and the tension of being a green shipmaster about to embark on his first voyage in command. We went into the first restaurant that we came to. We were both in a hurry. I ordered bacon and eggs. The bacon was tough and stringy. I chomped down on a piece. Dear God, my upper bridge work broke into two pieces. This voyage was starting off great. No clothes, now no teeth. Without the bridge I looked like a Jack-O-Lantern, two fangs, one on each side.

When we got back to the ship, I raided the Slop Chest for long underwear, oilskins, work shoes, and a razor. All hands were battening down and securing for sea. The ship was a beehive of activity. A tow boat was alongside, her stack huffing quietly. The pilot and I were in the saloon drinking coffee. Promptly at eleven, the Mate came in.

"The ship is ready for sea, Captain. The gangway is up, all lines singled up."

"Right, Oh, Mister. Let's go."

I couldn't get used to being addressed as Captain, but how sweet it was.

The pilot and I made our way up to the bridge. The Third mate and the helmsman were there.

"Mister, ring up Stand By on the engine, please."

"Stand By, Aye."

And off we went into a winter night. We dropped the pilot outside of

S.S. New York

My proudest possession

the harbor and hauled around on our Northerly course towards a point South of Newfoundland, where we would commence our Great Circle course across the North Atlantic, where the winter gales were ready to pounce on us out of the Northwest.

And pounce they did. That entire voyage was an unending struggle against the weather. Both of our port life boats were stove in. The port side accommodation ladder washed over board. All the wooden life rafts were smashed to bits and swept over the side. Day and night I kept to the bridge conning the ship; easing the helm and adjusting our engine speed to the weather. And still it blew, always from the port quarter. I began to think that somebody had put a curse on us. Part of an old sea chantey kept running through my head:

> *"AND OUT OF THE NORTH SHE COME. IT BLEW THE TAR RIGHT OFF THE SPARS, AND THE SPARS RIGHT OFF THE MAST. BUCKETS AND PAILS AND KEGS OF NAILS WENT BY IN THE WINTRY BLAST."*

In spite of the weather, we were making our Easting. Our Chief Mate, being a Bostonian, was a master at understatement. One wild night, he asked me to relieve him. The stern light had been washed out. I crawled into the wheel house. God, that wind was fierce.

"Mister, the hell with the stern light. No ship is going to run up on us in this weather. Let it go until the weather moderates."

He insisted, though, so out he went. The best part of an hour went by before he returned, soaked to the hide, a big lump on his temple. His only comment was,

"Wretched evening, Captain."

The next day Sparks brought me a message from our owners.

> *CANCEL BREST. PROCEED LE HAVRE FOR DISCHARGE.*

That was Ok with me, besides, Le Havre was an easier port to get into. Course was changed to our new destination. Nothing else changed. The weather remained foul. The wind was still Force six to eight, now a little more on our port beam. The ship was rolling her guts out. We entered the English Channel, hoping for a break. Nope. It got worse. The seas in those waters are different than the open Atlantic. Short, vicious waves that hit like solid iron. What little sleep I got was lying on top of my bunk with just my shoes off. Folded at the foot was a fancy blanket. It was royal blue, and had a big gold seal of the War Shipping Administration embossed on it. I'd just pull it over me for an hour or two. When I got up, I'd fold it up again. I didn't know it at the time, but the cabin steward spread the word below decks in hushed tones: *He ain't human. Hasn't been in his bunk since we left Charleston.*

One cold, miserable day we picked our way into Le Havre and dropped the anchor. Sparks had radioed our ETA, so some one had to know that we had arrived. There we lay for four days, licking our wounds. Then, one morning, out came a tow boat whose Skipper acted as harbor pilot. In short order he had us alongside. The French Agent put in an appearance and gave me a ride up to the Port Official's building. He told me that we were only to discharge enough cargo to lighten our draft enough to proceed up the Seine River to Rouen, where we would complete discharge.

On the way up the river, the pilot told me about a phenomenon that happens every day in the lower part of the Seine. It is called Le Muscaret, or The Bore, in English. It seems that it is caused by the down flowing river current meeting the rushing, incoming tidal flow. It creates a cresting wave which rushes down the river at incredible speed. It can be dangerous. We got up near Rouen about mid-afternoon. It is a tidal port, so the locks can only be opened when the tide is right. Set out into the river bottom are a series of pile clusters. The French call them *moles*. The pilot told us that a small boat would come out and take our mooring lines to the moles, where we would tie up, fore and aft, while waiting for the locks to open. This was accomplished in short order. The pilot warned me that we should have the engine ready, men standing by the lines, and be ready to take action if the force of Le Muscaret parted our lines. I was properly impressed, and made all arrangements. We were sitting in the saloon waiting for supper when the pilot jumped up.

"Here she comes, Le Muscaret."

We all rushed out. It was an awesome sight. A wall of water roaring down the river. The ship surged back on her moorings, but all was well. Le Muscaret disappeared down the river but not from memory. The pilot told me that there were two or three other rivers in the world that had a Bore. One was in West Africa, he thought.

The rest of our stay was quite ordinary. I took in the sights of Rouen, which fortunately, the Germans had spared. It is truly a magnificent city. After discharging, we steamed across the Channel and up into the Bristol Channel to Newport Mons, in Wales, for 2000 tons of slag ballast. Then to Cardiff to bunker for Philadelphia.

Back home via the Southern Route. It was just another voyage. Run of the mill for a tramp steamer, but to me it was the greatest experience of my life. Still is, too.

Tall oaks from little acorns grow.
David Everett

-4-

BACKWARD TO THE CAREFREE DAYS

My childhood was spent on the coast of New England, mostly within sight and sound of the sea. My father would point seaward and tell me that just beyond the horizon lay Spain, Portugal, Africa. I used to sit on the rocks and stare Eastward, conjuring up in my mind pictures of those far off lands. Some day I would go and see them for myself. I wondered if they would be like my geography books described them.

By the time that I had entered high school, I had become a confirmed reader of sea stories. I read everything that I could lay my hands on, pertaining to ships. I knew all about Donald McKay's famous clipper ships. I could quote from memory passages from their log books chronicling their record breaking voyages around The Horn. All the tales of the whaling ships were familiar to me. When the wind howled round the eaves at night during a Northeaster, I would imagine that I was a sailor making sail down in the Roaring Forties.

I was a great disappointment to my mother and grandmother who planned that after high school, I would enter The Massachusetts Institute of Technology and become an engineer. I was stubborn and wilful, though, as many are at sixteen. Without their knowledge, I canvassed all the shipping companies in Boston. Every Saturday I used to go to Boston calling at the offices of the Port Captains. A month before graduation I was promised a berth as Deck Boy. The ship was due to sail the day after our high school graduation exercises. I waited until the night before, and then announced my plans. Oh, the storm that raged. It went on and on, most of the night. My stubbornness prevailed, though, and two days later, a skinny, scared kid, I stood at the head of the pier and looked up the rusty sides of my new home.

I will never forget my first meeting with Mr. Kelly, the Chief Mate. The product of an Irish father and a French-Canadian-Indian mother, he looked like a mahogany skinned, ugly bull.

"So you are the new boy, huh? Stow your gear in the focsle and report to the Bosun."

Those were the only words of welcome that I received. He looked so cranky that I didn't dare to ask him where the focsle was. Instead, I timidly started forward. His roar brought me up short.

"Aft, you dummy."

I turned back and sneaked by him, half expecting a kick in the rear. Clutching my one suitcase, I made my way aft under the poop deck. Just inside

37

a big iron door, I spied the messroom. There was a little man in there noisily washing dishes. He was, like most of the mess boys of those days, a Greek. His name was George. (I later learned that no matter what their real names were, aboard ship all Greeks were either called George or Nick.) He showed me where the deck gang's focsle was. It turned out to be a long, dimly lit, room all the way aft on the starboard side. Double decker bunks lined the outboard side while crude wooden lockers occupied the inboard side. The place was deserted, everyone being on deck working. I quickly changed my clothes, and put on a brand new pair of dungarees. That big Chief Mate had taken all the starch out of me and now I didn't dare to go out. While I stood there, getting my courage up, someone entered. I couldn't believe my eyes because even though the doorway was of conventional height, he had to stoop to get through. He was stripped to the waist, and of all the fine figures of men that I've since seen, he outstripped them all. He looked like a combination Greek God and a professional weight lifter. The muscles across his shoulders rippled like brown snakes. He barked at me in a foreign tongue. When I didn't answer, he spoke again, this time in a guttural, broken English.

You are de new boy, ja? Vat's your name?"

He was a German, a native of Hamburg. I soon found out that almost the entire crew were Germans. This was back in the days when Immigration laws were not too rigidly enforced. Because this ship was regularly running to Hamburg and Bremen, it was natural that a good Chief Mate would take advantage of the fact that Germany had come upon bad times, economically, and hire some of the thousands of good German seamen that were on the beach in Hamburg.

My boyhood days were over. In one day, I was a man, doing man's work. Or so I felt. That night we all sat down at the long table in the mess room for supper. As befitted a boy, I sat at the foot of the table. The Bosun presided at the head. Then came the oldest Able Seaman and so on, down to the ship's boy, me. After swinging a chipping hammer all afternoon, my appetite was as sharp as a razor. The mess boy brought in a big pan of meat and gravy. The Bosun forked several pieces onto his plate and passed it on to the first AB. When it finally reached me, I stabbed my fork down into the thick gravy, drooling. There was no meat left, only gravy. I looked up the table. All hands were busy eating. The Bosun saw me looking at him and growled,

"Vat's the matter, boy?"

I replied that there was no meat and I was hungry. Mopping up the last of his plate with a piece of bread occupied him for a minute. Then he told me that on a ship, men eat before boys, and boys eat what the men leave, so if I wanted to eat, I'd better become a man. Brutal and direct.

Alright, I said to myself. *I'll show him. I'll learn everything there is to learn, and I'll work harder than anyone else. I will be a man.*

38

The next morning at dawn we sailed for Hamburg. As a ship's boy, I wasn't put on watch but was assigned to work on deck with the Bosun. He was a slave master and I his slave. The work was heavy. Great hawsers and coils of tackle had to be stowed below decks. All the cargo handling gear had to be put away. And always that big Bosun loomed over me. When lifting something heavy, he would always have his end up first. Then would come the, *Lift, boy. Vat's the matter? You tired?*

For awhile I hated him. I longed to push him over the side. I used to imagine how easy it would be. *Wait until he's close to the rail. A quick lunge and he'd be gone, off my back.* Then, without my quite knowing when or why, I began to admire him, and so commenced to emulate him. I didn't talk much because he didn't. I scrubbed my dungarees in a bucket every night because he did. Seemed a waste of time because by noon of the next day, they were dirty again. Still, he said that a good sailor started off the day in clean clothes. I took pride in doing good work, of being able to endure broiling sun and chill winds without complaining, because that's the way he was. Today, I am very grateful to him. He formed habits in me that have stood me in good stead ever since.

The days passed quickly. Because I didn't stand a watch, Sundays were for free. The first Sunday out, I wandered 'midships after breakfast. It was a fine sunny morning and we were about half way across the Atlantic. I could see the Third Mate up on the bridge, his officer's cap snowy white in the sunshine. *That's where I'll be, someday,* I vowed. The decks were deserted so I summoned up my courage and went up the ladders to the bridge. I sidled over to the Third Mate and ventured a "Good morning." Before he could answer, a roar behind me made me jump.

"Mister Mate, what is this boy doing on the bridge?"

It was the Old Man, himself. I looked for a way to escape, but the Captain was blocking the ladder. The Third Mate, Mister Brown, saved the day for me by saying that I had come up to learn to steer.

"Humph," grunted the Old Man. "I thought that this new generation knew it all. Well, boy, don't just stand there. Get into the wheel house and take the wheel. And mind your course."

Gee, I was actually being allowed to steer this great ship. The quartermaster relinquished the wheel to me and explained that the black lubber's line on the forward edge of the compass represented the ship's head and all I had to do was to keep the black line on the course. He showed me the one brass spoke on the wheel which, when pointing up, meant that the rudder was 'midships. At night the helmsman stood in darkness except for the dim light coming from the compass binnacle, and that by feeling the brass spoke, could tell where the rudder was.

And so the days went by. The work was hard, but little by little, the

39

strangeness was wearing off. I got to know all the rest of the crew, the firemen, the oilers, the cook. And slowly they came to accept me. I acquired a nickname, Slim, which was quite a compliment. Had I not been accepted, it would have been Skinny. The ship raised Bishop's Rock, the entrance to the English Channel. As we proceeded up the Channel, the Bosun spent most of the time trying to keep me on the job. The Channel was full of shipping and instead of working I spent my time staring at all the various types of craft.

"Bosun, what kind of ship is that?"

"That's called an English Drifter. Get back to work."

"Bosun, what's that one just over the port bow?"

"That's a Frenchman, home from the Grand Banks after twelve months fishing for cod."

So my education proceeded. Every day I learned something more about the sea and ships, and of how they were sailed. Although he never, by the slightest sign, admitted it, I think that the Bosun liked me. His gruffness and growling continued unabated, but he went out of his way to teach me the proper way to do things: How to splice, how to sew canvas, to reeve a tackle.

In a day or two we were up to the entrance to the Elbe River. The pilot came bobbing over to us in his little row boat, rowed by two apprentice pilots. The Bosun had told me that the Mate was very particular about boarding a pilot. Everything had to go perfectly. If there was the slightest slip up, or if anything was done in a slipshod way, there would be no living with him for days. The Bosun claimed that when Mister Kelly went into a rage, all the Indian in him came to the surface and he went on the warpath scalping everyone in his path. It was, therefore, a source of great pride to me that the Bosun let me rig the boat rope and stand by the forward end of it. When a pilot's small boat comes alongside a large vessel, it is necessary that he make contact well forward, up near the bow, on the lee side. Then it is the job of one of the apprentices to boat his oar and grab the boat rope. The rope must be rigged not more than a foot above the water's edge, not too slack so that it is in the water, and not so high that it can't be reached from a small boat. Then, after the rowboat has come alongside, the apprentice can grab it and gradually slack his boat aft, along the rope, until he reaches the Jacob's ladder amidships. It is the duty of the seaman on the ship to stand by on the forward end of the boat rope, holding one round turn on a bitt. He must lean over the bow and gauge the height of the waves and the size of the small boat. Then, as the occasion demands, slack off or pull in. A mistake in judgement would result in a second try with its resulting delay. I watched the little boat approach, never taking my eyes off of it. By the grace of God, I am gifted with side vision. I spied the Bosun, standing by the Jacob's ladder, frantically signalling me to slack off. I did, promptly. The rowboat made contact, slacked off down to the ladder, and made fast. The pilot came aboard and was greeted by the Mate. His affable,

"Secure, Bosun," was music to my ears.

Praise is a forgotten word aboard a ship. So is sympathy. The Bosun and I set about pulling in the ladder and the boat rope. We were in sight and hearing of the bridge so the Bosun had to confine his caustic remarks to a whisper.

"Dummer! Stupid boy. You will never be a sailor."

We stayed in Hamburg for over a week. It has always been a world famous sailor town, and tales of its attractions, told in the focsle, had inflamed my imagination. Two young German AB's offered to take me ashore with them the first night. I figured that they should know their way around, and gratefully accepted. The Captain returned from shore and we all lined up midships for a 'draw.' I drew the great sum of five dollars as an advance on my pay. When the Bosun shouted *'knock off'* at five o'clock, there was a dash for the messroom. Supper was over in a jiffy. Buckets clattered in the wash room as we scrubbed at the red lead, fish oil, and tar stains. On those old ships we had no such luxury as running water. As a matter of fact, it was an exceptionally good ship that allowed as much as two buckets of fresh water a day per man. And those had to serve for both bathing and washing clothes.

Promptly at seven we were off, ashore. I was a sailor, ashore in my first port. I adopted a salt sea rolling gait. Before we reached the city I was swaggering along with my hands shoved in my belt, for all the world like Sinbad the Sailor.

Despite my anticipation of seeing adventurous sights, our evening consisted of first going to the post office for stamps, and then for a stroll through the beer gardens surrounding Alster Lake, which is a beautiful lake right in the center of the city. There was an orchestra playing in one of them so we sat at a little table under the trees and drank a stein of German beer while listening to some Strauss waltzes. Back on board before midnight. An uneventful, and somehow, unsatisfying evening. I decided that tomorrow night would be different. If I only knew what the next night would bring, I would have stayed on board until the ship sailed.

That night I went ashore with one of the firemen and George, the messboy. They had both made several trips to Hamburg and claimed to be real old-timers in Saint Pauli, the waterfront district of Hamburg. It was a memorable night. First they took me to a cabaret, the New China. I was only a kid, and except for a few glasses of my grandfather's home brew, and the one stein of beer the previous night, had never had a drink. But now I was a sailor, a tough guy. Hadn't all the sailors that I had read about always gotten drunk when they went ashore? Well, by golly, what are we waiting for? We didn't have much money so we couldn't afford to buy drinks in such a fancy place. George got the idea to sneak out and buy a bottle of cheap brandy. Pretending that he was looking for some one, he sauntered out. We ordered three steins of beer from the waiter. While we were placing our order, two girls who had been

Joe Collins - Oiler
Hamburg - Seattle Spirit
1931

Joe had been first violinist on the Leviathon

My first ship

SS Seattle Spirit

Company: Seas Shipping Co. New York, NY
Master: Edward W. Myers (SS ROBIN MOOR)
Gross Tons: 5627

Home Port: Seattle, WA

Built: 1919 @ Seattle, WA
Dimensions: 410' x 54' x 28'

The Freighter, SS SEATTLE SPIRIT, was torpedoed by the German submarine U-124 (Mohr) at 0425 GCT on June 18, 1942 in the North Atlantic (50-23 North/42-25 West) while en route in Convoy ON-102 (#112) from Murmansk, Russia to New York via Reykjavik, Iceland in ballast. Ship cleared Reykjavik on May 29. Her complement was 37 merchant crew, 11 Naval Armed Guard, and 7 Canadian passengers. Three crew members were killed in the engine room by the explosion and one crew member, who had jumped overboard, died from shock and exposure.
Photo courtesy of Mariners Museum, Newport News, VA

The Bosun

Mr. Kelly and Red, a Deck Boy

Fishing Schooner off The Grand Banks, 1931

S.S. Seattle Spirit at sea, 1931

sitting at the next table came over. Very politely, they asked if they could join us. I was overcome with embarrassment. My experience with the opposite sex was practically nil, and where I came from, young ladies were more decorous. They were pretty, though, and I was flattered beyond words. My face crimson, I nodded, mutely. They seated themselves and at once started chattering like magpies. All this in quite good English. Their conversation, sometimes directed at us, more often to each other, sounded like the latest edition of the shipping news. They knew every ship that was in port; who was in the crew, how long they would be in port, everything. Amazed, I asked them if they worked in a shipping office. Evidently I had said something amusing, for they burst into gales of laughter interspersed with machine-gun German. One of them patted me on the head and said that this must be my first trip. When I admitted that it was, she moved her chair closer and asked if she could please have a drink. By this time my head was in the clouds. Here were two beautiful girls falling into our arms. Recklessly, I told the waiter to bring them both a beer. The one that had attached herself to me snuggled a little closer and said that she didn't like beer, and couldn't she have a small Grenadine? The other one echoed her. Nodding assent to the waiter, I boldly put my arm around my new friend. Just then George returned with the cognac. We dumped a dollop into our beers and took big swigs. A third fraulein appeared and latched onto George. He seemed delighted. Between guzzling beer and cognac, he barked away at her in his native Greek. She all the while smiling and bobbing her head, not understanding a word. Periodically, the waiter brought the girls more little glasses. There was music, noise, and confusion. The cognac slowly disappeared into the beer. The mixture burned its way down our foolish gullets. My memory of events from then on are dim. I recall the waiter totaling our bill by counting the saucers stacked in front of each girl. The amount was staggering. I craftily hid one mark, the price of launch fare back to the ship, in another pocket and laid the rest of my money on the table. My shipmates did the same. Our girls melted away. More waiters and the bouncer made threatening noises. Everything whirled round and round. I felt as if I was on a merry-go-round which spun faster and faster, propelling us through the door. Things steadied and I found myself sitting on the sidewalk. My shirt was torn and one knee showed through a hole in my pant leg. It would be sore tomorrow.

We picked ourselves up and started for the boat landing. There was a launch service that called at all the ships in the sprawling harbor, ferrying seamen to and from their ships. The launch would save us hours in getting back to our ship.

It was by then, very late, and the last boat was ready to leave. We stumbled aboard and took the remaining seats. There were seamen from half a dozen ships, all returning after a night in port. Danes, Japs, Frenchmen, Hindus, a floating League of Nations. Most of them were drunk and quarrelsome, excepting three or four little Japanese sailors. They sat quietly, like little mice, just opposite me, twittering away in their peculiar language.

We had no sooner pulled away from the wharf when my poor stomach rebelled at the beer and cognac diet. Without any warning, and without being able to control myself, I suddenly vomited. The poor little Japs were sprayed from head to foot. The one in the middle stood up, squeaked something and hit me, right on the nose. In seconds the whole boat looked and sounded like a first class war. Danes were walloping Frenchmen. Frenchmen were kicking Swedes, and George, the Greek, was rolling around with the three Japs, cursing and yelling in Greek and English. I felt as if I was being trampled to death. My nose was bleeding and my stomach retching. What a night! The launch finally pulled alongside of our ship. We crawled up the ladder, followed by the curses and taunts of the survivors. Making my way aft, I fell into my bunk, clothes and all. My last thought was, *Guess you're not a tough old salt after all.*

And so it went. My education. Changing from a boy to a man; from a landlubber to a seaman. Always having to learn the hard way. A bloody nose and a hangover taught me that getting drunk was foolish. Smashed fingers and an aching back--they taught me the proper way to do a job. A cuff on the side of the head taught me to listen instead of talking. A plateful of gravy taught me respect for my elders and superiors. All these things a boy learns at home and at school. I was learning them again, the hard way, and I wouldn't forget them.

There would be other ships and other ports through the years. New shipmates and new experiences. And from all of them I would learn something. Some day I would be Master of my own ship. And on what I had learned before might hang the lives of my crew and the safety of my ship. But all this was far ahead in the future. Indeed, my next voyage might well have been my last. From the Captain I learned how to keep my own counsel. How to conceal fear, and how to adopt the spurious air of unconcern and confidence that becomes infectious to the ship's crew. It all happened this way:

The sea never changes and its works, for all the talk of men,
are wrapped in mystery.

Joseph Conrad

-5-

FOG, THE CURSE OF ALL SEAMEN

On this voyage we were bound down the coast, South from Boston, to pick up cargo from New York, Philadelphia, Baltimore, and Norfolk. All the way home from Germany I had spent every spare minute at the wheel learning to steer. Practice makes for proficiency, as the saying goes, and I became adept at holding a course. I steered in all kinds of weather, always with the Mates cursing me. Because of their constant criticism I **had** to steer well. If I wandered off course a couple of degrees, their cursing could be heard all the way back to the poop deck. They watched the ship's wake like hawks. The slightest deviation from a creamy wake stretching as far as one could see in an unbroken straight line resulted in one of them storming into the wheel house roaring about, *Damned kids. What in the hell was the Merchant Marine coming to? Jesus, the Old Man is daft, allowing boys to take the wheel. God Damn it, boy, mind your course.*

I had gotten a chance to get home for a couple of evenings when we had returned to Boston. When my mother suggested that I take my bicycle on an errand to the grocery store, I said,

"What? A sailor ride a bike? I'm too grown up for toys. So I walked to the neighborhood store, knowing that I would meet several neighbors on the way. Sure enough, it was, *Hello, Frank, haven't seen you lately. Where've you been? Oh, I've been to sea. Made a trip to Germany. Just home for a couple of nights.* Or it was, *My, aren't you brown?* By the time I reached the store, I was swollen with importance. The clerk in the store asked me how the food was on the ship. *Not too good but you get so hungry that you don't care. There isn't enough, though.*

Home for two nights. Familiar faces and my mother's cooking were good. My feet still itched, though, and the next morning we cast off, headed for New York by way of the Cape Cod Canal and Long Island Sound. This route was miles and miles shorter than by going outside Cape Cod and across the Nantucket Shoals. These were bad waters so most ships engaged a Coast Pilot. Our Skipper had pilotage endorsements for these waters so he did all of his own piloting. By this time I was standing a watch, the eight to twelve. The Chief Mate had decided that I could steer so he had taken an Able Seaman off the eight to twelve and put me on. There was method in this because by putting an A.B. on day work, he got a lot more work done than he had from me.

44

Very shortly we ran into real Cape Cod fog. The fog around the Cape is so thick that you could cut it like soft, gray cheese. At eight o'clock in the morning I relieved the four to eight lookout on the focsle head. He warned me that the Old Man was on the bridge and to keep a sharp lookout. He went down the ladder to the forward well deck and disappeared in the fog, and I was alone. I leaned over the bow and strained my ears. Nothing could be heard except the hissing of the bow wave and the sigh of the damp wind through the fore stay. I paced back and forth between the two anchor chains for a few minutes, then stopped to listen again. Was that a bell that I heard? Nope. Pace back and forth again. Listen, stare. Nothing. Just the water rushing by the rusty bows. I wondered why the Old Man didn't anchor. Once I heard, way off to Starboard, the deep hoot of another steamer. I shouted up to the bridge pointing my arm in the direction of the whistle. The Old Man was invisible from where I stood, so at my shout, he sent the Third Mate up to the bow to see what I was yelling about. He listened with me for four or five minutes, both of us keeping our heads down below the bulwarks to keep the wind out of our ears. Grunting a warning at me to keep my ears peeled, he went back to the bridge. A glance at my watch showed that it lacked but a couple of minutes to ten. Time for me to relieve my partner at the wheel. Now came a combination of circumstances that happen every so often, and when they do, disaster is close aboard.

I relieved the wheel, repeating the course and glancing at the compass to see if she was on. I noticed that the engine room telegraph was on Stand By, but the thump thump of the revolution counter was pounding out Full Ahead. My partner repeated the course to the Third Mate who was standing just outside of the wheel house door, which was open. The Old Man was directly in front of me, leaning on the sill of an open window. The telegraph was at his elbow. After my partner repeated the course, he hesitated for a moment and then asked if it would be alright if he went to the bath room before he went on lookout.

The Mate said,

"Not by a damned sight. Take a bucket up on the bow with you. The Old Man pulled his head in and drawled,

"Let him go, Mister, we're all right."

So the stage was set. No lookout on the bow--thick fog. Vessel making ten knots in treacherous waters. From where I stood at the wheel, I could see out over the Skipper's shoulder. It was so thick, though, that nothing could be seen, not even the fore mast. All was quiet. The steady thumping of the revolution counter, by its repetitious noise was unheard. The slight noise made by the Mate shifting his position sounded loud. The sea was calm and the ship stayed on course with just a couple of spokes of wheel. The fog slid by closing us in. A false sense of security crept into the wheel house. Everything seemed so peaceful and cozy. As is the custom with all helmsmen, my mind emptied itself of all thoughts. My eyes, fixed on the compass, were slightly glazed. I was like a disembodied spirit. One little facet of my mind still functioned, that part of it that had to do with memory. I was back in that cabaret in Hamburg. Why, oh why, hadn't I been smarter? Why hadn't I asked my new found friend to take a walk with me? Maybe she would have asked me home with her. At that point my imagination leaped. Then I came hurtling back from my fool's paradise. A slight scraping of the Captain's foot brought my eyes back in focus. Over his shoulder I could see dry land. A black, shelving shoreline was dead ahead, not more than a few ship's lengths away! My heart jumped right up into my throat.

I stared at the Skipper, frozen with terror. I'll never forget his actions of the next minute and a half. The lesson has served me well ever since. With one motion, he flung the telegraph handle from Stand By to Full Astern. Then, sort of lazily, he flapped a languid hand at me and said, in the most normal tone,

"Better put that wheel hard astarboard, boy. Don't break it off, but get it over,"

I grabbed the midships spoke and wound her over. Two and a half full turns spun under my flying hands. The ship was light so she answered promptly. The bow swung faster and faster. The way was off the ship and she was now turning nicely. At that moment the fog shut in again. Our glimpse of the shore was only the result of one of those freaks of the fog. It had opened up like a long avenue down which could be seen, for one minute only, disaster. Then the gray, inpenatratable stuff came down again. In that short period a lot of thoughts went through that Skipper's head. Most of them I didn't realize for several years. First, he knew, to his everlasting shame, that he was way off his course. Second, he had only seconds to rectify his error. Third, and to me, the most important of all, that he was almost licked, but knowing all this, he still carried on in the best tradition. *Better put that wheel hard astarboard, boy!*

As the years went by I sailed with other Skippers, some kind, a few cruel and heartless, but all of them, with no exceptions, were excellent seamen and shipmasters. They sailed during hard times, in the midst of the country's worst depression. Ship bottoms were a glut on the world market, and ocean freight rates had sunk to an all time low. The focsles were full of seamen holding Second and Chief Mate's tickets, glad to have a berth. I was AB on one ship for over three years. All during that time we had the same three Mates and the same Captain. And all three of the Mates held a Master's ticket. Yes, in those days you had to be good to be Master. Consistently good, trip after trip. Drive, drive, drive. Shipowners had their back to an economic wall. To keep their vessels employed they had to have officers who could wring the last farthing from a Charter Party. Captains drove their ships and their crews unmercifully in fog and gales. They had to. If they didn't, there were hundreds on the beach ready to take their place. We in the focsle didn't complain too seriously. Sure, we growled and complained incessantly. All

U.S. Shipping Board freighter, Circa 1919

Victory ship operated by the Navy

sailors do. But we hung on because for each of us that were fortunate enough to have a berth, there were swarms of men on the beach waiting on the dock to take our place. I can remember docking in Baltimore in the early 1930s at daybreak. As soon as the gangway was lowered and Customs had cleared us, a horde of unemployed seamen poured up the ladder. They were hungry. So hungry that they were perfectly willing to take over the messroom, serve our food, wash the dishes, work on deck—anything to get something to eat.

Those were the times that bred the kind of shipmaster that I sailed with. They were my idols. They took chances, to be sure, sometimes against their better judgement. It's easy to say,

"Mister, it's getting thick. Slow her down.

Or, "Mister Mate, better drop the pick until it clears up."

That would be the sensible course to take, but there was an owner sitting at a piled up desk trying to keep that ship employed. She was due to load or discharge cargo on a certain day in a certain port. If she was late, another ship got her cargo and her Skipper hadn't produced. To this day that timeless sea chantey, a hold over from the Liverpool packet sailing ship days, still haunts me. *Drive her, Johnny, drive her.*

I remember another Captain that I sailed with who was one of that breed. That was the ship that I was AB on for three years. During that time I came to know him quite well. That is as well as one can where such a wide gulf exists between focsle and bridge. At one time or another I had been on all three watches. I had observed him in all kinds of weather. Had seen him make decisions in an instant, yet never flustered, never at a loss. I had seen him dock his ship against tide and wind with never a mistake.

A couple of nights I had stayed on the wheel all night because the weather was too wild for anyone to come on deck to relieve me, and all through those dark hours with the wind screeching through the rigging, I felt safe because of that dark form in front of me quietly peering out into the gale, occasionally giving me a soft command to, *Ease her a bit, boy.*

Some years later it came to me as a great shock to read of this ship. Shipping had been unusually bad that winter and I couldn't get a berth. I had to eat, though, and was lucky enough to get a job in an automobile assembly factory on the East Coast. My job was to put the left wheels on three hundred cars a day. When knock off time came, I was too tired to care about much of anything. However, one particular night as I stood in line waiting to punch the time clock, someone shoved a company published magazine in my hand. When I had finally fought my way onto a crowded bus, I idly riffled the pages. My glance was arrested by an article extolling the virtues of the company's trucks. They had, so the article read, been used to salvage all the cargo from my old ship which had been driven ashore on the East coast of South America, down South of Buenos Aires. There were pictures of the trucks ploughing through the sand and shale of a forbidding coast. Yep, it was my old ship. I never found out if the ship was saved or not. So many, many times had her Captain squeezed us out of tight corners. What had happened this time? Had his luck deserted him? He never counted on luck, just on himself. Now here was his proud ship, a wreck on the bleak shores just North of Cape Horn.

I never heard any more than that. What the details were, whose fault it was, I never heard. I still like to think, though, that it was no fault of his. He was too good a man to lose his ship. If he hadn't been, he'd have lost it long before, during the time when I was with him. But back to that foggy day, bound South from Boston. After such a close call, the only obvious thing to do was to anchor. But not us. Away we went, Full Ahead, and the devil take the hindmost. We were due in the next morning to load, and by God we'd better be there or there would be another Skipper on the bridge.

We docked on schedule, too, with all hands a little the worse for wear.

I know, now, that the Old Man, for all his air of unconcern, was a little the worser than any of the rest of us, although he'd cut off a thumb before exhibiting any evidence of it. This man, and many like him, were my teachers. I copied their speech, their manners, their beliefs. They were my gods. I had no others.

-6-

CROSSING THE EQUATOR

I have crossed the equator many, many times, always on an old freighter. I was on one ship for three years, sailing from East Coast ports to the East Coast of South America, so we crossed the Line twice each voyage.

When I was a youngster in school, I had read all the old tales of the Sargasso Sea, and believed them. I had read of how sailing ships had become becalmed and got stuck in the impenetrable seaweed, and of how the crew went crazy with thirst and died. And of how, many years later, another ship came upon them, the ship all over grown with seaweed, and the skeletons lying all over the deck. And what's more, I firmly believed it.

The Sargasso Sea is supposed to lie in the Doldrums, in the South Atlantic Ocean. The Doldrums normally extend from five degrees South of the equator to five degrees North of it, a distance of some six hundred miles. The Southeast Trade Winds and the Northeast Trade Winds blow steadily from Africa to the new world. Most of the year they don't overlap. Where they don't, that is the Doldrums and the Sargasso Sea. There is no wind there, just a calm sea with the sea languidly heaving under the thick seaweed. It is hot there--suffocating, breathless, like being in a hot tub. The only wind is that created by the forward motion of the ship. It feels like standing in front of an open furnace.

It is true, however, that during part of the year the two Trade winds drift North and South, and overlap. Then the Doldrums cease to exist for awhile, and the winds scatter the sea weed. So much for the myths that I had cherished.

I was standing the eight to twelve watch. The Third Mate, Mr. Crowly, had been on the ship for several years, so this business of crossing the equator was old hat to him. When I would be on the wheel, I would pester him incessantly about all the stuff that I had read.

"It's all a lot of nonsense, Slim. At the speed we're making, we should cross the Line the day after tomorrow. Just another day to sweat it out in this heat."

I guess that I only half believed him because as soon as,I got off watch at noon, I made a bee line for the messroom. The Bosun would surely give me the straight dope.

"Bosun, the Third Mate says that we will be crossing the equator the day after tomorrow. Will we get introduced to King Neptune and his Court?"

"Absolutely, Slim. The Mate always gives all hands the day off. He

49

even has the Second and Third Mates stand the wheel watches. You're in for a great treat."

Hah, now I was getting it right from the horse's mouth. When I came off watch at midnight, and turned in, my last thoughts were of the big day coming. It's a good thing that I didn't know what was in store for us.

I woke up a half hour later, soaking wet. The focsle was like an oven. The Doldrums at last! I couldn't stand that fierce heat and humidity, so I dragged my mattress out onto number five hatch and stretched out, naked as a jay bird. The Southern Cross was blazing in the sky above me.

Boy, I thought, *this is the life.*

And the skies opened up. It rained cats and dogs. In seconds me and my mattress were soaked.

So what? The big day is coming.

The next day was awful. I never knew that it could be so hot. The poor black gang crawled out of the engine room more dead than alive. The ship was wallowing among, making her eight and a half knots. It looked as though we were steaming through a nautical hay field. The seaweed stretched to the horizon, just as solid as the midwest prairies. The smoke from the ship's funnel went straight up, just as if we were stopped. I was standing wheel watch. Both doors to the wheel house were open, as were all the windows. The Third Mate and I were just as wet as if we were standing under a shower. Some of my enthusiasm was leaking out of me. The hell with King Neptune; let's get out of this Godforsaken part of the ocean.

After dinner it got worse. Stanchions, railings, bulkheads; all were so hot that you couldn't lay a hand on them. We lay around panting like hound dogs.

Time seemed to stand still, but supper time finally came. We dragged our way into the messroom, fearful of what our belly-robbing Steward had dreamed up. Bless his mangy soul. The food was awful, as usual, but there sat several large pitchers of strong, black, iced tea. I'd figure that we each drank two quarts.

The Bosun cleared his throat, rapped on his plate with his knife, and announced,

"Tomorrow will be a field day."

All hands groaned and cursed. I had never heard the expression, 'field day.' I took it to mean a day off for the festivities. I had a cruel awakening coming. He also announced that the Second and Third Mates would stand all the wheel watches so that all hands could participate. This all sounded great to me.

That night I turned in without a care in the world. Tomorrow would be *THE DAY!* It sure was, but not in the way that I thought. NO SIR!

"The next morning at breakfast, the Bosun again rapped on his plate.

50

Spitting out a few boiled mackerel bones, he said,

All hands midships by the fireroom fiddley by eight, sharp."

I slipped into the focsle and pulled on my best, shore going dungarees. Made by Sweet Orr, they were the best made. Triple stitched, and *no* rivets. I had washed most of the dye out of them so they looked real salty; what a deep water sailor man should be seen in. They were expensive, though, a dollar and forty cents from the slop chest. I had been saving them to wear ashore, but today was important, so what the hell. I also stepped into a brand new pair of Romeos. These were soft, light shoes, almost slippers. They were in great favor by sailors for wearing off watch. They were high sided, no laces, with elastic gores on the sides. They were no good to work in, but great for night lookout and wheel watch. Eight bells rang out from the wheel house. We all headed 'midships.' I couldn't help but notice that all my shipmates had on their oldest rags. And most of them had homemade wooden shower clogs on their feet.

Strange, I thought. *Here am I all dressed up like it was Sunday, and they look like a bunch of bums.*

The fiddley was just forward of the galley, and runs the width of the ship. There are two watertight doors; one on the Port side, the other on the Starboard side. Inside the doors there are about a zillion zigzagging, greasy, slippery metal ladders leading all the way down to the fireroom. I noticed that the Bosun had eight or ten five gallon pails and two fifty-five gallon drums lined up.

Must be for the festivities, I thought, smugly.

There we stood, the entire deck gang. Six A. B.'s, two Ordinaries, and the Bosun. There was no sign of the Mate or the Captain.

Surely, they would be the masters of ceremonies, wouldn't they?

Something was starting to stink.

"All right, gents, here's what we're going to do; what we always do on the equator. We are going to oil the decks. The Mate feels that the oil makes a good bond when the deck is hot, and he's right. Form a chain gang on the fiddley ladders. The watertender will fill the pails with hot oil. Then each of you will carry them up one flight to the next guy, and so on. The top man will empty the pails into these drums where I'll mix in the Stockholm tar and fish oil. Move it!"

I stumbled down the ladders to the fireroom in a daze. Never have I felt such heat. The hand railings were too hot to use. The watertender on watch spent most of his time standing under one of the ventilators. It was the only way that he could survive. But I had to stand at the foot of the lowest ladder, 'way away from any ventilator.

This ship, like most oil fired vessels burned Bunker C oil; thick black stuff the consistency of crude, cold molasses. Before it could be sprayed into the fireboxes, it had to be heated or it wouldn't burn. I don't know how hot it was, but it could burn you.

As fast as I could stagger up the ladder with a full pail and back with an empty one, that damned watertender was faster. He always had a full one waiting for me.

"Don't fill them so full," I gasped. "If somebody above me spills some, or God forbid, drops one, it'll kill the lot of us."

Thank God he did. They started coming only about two thirds full. I was actually on the verge of losing control of myself. I felt light headed, dizzy, faint. From up above I heard the Bosun sing out.

"All hands on deck."

I couldn't make it up those ladders. The watertender helped me over to a bench under one of the ventilators. Then he dumped two buckets of cool sea water over me.

As I look back, all of us were young and in the best of condition--Not an ounce of fat on us. How could there be, living on a diet of swill that stewards of those days put out? At any rate, I recovered fast, and crawled up the ladders. There was the Bosun stirring his brew like the witch in MacBeth.

"Step lively, gents. Dip out a pail full, grab a handful of those rags and head for the forward well deck. Turn to! I'll be right behind."

No mops or swabs with long handles; down on your hands and knees and rub it in well. This went on all day. Twice more, we had to reform the chain gang. Late afternoon saw us finishing up on the after well deck. The heat and work had taken it's toll. Exhaustion set in for real. At last the job was done. Now, though, we almost had a mutiny. The Bosun refused to give us any kerosene to clean up with. Two A.B.'s threatened to throw him over the side. The Mate, hearing the commotion, emerged from his lair in the chart room.

"Bosun, give'em a quart apiece, in their own buckets."

By the time we got halfway cleaned up, it was past supper time. I was just stuffing my ruined dungarees and Romeos out the port hole when the mess boy stuck his head in the washroom, urging us to hurry up. He got a bucket full of oily water dumped on him. And still ahead of me and my watch partner was the eight to midnight watch.

I came off lookout at ten o'clock and crawled wearily up to the bridge for two long hours on the wheel. The Third Mate was out on the bridge whistling and executing little dance steps. My partner mumbled the course to me and the Third Mate, and disappeared below. I gazed bleary eyed into the binnacle. The numbers wouldn't focus. My eyes were so inflamed by that damned oil that I couldn't see to hold the course. I called to the Third Mate and told him. He was furious.

"God damn it! I had to stand four hours on that wheel this morning. Now I'm stuck with two more. Get your ass over in the corner!"

The author, first trip as
A.B. 1932

On the Equator, 1933.
Author on the right.

As I huddled in a corner of the wheel house, half blind and aching in every joint, I reflected on the miserable day now ending. I now knew what a *'field day'* was. And that the *'Crossing the Line'* ceremonies *were* unique.

-7-

ON THE BEACH IN THE THIRTIES

And a bad time it was to be on the beach. There were no unions, then. The United States Shipping Board maintained seamens' hiring halls in the major ports. You would register in one, and then wait months to be called for a berth. And even then, the Mate might turn you down when you reported aboard.

I had paid off a ship as Ordinary Seaman. I still didn't have enough sea time to get my Able Seaman's certificate, but I did get my Lifeboat certificate, no mean feat. This was in the port of Boston. The Coast Guard gave the test and issued the certificate.

One morning I reported to the Charlestown Navy Yard for my test. A set of lifeboat davits was mounted on the edge of an open pier. Suspended from them was a lifeboat. A Chief Boatswain's Mate told me what I was to do. First, I had to recite from memory all the required contents of the boat. Then I would be required to issue the necessary orders to four Coast Guard seamen to launch the boat. And finally, I had to get into the boat and take her out, the four seamen acting as crew.

Sounds pretty straight forward, right? Wrong! I'll tell you why. Both the Coast Guard and the Navy despised us Merchant sailors. And the feeling was mutual. God knows why, but there it was. We even referred to the Coast Guard as the 'Hooligan Navy. '

After I had rattled off the interminable list of stuff required to be in the boat, the Bosun said,

"Go ahead and launch her."

The boat was hanging about four feet above the pier. I went over to the davits and slacked her off until she was almost level with the pier.

"What in the hell do you think you're doing?" barked the Bosun.

"I'm lowering her down so that I can climb in and put the plug in, that's what."

"H'mm, thought you'd forgotten it?"

I screwed the plug in, then made the bow painter fast to the bow and threw the slack out onto the dock.

"Now what the hell are you up to."

"I'm going to lead the bow painter *'well forward,'* just as the book says."

"Stop trying to do everything yourself. That's what these sailors are for."

54

OK, I thought. *Here goes nothing.*

"Lower away together."

Down she shot, splashing into the dirty, oily water. I slid down the after falls, grabbed the steering oar, and fended off. The four sailors followed me, just like four chimps in the circus.

"Cast off the painter, unship oars," and away we went, just like Lord Hornblower. My ego swelled to bursting.

"Stroke, stroke, stroke." I leaned on the steering sweep. Captain of the ocean seas, I was.

Out of the corner of my eye, I caught sight of the Bosun dancing up and down and waving his arms like crazy. Time to go back.

"Back water, Starboard, give way, Port."

We swung around like a top. I carefully steered her under the falls, which were immediately hooked on. The five of us swarmed up the falls and two blocked her.

"How'd I do, Bosun?"

"Well enough," he grunted, grudgingly.

"Seeing as how you're so skinny and pitiful looking, I'm going to do my first good turn of the month. You passed! Go get your certificate."

Well, now, I had a little edge on getting a berth, because Federal law required a high percent of the crews of American flagged ships to have life boat tickets--or so I hoped.

Listening to other sailors talk, I found out that the best way to get hired was to be on the pier when a ship arrived, and go right aboard and hope to see the Mate. So every morning before seven I was on some pier waiting for a ship to berth. Under my arm would be a copy of the Boston Post. It published a daily ship arrival and departure report, and it dictated to what pier I would go.

That morning I headed for the Hoosac piers, over in Charlestown, on Water Street. Two ships were due in between seven and eight. One was a big Black Diamond Line ship. I stood gazing up at her as she was making fast.

God, she was huge! It sure would be fine to sail on her, I thought, as I scooted up the gangway. I made a bee-line for the saloon pantry knowing that the Mate would be at breakfast. I stuck my head in and asked the mess man where the Mate's room was.

"Port side, right around the corner."

I stationed myself right outside his door.

"Vot you vant, boy?"

There he stood, a big pot-bellied square head.

"I'm looking to sign on,"

"Ya, Vat ships you been on?"

"Just one, as Ordinary. I have a letter from her Mate."

"Ve don't need boys. Ve yust need two A. B.'s. Goot bye."

Better luck next time, I muttered, as I headed down the gangway. A big tall figure rushing up the gangway damned near knocked me overboard. By God, it was Dave Merson. He had been the other Ordinary on my last ship, and we were close friends.

"Dave, how's things?"

"Can't seem to get a berth, Slim. Things are bad. Any openings on this ship?"

"Only two A.B.'s, Dave."

Dave had been going to sea for two or three years but would only ship as Ordinary. I suspected that he couldn't read, so couldn't get an A.B.'s certificate. Any ways, he liked day work instead of standing a watch. He was some figure of a man; six feet four or five, and arms and shoulders like a gorilla. Getting ahead of my story; years later, in the early forties, Dave died a horrible death. He was on a NorGulf ship down in the Caribbean. One morning she was torpedoed. Dave and another sailor were down in #5 lower hold stacking dunnage. The ship rolled over and sank in minutes. They both went down with her. Another of my shipmates gone.

We stood at the head of the gangway, talking.

"Slim, let's see if we can bum some breakfast off this ship."

"OK by me, Dave. The crew's mess is right here, amidships."

In we went. Dave boomed out that we were on the beach and hungry.

The Bosun came to our rescue.

"Sit down. Help yourself to whatever's left. Mess, give these two birds a bowl and a mug of coffee."

There was nothing left but cold oatmeal and bread. It was filling, though. The crew all piled out to go to work, watches having been broken. Dave pulled out his pipe and sat there, sucking it.

"God, I wished that I had some tobacco."

I remembered that pipe, always stuck in his mug.

"Here, Dave, have a cigarette."

"Can you spare two?"

"Sure."

He crushed them in his big paw and stuffed them in his pipe, paper and all. Lighting up, he leaned back contentedly.

"This ain't so bad, Slim. Let's sit awhile. It's colder than hell out there."

However, the messboy drove us out in no uncertain terms. Back down the gangway we headed, and sat down on a pile of bales of wool in the cargo shed. We took council on how the hell we were going to get a ship. Dave came up with a beaut.

"Slim, you will agree that the best paying, the best feeding ships are the tankers, right?"

56

"Sure, I've heard their praises sung in the focsle, too. And they're the best to work on. No damned booms to raise and lower, no hatches to batten down, no dirty holds to clean. Just watch and watch, maybe a little soogying and painting. But why even talk about it? Those guys never pay off. They have to die of old age and get carried off."

"Yeah? Well how come we've heard so much about them? We heard it from guys that had sailed on them, and for whatever reason, paid off. Maybe they got fired. Now here's what we'll do. We'll concentrate on tankers. Some of them dock right over in East Boston. Let's head over to the Standard Oil piers and see what's what."

I didn't put much faith in his scheme, but anything was better than freezing to death in a cold, dank cargo shed.

"I'm with you, Dave. Let's go."

I followed him for miles, it seemed. His great, long legs ate up the distance effortlessly.

"Slow down, Dave. I can't keep up."

He leaped over a snow bank and waited for me to catch up.

"How much further, Dave?"

"Right up around the next corner, kid."

Well, at least I wasn't cold anymore.

We rounded the corner and there was the Standard Oil pier, an enormous complex of tanks and big pipes running all over the place. It was completely enclosed by a high, chain link fence. We peered through the fence, and sure enough, there was the stack of a tanker tied up to the pier.

There was no mistaking her distinctive stack markings; she was a Standard Oil tanker for sure.

"Let's go aboard, Slim. This could be our lucky day."

We followed the fence to the gate. It was shut. An old watchman came out of the gate house.

"What do you two gents want?"

"We are two out of work sailors looking for a berth. Would you know if the Chief Mate is aboard?"

"He's aboard, alright, but you can't go beyond this gate."

"Why not? We just want to hit him up for a job."

"All the hiring is done by Moe."

"Who is he, and where do we find him?"

"He runs the clothing store just up the street."

All this sounded pretty strange to us, but we set off for Moe's. It turned out to be a little, dingy store front. Piled up inside the one, dirty window we could see dungarees, work shoes, oil skins; all the gear needed by seamen.

"Slim, there's something fishy, here. Let's go in and find out."

"I'm right behind you, Dave."

57

In we went. The little bell over the door tinkled faintly. The place seemed deserted. Then a rear door opened and in waddled an enormous fat man.

"Good morning, gentlemen, what do you need? Some fine new, blue work shirts, maybe? Over here we have a new shipment of extra special work shoes. They'll last a lifetime."

"We don't need any clothes; we need a job on a tanker."

"Oh, well, let me explain how that works. The Standard Oil Company has honored me by appointing me as their representative for procuring unlicensed personnel for all their ships that dock in Boston. Are you, two, deck or engine?"

"We're both deck, Ordinaries."

"Good! Step over here and we'll get you all fixed up."

It soon became clear that we were expected to buy forty bucks worth of gear that we didn't need, and didn't have the dough for, anyways.

"Dave, when I was a kid I read about the Crimps in Frisco during the Clipper ship days. They would shanghai sailors and deliver them aboard ship for so much per head, paid by the ship owner. Here we are supposed to pay, ourselves, to get ourselves shanghaied. Tell him to stick his jobs up his fat backside!"

And Dave told him just that.

Back out on the sidewalk, again.

"Slim, it must be noontime because I'm hungry. Let's we head over to Scollay Square. There's a joint over there where you can get a big plate of baked beans and a hot dog for fifteen cents."

"You're nuts, Dave. By the time we walk that distance, it will be supper time. I'm going to catch a street car for home."

"OK, Slim, but could you spare me a half dollar? That will do me for supper, and I'm sleeping on the cuff at the Sailors' Haven."

We agreed to meet the next morning at the hiring hall, and I went home to a depression supper of finnan haddie, which is a very tasty dish to a young seaman. My mother used to cream it and pour it over two, big, boiled potatoes. To a New Englander, there is no finer fare.

The next morning I was at the hiring hall bright and early. It was snowing cats and dogs. Six or eight of us were sitting around telling lies about the ships that we had been on. One young guy was boasting that he had just got his A.B.'s ticket. My ears pricked up when he told how the examiner was about to turn him away because he didn't have enough sea time, but he convinced him that he did by counting the time that he had sailed coastwise.

There was no sign of Dave, so I shot out the door heading for State Street and the offices of Rogers and Webb, the operators of the Yankee Line. My last ship had been a Yankee Line vessel.

I was like a drowned rat when I got there, but no matter. They were very kind to me and wrote out the precious letter at once. I took the opportunity to hit them up for a job. No luck. They told me that they were operating four ships. They were the Seattle Spirit, Westpool, West Harcouver, and a small four hatch laker that was being laid up for lack of cargo.

I was starting to realize that I shouldn't have signed off the Seattle Spirit. Berths on the Yankee Line were much coveted because of the exchange rate prevailing in Germany. Because inflation had gotten out of control, the dollar's value had soared in Germany, and would buy a hundred dollars worth of goods and services, meaning booze and women. Oh well, no use crying over spilled milk.

Now for the A.B.'s exam. It would be oral, but from what I could gather, it was no cinch. It included knots, splices, steering commands, memorize all the quarter points of the compass, about one hundred and twenty eight of them. A waste of time because all ships were now using degrees.

Dave finally showed up with a hangover that you could hang your hat on. He said that he had met a couple of shipmates that had just paid off a ship, so they made the rounds of the speakeasies. (Prohibition was still in effect, in those days.) We pored over the shipping news in the paper.

"Slim, look here. The West Harcouver is due in from Bremen, tomorrow. (So he could read, after all.) She's docking at pier forty-two. Let's we meet her."

I told him what I had learned at Roger and Webb.

"It's a waste of time, Dave. Nobody will be paying off."

"Yeah, but maybe the Mate will be firing a couple."

I reluctantly agreed to meet him the next morning.

Seven o'clock the next morning found the pair of us watching a tow boat pushing the West Harcouver into pier forty-two, Charlestown. We had to wait quite awhile for Immigration to clear the ship. Finally, the gangway was lowered and up we went.

The Mate was right at the head of the gangway. Dave ploughed right ahead with his pitch. Surprisingly, the Mate invited us to his cabin. There, we presented our discharges and waited. I cleared my throat and said that I would have my A.B.'s ticket in a day or two.

"I have one job open, Ordinary Seaman. You're hired," said he, pointing at Dave.

I swallowed my disappointment and backed out of the room. In a minute, Dave followed me.

"Slim, the ship is paying off this afternoon. I'm going ashore to get my gear. Too bad that we couldn't ship together."

"Dave, you need the job worse than I. At least I've got a home to go to and enough to eat. Good luck."

Just then a slick looking critter came out of the galley. He even had a waxed mustache, for God's sake!

"You guys looking for work?"

"I am," said I.

"Well, I'm the Chief Steward, and I need a good crew's messman."

"Slim, grab it," said Dave

"Dave, I'm no messman. Besides, I hate washing dishes."

"So what? Make one quick trip, and maybe a job on deck will open up."

He had a point, at that.

"Mr. Steward, I never sailed in the Steward's department, but if you will have me, I'd like the job."

I struck a deal to report for work the following noon. That would give me the morning to take the exam for A.B. Dave and I parted, both of us to go and pack our sea bags. I spent the evening studying. I felt that I was ready.

The next morning I caught the street car for Boston. I went straight to the ship and dumped my gear back aft. The saloon messman and I were to share a tiny coop. He came in while I was unpacking, and we got to talking. I had grave doubts about sailing as a messman, and said so. He peeked out the door to make sure nobody was listening.

"Watch out for that Steward. He's no damned good. In fact, he's an evil, no-good bastard."

"What do you mean?"

"Never mind. Just remember what I told you."

And with that, he sidled out the door and was gone.

I put the Steward out of my mind and headed over to Boston. Two hours later I was the proud holder of a crisp A.B. certificate. Heading back to Charlestown and the ship, I fell to wondering. Am I doing the right thing? My heart wasn't in it that's for sure. All I ever wanted was to sail on deck. My doubts increased as soon as I got aboard. The Steward was waiting at the head of the gangway.

"Get your ass in the messroom. The crew are waiting on themselves."

I scurried in. Everybody started yelling at me.

"More coffee, here. How about some butter? Where's the bread? Shake a leg, Mess."

By the time they finished eating and filed out, I was fed up.

Nothing but a damned servant, I muttered.

By the time that I got all those damned greasy, dirty dishes washed and the messroom cleaned up, it was time to get ready for supper. The Steward came in to show me how to make the coffee. This ship had a proper coffee urn like you see in a lunch room.

"This crew is very fussy about their coffee," he said.

"No wonder," I thought. "They need it to wash down the garbage that he was feeding them."

Green water coming aboard abreast #3 hatch

More of the same

Promptly at five o'clock they all piled in on me, again.

"Who made this God damned coffee? It's worse than dishwater. Mess, you'd better straighten out, fast. We ain't going to up put with this any longer."

"Neither am I," I said to myself.

About five thirty the Steward came into the messroom. I was washing the dishes.

"You'll have to speed it up, here. The lights go out at seven!"

"Lights out, how come?"

"The Chief Engineer shuts down all auxiliaries at seven; water pumps, generators, heat, everything."

"But why?"

"To save fuel oil, of course!"

I had heard that many ships did this. All British ships had been doing it ever since steamships came on the seas.

I finished up as quick as I could and went back aft. It was a bitter cold night. I poked my head in the deck focsle. A half dozen men were sitting around a table on which sat a kerosene lamp.

"Come in, Slim. Pull up a bench."

What a way to spend an evening. The one radiator was already clicking as it cooled down. The Bosun asked me what I thought of the Steward.

"I don't know him yet, so I don't have an opinion."

"Well, you watch your step with him. If he makes a pass at you, let me know. It's just about time that somebody layed one on him."

"I don't understand."

"He's a wolf. He likes boys!"

That was enough for me. I said so long, packed my sea bag and headed for the gangway. Dave came with me.

"Slim, stick around. If that old queer so much as looks at you, I'll break him in two."

"Thanks, Dave, but me for the beach, again."

We shook hands and off I went. I didn't know it then, but Dave and I would be shipmates again, on another ship, a year or so later. And, as always, he would be a strong anchor to windward.

-8-

SAILORING DAYS-MONKEY BUSINESS

Way back in the early thirties I was A.B. on the same ship for three years. Not because it was such a good ship. The Depression was going full blast. If you quit and paid off a ship, you'd be lucky to get another berth in a year. This ship was on a regular run. Boston, New York, Philly, Baltimore, Norfolk, a couple of Carolina ports, then to Jacksonville for a deck load of lumber. First port of call, foreign, Pernambuco, Brazil. (Now called Recife.) This backwater was almost on the Equator. Then South, along the East coast of South America, calling at Rio, Santos, Bahia, (Now called Salvador.) Rio Grands de Sul, Montevideo, and finally the paradise of South America, Buenos Aires.

We would then reverse our route and call at the same ports, loading for the States. Our last Brazilian port would often be Para, a thousand miles up the Amazon River.

Because I had been on board for so long, I was on the eight to twelve watch, the best one. In those days there were only two A.B.s on a watch; one on the wheel and one on bow lookout after sun down. Even then, if it was a clear night, the Mate would have the lookout overhauling a life boat or stacking dunnage in the Shelter Deck. All Mates in those days were work crazy. They worked themselves from four, AM to eight, PM, seven days a week. The Mate on this ship even worked all during his bridge watch. He was a marvel with a needle and palm. He'd sit on a stool, out on the bridge wing, and hand sew life boat covers, wire reel covers, ventilator covers, and anything else that needed stitching. His name was Mister Bang, and he was a native of Schlesvig-Holstein, which used to be a country between Denmark and Germany.

As I look back, Mister Bang was the finest seaman that I have ever known. He went to sea when he was twelve years old on German square riggers. Down around Cape Horn to Chile to load Nitrate for Germany. For a year or more I was on his watch, and in those dark, quiet hours, he would tell me stories of his young days on those hard driven wind ships.

I remember one in particular. It was his first trip, and he only a child.

62

On the way down to the Horn it kept getting colder. Down in the Roaring Forties it was constant gales. Make sail, reef down, all hands. There were only two watches in those days. Four hours on, four hours below, interrupted by the constant, *All Hands*.

To set a reef or furl, the sailors had to climb the ratlines to the crosstrees; scramble out on the yard while standing on a swaying foot rope strung under the yard. Then they would lay their bellies on the yard and fist the sail which would be flapping wildly in the winter wind. The heavy storm canvas used down in those latitudes was thicker and coarser than any sails seen today. Sometimes the hands would spend a whole watch clawing at the canvas, only to have it blow out of the gaskets and flap away down wind. No seaman of those days ever had any finger nails. Their finger tips were just calloused balls.

Mister Bang's ship was way down near Cape Stiff when the cry came again, *All Hands*. Up and up they went; the icy wind tearing at their clothes. The higher they went, the more the movement of the ship increased. He got violently sea sick and threw up. The poor kid spent the whole watch up there fighting canvas. At last, half dead, they made their way down to the deck. He was just about to stagger below when the Chief Mate fetched him a clout on the head.

"Come with me, boy."

That damned Mate flung him down on the deck which had a puddle of frozen vomit.

"Scratch it up with your finger nails before you go below."

He spent his watch below, hopelessly scratching with no finger nails. Only twelve years old!

Ships, in my early days, were largely self supporting, both on deck and in the engine room. All the cargo handling gear, now furnished by the stevedoring companies, was made by the Bosun, as were all mooring lines and springs. The black gang also did all their own repair work, fabricating many parts on the engine room lathe. We even made our own paint.

I remember on one voyage, we were due to sail from Buenos Aires at five, PM, and then couldn't because of low water. Of course, everybody had spent all their pesos. And here we had another night in port. I got up my nerve and decided to hit up Mister Bang for a loan. I went midships and timidly knocked on his screen door.

Come in, Slim. What's on your mind?

"Well, you see, Sir, Earl and I would like to go ashore but we're broke. Could you please, maybe, spare five bucks?"

"Why, I guess so."

He opened his desk drawer and rummaged around through an assortment of nails, light bulbs, paint brushes, and God knows what other junk, the accumulation of ten years as Mate.

"Here we are," said he, pulling out a crumpled five dollar bill.

As I stretched forward to take it, he grabbed me by both shoulders and flung me right through the screen door. I slammed into the steel bulkhead and slid down to the deck, with pieces of the door hanging from me.

"That will teach you to take your hat off before you enter a Chief Mate's cabin. Now fix the door before you go ashore."

Never raised his voice; never even got up from his chair. He wasn't mad either. Discipline and manners.

The food on those rust buckets, or the lack of it, was the constant subject for belly aching. Ships were then manned by thirty men, and the Steward was allowed twenty-nine cents a day per man, and that was for three meals. A boiled mackerel for breakfast—never an egg. Dinner would be old bull liver, tough as shoe leather. Supper—rancid cold cuts and bread. The Steward bought his beef in the Argentine— Bull necks and a few forequarters. Milk for coffee was a half can of condensed milk poured into a gallon pitcher of water. All of us used to stock up in Jacksonville. Cans of sardines, deviled ham, jam, etc. The first thing that I did when we arrived at Pernambuco was to run up the dock and buy a dozen eggs. Back on board I'd stick a steam line in a bucket, boil them, and have a feast. I could get the dozen eggs and a bushel basket full of oranges and papayas for a pack of cigarettes, which cost me six cents from the slop chest.

Mister Bang was a nut about the condition of his bowels, so he used to stock up on corn flakes and bran which he kept in the sideboard in the officers' saloon. Being on the eight to twelve watch, I used to cut through the saloon at twenty minutes to twelve every night to call the Second Mate for his watch. On the way through, I'd snatch a box of corn flakes or bran and a full can of milk. I hid them out on deck. When I was relieved at midnight, I would sit out on number five hatch and eat it all, disposing of the evidence by throwing the empty box and can over the side.

For weeks I heard the Mate raving about the thief on board and what he was going to do to him when he caught him. He never once suspected his star pupil, me.

Then came my down fall. The saloon messboy told me in great confidence, that the Steward had acquired several gallon cans of strawberry and raspberry jam. He was doling it out very stingily to the officers. Once a day they each got a little saucer of it. Oh, boy, jam. My mouth watered. For several nights I searched through the saloon and the officers' pantry. Couldn't find it. I finally got the messboy to tell me where it was. Hidden in the galley behind the coal scuttle. The next night the Mate had me greasing cargo runners instead of standing lookout. By midnight my dungarees were soaked with dirty, black oil. No matter. I stole into the galley, which was never locked. Feeling around in the dark, I found the jam. Armed with almost a full can and a fistful

Mr. Bangs, the finest seaman that I ever knew.

of pilot crackers, I hoisted my backside up onto the cook's scoured clean chopping block and had a feast, scooping out the jam with the crackers. When I could eat no more, I put the jam back behind the coal scuttle and sneaked back to the focsle. My watch partner was still awake and smelled a rat, but I told him nothing. I was on to a good thing and wasn't about to share it with him.

I had slipped up, though, and badly. I never thought about my oily dungarees, and in the darkness, had smeared black oil on the cook's chopping block. The next day the Steward, who was no dope, started playing detective, asking questions of the Engineers and Mates about who had a dirty job last night. When he got to Mister Bang, the cat was out of the bag. They set a trap for me.

The galley ran athwartships and had a steel door on each side, which, in good weather, were hooked open. The next night I was perched up on the chopping block again, stuffing jam and crackers when, **Clang.** Both doors slammed shut. The Steward was yelling outside of the port door and the Chief Mate was bellowing outside of the starboard door.

"We caught him, We've got the son of a bitch."

In they came, their flashlights blinding me. The Mate belted me off the chopping block. Then that belly-robbing Steward started kicking me. I kept trying to roll out of his way until he hit his foot on the stove. He only had a pair of carpet slippers on, so he damned near broke his toe off. I scooted like a rat out the door and escaped. The Mate never once said a word, but for a long time he was very cool. He knew damned well that not only was I the jam thief. I was also the skunk that ate up all of his corn flakes and bran, making him constipatd the whole trip.

It was on this trip that I hit on a business venture. An A.B.'s wages then. were $57.50 a month, not much. There were two large pet stores in Boston. I went to see them and struck a deal. They would pay me $5.00 apiece for marmoset monkeys, and $10.00 apiece for spider monkeys. I could buy them in Bahia for a pack of cigarettes, each. The next trip I stocked up; six marmosets and three spider monkeys. I wasn't too popular in the focsle. In those days eight of us lived back aft in a focsle. I tied strings around the monkeys' loins and secured them to the edge of my bunk. Surprisingly, they were quite clean, although the rest of the crew gave my bunk a wide berth. Fortunately, when we arrived back in Boston it was summer time. Monkeys are very susceptible to pneumonia.

My first venture in the monkey business was a success. The sixty bucks that I received was more than a month's pay. During the next two or three trips, I did pretty good. However, as winter in the Northern latitudes set in, I had troubles with the monkeys getting sick. At last, I hit upon the solution. I started keeping them in the steering engine room. The steering engine is a huge steam engine that turns the rudder. It is located all the way aft, in the stern. It was always very warm and steamy. The monkeys seemed to thrive in there. My shipmates were quite happy to get them out of the focsle. Then, disaster struck. One of the black gang decided to get in on my action and make a quick killing. He bought a small ape, about the size of a three year old kid. He chained him up in the steering engine room, where he spent all of his time trying to get at my little guys. We started North from Brazil. When we got into the Doldrums, just to the North of the Equator, the heat was fierce. Just about that time, the Chief Engineer ordered the Third Assistant Engineer to do some repair work on the steering engine—on his watch below, of course. He stood the eight to twelve watch, so about one in the afternoon, back aft he would come. He hated that little ape with a passion, and would torment him by yanking on his chain. The heat in that steamy room was getting to him, so, after a couple of days, he showed up with a big oscillating fan which he had unscrewed from the bulkhead in his room. He set it on the deck and turned it on. It really made an improvement, not only for the Third, but for the monkeys and the ape. That little ape was something to watch. He would parade in front of the fan, holding up first one arm, and then the other, letting it blow into his armpits. That damned engineer was a cruel bastard, and he would reach over and shut the fan off. Mr. ape was pretty smart, though, and right away he learned how to throw the switch back on. The next afternoon that lousy engineer decided to outfox the ape. He wired the switch so that the ape would get a hell of a shock when he tried to turn the fan back on. It worked, alright. That electric shock knocked him flat. He picked himself up and walked slowly over to where the Third was on his knees, fixing a pipe. Leaning over, he opened that great mouth of his and bit the entire calf muscle out of his leg. We heard him screaming and ran in. He was rolling around in agony and bleeding something awful. I ran midships and got the Mate. He was a pretty good first aid man; tied off the blood vessels with sail twine and bandaged him up. Four of us carried him to his room from which he never emerged until he went down the gangway to the ambulance, in Boston. That was the end of my monkey business. Mister Bang shot the ape, strangled my monkeys, and threw them overboard. There would be no more livestock brought aboard this ship. He wouldn't even allow a Brazilian canary aboard.

There's many a slip. Twixt the cup and the lip.
English Proverb

-9-

WHEELING AND DEALING IN THE FOCSLE

After my monkey business fizzled out, I cast around for some enterprise to take its place.

I was still A.B. on the same ship, running between US East coast ports and South America. It was 1933 and my $57.50 per month didn't go far in the flesh pots of Buenos Aires. Radios had grown by leaps and bounds from the home made crystal sets of a few years ago. Now, in spite of the depression, almost every home had its Philco or Atwater Kent. Amos and Andy were heard nightly, the Lucky Strike Hit Parade kept everyone glued to their sets every Saturday night. The radio stores were doing a land office business in small cheap sets. The more I pondered, the more it became clear. My fortune would be made.

We had just paid off after a four month voyage. After slop chest deductions and *'draws'* in various ports, my pockets burned with well over a hundred bucks.

We were docked over in Brooklyn at the foot of Hamilton Avenue. Right after supper I hustled down the gangway, heading for the Hamilton Avenue ferry to Manhattan. Dropping a hundred reis coin in the hopper, aboard I went. In those days Brazil had a money system that was strange. Their standard was the millreis, or one thousand reis. One millreis was worth about twelve cents, US. Their one hundred reis coin was the exact size of our nickel and worth a little over one cent. They worked great on the nickel ferries and subways.

When the ferry docked in Manhattan, I scooted off and headed for Cortland Street. In those days, Cortland Street was lined with cheap radio stores selling brand names that nobody ever heard of, but they worked—for awhile. Trying to be very canny, I went in one store after another, comparing prices and sound volume. Volume was important. I wound up buying ten small, Dewald radios for twelve bucks apiece. When turned up they could be heard for blocks. Perfect for my as yet undeveloped market.

Back on the ship, broke but hopeful, I hid the radios under the spare mooring lines up on a shelf in the steering engine room. Lying in my bunk that

67

night I mused on the future. It looked rosy, indeed.

On our Southbound voyage we would stop at six or seven Brazilian ports from Pernambuco in the North to Buenos Aires and those would be my markets. The competition in the whorehouses in those ports was fierce. One would tout that they had a couple of Chink girls, and for awhile would get the lion's share of the trade, only to lose it to another house whose runners extolled the added attraction of a free bottle of Brazilian beer—-on the way out, of course. These runners would board every ship the day she docked. Passing out cards in the focsle, some with pictures on them, they vied for our trade. Having had some small acquaintance with most of them, they would be my targets. I reasoned that a whorehouse having a radio blaring out Brazilian music would surely grab off a big share of the trade. Then, after a couple of trips, when the radios wore out, repeat business. I couldn't lose. Sinking into an untroubled sleep, I was well pleased at my uncanny grasp of supply and demand.

In due course we sailed. Down the East coast, loading in Philly, Baltimore, Norfolk, Wilmington, Charleston, Brunswick, Georgetown, and finally Jacksonville for our usual deck load of lumber. Then it was South on the Great Circle route to Cape San Roque, the Northern bulge of Brazil, right on the Equator. We made a fine summer passage, roasting in the Doldrums, then Picking up the Southeast Trade winds. Our focsle, being on the starboard side, aft, was, as usual, a furnace but nothing bothered me. The vision of all those millreis that I was going to get made it all bearable.

Because I had spent most of my pay on radios, I hadn't had much shore leave in our East coast ports, but did manage to acquire about a million crab lice in Jacksonville. My crotch was scratched raw, aggravated by the terrible heat.

One night I was at the wheel, all alone in the wheel house. The Third Mate was way out on the Port bridge wing, draped over the wind dodger and probably fast asleep on his feet. The sea was slight and the ship stayed on course with only an occasional spoke or two of wheel. I had my dungarees down around my ankles, and was busy catching crabs by the dim light from the binnacle. Whenever I caught one I'd crack him with my finger nails and place the corpse on the binnacle glass so I could keep score. I had just dispatched number twenty when a strange, faint sound stole into my consciousness. It couldn't be! I was hearing, faintly but unmistakenly, Amos and Andy. I craned my head first one way, then the other. Where was it coming from? The Old Man's quarters were just under the wheel house. On the starboard bulkhead, just out of my reach were three brass speaking tubes. One to the Captain's stateroom, one to the engine room, and one to the radio shack back on the boat deck. By God, the sound was coming from one of them. I had to let go of the wheel and hobble over, my pants still down. I flipped open the Old Man's tube and the sound poured out. He had one of those new fangled short wave radios and here was Amos and Andy, plain as day. I stood there entranced, my ear glued to the tube. I got so interested that I forgot the wheel, my pants, the crabs, everything. Suddenly I heard a footstep. There was the Old Man peering into the binnacle. He reached out a finger and tentatively poked at the dead crabs. Holy Smoke! I eased the cover back on the tube, reached for my pants, and sidled over towards the wheel. He peered intently at me and said, "One of those critters is still alive. Be so kind as to kill it."

As he got to the end of the sentence, his voice had risen to a roar.

"YES, Sir," I muttered, trying to get the ship back on course, pull up my pants, at the same time searching for the live crab. Whew! I got off easy from that one.

The very next day the Mate switched me to his watch, the four to eight. He made no explanation, but he obviously wanted me where he could keep an eye on me. My new watch partner was an old hand by the name of Moody Harrison. He had been going to sea for some twenty years and was a fine seaman, although he had one peculiarity. He hated all Captains. He used to reminisce about all the ships that he had been on. Without exception, at the end of his story, would come a comment like, *A pretty good ship but the Old Man was a real bastard.* This ship was no exception, Even though he had practically no contact with the Captain, he spent most of his time cursing him.

Now, unbeknownst to us, the Old Man had made some new friends who were salt water fishing nuts. They had filled him full of tales of trolling in the Gulf Stream for those big Sail fish and Marlins. He decided that the South Equatorial Current, through which we were steaming, should be just as good as the Gulf Stream, so afishing he would go. Right outside of his room on the boat deck, starboard side, was a contraption called the deep sea sounding device. I sailed on a lot of those old freighters and can only remember one instance where it was ever used, and even then it was useless. It consisted of a pedestal riveted to the deck. On its top there was a drum on which was wound about a mile of steel piano wire. This drum had two cranks on it and a clutch release. The lead itself resembled a conventional hand lead only much heavier. Its bottom was hollowed out to be packed with tallow to which a sample of the bottom would adhere. On the side of the lead's shank were three spring clips into which was snapped a graduated glass tube, open at the bottom. The inside of the tube was coated with a chemical that turned brown when exposed to sea water. Suspended from the ship's rail was a pipe boom with a small block shackled to its outer end. To operate this device, the piano wire would be rove through the block and shackled to the lead. Then the boom would be swung outboard, well clear of the ship's wake, and the clutch released. Down would go the lead, the wire leading far astern. Then it was cranked back on board. The discoloration in the tube was read off on the graduated scale, giving the depth in fathoms. The sand, mud, shells, clay, etc. adhering to the tallow, and the depth were compared to a chart of the area, and presto, you had the ship's position—sometimes.

Anyways, the Old Man got a big S shaped meat hook from the Steward's meat box and fastened it to the piano wire. Then he had the Bosun unship the big brass ship's bell from the focsle head and hang it on the bulkhead, right outside of his stateroom port hole. Some way or other, he rigged the piano wire to the clapper on the bell. He was ready to go fishing. Out swung the boom, and overboard went the big meat hook with a chunk of salt pork lashed onto it. He released the clutch and away she went. He was in business and settled down to wait for a big one to strike. Nothing, day after day. It took him over an hour to crank in to replenish the bait, cranking against the ship's speed. Still no bites. Then my scheming watch partner came to his aid. He stole two boat hooks from one of the life boats and lashed them together, doubling their length. He and I were called at twenty minutes to four in the morning to go on watch. Jumping out of his bunk, Moody eased his long pole out of a port hole and snagged the wire. Very carefully, he pulled it into the port. Grasping it with both hands, he gave it several mighty tugs. We could hear the big bell clanging way up on the boat deck. Carefully releasing the wire, Moody sauntered midships and mounted the ladder to the bridge to relieve the man at the wheel. There was the Old Man, naked as a jay bird, cranking away and yelling, *I've got one, and he's a big son of a bitch, too.*

Moody worked this stunt for three nights, hand running. After that, the Old Man had the Bosun secure the sounding gear and take the bell back to the focsle head where it belonged. No more fishing for him.

Back to business. We headed into Pernambuco, a God forsaken place, if there ever was one. The port was an artificial one created by man made breakwaters. A strong current set vessels against the dock, and for that reason, a native docking crew boarded us out in the harbor, and helped us to make fast, fore and aft, to large buoys lying off the dock and parallel to it. Then, all we had to do was to slack off on the lines and the current would put us alongside. Sailing was the reverse. Let go everything ashore, heave away on the buoy lines, and away.

The heat, as always, was fierce. Air conditioning was unknown, back in those days, and down there on the Equator it seemed as if you couldn't breathe. The focsle was like an oven. At sea we could rig wind chutes out of the port holes, but in port there wasn't a breath of breeze. Somehow, we survived, trip after trip.

Right after we docked, up the gangway came the usual immigration and customs ghouls, and as usual, made a bee line for the Old Man's office to receive their cumshaw. Nobody could board or leave the ship until they departed. As they went down the gangway, up poured the usual horde of blood suckers, pimps, a traveling hair cutter, one pack of cigarettes for a fast cut, sitting on number five hatch. Salesmen staggering under a gigantic load of bird cages full of tropical birds of every color—not for me, though. On my first trip

I had bought two yellow canaries. The next day they changed to mouse colored sparrows that had been dusted with Saffron powder. Then there were the booze salesmen. They were the best; Johnnie Walker, black label, the very best American Ryes, Gordon's gin, British rum, all the very best. The bottles were authentic, but the contents, Wow! They all contained a native drink called Casash, as near as I can spell it. This vile, poisonous stuff was made from fermented sugar can pulp and God Knows what else. It was over a hundred proof plus some narcotic, because it not only made you stinking drunk, but stark, raving crazy, to boot.

Singling out one of the pimp runners with whom I had a nodding acquaintance, I motioned him to follow me. When no one was looking, we ducked into the steering engine room. With a great show of stealth, I dug out one of the radios and plugged it in. He pretty near fainted with greed. The haggling began. Whenever he seemed to cool off and stand pat, I'd switch stations. I finally agreed to let it go for sixty bucks in millreis. He whipped out a piece of cord, made a sling, and hung the radio under his armpit, under his jacket. He sauntered out on deck, slipped down the gangway, and was gone. But I had a great fistful of millreis which I would exchange for Argentine Pesos in Buenos Aires. Things were looking up. I had half of my investment back and still had eleven radios left.

Pernambuco was a small place, so not wanting to glut the market, I decided to pull in my horns and be content with selling just the one this trip.

The first and only night in port I got stuck with the midnight to eight AM gangway watch. Long about one o'clock the crew started to straggle back aboard. I could hear them from way up the pier. Drunken singing, cussing, arguing, and being sick. A normal first evening in port.

The next morning at breakfast, I had to listen to the usual rehashing of their adventures of the previous night. A disturbing note crept into their tales. It seemed that most of them had hit what was supposed to be, *The joint.* It had an American radio. Trouble was, when it came time to pay up, the going price had doubled. I'd have to watch my step. If they ever found out that my radio had caused them to pay through the nose, I'd be in bad trouble. I would have to play a lone game and keep my trap shut.

In quick succession, we hit all the ports, Southbound. In Bahia I unloaded two radios. None in Rio, because we lay way out in the roadstead at anchor, discharging into lighters. In Santos business peaked. Santos, up a dirty river was, and probably still is, the largest coffee exporting port in the world. Even way back then, the entire port area was honeycombed with underground conveyors, bring bags of coffee to the ships from assembling yards on the outskirts of the city. That damned city was almost my downfall. In quick succession, I sold six radios. Then I made a bad mistake. I put one of the radios on the shelf next to my bunk, and was enjoying the Brazilian tangos. A watertender and an A.B. came into the focsle and stared intently at it.

"Where'd you get that radio?"

"Cortland Street in New York, why?"

"Well, we were in the Trocadero last night and they had its twin, and we got way overcharged. Special entertainment, they said. You skinny bastard, you sold it to them."

The cat was out of the bag. The more I tried to lie my way out, the deeper I buried myself. I hotfooted up to the Mate and begged for a day off. I got it, too. I figured I'd disappear for a day before somebody flattened me.

Four of us, Charlie Wilson, an oiler, Little Joe, a watertender, Bill Welch, an A.B., and I, went ashore right after breakfast, dressed in our best shore suits. We were headed for the cog railway terminal. Some years before, some very clever German engineers had carved a railway line right up through the mountains to San Paulo, then the capital of Brazil, and known as the richest city in South America. The cars were mostly glass and what views! Up and up we went at about a forty-five degree angle. The seats automatically canted so that we were always sitting level. We passed on the very edge of gorges thousands of feet deep. We could look way down on the tops of tropical jungle, and on the other side, look up at the rocky heights. The porter who served us *cafe con leche*, claimed it to be one of the engineering feats of the world. I believe it. When we arrived at San Paulo, we became true tourists. We visited the snake farm and saw venomous snakes being milked for their venom. We walked miles gawking at the breathtaking white buildings, had a fine lunch, and even poked our noses into a first class gambling casino where we shot a few millreis on the chuck-a—luck machines. Late afternoon saw us boarding the cog railroad for the trip back down to Santos. It was then that we realized why San Paulo was built up in the mountains. It was so cool. The lower we went, the hotter it got.

I had three radios left. No sense in trying to sell them in Montevideo. In those days Uruguay had a very unfavorable rate of exchange. We had to pay $1.10 US for one of their pesos. Consequently, we seldom went ashore, there. I managed to peddle one radio in Rio Grande du Sul. Two left, and we were on our way up the La Plata River to Buenos Aires. We were to dock in La Boca to discharge our deck load of lumber. In BA the Customs were the worst. The entire port area was completely fenced off, miles and miles of it. This immense area was patrolled by Marineros. They were uniformed similar to our Navy sailors. Like the cops in Spain, they always travelled in pairs. They had the authority of God Almighty, and what was worse, they were absolutely in corruptible. Don't **ever** try to bribe one; they'd hang you.

I made sure that the radios were well hidden before we docked. La Boca was the very worst part of Buenos Aires. Life was cheap on its waterfront streets. I decided to stay aboard until the lumber was discharged, and the ship moved to the Darsena Sud, quite near to the center of the city. As soon as we shifted ship, I headed for the Avon Bar, a famous hangout for Merchant seamen. At the Avon, I got a favorable rate of exchange for a fistful of Millreis and settled down with a stein of superb German beer. Buenos Aires, in those days, had a tremendous German population. They operated breweries, restaurants, and God knows what else. I was enjoying my first beer and munching on free peanuts. Every bar in BA had peanuts, and their floors were a couple of inches deep in peanut shells. They served in place of sawdust used in our saloons before Prohibition. I gazed around the smokey room. Nothing had changed since the last trip; same whores, same ferret faced waiters. American sailors had nick-named all the whores. *Mussolini* was an Italian. *The School Teacher* wore glasses. Then there was *Fat Annie* and *Bullshit Annie,* who got her name in a peculiar way. When she first entered the profession, she didn't know a word of English, only Spanish, so she asked a Spanish speaking seaman for a polite expression that she could use when she approached a potential score. He, with tongue in cheek, told her that the finest greeting to an American or Limey was, *Bullshit!* She was a big strapping dame with a voice like a fog horn. She would get herself half drunk, sidle over to a table full of Yanks or Limeys, and roar, *Bullshit.* Oh, I forgot another one, *Madame Ruby.* She always wore a red dress and was very haughty.

I ordered another beer and got to talking with a German at the next table. It turned out that he wasn't a seaman at all but worked for the Hohner Harmonica company, a German company that made and sold, all over the world, high quality harmonicas and accordions. Very casually, I let it slip that I just happened to have two first class American radios. He bit like a trout in Spring. Would I consider selling one? I said that I was most reluctant but would be interested in a trade for harmonicas and accordions, but that it would have to be good because if those Marineros caught me smuggling radios ashore, it wouldn't just be a fine. They'd lock me up in their stinking hoosegow and throw away the key.

We finally struck a deal, two dozen big harmonicas and two accordions for the two radios, delivery to be made in the Plaza of the Venticinco de Mayo. Of course I didn't trust him and he didn't trust me, even though I was quite sure that he was stealing the stuff from his own company.

The next night after supper, I rigged up a sling under my armpit for a radio, put my jacket over it, stuffed five packs of Lucky Strikes in each sock, and headed up the dock towards the gate. The ten packs of cigarettes were worth five bucks in pesos and would buy me a first rate dinner at the Immermann Hotel; bife con huevas with all the fixings, and enough left over to light up the town till the wee hours. I was pretty shaky going up the pier. I felt that damned radio getting bigger and bigger, and bulging suspiciously out of my jacket. The area was crawling with Marineros, always in pairs. Each time that

I got near two of them I'd gradually bear to starboard so that the radio was on the side away from them.

"Buenos Noches," I'd croak.

They would raise two fingers to their caps as I slithered by. *Whew, I had made it!* I jumped on a street car and headed for the rendezvous. There he was, right on time, with a big cardboard box containing half the loot, one accordion and twelve beautiful harmonicas. We made the exchange and scheduled a repeat performance for the next night. I couldn't go back to the ship until very late. What the rest of the crew didn't know, the better. I caught a taxi this time. What the hell, I was in funds. Stepping out at the Immermann, I went through the ornate lobby to the desk. I slipped the desk clerk a peso and announced that I was here to have a leisurely dinner and wanted to check my box.

"No problem," said he.

Boy, what food those German chefs could dish out. I even finished up with a cigar that came in a long, skinny bottle.

Now for the bright lights. I must have hit every bar and cabaret in BA. About three, AM I'd had it. Back to the Immermann for my box and another taxi to the ship. The Marineros never bothered about stuff being carried on a ship, so right up to the gangway we drove. I got out with some difficulty, caused by the liter or so of Canya sloshing around in my innards and interfering with the steak and eggs. Canya being a cheap, potent Argentine brandy. Back aft I went to hide my loot in the steering engine room, then into my bunk for three hours before the Bosun hollered, *Turn to.*

The next night was a repeat performance. That German was an honest crook.

The following morning the Bosun gave us some surprising news. There was something wrong with one of the ship's boilers so we were ordered to finish discharging, load for Boston, only, and proceed direct to Boston on two boilers. Had I ever been lucky. I had originally planned to dispose of the remaining radios when we called at the Brazilian ports, Northbound. Boston, being a very cultural town, was full of high class music stores who would be very happy to take my harmonicas and accordions for a nice fat profit.

My only problem would be a good hiding place in the steering engine room because the Boston Customs men were real Irish bastards. Then, too, I was faced with the problem of smuggling my loot ashore. The harmonicas were easy. Stick a few at a time in my pockets. The accordions were going to require some thought. They were pretty big, and I couldn't just sling them over my shoulder and walk down the gangway...or could I?

Sailing day finally arrived. Pilot aboard, lines singled up, all hands standing by, fore and aft; let go forward, let go aft, slow astern. Round she swung and down the La Plata River we slogged. Maximum speed, six knots.

Let me tell you, BA to Boston at six knots is one long voyage. The ship wouldn't steer well and wallowed along like an old barge. Watch on, watch off, seven days a week; lousy food, constant heat. It was no wonder that everybody got cranky and short tempered. Fights broke out. Almost daily, the challenge was heard, *Step out on deck.* We had all told and retold our worn anecdotes and were heartily sick of them. We got sick of the sight of each other. Personal habits, once unnoticed, grated on nerves. It was a relief to finally sight Boston Light and the pilot boat. We docked at the old Army Base Piers in South Boston, tied up, and at last heard the telegraph ring, **Finished with Engines.**

The next day the Shipping Commissioner came and paid off the crew. The Old Man sat at the head of the table in the officers' saloon, piles of bills and stacks of coins in front of him. He and the Commissioner would check off a name on the payroll, made out by Sparks, call out a name, and we would shuffle forward and receive our pay and discharge certificate. Many of the crew packed their bags and disappeared down the gangway. A hard nucleus remained, though. All the Mates, all the Engineers, a few of the black gang, Moody, one Ordinary seaman, and of course, me.

All during that long Northbound voyage, I had wrestled with the problem of getting those accordions ashore. My choices narrowed down to three. I could declare them and pay the duty, which ran against my larcenous soul, or I could try bribery. That was too risky. If I picked the wrong man, the consequences would be dire. The accordions would be confiscated; I'd have to pay a fine equal to double the duty, and I could be charged with attempting to bribe a Federal officer. My third scheme was too crazy to even consider. I would become a blind beggar—maybe. Sling an accordion over my shoulder, hang a tin cup around my neck; then, complete with black glasses, stroll down the gangway and out the gate. Insanity! But?? The Customs rats would never know that I was a seaman. They would figure, just another itinerant beggar...or would they? Anyway, my first option had expired. All foreign purchases had to be declared prior to docking, and I hadn't declared them. Another knotty problem reared its ugly head. Each accordion was in an expensive fiber case. I couldn't carry one down the gangway in its case. That would be a dead give away. Blind accordion players didn't go around carrying their instruments in expensive cases. I felt like a rat in a trap.

We were to stay in Boston for at least ten days, because after discharging, we were to shift ship to a repair yard to have our boiler fixed. Bingo! There was my solution. The repair yard would probably have only one Customs guard, maybe none. I was all set.

I had persuaded the Bosun to give me the midnight to eight AM gangway watch, so I had all day to myself. The next morning I turned in after a quick breakfast. By noon I was up for dinner, and one o'clock saw me heading for the street car to Boston, three harmonicas stowed safely under my coat. Getting off at the South Station, I walked up to the Boylston Street, Tremont Street area, where all the fine shops were. Sure enough, there were several swank music stores with baby grand pianos, cellos, and violins in their windows. I picked out the swankiest, drew a deep breath, and sailed through the glass doors. A stuck up salesman asked if he could help me.

"Thank you, but I'd like to see the Manager"

"I'm the Assistant Manager, how may I serve you?"

Boy, he sure was high-faluting. I hid my hands so he wouldn't see the broken nails and heavy callouses. I drew out a harmonica and offered it to him. He extended a limp white hand. Turning it over and over, he blew a few notes.

"A Hohner, and a nice one. Where did you get it?"

"Germany," I answered, promptly. "I've been studying over there and brought a few home to help pay for my studies."

"Why don't we step into my office and discuss this further."

By Godfrey, before I got out of that little office, I had sold all twenty-four of them for seven bucks apiece, C.O.D. Hurrying back to South Boston, I loaded up with the remaining harmonicas. I had them taped up and down both legs, in my pockets, and one up each sleeve. If the wind ever blew up my pants legs, I'd sound like Sousa's brass band passing by.

Back on board in time for supper. One hundred and sixty-four long green ones in my kick. Then my greedy mind started working. *Why, oh why did I sell them all to the very first store? I should have shopped around.* Actually, I did very well for those lean, hungry days.

I spent the next few nights making a blind man's cane out of a piece of dunnage. I painted it white and hung it up in the fiddley to dry before daylight. I had the Steward buy me a pair of black, opaque glasses on one of his trips ashore. I was ready. As soon as we shifted to the Bethleham repair yard, it would be go for broke.

The next day I went to town again. I had to strike a deal for the accordions before smuggling them ashore. I would look foolish, if not suspicious, wandering around the swankiest section of Boston with a big piano accordion hung over my shoulder. This time I bypassed my harmonica customer and started to look in the windows of the other music stores. By God, in the second or third store, there, smack in the middle of the window, was an exact duplicate of mine. Shiny black, lots of bright nickel, generous inlays of mother-of-pearl. They had rigged up a spot light so that it glittered and shimmered like the stars. It was positively beautiful. And so was the sign, **Special, $495.00.** In I went. This time, quite by coincidence, the owner himself came to help me. Hiding my hands again, I said that I was interested in the accordion in the window. He shut off the spot light and plucked it off the stand.

A day off in Santos, Brazil

Moody again

The Liar's Club meeting on #5 hatch. The author third from right.

Christmas Day in B.A.

"Here, try it. It's the only one that I have. They are most difficult to get. Have to import them from Germany, you know, and that chap Hitler is causing us no end of difficulty."

Music to my ears! He kept urging me to try it, to listen to its superb tone, to note how responsive the keys were, on and on he went. I muttered something about a sprained wrist, still keeping my paws in my pockets. I'm the world's worst haggler, but I gave it my best shot. I said that the price seemed way too high.

"My dear young Sir, you must realize that with the ocean shipping charges and the exorbitant import duty, that instrument actually cost me $400.00."

I could hear the angels singing. How sweet it was. Very gently, I let it be known that I was selling, not buying. I used the same story—studying in Germany, felt that it was time to come home, *That chap Hitler, you know. Bought two accordions home with me, needed the money, etc.* Blessed be the Saints that watch over such as me. I struck a bargain, $325.00 apiece, C.O.D. Now all I had to do is work my blind man's stunt, twice. The old butterflies started flapping their wings in my stomach. They never stopped until the big day arrived.

The Mate and the First Assistant Engineer had hired all the crew replacements, so the focsle was full again. I wanted to rehearse my blind man's act but didn't dare to. There was no privacy.

The next morning a tow boat came alongside. The usual, *All Hands, Fore and Aft* echoed through the alleyways, and we shifted ship over to the repair yard. Just as soon as we docked, I hurried down the gangway to scout for Customs men. I couldn't find a single one but that didn't mean that they weren't lurking around. There were two gates, manned by timekeepers checking the workmen in and out. Not too bad, I decided. I couldn't stall any longer.

I was heading back to the ship. Up ahead of me was a workman trudging along pushing a two wheeled cart with big wooden wheels. It was piled high with pipefitting tools, pieces of pipe, and God knows what else. As I drew abreast of him, damned if it wasn't Frank Rogier, a Belgian watertender that I had been shipmates with on another ship. I banged him on the back and we shook hands. He had been a good friend and many a stein of beer we had dumped together. He told me that he had married and had quit the sea. I offered him a cigarette, which he accepted, gratefully. Sort of apologetically, he remarked that he was reduced to rolling his own. Shipyard pay, in the days before the unions wasn't too hot. We were leaning against his cart, smoking, and reminiscing, when all of a sudden, a blinding light hit me.

"Frank, old buddy, how would you like to latch onto ten cartons of cigarettes?"

"What have I got to do?"

"Well, I've got two large packages to get off the ship. Could you hide them, one today and one tomorrow, under that junk on your cart?"

"Piece of cake, pal. The one Customs guard we have is stinko by three in the afternoon."

Boy, oh boy! I could bury the blind man act deep, as it should be. I was nuts to ever think of it.

Rogier was working on our ship which made it easier. Between noon and one, while everybody was eating dinner, he and I scuttled down the gangway with an accordion and buried it under the stuff in his cart. At three-thirty, he boldly pushed it out the gate where I was waiting in a taxi. Off I went to Tremont Street, whistling all the way. The next afternoon we repeated the performance. No Sweat! Finished—Done—Finito.

Blessed is he that is brief. For he shall long be remembered.
Anon.

-10-

FOILED IN BRAZIL

There is a sequel to the story of my radio business. One that gave me great satisfaction.

After my success in disposing of the harmonicas and accordions, I took the time to think. My nerves had been badly frayed. Thoughts of the blind beggar haunted me. What if the Customs sleuths had asked me to play a tune? I couldn't have played a note. Didn't even know how to pump the damned things up. It seemed to me that I had pushed my luck just far enough. I also reasoned that the radios I sold in Brazil hadn't yet worn out, or gone on the fritz. I had better lay low, at least for this next trip. No dealing and wheeling.

One of the A.B.s that shipped over was the same guy that got so mad at me in Santos. He was a tall, rangy Norwegian by the name of Otto. He and I had never gotten along. In fact, we had crossed swords, once. I came off a bad second. He had banged me up pretty good. I never could get inside those long arms of his.

In due time we sailed for New York. Otto never let up on me, still making wise cracks about all the dough that I must have made, and what a dirty louse I was to sell cheap, junky radios that would wear out in no time.

One night in New York I was lying in my bunk reading. It was late, but most of the crew were still ashore. Our focsle was empty except for me. I heard footsteps and a thump. No question about it, the sound was coming from the steering engine room. I stole out in my bare feet. Peeking around the corner, I saw Otto heading up the after well deck towards the gangway. I quickly ducked into the steering engine room. There on the deck was a big carton with Philco stenciled on the side. *H, ho, so that's what he's up to.* I crept behind the engine and waited. Pretty soon, back he came, carrying another one. And then a third. Damned if he didn't hide them in the very same place that I had used.

While he was bunking them away under the mooring lines, I tried to ease one of my legs out straight. It was becoming cramped. My bare foot grazed a steam line. I yelped like a billy goat. Otto shot around the engine and glared down at me.

"What in the hell are you doing here?"

I had no choice but to brazen it out.

"Seeing what you're up to, that's what."

"If you ever tell anyone about these radios, I swear I'll stick a knife right through your skinny carcass."

He meant it, too.

"Otto, I have no intention of telling about your scheme, but why buy such expensive ones?"

"I'll tell you why. I believe in giving fair value, not the junk that you were peddling. I paid forty-five bucks apiece for those beauties."

Such noble thoughts, I muttered to myself.

Nothing more was said, but I watched him like a hawk in every port. No action until we got back to Santos. There, I saw him in deep conversation with one of the pimp runners. Pretty soon they sneaked into the steering engine room. *This is it,* I muttered to myself.

We had all been going ashore every night. At supper, Otto guessed that he'd stay aboard. He turned in early. I, too, drew the curtain across my bunk, but not to sleep. All was quiet. He and I were the only ones left in the focsle. It seemed hours before I heard a whistle from out on the dock. Otto was silently climbing down from his upper bunk. He pulled on his dungarees, picked up a heaving line, and sneaked out. Pretty soon I heard him moving around in the steering engine room. Then I heard him going up the ladder to the poop deck. Out I crept and went up the ladder. When my head got level with the deck, I stopped. I could see the action perfectly even though it was pretty dark. Otto was lowering the first radio down to the dock. A dim form untied it and stuck a fist full of millreis notes between the strands of the heaving line, which Otto quickly retrieved and pocketed. As he lowered the third one, I backed quietly down the ladder and went back to the focsle. Pretty soon, in came Otto with a big grin on his square headed puss. I was sitting on the edge of my bunk, puffing on a cigarette.

"Look at that, you cheap bastard. Eight hundred millreis apiece. Ninety-six bucks, each. Give 'em quality, that's the secret."

I must say that I sort of envied him. There he sat at the focsle table gloating and fingering the brand new crisp one hundred millreis bills. All of a sudden he let out a scream of anguish.

"Oh, my God, oh, my God! the dirty cheating crook."

On and on he went, finally subsiding to incoherent moans.

"Otto, what's the matter? You sound like you're dying.

"Look," he moaned, flinging a note on my bunk. As it landed one of the zeros fell off. They were ten millreis notes with a zero glued on. Instead of ninety-six bucks apiece, he got nine dollars and sixty cents. Quality, indeed!

Otto, the radio mogul

Home is the sailor. Home from the sea.
        Robert Louis Stevenson

-11-

A.B. ON A SHIP TO NOWHERE

I've mentioned before, about the old rust buckets that I sailed on during the great depression of the thirties, and of how bad things were. Our existence was tolerable, mainly because we had grown up in that era and didn't know anything different. There was one time, though, that the direct effects of the world wide economic slump came home to roost.

I was A.B. on an old West Coast Shipping Board ship. She was docked in Brooklyn where her cargo was fully discharged and the crew paid off. The Chief Mate announced that due to lack of cargo, she was to be temporarily laid up. He offered the job of ship keeper to another AB and myself. The Second Mate was to be in charge. The vessel was towed to an obscure berth way out in the wilds of Brooklyn. Her boilers were blown down and the black gang paid off. Just the two of us and the Second Mate remained. It was mid winter, cold and snowy. There was no light or heat, and the deserted focsle was like a black tomb. We tried to make do with one kerosene lantern. The Second Mate, Mister Brooks, brought his new bride aboard. His room was about the size of a small bathroom, but they, too, made do.

Moody and I were in a hell of a fix. The lack of heat was the worst. We swiped extra blankets from the empty bunks and piled them on us. My head got so cold that I took to sleeping with an old Navy woolen watch cap pulled down over my ears.

Our pay had been cut to forty bucks a month, out of which we had to feed ourselves. The Second's wife had fired up the galley stove, so they were doing pretty good, but she wouldn't let us use it, damn her.

Adding insult to injury, we were required to work on deck eight to five, six days a week. That damned Second Mate decided that we would chip rust underneath the cargo winches. There we were, on our hands and knees, in the frozen snow, banging away with chipping hammers. Once an hour the Second would leave the warmth of the galley to check on us. After the first few days he separated us, one on the forward deck and one on the after deck.

At noon, Moody and I would huddle in the crew's messroom, back aft, and eat a couple of cans of sardines and a nine cent loaf of bread. We had no way to wash, so after a few days, we were filthy, plastered with rust and dirt.

At knock off time it was already dark and cold. The pair of us would head down the gangway and up to a cheap, crummy cafeteria. I usually had bacon and eggs with a double order of rancid fried potatoes. That forty bucks had to stretch for a month.

That lousy Second Mate decided to let us knock off at noon on Saturdays, not because of any consideration for us. It was so that he and his new wife could head way up in the Bronx to spend the weekend with her folks. His last words each Saturday were,

"Now, you are not to leave the ship except to eat, and then one at a time."

Just as soon as they were out of sight, we headed for Manhattan, our dirty clothes in a shopping bag. After the first week we were both pretty ripe. People on the bus gave us a wide berth.

We were bound for 25 South Street—The Seamen's Church Institute, a world famous place known to seamen of all nationalities. It was run by an equally famous person, Mother Roper. 25 South Street was a many storied building that housed a multitude of amenities for merchant seamen. A private room cost thirty-five cents. Of course it didn't have a window and was the same size as a solitary confinement cell but, all important to us, it was warm and clean.

As soon as we checked in, we would head for the showers carrying our filthy work clothes. A good half hour under the hot water washed away the grime and eased tired muscles. Then we scrubbed our dirty clothes. Supper was in the cafeteria and was great. The cost? Practically nothing. We would spend the evening in the reading room. It would do credit to a public library, with the emphasis on things maritime and religion. And then to bed. Ah, those clean sheets and plenty of heat.

Sunday morning we wandered up and down South Street gawking at the ships tied up at the many piers fronting the East River, Sunday noon featured a big dinner, courtesy of Mother Roper. Late afternoon saw us heading back to Brooklyn. We had to get back before Mister Brooks or he'd have a fit. It was some let down to crawl back into that black, cold focsle.

Such was our routine for several weeks. Spend the evenings in the greasy spoon; the weekends with Mother Roper. No drinking or helling around. We couldn't afford it.

About three more weeks went by. We were really getting stir crazy. Nobody to talk to except each other. Always broke, and always cold and hungry. Then came a change in the monotony. One cold morning we were banging away with the chipping hammers when the toot-toot of a tow boat caused me to look up. Around the sea end of the pier appeared a decrepit, rusty old stem winder coal collier, pushed by two tow boats. I could just make out her name, almost obscured by the rust caking her bows, **PENOBSCOT.**

I went over to the side to see her better. The tow boat Skipper hollered over and asked if we would receive her lines. He had orders to tie her up to our ship. The Second Mate came out of the galley and took over, shouting all kinds of useless orders. Moody and I went forward to take her lines. As she came alongside damned if there wasn't a man and a woman on her focsle head, passing the lines down to us. We tied her up forward, then went aft to repeat the performance, and there were the same couple expertly slinging over the heaving lines, then slacking off on the big hawsers. They moved like a well trained team. After she was all tied up, they came over and introduced themselves. He was the Master of the **PENOBSCOT** and she was his wife. The ship belonged to the Sprague company, big coal operators. Sprague also operated the American Republics Line which our ship belonged to. The **PENOBSCOT**, like us, was being laid up for lack of cargo. She was an ancient tub, but beautifully constructed. Later on, I got to know them better, and they would have Moody and me over for supper. The Skipper's quarters were sumptuous. They were just under the wheel house and spanned the entire breadth of the ship. Beautiful dark paneling and lots of brass. Expensive black leather settees added the final touch. It was such a surprise to step from a rust pitted deck into such opulence. The Captain's wife had installed a small coal burning stove on which they did all of their cooking and it kept their quarters toasty warm. It was such a treat to be invited over. I'd sink into a deep leather chair. The stove would be rustling quietly, and the soft glow of the brass lamps hanging in gimbals reflecting from the polished wood paneling created the illusion of being at sea on one of the posh British ships plying between London and India.

The Captain had been all over the world. His Master's ticket was completely covered with pilotage endorsements for every port from Maine to Florida. He would reminisce about some of his voyages till late at night when his wife would shoo Moody and me out.

A couple of weeks passed. Each weekend I spent considerable time in the library at 25 South Street studying for my Third Mate's ticket. They had all the books but it was tough sledding with nobody to guide me. Surprisingly, Mister Brooks offered to help me. He got so interested in coaching me that he unlocked the chart room and really schooled me in chart navigation, dead reckoning, compass error, stuff like that. He even offered to guide me in celestial navigation when and if we ever got to sea again. He could be a cold hearted bastard to work for, but even so, I've always been grateful for his help.

One cold morning I crawled between the winches, chipping hammer in hand. As I got down on my knees, a terrible pain shot through my left knee. It was so bad that I felt weak and sick to my stomach. I looked around to see if the Second Mate was in sight. No sign of him so I quick headed for the door to the shelter deck. Once inside, I pulled off my jacket and pants. Had to because I was wearing long johns. Peeling them down I peered at my knee. There was a great festering boil, all red and purple. I hauled my clothes back on and hobbled over to the bulwarks and over onto the **PENOBSCOT**. I asked the Captain's wife if she would look at my leg. She fussed around for awhile, then applied some tarry smelling stuff which she said would draw out the pus. She was very skillful and bandaged my leg as good as a doctor could have done. That night I couldn't sleep. It wasn't the cold this time. My leg was killing me. I couldn't turn over without my knee hurting, and it was throbbing something fierce.

By the end of the week I was at the end of my rope. There were at least six boils on my knee. I had to cut a hole in the knee of my long johns because the pressure hurt too much.

The Skipper's wife said that she didn't like the looks of my leg. All the boils had run together and my entire knee looked like a piece of rotten meat. She told me to come back after supper. I couldn't even walk up the pier to get any supper.

That night when she looked at my leg she said,

"You're for a doctor. There are black streaks running up your leg."

She and the Captain had an old Model A Ford out on the pier. They helped me down the gangway and into the car. They took me to a family doctor somewhere off Columbia Street. He looked at me, all the while talking to himself. Getting off of his stool, he left the office. When he returned, he was carrying a bowl and a tray of shiny instruments.

"Son, take a good grip on the arms of your chair. I'm going to have to hurt you, bad."

Swift as lightening his hand reached for the tray and passed twice over my knee. Oh, my God. I thought that he had cut my leg off. The Skipper's wife was standing behind me holding my shoulders. I damned near keeled over, and was soaked with sweat. I ventured a glance at my leg. He had made two great, criss-cross slashes. Now, he took tweezers and pulled away the skin. Then he cut it all off with a pair of scissors.

"Hang on, son, this will finish it up."

And he pulled out the cores of all those boils. When he finished, I was as weak as a new-born kitten.

With my leg heavily bandaged, I tottered out to the car and back to the ship we went. Somehow, I got back into my long johns and turned in. Believe it or not, I felt better.

The next morning Moody had gone up to the greasy spoon early. He brought me back a great breakfast, all packed in cardboard containers. Oatmeal with real cream, bacon and eggs, home fries and coffee. It was all stone cold but I downed every crumb. Pretty nice of him. I owed him a few big ones.

Moody and me

**Moody Harrison on #5 hatch down in the
South Atlantic**

The doctor had given me strict orders to keep the bandages soaked with a weak solution of Epsom Salts and hot water. But where to get hot water? My good nurse solved that one. She and her husband were lugging jugs of water aboard the ship daily, for cooking and washing. She informed me that there would be a dipper of hot water on her little stove, and for me to help myself whether they were on board or not. Pretty nice of them, huh? Every couple of hours I'd make my way over to their ship, carry the dipper out on deck and pour the solution over my knee. Don't you know that after a few days my leg started to heal. No new infection, and the pain was gone.

One day the Chief Mate appeared. He told us that the ship would be going back into service, but not right away. He had gotten permission from the home office to hire about fifty unemployed seamen who were on the beach. He was going to have them chip off the rust in all the holds and 'tween decks, and then red lead and paint them. This was going to be some big job, and the only reason the company had agreed to such an expense was the big damage claims pouring in from the coffee importers. Coffee was our main Northbound cargo, and even though it was standard practice to use hundreds of straw mats while loading to keep the coffee bags from touching any metal, the claims had been soaring. A bag of coffee weighed one hundred kilos, so if it was condemned or degraded, the cost to the company was substantial.

This big chipping job was to be done with air hammers, which had recently made their appearance on ships. I hated them. They were identical to riveting hammers and would sure knock off the rust but they were hell on the poor soul operating them. We had air outlets located all over the ship, and a big steam operated air compressor down in the engine room. The good news was that the Third Assistant Engineer, a watertender and oiler would be summoned back to get steam up on one boiler. That meant that we would have light and heat again.

The next day, the black gang raised steam, we got heat and light in the focsle, and the bed bugs came to life. The freezing cold had sort of numbed them, I guess, but now they were ready to eat Moody and me alive. Moody had been reading a book by Lowell Thomas, *The Seadler*. It was the story of Count Felix Von Luckner, and of his exploits in command of a square rigged armed raider during World War I. In the book, Von Luckner digresses back to his early days as a foremast hand. While he was on one ship, a shipmate who hated the Skipper caught a match box full of bed bugs and turned them loose in the Captain's bunk. Moody, who hated our Skipper, decided to do the same thing. For several nights he was forever snapping the lights off and on, flushing out hungry bugs. Like Von Luckner, he put them in a match box. I could hear him muttering, *I'll fix the old bastard. I hope they eat him alive. Serves him right. Won't allow the Steward enough dough to keep us from starving. Oh, you're going to get it good.*

One morning we were sitting in the greasy spoon. I asked him how his trapping was going.

"Got the match box full. Course every time I slide it open to add more, a few escape, but I'm just about ready."

"Yeah, well how do you propose to get into the Old Man's cabin? It's locked, you know."

"By God, I never thought about that."

He looked kind of crushed, so just to cheer him up, I let it be known that the Second Mate had all the ship's keys.

"But how can I get them away from him? That bastard probably sleeps with them around his neck. Look how he keeps the galley locked"

"You'll figure out some way. Let's go. It's almost eight o'clock. If we're one minute late, the keeper of the keys will eat us alive."

And then an idea hit me.

"Listen, Moody. Why not turn your bugs loose on this lousy Second Mate? And you would kill two birds. That snooty wife of his could have let us use the galley stove once in awhile. What do you think?"

"Slim, that's the best idea that you ever had. Those bugs are starving. They'll eat them alive."

On the way back to the ship he made his plans.

"Every couple of days, they go ashore in the afternoon to buy groceries. That's when we'll get 'em."

And that's just what he did. While they were ashore, I took up station as lookout at the gangway, armed with a chipping hammer to give the alarm. Moody slipped into their cabin and turned the bugs loose in their bunk. Thank God that they had left their door unlocked.

The next morning we spied the pair of them coming down the midships deck towards the gangway. They were each carrying a suitcase.

"Slim, we're moving ashore until the ship is back in service. I'll expect you and Moody to work hard and no goofing up."

He tried to give me a stern look, but the red welts all over his face and neck made him look like a sad clown. Ha, ha.

The Mate and the First Assistant started filling out the crew. I woke up one morning sick as a dog. Flu, I guess. All those freezing nights plus a badly infected leg had caught up to me. I managed to get through the day, somehow, but the next morning I was worse. Shivering one minute, sweating the next. In desperation, I went to see the Mate.

"If you're sick and can't work, pay off."

He was some cold hearted bastard. Pay off I did and rode a train back home to Boston. Thanks to my mother I made a fast recovery. I swallowed my pride and called the Boston office and asked for my job back. Two days later I got a postcard from the Mate. Scrawled on it were two words, **Come back.**

And back I went, of course. Jobs were few and far between.

I believe that our Heavenly Father invented man
because he was disappointed in the monkey.
                                   Mark Twain

-12-

SKULLDUGGERY IN THE FOCSLE

I suppose that it is a sign of old age to compare the good old days to the present ones. I'm no exception. Nowadays, television, movies, novels...they're all quite explicit about sex, violence, homosexuality. The most intimate, and sometimes sordid practices are commonplace. It was all so different back in the thirties when I was a naive young seaman. Even though we thought we were worldwise and sophisticated because of sailing to foreign lands and glamorous ports, the truth was we were abysmally ignorant of the realities of human behavior.

Take me for instance. Brought up in a small New England town during the years of prohibition. Drinking was evil. Sex only took place after marriage. Any deviation, sexual or otherwise, if it existed, was never mentioned; swept under the rug.

Thus, when I went off to sea at the tender age of sixteen, I was truly a babe in the woods.

On those old prewar freighters there were no luxuries. Six Able seamen and two Ordinary seamen lived back aft in a crowded focsle. Iron bunks, two tiered, lined the outboard side. Small wooden lockers took up most of the inboard bulkhead. The deck was concrete, cold to the feet.

I was about eighteen and had just gotten my Able Seaman's certificate. I had been to the North European ports several times, and was now on a regular run to the East Coast of South America. I fancied myself to be an old sea dog. Hadn't I sampled the flesh pots in dozens of ports? And hadn't I listened to interminable boasts of sexual prowess and endurance? Broad hints and coarse jokes were told of *wolves,* men who preferred other men instead of girls.

Being young, and I suppose, innocent looking, I was the butt of many of them. *Watch yourself, Slim. Don't let a wolf catch you in the shower. It was difficult for me to believe that such critters existed, but there must be some truth to it.*

On this particular ship, I had a lower bunk parallel to the ship's side. All of us had hung blue denim sheets on a wire along the side of our bunks to

87

screen out the glare of light bulbs which burned day and night. On the outboard side of my bunk I had rigged up a shelf extending out a couple of feet to the ship's side. On it I kept cigarettes, a magazine, a book or two, and a big, two gallon clay jug. We used to buy these jugs in the open air markets in Brazil. They were ideal for drinking water. They were very thick, and being unglazed, would sweat, keeping the water cool. They were very wide at the base with a long neck. In a heavy sea they wouldn't upset.

Right outside of my bunk was a sturdy wooden bench which the occupant of the top bunk stood on to get into his bunk. About three feet in front of the bench was the bulkhead separating the focsle from the steering engine room. On this bulkhead was a large steam radiator, our only source of heat in the winter.

The sailor that had the bunk above me was something of a mystery. He was a naturalized Swede with bright red hair, Red Swensen. He had joined the ship in New York, and this was his first trip with us. Our ship, like most ships in those days, had a good sprinkling of Scandinavians. They were damned good seamen, and had learned their trade in sail. Red was no exception. He could splice blindfolded, and could use the palm and needle like a seamstress. I can see him, now, sitting on a hatch, his needle flashing in and out as he repaired a tarpaulin.

As a first tripper, he got the twelve to four watch, which nobody wanted, so we didn't see too much of him. The twelve to four were either on watch or trying to sleep.

Red had an odd affectation which led to considerable speculation. He was never seen without a white officer's cap from which the gold braid had been removed. Rumor had it that he had been Mate on tankers and had gotten into some kind of trouble. Also, he was older than most of us, somewheres in his mid forties, I'd guess.

Our final port of departure was Jacksonville, as usual, and once out of the Saint John's River, we headed South on the Great Circle course for Cape San Roque, the Northern bulge of Brazil.

On we steamed, with the weather getting hotter and hotter. Air conditioning was far in the future, but we managed, while under way at least, by rigging a wind shute from a port hole to our bunk. Made out of a denim sheet sewed into a long tube, they created a nice breeze. Not so, however, when in port. When it was summertime in the Southern hemisphere, we sweated it out in those hot, humid Brazilian ports. There, we would sleep stark naked with a pillow between our thighs to soak up the sweat.

When we arrived at Santos and tied up, the heat was fierce. It seemed to beat on your head like a hammer. We were young, though, and took it in stride. After all, this was normal for Santos, so we went about our business as usual.

We were due to stay in port for three or four days so the Old Man gave a draw. Not for me, though. I had an outlet for Lucky Strikes. The bartender in one of the waterfront bars. He had connections with the Customs guards so instead of having to run the risk of smuggling them ashore, he came down to the ship, slipped his friends the usual bribe and boldly walked out the gate with a bag full of my smokes under his arm. And I was left with a fist full of Brazilian cabbage.

That first day the Mate had me working aloft in a Bosun's chair all day in the broiling sun. By five o'clock I was beat. Dog tired, I made it to the messroom for the usual slop. After supper everyone was washing up and changing clothes to go ashore. I just didn't have the energy to go, so I crawled into the washroom for a shower. These old ships had only salt water showers, pumped directly from over the side. Without remembering that we were up a dirty river, I stood under the shower and pulled the chain. Dirty, filthy river water cascaded all over me. Some kettle of fish. Luckily, I had one bucket of fresh water under my bunk.

My spirits perked up a little, so I guessed that I, too, would slip ashore. Jumping into clean pants and shirt, I headed for my favorite joint where my friend the bartender held sway.. I got a nice table in a corner and settled down with a gin fizz. It slid down my parched gullet and called for another. I was feeling better by the minute. Two good looking bimbos were eyeing me from the next table, or rather they were eyeing the pile of dough lying on the table. I waved them over and ordered gin fizzes all around.

They must have been recent converts to the oldest profession because they couldn't speak five words of English, just Portuguese. We were having a fine time talking a blue streak, nobody understanding a word, when who do I spot but Red Swensen. I tried to catch his eye to invite him over. The girls saw what I was up to and grabbed my arm, all the while keeping up a torrent of Portuguese. Being curious,I waved over my friend the bartender to act as interpreter. He listened to the dames for a minute and then said,

"That guy no good; bad, no like girls."

Can't be, I muttered to myself. *Who ever heard of a sailor that didn't like girls?* But what with the gin fizzes and other distractions, the matter slipped from my mind.

When the Bosun yelled, *Turn to,* the next morning, I was in worse shape than the day before. All that damned gin had turned to poison. How I ever got through that long, hot day I'll never know. *Never again,* I vowed, a solemn oath that sailors have been breaking for a million years. But I kept it, at least for one night. Wild horses couldn't drag me ashore.

I struggled through supper, washed up, and spent the evening sitting up on the poop deck where an awning had been rigged. The sun dropped below the horizon and I went below for some badly needed sleep. Shucking off my dungarees and singlet, I stretched and sighed, *This is more like it. A sensible sailor would stay aboard and save his money; not go whoring around these dirty jungle ports.*

I thrashed around for awhile fighting the heat, but finally fell asleep. The focsle was deserted, and all was quiet and peaceful.

Long about midnight I awoke and peeked out of my curtain. Still deserted. I had a smoke and reflected on how smart I was. All my dopey shipmates ashore guzzling booze and chasing whores when they could be peacefully snoozing like me. I stubbed out my cigarette and rolled back in. It was cooling off nicely. Off I slid into a sound sleep.

A long time later something brought me wide awake. I listened. It was Red, sitting on the bench right outside of my curtain. He was drunk and muttering to himself as he struggled out of his shoes. I could see the outline of his head and shoulders through my curtain. He was talking to himself and weaving around on the bench. And me lying there, naked as a jay bird. The focsle was still deserted except for Red and I.

Then he leaned against my curtain, his head bulging against the cloth. To my horror, I felt his hand creep under the curtain and up my leg. Without thinking, I rolled over on my right side, grabbed my big water jug by the neck with both hands, and swung with all my strength. **Blam!** I nailed him on the back of his head. He pitched forward. I tore the curtain aside, and there lay Red, blood streaming from his head. What I didn't realize at the time was that as he flew head first off the bench, he dove headlong into the radiator.

My God! He looked dead to me. I didn't know a thing about first aid, and any way he looked far beyond first aid, or fifth aid, for that matter.

I was starting to shake. I pulled on my dungarees and ran midships for the Mate. Back in those days the Chief Mate was a real father figure. He handled all disciplinary problems. He ran the ship singlehanded. And those old-time Mates were equal to it. The Old Man was a mysterious figure, seldom seen, yet always there to make the decisions or to take the rap. The Mate was the man you went to.

I pounded on his door. Thank God he was aboard. When he opened it, I started shouting.

"You had better come back aft, Mister Mate. I think Swensen is dead."

"Calm down, Slim. What happened to him?"

While I was spilling out my story, he was pulling on his pants. Back aft we went. We both ran into the steel door off the well deck at the same time. He flung me aside and charged through the door. I picked myself off the deck and followed him. When we entered the focsle, Red was laying on his back. A drunken oiler and an AB were squatting over him. They had rolled him over. Boy, what a mess. His forehead was all caved in; his eyes were half open and showing only the whites. The Mate ran his hand over the back of his head

90

where I had hit him with the jug. He raised an eyelid and peered in. Straightening up, he ordered the two drunks to run up the dock and tell Customs to send an ambulance. As soon as they had left, he turned to me and said,

"Tell me exactly what happened."

I did, leaving out nothing.

"Slim, listen carefully to me I have known Swensen for a long time. What I know about him will remain unsaid. All you know is that he fell while climbing into his bunk. Savvy?"

I did just as he said. The ambulance came and took Swensen away. The next morning I had to go up to the Mate's room. There were two uniformed policemen there. The Mate, who spoke pretty good Portuguese, acted as interpreter. I repeated my story. *Heard a thump. Looked out and there he lay.*

The next day we sailed for Montevideo and Buenos Aires. Northbound, we called again at Santos to load coffee for the States. Not a word did we hear about Swensen. Not then, nor ever.

What happened to Red Swensen, I never heard, but to me he was an evil man, possessed by evil forces.

"Ships that pass in the night, and speak each other in passing.
Only a signal shown and a distant voice in the darkness."

Henry Wadsworth Longfellow

-13-

THE WHALING SHIP TAMERLANE

This story contains such a fascinating series of events that I pass it on to you.

It is difficult to know how to begin. Sometimes the end seems to be the beginning, and visa versa. Perhaps I should best start in New Bedford, Massachusetts, back in October, in the year of our Lord, 1850.

In that month the Tamerlane weighed anchor in the roadstead and set sail on a voyage that was to last over three years and cover two thirds of the earth's watery wastes. There was a young foremast hand signed on the ship's Articles. His name was Samuel Harris. For upwards of three years he faithfully kept a journal of his travels, his doings, and his thoughts. This journal has a violent ending, one which puzzled me for many years. Some small part of the mystery I have managed to piece together. The remainder must remain anyone's guess, hidden by a hundred and forty years of obscurity. First, I must explain how I came to know that this particular vessel cleared the harbor of New Bedford in October of 1850.

My wife's father was also a seafaring man. A native of Holland, he sailed for many years on Dutch ships, mostly in the Dutch East Indies. After some years at sea, he came ashore in America and settled on the East Coast. Some time ago, he acquired the journal from a dying merchant seaman in the Norfolk YMCA. How this sailor obtained the journal must forever remain a mystery.

The journal bespeaks a man of above average intelligence and education for seamen of those days. His english grammar was good, his descriptions clear, and his youthful imagination most refreshing.

Some years after I had read the journal, or log book as it really is, I was cleaning out some old papers and letters from the attic. As is always the case, instead of getting on with the job, I found myself reading the yellowed old papers and debris of two generations. I had emptied a drawer of it's contents and was leafing through the pile of trash when my eye was caught by the words, *The Silent Pilots*. I had picked up an old magazine, The Outlook, issue of January 27, 1915. *The Silent Pilots* was an entertaining article about ships' figureheads, and of how they had all but faded from existence in this day of steamships.

It went on to say, that being as they were, mounted on the bows of sailing ships, they were invariably lost when the ships were. However, it stated, there had recently sprang up a fad among wealthy North Shore of Boston residents of collecting ships' figureheads. One of the finest collections was owned by a Mr. Robert S. Peabody, of Marblehead. His best figurehead, the article continued, was from the New Bedford whaler, the Tamerlane!

By golly, I thought. *That's the same ship that young Harris sailed on, and whose journal is in my desk.*

I sat down on the floor and continued reading. The account went on to say that this same ship, the Tamerlane, was the one made famous in Frank Bullen's book, *The Cruise of the Cachelot.* I rocked back on my heels in that dusty attic, lost in thought. What boy had not read *The Cruise of the Cachelot?* When I was a small lad, my imagination had been fired by the doings in that tale. Harpooning the wily sperm whale in the South Pacific; pursuing bowheads in the Arctic Ocean; tales of adventure that made a young boy's heart leap and made him vow, *I'll be a sailor, too.*

This was happening in the year 1990, seventy-five years after the magazine had been published. Holding it, I slowly went down the stairs, all thoughts of cleaning the attic forgotten.

Going to my desk, I took out the journal. It was written in what must have been the 1850 counterpart of our common ten cent note book. The cheap, cardboard binding had come unbound and was hanging by a few shreds. It was stained and tattered. I stood there thinking of the miles and miles of ocean that it had travelled, and of the years that it had lain in another seaman's sea chest. I thought of the focsle on that whaling ship--dark, unheated, no light except a whale oil dip; and I pictured Harris straddling his sea chest, faithfully putting down in his journal, his life. I could see him, tired, wet, hungry, yet finding the time to set down a brief account of the day's events.

One entry reads, *Sweetened water and bread for breakfast The crew most exasperated.*

He didn't explain that sweetened meant with crude molasses, and that bread meant hard, stale, weevily, ship's hard tack. And this up in the Bering Straits, between Russia and Alaska where the waters and the winds were icy and the cold crept into your very marrow. And that day or night the cry of, *thar she blows, b-l-o-o-w-s.* Or, *All Hands,* meant more cold hours, more misery, hauling on a wet line or oar, with the big, gaping sea boils on wrists and ankles making every movement agony.

I opened the cover, being careful not to tear it. On it's inside Harris had kept his account with the slopchest. It was a pitiful little budget covering three long years. The items represented his total purchases, and so represented all his earthly possessions, because one can assume they whatever he started out with had either worn out or been washed overboard during the innumerable gales encountered.

I have said that between the lines of a ship's logbook there can be found a world of adventure. As I read those brief entries, I tried to picture what happened. I put myself in Harris's shoes 'way back there in 1850 on board the Tamerlane. She was bound South from New Bedford, down across the Gulf Stream, then struggling through the Doldrums and Horse Latitudes till she reached the Roaring Forties. And still South until they sighted their first landfall, Staten Island. This was not the Staten Island a ferry boat ride distant from New York City. This was a bleak, windswept rock just North and East from that devil, Cape Horn, called Cape Stiff by the windship sailors.

Before reading further, I resolved to try to unravel the mystery of the last entry in the Journal. It was fairly safe to assume that if Mr. Peabody was one of those wealthy, North Shore collectors of figureheads in 1915, he was not then a young man. And all these years later should see him quietly sleeping in some New England graveyard. Nevertheless, I drew a sheet of paper and addressed a letter simply to Mr. Robert S. Peabody, and, or descendants, of Marblehead, Massachusetts. In it I told of all that I have just related, together with the last entry in the journal, and asked how he had come by the Tamerlane's figurehead. I didn't hold out much hope of the letter ever reaching a recipient, but sent it anyways with some little hope and an insatiable curiosity. I then turned back to the journal.

As I said previously, sometimes the end of the story seems to be the beginning, so I had better set down here the last entry that Harris made in his journal in order that the reader may get some sense of continuity

> **Monday, 12th--At about 1/2 past seven a. m. came in sight of McCorley's Island, commonly called Goat Island. At 8 felt a tremendous shock...**

And there the journal ends.

Did the ship strike a reef and founder? And if so, how was the journal saved? Did Harris get home safely or was he lost in the Pacific Ocean?

It was this curiosity that prompted me to write Mr. Peabody in the hope that some light would be cast upon the mystery.

Imagine my surprise, when, some weeks later, I received an answer. It was from Mr. Peabody's son, himself now middle-aged. He told me that upon his father's death, all but one of his figureheads had been presented to the Peabody Museum. The figurehead from the Tamerlane he had kept, and it stands to this day over his front door in Marblehead. Then, to my utter surprise, he went on to say that he knew me, and also had known my father very well, and that it was he who had given me my first job on my first ship, the S.S. Seattle Spirit!

It's a small world. Peabody and Lane are steamship agents and operators in Boston, and Mr. Peabody and Mr. Lane had given me my first berth on one on the Yankee Line vessels that they operated between East Coast ports and Germany. I had never connected the Mr. Peabody that I knew with the Peabody in the magazine, although the Peabodys are a very old, illustrious family. A small world, indeed.

At the end of his letter Mr. Peabody said that as far as he knew, the Tamerlane was broken up in New Bedford, her home port. It was there that his father purchased her figurehead.

It was such a pleasant surprise to hear from him and to learn that he still had the figurehead of the Tamerlane, that it was some little time before I again tried to surmise what had happened to her. Obviously, she wasn't lost on Goat Island; otherwise Mr. Peabody would never have acquired her figurehead. And if she didn't founder that morning, why did Harris stop keeping his journal? He had been so faithful for upwards of three years that it seemed only logical for him to continue to the end of the voyage. To be sure, in his journal, he had skipped days every now and then. I imagine that his original intention had been to keep a daily diary. However, having been a seaman myself, I can well understand why he occasionally skipped a few days.

In these days of steam and modern comfort, it is difficult to realize the hardships of a wooden sailing ship. When the seas started to make up, the focsle stove was the first to be doused. The danger of fire was ever present, and the comfort of a foremast hand meant nothing. Then, there were the days and days of gales down at Cape Stiff. The hoarse bellow of *All Hands* was a nightmare, repeating itself watch after watch. After a few days of such fare, it is no wonder that Harris skipped a few entries.

Imagine trying to set down the day's activities after having spent three or four weeks on *four and four,* which meant four hours on deck, then four hours below. That only happened in good weather, or during long prevailing winds from the same quarter. Down around Cape Horn, or up in the Bering Sea, the sailor's four hours below in the dubious comfort of an unheated focsle was interrupted every watch by the cry, **All Hands.** Struggling into boots and jacket, clawing his way across a windswept deck, cold and icy; then up the shrouds to take another reef. Fingernails torn off; hands numbed. Misery and weariness were constant companions.

In my days at sea, the comforts were luxurious compared to Harris's fare, yet that same hoarse cry, **All Hands,** is still fresh in my ears and evokes the same memories. Yes, *All Hands* is a command that no seaman ever questions. Maybe people and businesses ashore could well profit by the unflinching obedience that such a command produces. Of course, there is a difference, in that at sea, *All Hands,* meant that the ship and the lives of everyone on board were in danger. Failure to obey could well mean death for all hands. But isn't that true of modern business? Economic death means that every employee is thrown to the wolves of unemployment. In my opinion, the loyalty and obedience exhibited by ignorant seamen could be emulated with far reaching results by landsmen. Probably I'm prejudiced, but there it is--Sailor's philosophy.

Later on, Harris noted in his journal the following hair raising event:

> **July, 1851, Monday, 14th -- At 6 P.M.** came to anchor in Alaska Bay in company with the ship Copia, of New Bedford, Bark Anadir, Do, Brig Sirno of Woahoo, also the Bark Sussex, of Hobart-on. The Hamilton at anchor in a small bay to the windward of us, also the Starbuck, and another ship, name not known, not yet anchored. From the Brig we learned that the ship Armeda (of New London), was lost at a place about 40 miles distant from this bay. She was driven on a dangerous reef and became an unmanageable wreck in a short time. There happened to be an English whaling ship in sight at the time. She saw the signals of distress, and immediately came to the assistance of the wrecked mariners. With the united exertions of both crews they were saving some of the most valuable articles when they were boarded by a horde of savage natives who had come off in their canoes for the purpose of plunder, and immediately began to strip the ship, and to drink the Old Man's rum, whereupon a scene of the most bloody description ensued. The Captain of the Armeda felled an Indian to the deck while the latter was leading his followers on to ransack the Cabin. The savage instantly rose again and plunged a dagger to the heart of the nearest man, (a foremast hand). The Captain had frequently requested them to leave the ship but they could not be induced to go. Now commenced an indiscriminate slaughter of the savages, carried on by the crews of both ships wrought to an almost indescribable fury by the cruel death of their comrade, nor could they be restrained as

they seized upon harpoons, lances, cutting spades, hatchets, and various other whaling implements, and rushed madly on the natives, some of whom stood with their daggers drawn ready to receive them, while others of them were attempting to escape in their canoes, but in this they were foiled. They had brought off some of their females in all their canoes but one. They, upon hearing the uproar, and as they had remained in their canoes alongside, immediately shoved away from the ship and paddled towards land with all their might, thereby abandoning the poor wretches to their fate, which was awful. The exasperated seamen attacked them at the main mast with such over whelming vigor that they drove them forward on the forecastle.

The shout was vengeance, and a terrible vengeance it was. While some of them were pierced through and through with harpoons and lances, others were nearly cleft in twain by spades and hatchets. When they were fairly cornered they fought with the most desperate bravery, having no other weapon than their knives but they were (of course) no match for the weapons used by the seamen. Some of them even fought with their bowels hanging out nearly to the deck, some with their skulls open and their own blood streaming over their faces and fairly blinding them. Some, after being maimed in the most horrible, manner fell upon the deck seizing whatever missile they could to hurl at their opponents. Some sprang overboard badly wounded and were either drowned or dispatched by men alongside in whale boats.

The canoe which had been left by the squaws was filled with so many savages attempting to escape that at a short distance from the ship a tremendous wave over-topped them and they all sank with the most thrilling shrieks and groans to rise no more. It was impossible to tell how many were killed, as many of the men were employed in throwing the bodies overboard for some time, but there must have been a great number as the blood poured out of the scuppers constantly during the combat, and there were two or 300 of them aboard, some few of which escaped by means of broken spars and planks, and rallied all the remaining natives on shore to the rescue.

Soon the water was covered with canoes, so many of them that (as they were also armed with their fighting implements) the Captain was obliged to abandon the wreck, and that without saving scarcely anything of much value.

Such events, though not commonplace, were part of a whaler's voyage.

In those days hundreds of whaling ships cleared New England ports for three and four year voyages. If we could read between the lines of their log books what stories would come to light! All of them, in their wanderings from the South Atlantic to the North Pacific, then over to the Sea of Japan, sailed arm in arm with adventure, danger, and death. It was their way of life, but their log books were meager and barren.

Footnote: Harris's journal was fast deteriorating, so I donated it to The Nantucket Historical Society, where it is on display.

Cleanliness is next to Godliness.
Anon.

-14-

"FILTHY MCNASTY"

One time, back in the thirties, I was an A.B. on an old cargo ship running to ports on the East coast of South America. It was a good ship, manned by good officers.

We were homeward bound, having departed from Santos with a big load of coffee. I had been on the ship for several voyages, so I had gradually worked up through the watches, to the coveted 4 to 8 watch. To my way of thinking, it was the best watch for several reasons. First, my partner and I only had to work on deck with the Bosun for one hour, four to five in the afternoon. Second, whichever of us was on the wheel got relieved by the other for supper. This broke the tedious business of standing wheel watch. Third, when we finished breakfast at 8:30 A.M. we could get two or three hours sleep before it got too hot. Also, the focsle would be empty except for the two A.B.s on the twelve to four watch, and they were always sound asleep. And last, and most important to me, we were on the Chief Mate's watch. Mates, in those days, were, without exception, the tops in seamanship and ship maintenance. Our Mate was the best of the best, and I picked his brain incessantly while I was on the wheel. It was mid June, and full summer had arrived when we docked in Brooklyn. It was my turn to stand the night gangway watch. After supper I went amidships to get my orders from the Mate. I knew them by heart, but this was a little ritual that he never failed to repeat in every port.

"Keep a close watch on the mooring lines, slacking them off when the tide rises, heave them in when it falls. If the temperature was below freezing, check the cargo winches and windlass every half hour to make sure they were slowly turning over. Keep the gangway lower end exactly one foot above the string piece. Call the Mate on duty for any emergency. STAY AWAKE! No napping in the fireroom fiddley, hear?"

After the lecture he leaned on the rail outside his room and lit his pipe.

"Slim, you're pretty friendly with the two Ordinary Seamen aren't you?"

"Yes Sir, they're two good men."

99

"Yes, I know they are, but unfortunately I've got to let one of them go when we pay off tomorrow."

"Mister Mate, those two guys never missed a day in port. When the Bosun yelled, *'Turn to'* in the morning, they were always there. They pull their weight and then some. Why?"

"Well, the home office has some big shot vice-president that has a son that needs a little touch of hard work, so we're stuck with him for one trip, that's why."

I talked to myself all through the night about this injustice. Two good, steady men, and one of them had to go. They both held A.B.'s tickets and were fully trained seamen--men that any Mate would be glad to have on board. They worked day work with the Bosun, and believe me, they earned every penny of the $47.50 a month that they were paid.

The next day it happened just like the Mate said. The two Ordinaries flipped a coin and the loser packed his sea bag and went down the gangway.

The following day the new Ordinary showed up, carrying an expensive pig skin suitcase. I was in the focsle trying to sleep after having been up all night. This critter didn't look too hot to me. He was about eighteen or nineteen years old. He was all dressed up in a white shirt and suit. When he spotted me he asked where he could stow his stuff and where was his bunk. By tradition, the two ordinaries got the worst bunks in the focsle. There were a total of eight bunks in the focsle of this ship. Six of them were on the Starboard side, nearest the port holes, a godsend when down in the tropics. The two ordinaries' bunks were up against the bulkhead separating the focsle from the steering engine room. They were hot and they were noisy. That big steering engine made one hell of a racket, day and night. They were also the first two bunks from the door, so there was constant traffic by them from men going and coming on and off watch. This new hand got the bunk nearest the door.

"When do I go to work?," he asked me.

Before I could answer, the Bosun came in. He was a big Norwegian and stood for no nonsense from anyone.

"Get that fancy suit off and get out on deck. There's work to be done. Hurry it up."

When our Northbound cargo was discharged, the ship immediately started loading. When it was loaded we sailed down the coast picking up cargo wherever offered. By the time we sailed from Jacksonville, our last U. S. port, the heat was something fierce. We were bound South on the Great Circle route to Cape San Roque, in Brazil. Now that we were at sea, the Bosun broke out the air chipping hammers. The after well deck was to be chipped clean of all rust and then given a coat of fish oil, a coat of red lead, and finally, a coat of an ungodly mixture of Bunker C fuel oil, stockholm tar, and whatever else that the Bosun could dream up. Our new Ordinary was one of the poor souls that would operate a hammer. The other Ordinary would also participate.

These hammers were just the same as a riveting gun. They were powered by eighty pounds of air pressure. When the chisel was pressed against a rusty deck, the rust and dirt would fly up in a cloud, enveloping the poor devil operating it. Our new Ordinary had on his only pair of dungarees, and was stripped to the waist. In a matter of minutes he was as black as a Negro from the waist up. When noon time came he sat down to dinner without even washing his hands. After supper he fell into his bunk, dirt, rust, and all. This caused quite a stir amongst us. When eight men live in close quarters, especially in the tropics, one stinking apple can quickly spoil the barrel. I took it upon myself to have a word with him. The next night when I came off watch, I invited him to come up on the poop deck with me. Boy, he was getting pretty ripe! I started my little lecture. It quickly developed that he had no conception of keeping his clothes or himself clean. At home, he always had a drawer full of clean shirts and underwear. When his mother got after him, he would reluctantly take a bath on a Saturday night. When I pointed out that we had no bath tubs, he looked amazed.

"How do you take a bath, then," he asked in a plaintive whine.

"In your bucket, of course," I retorted.

He just shook his head and announced that he couldn't do that. I was starting to get a little annoyed.

"Listen to me, you damned fool. You're starting to stink like a pole cat, and whether you know it or not we're not going to stand for it."

He just laughed at me.

"I don't take orders from you, so just leave me alone. I didn't want to come on this stinking old ship in the first place."

I gave up and went below. The more I thought about this matter, the more I became convinced that something had to be done, but what?

The next morning at four A.M. I headed for the bridge to stand my two hours on the wheel. The weather was fine, and the ship was working easily. She was staying on course with just a spoke or two of wheel. The Mate was busying himself stoking up his little percolator. I waited until he had downed his second cup and had got his pipe drawing good. I cleared my throat, nervously. And I was nervous, too. No seaman worth his salt ever ratted, and I was about to do so.

"Mister Mate, we've got a problem back aft."

I told him about the Ordinary who, by this time, I had nick named 'Filthy McNasty.'

"Slim, you do have a problem, but I have the solution."

"What is the solution, Sir?"

"You'll see, very soon. Mind your damned course."

The next day was Sunday, a day off for the Ordinaries. It had always been the custom for the Mate and the Bosun to make a surprise inspection once or twice a trip. They always showed up on a Sunday. It was never a thorough inspection. They would go into the mess room and see if the dishes were clean. As for the focsle, they would just look around, examine the paint work and the deck. Maybe the Mate would remark to the Bosun,

"Bosun, the next rainy spell that we run into, you should soogey out this place." Or, "Bosun, this deck could do with a fresh coat of paint."

Then they would be gone.

This particular Sunday morning was something else--was it ever! The two of them came through the door, the Mate leading the way. The first thing he saw was Filthy lying on his bunk, just as dirty as when he had knocked off the previous day. He was sound asleep, and this was about ten o'clock. The two A.B.'s on the twelve to four were up and watching closely. They were two old hands and tough as nails. The Mate leaned over and took a good grip on Filthy's mattress. He gave a good heave and dumped him onto the deck.

"Get up you dirty bastard. Get out on deck. You're a disgrace."

Filthy scurried out.

"Bosun, what do you recommend?"

"Sand and canvas, Mister Mate."

Now, I had never heard of that expression. What did it mean? I looked over at the two A.B.'s. They both had broad smiles on their mugs.

"Slim," the Mate said to me, "Go amidships and tell the Chief Engineer that I want water on the after deck, full pressure."

The Mate left. The Bosun sent one of the A.B.'s up forward with instructions to bring back several pieces of sail canvas and a bucket of sand.

When I got back, the Bosun was dragging a two and a half inch fire hose from it's rack under the poop. He had just got it straightened out, with no kinks, when the pressure came on. Filthy was sitting on the after end of number five hatch watching the Bosun with great interest. The salt water shot out of that nozzle with such force that it almost upset the Bosun. He whirled around and turned it full onto Filthy! He was washed off the hatch and was pinned up against the hatch coaming, spluttering and choking. He kept trying to get up, but each time, the Bosun would hit him again with that solid stream of water, knocking him back down. By God, I thought that he was going to drown him.

The A.B. arrived back with the canvas and the sand. Without being told, he pounced on Filthy and ripped his shorts off. Then he and his watch partner went to work on him. They scrubbed him with that coarse canvas, taking big chunks of skin off in the process.

They would sprinkle sand on him and then scrub. Filthy kept trying to get away from them, but each time he managed to get up, the Bosun would knock him down again. One time he washed him into the scuppers. He damned near went overboard, because abreast of the hatch there weren't any bulwarks, just two lengths of waist high chain strung between stanchions. Poor Filthy was crying and hollering something fierce, but they weren't done yet. They rolled

102

him over on his stomach and went to work on his back, arms and legs. He was starting to look like a piece of raw meat!

I had had my fill.

"Bosun, how about calling it quits?"

"Yeah, Slim, I guess he's had enough. Knock it off, men. Slim, go 'midships and tell the Chief that we are finished with the water on deck. And while you're up there, go up and see if Sparks will open the slop chest and get this skunk some work clothes. I'm going to throw overboard everything he owns."

Boy, talk about justice! This tale has a sad ending, though. Filthy never learned. For the rest of the voyage he was always scrubby. He would clean up a little bit whenever one of us would say to him, *SAND AND CANVAS.*

When we got back to Boston, he was the first one down the gangway. Didn't even wait to sign off and collect his pay.

It is human nature to think wisely and act foolishly.
                                    Anatole France

-15-

GOLD...COIN OF THE REALM
(AND OF GOOD SEAMEN)

Years and years ago, when I was a young Able Seaman, I quickly discovered what seemed to be a very sensible practice indulged in by most of the crew. When ever they went ashore, they would slip a five dollar gold piece into the watch pocket of their pants or dungarees. There was good, solid thinking behind this. Ships would frequently sail on very short notice. Sometimes it was because expected cargo hadn't shown up. On other occasions cargo had either been loaded or discharged faster than the Mate had figured. In any event, it could be ten o'clock in the morning and the ship not due to sail until midnight. No matter...The Mate would take a piece of chalk and change the sailing time on the sailing board from midnight to 1:OO PM.

Because of this practice, seamen were forever being left behind. Now, this was not too bad in an American port. The stranded seaman merely went up to the Agent's office and got a train or bus ticket to the ship's next port. This worked fine, and usually the missing man would be standing on the dock when the ship pulled in.

Missing a ship in a foreign port, though, was a different kettle of fish. When a man went ashore in the daytime, he was, without exception, off watch. He was either a watertender--fireman, who stood sea watches both at sea or in port, or he was an Ordinary Seaman standing the night gangway watch, or maybe a mess boy or cook, slipping ashore in between meals. Anyway, they went ashore and got left on the beach. Because they were only going for a couple of hours, they never had their seamen's papers with them. Neither did they have much money. Caught in a foreign, out of the way, backwater port, they frequently stood forlornly on a vacant pier from which the ship had long since departed.

What was he to do? No money--dead broke, no papers, and often the port was too small to warrant an American Consul. Somehow, or other, he had to find his way to the nearest port where there was an American Consular office. There, they would arrange for him to sign on another ship which was short of a full crew, or maybe they would put him on a train to his ship's next port. All this took time, and the poor castaway had to eat and sleep. Hence the scheme cooked up by some forward looking sailors. Gold, especially American gold was universally accepted, no questions asked. Paper currency, American, that is, worked OK in the waterfront joints, but at the train and bus stations, restaurants, and stores, it was looked upon with suspicion--too many counterfeits. Gold was the answer, no question about it.

But not me. I was smarter. I took a five dollar bill, folded it very carefully down to the size of a postage stamp, and stuck it into the watch pocket of my shore-going dungarees. Drunk or sober, dead broke at 4:OO AM, it would never, never be used except for missing the ship. Smart aleck, that was me.

A week or two later, the dungarees needed a good scrubbing. Forgetting completely about the five dollar bill nestled down in the watch pocket, I used my knife to cut up half a bar of strong washing soap into little slivers, and dumped them into my wash bucket. Then for good measure, I added half a cup of 'soogey' powder, a strong washing powder containing lye. It would take the skin off your hands. I stuffed the dungarees into the bucket, filled it with water, and carried it into the wash room where there was a live steam line. I stuck the steam pipe down into the bucket, turned on the steam, and let it cook and bubble all night.

The next morning when I came off watch at 8:OO AM, I wolfed down a quick breakfast and went into the wash room. Shutting off the steam, I fished out the dungarees with a stick, and spread them out on the scrubbing bench. Using a scrubbing brush, I set to work. I was happily scrubbing away, when, all of a sudden, a sad little piece of white paper floated out of the watch pocket. My God! It was the remains of my five dollar bill!

I carefully unfolded it. It was just as white as snow.

I spread it out carefully, to let it dry, and finished my scrubbing.

Some weeks later I was telling Sparks this sad little story. He asked to see the remains of the bill. There were absolutely no markings on it. Just a piece of white paper. Don't you know, he took it ashore in Buenos Aires, went to the Bank of New York, and they cashed it! Sparks charged me a one dollar
'handling' fee.

After all this happened, I came to the conclusion that my shipmates were right, after all. Gold was the thing. The first thing I did when we got back to the States was to go to a bank and buy a five dollar gold piece.

I carried that little coin, it's only the size of a nickel, all through World War II, and long after.

When I finally came ashore, my son was in the Marine Corp. The time came when he was posted overseas, to the far East. While I was driving him to the airport, I told him the story of the little coin, and presented it to him. He carried it all over the East, and, like me, never had to use it. Recently, I talked with him about the coin. I advanced the proposition that now that the need for it had past, how about giving it back to me.

"No way, Pop. You're acting like an Indian giver. You gave it to me with no reservations. The fact that it is now worth a lot of money, has nothing to do with it." And of course he's right. What would I do with it, hoard it?

If man could be crossed with the cat, it would improve man, but it would deteriorate the cat.
Mark Twain

-16-

THE GOOD OLD DAYS (YEAH?)

A lot of my younger colleagues have listened patiently to my groaning and moaning about how bad conditions were on board ship back in the thirties. I suspect that they were just too polite to tell me what they really thought; that old age and overwork had addled my brain, and that I exaggerated out of all proportion to the truth. Well, here's another little incident to support my case.

Back in those days I was sailing A.B. on the American Republics Line ships running to the East Coast of South America. These ships were all either Hog Islanders or West Coasters. They were built in 1918-1920. They had been ordered for use in World War I, but the Armistice came along before they could be used. Because of this, the government had no use for them, so they chartered them out to various steamship companies at bargain prices. Even though they were wartime built, they were good, well found vessels.

The usual route for our ship was to sail South from Boston, picking up cargo all the way. The last stop was Jacksonville, Florida, where we always took on board a deck load of timbers consigned to La Boca, a part of the port of Buenos Aires.

We arrived off the entrance to the Saint Johns River at daylight and boarded a pilot for the trip up river to Jacksonville. The lumber terminal where we were to load was miles from the city. It was just an open field on which were stored thousands and thousands of board feet of lumber.

As soon as the pilot came aboard, watches were broken and all hands were called to top the booms. Then the Bosun had us stretch old cargo runners thwartships on the decks. Our deck cargo of timbers would be loaded on top of these wires. Then they would be thrown over the deck load. One end would be made fast to the deck with a big turnbuckle. Then the other end would be rove through a couple of snatch blocks leading to the nearest winch. The winch would heave away until the wire was good and taut. Then it would be stopped off and made fast. It was a very efficient way to secure a deck load.

We finished laying out the wires and stood by, fore and aft to tie the

107

ship up to the dock. As soon as she was secured we went to breakfast where the Bosun laid a beaut on us. The lumber consigned to our ship had not arrived, and wouldn't until the next day.

Hooray! A night in port.

"Hold it," he said. "The Old Man has decided to have the ship fumigated! All hands have to leave the ship at 8:30 A. M. because the fumigating chemicals are poisonous."

So, he concluded, all hands were to report midships to receive a draw. We all piled out of the messroom and went forward to the saloon. By coincidence, I was first in line. The Captain and his clerk, Sparks, were sitting at one of the tables. In front of the Old Man were several stacks of half dollars. It didn't sink into my thick head what was coming. Up I marched and said,

"I'll draw ten dollars, Captain. Where do I sign, Sparks?"

The Captain gave me a nasty look and snarled,

"You'll take what I give you. This isn't a draw. While this ship is being fumigated, she won't be feeding. All hands, including the cook will be off this ship by 8:30, and will not be allowed back aboard until 7:00 P.M. Here is fifty cents for your dinner and supper! Next."

I stumbled out in a fog. Fifty cents??? And us 'way out in the countryside, nine miles from nowhere. What to do? In those days you either put up with it or paid off. We couldn't even do that. We had signed offshore Articles back in Boston. Even if we jumped ship, we would forfeit what pay we had already made, and worse, we'd be black balled throughout the company, and in those days jobs were precious.

There we were, the whole damned crew, down at the foot of the gangway, jawing away and talking to our own belly buttons about what a cruel world it was. Someone spoke up and said that about a mile up the dirt road, there was a little store. So, what the hell. We set off in little groups. It was full summertime and hot as hell. Our feet kicked up the dust and it got in our throats something fierce. Every once in awhile a colored guy driving a mule and rickety wagon would pass us. We would ask for a lift but they would just cluck to the mule and go by. After what seemed to be an age, but was probably about two hours, the little store appeared up ahead. We all trooped in. Coke was a nickel a bottle. God, but it went down good. There we sat, out on the porch, wondering what to do next. We all had about three Cokes which left thirty-five cents apiece which had to go for both dinner and supper. We were in some pickle. Suddenly, one of the oilers spoke up.

"Hey, listen up. Let's find the nearest ship and put the arm on them. We can even offer to work for our food. How's that?"

Everybody started talking at once. Most of them went for the idea, and off they went. No sooner were they out of sight, when around the curve came Mr. Sax, the Chief Engineer. He looked like a wilted turnip. He waddled in the door looking for a cold Coke. I slid in right behind him. Making sure that none of my friends heard me, I put the old arm on him.

"Mr. Sax, could you please see your way to loaning me a few bucks?"

"Slim, I could, but if that crew out on the porch find out, they'll never let me alone."

"Chief, they'll never get it from me, I promise."

"Here's a ten spot, but remember, not a single word to those wolves out there."

I carefully folded the ten dollar bill and stuck it my watch pocket.

"Thanks, Chief. Mum's the word."

I sauntered out and rejoined my companions. They were getting itchy and decided to see what was up the road. I begged off and rejoined the Chief.

He was a pretty fat specimen, and hated any physical effort.

"Slim, I've phoned for a taxi. Want a lift up town?"

"Bet your life, Mr. Sax."

A dilapidated model A soon showed up and off we went. We hadn't gone very far when up ahead I spied my shipmates slogging along through the dust. I scrooched down below the window so they wouldn't see me, and we rattled by leaving them in a cloud of dust.

We finally reached a point outside the city. The road became paved as we approached civilization.

"Where do you want to go, Slim?"

"I'd like to stop in at the YMCA, if it's all right with you, Mr. Sax."

"Driver, drop my young friend, here, off at the Y."

At the Y, I said so long to the Chief, and thanked him again. Inside, I marched up to the desk and showed my YMCA card, issued by the Newton Mass. YMCA.

"Glad to see you-all, Yank," drawled the clerk. "What can I do for you?"

"I'd like to take a swim."

"Sure thing. That will be twenty cents for a towel. Go right through that door over there and down the stairs. Take any locker that's open."

I raced down the stairs, unbuttoning my shirt as, I went. No swimming trunks in the Y's of those days. You went in balliky bare. It was great! Made you feel like a seal. I fancied myself quite the diver and swimmer, back then. There were three or four other young guys in the pool. They watched closely as I launched myself off the diving board in what I thought was a pretty fair front jack. When I hit bottom, I pushed hard with both feet and shot out of the water at the edge of the pool with enough momentum to wind up standing on the edge. One of the little tricks that you learn in any Y. Seeing that I had the attention of my audience, I tried a half gainer, what we used to call a Flying Dutchman.

"Not too bad," I thought, smugly.

I walked over to where they were sitting and said hello. One of them said,

"Hya, Yank. I'm Pete. This is Joe, and this is Jeff. We all work here." Jeff spoke up with the heaviest Boston accent I ever heard.

It turned out that he was a graduate of Springfield YMCA College, located in Springfield, Mass. He turned away, did two beautiful hand springs, leaped up onto the diving board and executed a perfect two and a half somersault. When he entered the water there wasn't a ripple! So much for me and my fancy diving. While he was racing up and down the pool, his friends explained that he was the Athletic Director of the Y. No wonder he was so good. Every graduate of that school not only excelled in a variety of sports, they were also accomplished acrobats.

I spent most of the afternoon in the pool with my new found friends. Hunger was getting the best of me, though, so I took my leave. I wandered around Jacksonville gawking at the sights. In those days the South was rigidly segregated. Negroes had no right nor privileges whatsoever. Their kids couldn't play in the public play grounds. They never dared to take a drink of water from a drinking fountain. All restaurants were closed to them, as were most stores. Movie theaters were off limits to them, also. Only the most menial jobs were open to them. All in all, they were forced to lead a pretty lousy life. Coming from way up North, I had had no exposure to this vile stuff. I consoled myself with the old expression, *'When in Rome do as, etc.'*

I spotted a likely looking cafeteria and sailed in. Everything looked so good, and I was so starved that I kept piling dishes onto my tray. By the time I had pushed it down to the cashier, I could hardly lift it. Lift it I did, though and made my way to an empty table where I ate my way through every dish. Someone had left a newspaper on the table so I got to reading it. Being a perfect stranger to Jacksonville, there wasn't much of interest in it. I was about to fold it up when an ad on the back page caught my eye. It was an ad for a movie theater. Big black letters proclaimed that the Mills Brothers were appearing there. By God, that's just where I'd go. I was an avid fan of theirs and listened to them on the radio whenever they were on.

I ambled out onto the street and hailed a cab. Settling down on the back seat, I gave the driver the name of the theater. He turned around and gave me a nasty look.

"Look, buddy, you don't want to go there."

"Yes, I do," I said. "Why shouldn't I?"

"It's your business, young feller, but you Yanks sure don't have much sense."

He slammed the cab in gear and shot off, pretty near breaking my neck. He looked at me in the mirror.

"Are you sure that you have the money to pay for this ride? It's way out of town, down near the lumber docks."

"Ski"-Ordinary Seaman

I waved a five dollar bill at him and said,

"Keep going, pal."

Shortly, the paved road gave out and we were back in the dust. There weren't many houses, and what few we passed were dilapidated shacks raised up on stilts. It was still daylight so I could see that the inhabitants were all colored. We rounded a turn and rattled into a sort of small town. The street was crowded with people, all colored. The driver pulled up in front of a rather large building with a marquee built onto the front. A big sign proclaimed, *'The Apollo Theater proudly presents The Mill Brothers singing their favorite songs.'* I paid off the cab driver and walked up to the ticket booth. The colored girl inside the booth looked at me in amazement.

"One ticket, please," I said.

"That will be fifty cents, one balcony ticket."

"I don't want a balcony seat. I want a seat downstairs, right up front," I demanded.

"Sorry, downstairs for colored, only. White folks have to sit in the balcony!"

Feeling out numbered, I picked up my ticket and slunk upstairs. There were five or six Negroes already up there. They all turned and stared at me, then got up and walked out! Wow, was I ever getting the full treatment. At first I was annoyed, but then I began to realize a little bit what the word discrimination was all about. These poor folks had a perfect right to retaliate in any small way that they could. And I didn't blame them. So I settled back and enjoyed every single minute of the Mills Brothers and their marvelous voices.

That experience has never left me. After the performance I started back to the ship. As I trudged on through the dust, great and noble thoughts swept through my mind. One of them still sticks, the one that goes, *Man's inhumanity to Man.*

You can put blind trust in God,
but with men, keep one eye open.
Anon.

-17-

THE COOK GETS EVEN...OR DID HE?

Back in the early thirties, I was once again an A.B. on an old West coast built Shipping Board freighter. All these ships had what is called a shelter deck. This cargo deck was on the same level as the main deck, and ran all the way from the after bulkhead of the forward well deck aft to the forward end of the after well deck. It passed under the bridge structure into #3 'tween deck and then under the midships housing.

I had heard that they were built with this shelter deck to cut down on the Panama Canal tolls, which were based on the ship's cargo capacity as measured below the main deck. It was very inefficient because all the cargo had to be hand trucked from the two watertight doors in the after bulkhead of the forward well deck, or lowered through #3 hatch 'tween deck. The after well deck bulkhead also had two watertight doors, one Port, the other Starboard. Inside the Starboard door the builders had created a large room walled off from the cargo compartment. Into this room they had installed the Steward's chill room and freeze room. They had thick wooden doors like those you used to see in a butcher shop. The chill room was kept at 35-40 degrees, and was used for vegetables, bread, etc. The freeze room was for meats and fish, and was kept at 0 degrees, or lower. Also in this room, secured to the bulkhead were all the tools and apparatus needed to convert the ship from an oil burner to a coal burner. Hanging up there were big cast iron grates to be used in the fire boxes. Also hanging there were the long *'slice'* bars. These were fifteen or twenty foot long pokers. They were to be used to stir up the coal fires and to rake out the ashes. All this stuff had been hanging there for years, ever since the ship was built. And last, in this room was an exit from the engine room. It was used by the unlicensed black gang going and coming on and off watch. It was also used by the oiler on watch, who had to come up out of the engine room every two hours and go all the way back aft to oil the steering engine.

Back in those days ships only carried one cook and one Steward. Between them they prepared the meals for thirty to thirty-four men. It was the cook's habit to go down to the chill room every morning and gather together the

112

bread and whatever else we were going to get for breakfast. Then he would go into the freeze room and take out what frozen meat was slated for the day. This he would leave on a chopping block for the Steward to cut up later in the morning. On this particular morning, down he went, clad, as usual in a singlet, white pants, and an apron. As six o'clock rolled around, he was in the freeze room lifting down a fore quarter of old bull beef.

It was time for the four to eight oiler to come up and oil the steering engine. This particular oiler was something of a mystery man. He had been on the ship for three or four years. He had no friends, and obviously didn't want any. Whenever he went ashore, he went alone. Where he went and what he did, no one knew. His bunk in the black gang's focsle was the last one aft. It was a little isolated from the rest. After breakfast he would wash some clothes and then turn in. Because the sheet across the side of his bunk was always drawn, you couldn't tell if he was sleeping, reading, or what. He was a short, powerful man, with very muscular arms. In the past, a few of the crew had come aboard half drunk, looking for a fight. To their sorrow, they had made the mistake of tormenting him. He had come out of his bunk as silently and swiftly as a tiger. Not a sound escaped him as he proceeded to methodically thrash them. The word got passed, and everyone gave him a wide berth.

In those days there were a lot of strange men sailing the ships. Some were on the run; some had done time, and others were just born loners. He might have been all three. Without any of us knowing why, he had developed a silent hatred for the cook. We never found out why.

Four bells rang out from the bridge, to be echoed by the First Assistant Engineer beating it out on a crowbar hanging in the engine room.

What happened next is conjecture. There were no witnesses. The cook didn't return to the galley. It was sometime after eight o'clock before the Steward missed him. He looked into the cook's room. His bed had been slept in, but no sign of him. He ran up to the officers' saloon and told the Mate about the missing cook. The Mate followed him out, all the while shouting questions. It didn't take the Mate long to figure out where the cook was.

"Steward," he said, "Let's you and I take a peek into your refrigerated rooms."

When they got down to the shelter deck, the Mate noticed that the doors to both rooms were dogged fast. The two of them undogged the chill room door and looked in.

"He's been here, Mister Mate. See, he's got the bread and butter in his carrying pan."

"There is something fishy here, Steward. Open up the freeze room."

And there was the cook, draped over a bench. His bare arms and shoulders were blue, and both ears were snow white, a sure sign of frost bite. He was conscious, though, so they dragged him out on deck and commenced rubbing him. Several of us that were off watch gathered around them. That poor cook's teeth were chattering so badly that the Mate shoved a towel in his mouth so he wouldn't bite his tongue off.

Our Chief Mate was an old hand, and no dummy. It didn't take him two minutes to figure out that the only person that could have done the job was the four to eight oiler. He went storming into the black gang's focsle and yanked the sheet off the oilers bunk.

"You locked that poor cook in the freeze box. Why did you do it? Another hour and he would have been dead. Speak up, man."

He was wasting his breath. The oiler just looked at the Mate with his inscrutable black eyes.

"Don't know what you're talking about."

And that's all he ever said.

As for the cook, he lost the lower part of both ears. They just fell off after a week of intense pain. Stick around, though, there's more to come, and worse, too.

The ship's galley was located midships just aft of the fireroom fiddley. It spanned the breadth of the ship and had steel half doors on each side. The galley deck was terra-cotta tile. The deck was pitched to a big drain in the middle. Once a week the cook would put a big kettle on the stove, half fill it with water, and then dump a whole can of lye into it. When it was boiling hot, he would gingerly lift it off the stove. Then, standing first in one door and then the other, he would slush it on the galley deck. That smoking hot lye would eat off all the grease and dirt, carrying it down the drain and over the side. The tile would look spanking clean as if it had just been laid. When the deck dried he would rinse it off with a couple of buckets of water, and go for his afternoon's nap.

A week later we were in some filthy port discharging. Watches had been broken, and we were all on day work. As usual, the First Assistant had assigned the four to eight oiler as Deck Engineer. His duties were to oil the steam cargo winches. He went forward and aft all day, oiling and checking the winches.

It happened about ten o'clock in the morning. The cook had his big kettle of hot lye bubbling on the stove. He peeked out of the door. The four to eight oiler was coming down the midships deck, an oil can in his hand. He was stripped to the waist, the tropical sun was blazing down. The cook ducked back into the galley, grabbed the kettle, and flung the contents all over the oiler! Pandemonium broke loose. The oiler was rolling around the deck screaming. His skin was already peeling off his shoulders and arms. His entire scalp would later slough off. Men appeared from everywhere. The Mate as usual, took charge. He and the Old Man jumped on the oiler and rolled him in a sheet. An ambulance arrived and took the poor man away. Then, the Mate and the Captain went to work on the cook. They knew very well of the hatred that the cook had for the oiler, but they couldn't trip him up. He stuck to his story. They tried

114

Taking our departure on a pre-war Shipping Board freighter.
Two of the cargo booms on the after deck have been cradled,
the others are still up.

and tried but he just repeated his story.

"Why hadn't he dumped the kettle on the galley deck and let it run down the drain?"

His answer,

"I didn't want it to go down the drain and out the overboard scupper because the scupper was right over the gangway, therefore I decided to put off the job until another day."

Nobody believed him, but there was nothing else they could do.

The matter was closed and the ship sailed down the coast for her next port, leaving the oiler in the hospital.

A couple of weeks later she was Northbound, picking up cargo at the same ports where she had discharged. Much to our surprise, there on the dock was the four to eight oiler, waiting for us. As soon as the gangway was down, up he came, carrying his battered suitcase. His head was swathed in bandages. He would never again have a hair on his head. He had a shirt draped over his shoulders. They, too, were heavily bandaged. He never spoke a word to anyone, just went back aft, changed into dungarees, and went back to work, oiling the winches. A strange, silent man--dangerous, too. At long last, we battened down the hatches and sailed for the States. We were four or five days out when another tragedy occurred.

One morning the four to eight oiler left the engine room about ten minutes before six A.M. This was later verified by the First Assistant. He went up into the shelter deck room and took down one of those long, heavy slice bars. Then he backed into the shadows and waited. Promptly at six, down came the cook. Suspecting nothing, he set down his pan and started to undog the chill room door. Behind him the oiler swung that slice bar in a great arc about two feet off the deck. It struck the cook in the back of both legs, breaking both of them. In fact, the Mate later said that they were almost cut off! He then went aft, oiled the steering engine, and returned to the engine room.

Once again, the Steward missed his cook and summoned the Mate. Together, they went down to the shelter deck and found him, unconscious and bleeding badly. They carried him up to his room on a spare hatch cover. The Mate and the Old Man sewed up the awful wounds and set the legs in home made splints. They could do no more.

This business had gotten badly out of hand. The Captain decided to conduct a formal investigation. He called for a meeting to be held in his office. Present beside himself were the Chief Mate, the Chief Engineer, the First Assistant, the Steward, and the four to eight oiler.

All the facts about this investigation I later got from the Mate. I was on his watch, and he enjoyed talking to me during the long, dark hours when I was on the wheel.

The Captain closely questioned the Steward and the First Assistant.

They told a straight forward story about what little they knew about all three incidents. Then the Old Man turned his attention to the oiler.

"Matthews, it's obvious that you have committed a serious crime. What have you got to say about it?"

Matthews turned those inscrutable eyes on him and growled,

"I don't know nothing about it, and that's all I've got to say."

By God, he got away with it! When we got back to New York, the Old Man summoned the police. They spent one morning questioning all concerned.

"No direct evidence, Captain. No witnesses. We bid you Good Morning."

And that was the end of it. I paid off and got another ship.

116

You aim for the palace and get drowned in the sewer.
                    Mark Twain

-18-

THERE JUST AIN'T NO JUSTICE

When the first iron ship ever built slid down the ways she surely had on board a couple of cases of the most diabolical invention ever contrived by man, the chipping hammer.

The very minute a new ship entered salt water, she started to rust. Her hull, her decks, her deck gear, the housing, everything immediately started to pit and corrode. It was an insidious process, and woe be to the Chief Mate who didn't take immediate steps to stem it. He would never succeed in keeping ahead of it, but try he must.

It was a never-ending task. Chip off the scaling paint and rust. Wire brush the exposed surface. Rub in some fish oil, then give it two coats of red lead, and finally, a coat or two of paint. A few months later, repeat the whole damned thing.

These chipping hammers were somewhat similar to an ordinary carpenter's hammer, except that they didn't have a round head for driving nails. Instead, they had two sharp heads. One was vertical, the other horizontal, enabling the operator to hopefully deflect the flying rust and pieces of paint away from his eyes, goggles then being unheard of.

On ships all over the world the battle against rust went on unrelentingly. At sea the deck gang swung their hammers day and night on the decks. In port stagings were rigged over the side and the hull was attacked. Every ship, in every port, had a mottled look. One section of the hull would be bright red, the next bare, awaiting a fresh coat of red lead. Then would come a strip of fresh black paint, followed by a rusty section. It was a hopeless battle, and still is. Over the years the ships' hulls got thinner and thinner until they were sent to the breakers yards to be broken up for scrap.

As if this wasn't bad enough on the overworked deck gang, a new device appeared on ships. The old chipping hammer, despised by a whole generation of seamen, disappeared almost overnight, to be replaced by a contraption far, far worse. It was the pneumatic air hammer. It was very

117

similar to the pneumatic riveting gun, except that the hammer in a riveting gun was fixed in the end of the gun, and only went in and out an inch or so. In these new chipping hammers, the operator slipped the chisel into the end of the gun. When he pressed the trigger, he had to hold onto the chisel with his other hand, or it would fly out like a projectile.

Chief Mates on every ship at once put these hammers at the head of their stores lists. Down in the engine room the black gang installed a powerful steam driven air compressor from which they ran pipes all over the ship to outlets. Then, a long, heavy rubber air hose would be snapped onto an outlet. The engine room would start up the compressor and run it up to eighty pounds per square inch. You would then be ready to go. The vibration was fierce! Your arms and shoulders would absorb the worst of it, but it was anything but fun. A cloud of rust and dust blew back in your face and eyes, (No goggles yet.) and mixed with the sweat. In a matter of minutes you would look like a black man. Truly, a hell of a way to make a living.

It was about this time that I was A.B. on a West African Line ship running to West African ports. As ships went, back then, it wasn't too bad a berth. We got Shipping Board wages, $57.50 a month for A.B.s, which was more than a lot of Lines were paying. The food, of course, was just as bad as on all ships, but we were young and hungry, and didn't know any better.

When I signed on, I was lucky. The Bosun assigned me to the eight to twelve watch, which was the most coveted because you got to sleep right through from midnight to 7:20 A.M. My watch partner was on the elderly side. He had been going to sea for about a hundred years, and was an excellent seaman. However, he hated physical work.

The Mate was well aware of this, so he cooked up a beaut. He declared that my partner would stand all four hours of the morning watch on the wheel, and I, who was young and able, would spend the four hours up in a bosun's chair chipping the foremast, red leading it, and painting it.

We were down in the South Atlantic, and the heat was fierce. Promptly at eight A.M. I went up the foremast ladder to the crosstrees, a coiled gantline over my shoulder. I shackled the gantling block just under the crosstrees and rove the gantline through it, pulling on it until the end reached the deck below. The Bosun was down there. He made fast the end to a bosun's chair. Then he made fast the air hammer to the side of the chair, and hoisted it up to me. He also sent up a heaving line that I could use to hoist up a pot of red lead when I needed it. I pulled the standing part of the gantline through the rope bight on the chair and tied a bosun's chair hitch so that I could lower myself.

Gingerly, I eased myself into the chair and fired off the air gun. Holy smoke! The impact of the gun against the mast sent me sailing out three or four feet away from the mast. The Bosun was watching me, and yelled up that he would send up a length of one inch line that I could use as a frapping line to

118

Looking aft on a pre-war freighter

prevent me from sailing through the air as if I was in a giant swing. He did, and I passed the line right around me and the mast. I drew it as tight as I could, made it fast and went to work.

The work went slowly. As the morning passed, it got hotter and hotter. At ten o'clock I heard the Bosun sing out to the two Ordinaries, *Smoke O,* meaning coffee time. Not for me, though. On his way down the forward deck, he told me to stay where I was, that it would take too much time to lower me down just for a ten minute break. And I was dying for a long drink of cool water. No dice, though. It would take me a couple of hours to chip two feet. Then the Bosun would send up the red lead. For both chipping and red leading, I would have to haul myself around the mast, plastering myself in the process. After a few days I had gotten down ten or twelve feet. The lower I got, the more I sailed out away from the mast. If the hammer didn't do it, the roll of the ship did. The mast was more than two feet in diameter. I took to trying to grip it with my feet to minimize my swing. After a couple of days my crotch was aching from trying to hang on with my feet.

Every morning I could look over towards the wheel house and see my partner at the wheel. He would leer at me and thumb his nose. Then he would peek out of the wheel house door to see where the Third Mate was. If the coast was clear he would light up a cigarette and blow the smoke at me, the louse.

After a week of this I was getting desperate. The beginning of a way out was starting to ferment in my head. What could I lose? Anything was better than hanging up there day after day like a damned monkey in a tree.

The next day I waited until I heard the Bosun shout, *Smoke O.*

I looked down at the forward deck. It was deserted. I looked 'midships. Not a soul in sight. Now was my time. Each day before going aloft the Bosun would give me three chisels that the engine room crew had sharpened. I put one in the gun, aimed it over the side and pressed the trigger. Away it sailed over the side and into the water. I saw my partner watching me. Thumbing my nose at him, I shot the second and third one overboard.

"That'll fix'em," I muttered. "Now the Mate will have to buy more of them, and until he does, I'll be rid of this job."

It wasn't to be. I saw the Mate coming up the forward deck. He had been watching me from his port hole.

"Slim," he hollered. "Send down your heaving line. I have three new chisels for you. The black gang can make them just as fast as you can shoot them over the side. By the way, you're making good progress. On the voyage home you can start on the after mast!"

And that's just what I did. As I said, *There just ain't no justice*

119

Big shots are only little shots that keep on shooting.
Anon.

-19-

THE RIGORS OF A LIFE AT SEA

Ever since I could read, I had an all consuming ambition to go to sea. I read everything that I could lay my hands on that pertained to ships and the sea. This was back in the twenties, and most of the stories were about sailing ships. I read about the whaling ships. I devoured the tales of the big, sleek Clipper ships, square rigged and built for speed. By the time I reached high school my goal was firmly set. I would go to sea.

Alas, the days of sail had all but come to a halt. The day of Steam had arrived to stay. No matter. The call of the sea was loud and clear. If it was to be on steamships, so be it.

When I reached my junior year in high school, I was only fifteen years old. Back in grammar school my teachers had advanced me by a year and a half. My folks were flattered, feeling that their son was a smart boy. However, looking back, it was a mistake. Being so young, I missed the social side of high school. Girls, dances, proms were not for me. I still thought that guys that associated with girls were sissys. I still had a long way to grow to maturity.

We lived in Massachusetts. That state operated the school ship Nantucket. She was an old, square-rigged barkentine, that had been equipped with an old fashioned horizontal, steam reciprocating engine. This was used to teach the engineering students. The ship acted as both barracks and classrooms. All winter she would lay tied up to a wharf in Boston. A temporary wooden structure enclosed her decks, furnishing space for the classrooms.

The course would last for two years. At the end of that time, students were graduated with either a Third Mate's ticket or a Third Assistant Engineer's ticket. Each summer, the ship went on an extended cruise, during which practical experience in seamanship and ship handling was acquired.

In the fall of 1930, I started my senior year. Without my folks knowledge, I applied for admittance to the Nantucket. Several weeks later I received notice to report on board the Nantucket on a Saturday morning for a physical examination.

120

That morning is still very vivid in my memory. It was unusually cold, and a damp wind was blowing. There must have been twenty or thirty other boys. An officer directed us to a drafty, cold classroom, where we were told to strip. There we stood, naked as jay birds. It sure was cold, and the goose pimples grew. One by one we slowly passed into a smaller room where the ship's doctor presided. My turn finally came. The examination was very thorough. When it was over, I was passed through another door, and told to get dressed and wait. Sometime later, the doctor stuck his head out of his door and called my name. I went in and was told to sit down. He perched on the edge of his desk and looked me squarely in the eye.

"Son," he said. "I'm sorry, but I cannot pass you!"

"Why, doctor? I'm as healthy as a horse."

"Yes, you are healthy enough; it's not that. You see, life at sea is very rigorous, and requires a very strong, sturdy body. You are tall and thin. Believe me, I know what I'm talking about."

I pleaded and begged, to no avail. I pointed out that I had been active in YMCA sports since I was twelve years old; that I was on the swimming and diving team, and that I had five silver cups for field sports. The answer was a firm no. Somehow or other, I found my way home. Tears had streaked my face. I wiped my face clean with a handful of snow and went in to the house. I never told my mother of my defeat and disappointment. I ate a quick supper and went up to my room. Right then and there I vowed that I would go to sea, no matter what.

All through the winter and spring I canvassed the steamship companies and agents in Boston. Each Saturday saw me on the street car by seven o'clock. At every turn I was rebuffed. The great depression was in full swing, and able bodied men couldn't get work, let alone a half grown kid. At last my persistence paid off. I got the promise of a berth on a Yankee Line steamer, the S.S. Seattle Spirit, trading from East Coast ports to Hamburg and Bremen.

The day after graduation exercises, I sailed out of Charlestown on my first ship. Every night when I rolled my tired, aching body into my bunk, I thumbed my nose at that smart ass doctor.

"It's only the beginning, Doc. You ain't seen nothing, yet!"

Fate and the good Lord who watches over such as me were good to me. Years later, when I got my first command, the first thing I did was to, once again, thumb my nose at that long ago doctor. I suppose that maybe I should have been grateful to him. Maybe I wouldn't have made it without my all consuming desire to prove him wrong. In any event, I did make it. And for all the gold in Fort Knox, I wouldn't have missed a day. So there, Doc!

Man doth not live by bread alone-especially whole wheat bread.
Denis W. Brogan

-20-

BREAD, THE STAFF OF LIFE (MAYBE)

Back in 1931, when I first went to sea, there were no super markets such as we have today. Bread was bought at a bakery where it was made. Meat was bought from a butcher shop. Fish from the fish market. Vegetables and fruit from the corner fruit stand. Bread and rolls were always white and unsliced. The day of whole wheat, rye bread, or *'vitamin enriched'* bread was far in the future.

All ships baked their own bread. They were big, long loaves, and tasted great the day they were baked. However, they were kept in the Steward's chill box where they soaked up the odors of onions, turnips, or whatever else was in there. Then, that bread was edible, but barely so.

Stewards of those days were properly called *'Belly Robbers'*. They had to be on the daily food budget allowed him by the Company. It was twenty-nine cents per day per man! And that was for all three meals for hungry men doing hard manual labor! Those old Stewards did all their own buying. There were no such critters as port stewards, back then. So, even though we cursed them, they were not to be blamed. It was the time of the Great Depression, and hungry bellies were the order of the day.

We were docked in New York, and the Steward was stocking up on staples. We knew because the deck gang had to carry the stuff aboard. One miserable job that we hated was taking aboard bags of hard coal for the galley stove. We hoisted them aboard with the winches at number three hatch, and then had to manhandle them up onto the boat deck. They were burlap bags and weighed a hundred and fifty pounds apiece. By the time we were through, we were as black as Negroes. Then, every few days the watch on deck had to go up there and empty two or three bags down the chute that led to the galley.

Unbeknownst to us, the Steward, in one of his forays ashore, had stumbled upon a bakery that had suffered a bad fire. The bags of flour had been wetted by the fire hoses. For this reason, the Steward was able to buy them for a song. His only problem was that he had to take all of the bags, and he didn't have the space to store so many of them. He solved that problem by having us put them in the slatted boxes on the boat deck where potatoes, onions, etc. were stored. We dumped them in and forgot about them.

Some weeks later we were at sea, again. Day after day, bad weather plagued us. We were taking green water over the main deck, and the spray went up and over the boat deck. The Bosun had the watch on deck put extra lashings on the life boats.

At last the sun came out, again, and the wind and seas subsided. As we went about our business, the smell of bread baking wafted across the gentle breeze. Our mouths watered.

Wow! Fresh bread for dinner.

When eight bells rang out, we all piled into the mess room. All hands reached for the bread at once. The Bosun whacked several hands with the back of his knife. The messboy had sliced a loaf into thick slices. The Bosun took one and, from long habit, held it up to the light and peered intently at it. He was looking for any hidden cockroaches. We all did this at every meal. The Bosun roared,

"Mess, get your ass in here. What are all these brown spots in the bread?"

"I don't know, Bose."

"Well, get your ass midships and tell that damned belly robber that I want to know. Git!"

What we didn't know was that those bags of flour that had already gotten wet once, had gotten wet again by sea water during the storm. It was all moldy. Shortly, the mess boy returned with the Steward in tow.

"Something wrong with the food, Bosun?"

"You're damned right there is. What are all those spots in the bread?"

"Why, Bosun, I'm surprised at you. Surely you have heard about the newest breakthrough in bread making. It's been in all the papers and on the radio. It's called *'whole wheat'* bread. The wheat is milled with the husks on. The husks cause the brown spots. Medical science has just stumbled onto something called vitamins. They are essential to good health, and are found in the husks of wheat. Naturally, when I heard this, I went right out and bought whole wheat flour. Nothing but the best for you guys."

That damned fool Bosun didn't want to reveal his ignorance.

"Why of course, Steward. I should have known. I've read all about it. Fine looking bread, Steward. Many thanks."

And we swallowed this nonsense, along with the bread, hook, line, and sinker. *Ignorance is bliss,* or so said some smart aleck poet.

WHITE SHEETS... BLUE SHEETS

I first went to sea in 1931. A few years before my time, ships were more fully manned than in the thirties. The stock market crash in 1929, followed by the Great Depression, resulted in steamship companies shortening sail. The quality and the amount of food diminished. Mates and engineers had their stores lists radically cut. Last to go were the so-called petty officers. At least their rating disappeared. The first to go were the quartermasters. There were three of them on every ship. They did all the steering when the ship was at sea. In port, they stood a round the clock gangway watch. It was a soft job and much sought after. They simply disappeared from crew lists.

The petty officers on a cargo ship consisted of the Bosun, the three quartermasters, and the three oilers. How the oilers were so classed is a mystery, nevertheless, they were. These few men enjoyed certain small privileges that assumed an importance beyond what they really rated. For example, they had their own messroom amidships. And get this; they were issued white bed sheets. Now, this might seem of no consequence, but it was.

Those white sheets became a badge of class. The rest of the crew were issued blue denim sheets, and they were entirely suitable. Those seven men felt that they were a special breed. The only one entitled to feel that way was the Bosun. On all ships, without exception, he was the best seaman.

First, the quartermasters were done away with. Next, came their amidships messroom. And last, their messboy was done away with. Yep, they had their own messboy to wait on only seven men.

By the time that I came along, the oilers were bunking back aft in the black gang's focsle. The trouble was, though, they were still being issued white sheets. Once a week we all had to parade amidships, carrying our soiled bedding. The Steward counted what you turned in, and gave you back the same. Those damned oilers would flaunt their white sheets and look down their noses at us second class citizens.

I know that all this sounds childish, but it was very real.

-22-

THE NORTH ATLANTIC CONVOYS

Many tales have been written about the seamen who manned the merchant ships which carried the goods of war across the North Atlantic during World War II. British authors have written their stories about their men and ships. They've done it well, too. Books and stories by American authors have been few. Some were non-fiction telling of heroism of the merchant sailor adrift in a life boat after a torpedoing, or gallantly defending his ship with the pitiful little pop guns which were all that was available in the early part of the struggle. Others used fiction to dress up a bit, the horrid business of war at sea. A girl at home, a war acquaintance in Oran; maybe an attractive refugee encountered during the blackout in London. Most of them portrayed the Merchant Service in its true colors; a vital cog in the machinery of war. Its heros and cowards praised and damned, no better nor worse than any other cog in that vast machine that finally restored peace.

Being myself a member of the Merchant Service before, during, and after the War, and being, too, an avid reader, I have sought out those tales in books and magazines. Reading them, I have lived, again, or existed again, through those years from 1939 to 1945. But, though in each tale, I came upon something familiar, something poignant, some vital thing seemed to be missing. The more I thought about it, the more perplexed I became. One day it all came to me. Nothing exciting ever happened to me! I sailed the convoys all through the war and was never torpedoed, never was sunk by aircraft or had the guts ripped out of my ship by a magnetic mine. I had nothing to tell, just a never ending series of voyages. Cargos loaded and cargos discharged.

My story of the war at sea wouldn't interest anyone. Whenever I reminisce on those years, the first thing that comes to my mind are Winston Churchill's words, **Blood, sweat, toil, and tears.** That's all that I had for five long miserable years. No hair raising experiences, no medals. Just work and work and more work, with bad food, little sleep, and plain common, down to earth fright, always with me. I'm going to tell it anyway, feeling that there were a lot more like me. Not only those who sailed the ships, but the other forgotten men and womenwelders, ship fitters, craftsmen of all kinds who forsook their homes and families to come to the ports where the ships were being built. They reaped the dubious rewards of overtime and double time while their kids grew older and their wives bitter.

About the time of the Sudetenland incident when Germany had stopped rattling her sword and had drawn it full length, I had paid off a ship and come home. My son was four years old and I hardly knew him. My wife and I talked for a long time one night. We were trying to buy a little house and the mortgage payments were a heavy burden. We figured that we could still hang on to the house if only I could get a job right away. It would mean pulling the belt a notch or two tighter but at least I'd be at home with my family.

I was lucky enough to get a job in one of the local ship repair yards as a rigger. I mistakenly assumed that the work would be much the same as on board ship; splicing wire and rope, refitting life boats, hoisting stores, rigging derricks, and the like. No dice. That was *fancy rigging* and belonged to the old time riggers. My next six months were spent deep down in the dry dock, up to my ankles in freezing water. Mostly, I dragged heavy tackles and chain hoists through the muck. The leading man rigger was like a Bosun, never satisfied. *Where have you been? I've been waiting for twenty minutes for that tackle.* But the pay was good. I worked almost every Saturday and Sunday, and some weeks a couple of half nights. And the very best of all, I went home every night to my little New England clapboard house with its old fieldstone fireplace. Banging my lunch box down and getting out of my overalls, I would bellow for Junior to come and help me build a fire. While supper was cooking, I'd tell him a sea story of some far off place that I had visited, or about some ship that I had been on. Outside the thermometer would be going down to ten or more below zero and I would be going down the hill at five in the morning, but what the hell. The sailor was home from the sea. No ship could equal that.

It is a good thing that we can't look into the future. Good because I was living like a king. A small, insignificant king, maybe, but our mortgage was inching down, our bills were being paid, and a savings account was showing signs of life.

Full summer had come. My garden occupied me, I had shingled the roof, and more than a cord of wood was put by for the winter. I had even contracted to paint a neighbor's house in my spare time. The sea was never like this, nor would I ever return to it. Or so I thought, that last summer.

One night I came home from work to find an official looking letter on the mantel. Seamen were becoming scarce. Men holding a ticket were badly needed. There followed a list of the benefits to be derived from a job afloat. *Phooey, I know all about those benefits.* Still, I couldn't help but notice those wage scales. I compared a Second Mate's pay to my rigger's pay. I reasoned that I could pay off the mortgage in one year instead of ten. I burned the letter in the fireplace that night and vowed, **Never again.**

Another letter arrived. It told of War Bonuses. This was something beyond imagination. While I mucked around down in that dry dock, Second Mates were being paid like oriental potentates. My wife and I had words, unpleasant ones, and the subject became closed. I couldn't stop thinking, though. It seemed to be the chance of a lifetime to get my head above water, to pay for my house, and buy all of the things that we never had.

Coming home one night, my thoughts fell into place and I reached my decision. Back to sea I would go and every penny would be well accounted for.

The next few days weren't pleasant ones. My interest in the dry dock waned until it became unbearable. At home matters had reached an impossible state. I was an unfeeling husband and father to even contemplate leaving a steady job to return to sea, especially when war seemed imminent. But away I went, Third Mate on a freighter bound for God Knows where.

It was a different life at sea than the one that I had left the year before. Then it was a quiet, well ordered existence. Watch on, watch off—the rare sight of another ship to relieve the monotony of the horizon—the eternal discussions about ships or women. Yes, it was all different now. A man's life belt was always with him. Night watches were no longer spent in peaceful contemplation of sea and sky. No more did dreams of home or the next port whisk the hours by. Now, it was a grim, deadly business. My bridge watch was the eight to twelve. By seven-thirty at night I would be stepping out onto the lee side of the boat deck, bundled to the eyes against the bitter cold. There I would huddle in the pitched blackness getting my night vision. The Coast Guard had furnished us with booklets explaining the intricacies of night vision. They explained that when one's eyes were seeing with their night cells, one was truly color blind. If colors could be distinguished, part of the night vision was lost. Their tests had proved that the mere flare of a lighted match destroyed most of the eye's ability to see in the dark. All this was most important, now, because our very lives depended on a good lookout. That was why I spent that half hour on the boat deck before relieving the Chief Mate at eight o'clock.

All through the watch I prowled from the port wing through the wheel house to the starboard wing, powerful night glasses sweeping the horizon. My life belt was hung on the Pelorus stand in the starboard wing. Quite unconsciously, every time I passed it, my mittened hand stole out to make sure that it was still there. In such bitter weather, a man in those waters started to die when he went in and would be dead and frozen inside twenty minutes, yet knowing this, man is a tenacious animal and clings to life, even the extra twenty minutes that the life belt would afford.

The Old Man prowled the night watches, too, uneasy and apprehensive. Submarines were taking a fearful toll of shipping and we, like all the other freighters of those early days were virtually defenseless. Our speed was nine knots at best so we couldn't run away. Our armament consisted of two little machine guns and an antiquated swivel gun on the poop deck, vintage the first

World War. The Old Man was worried and scared just like the rest of us, but kept his fears to himself. For many years he had been Chief Mate on coastwise tankers. Ten years ago he had retired. Now, in his seventies, he found himself pacing the bridge of a worn out old freighter loaded to her beams with ammunition. In the nighttime he and I used to talk about why we were out there. He, like myself, had been dazzled by the high pay and fat bonuses. We both disavowed patriotism, he snorting that most heros were dead and that a whole chest full of medals wouldn't buy a pipe full of tobacco. I like to think, though.that he was just covering up his true sentiments as all seamen do. He had been living comfortably in retirement. His children were all grown and married, and his pension and savings were more than adequate. Why did he come back? Excitement? Adventure? He had had a lifetime of both. Money? He didn't need it. No, it was none of those. Even though it was farthest from his thoughts and was something that he was absolutely unaware of, the truth of the matter was that he was an American. His country was threatened and he didn't want to be left out. The was a job to do and so here he was, an old man who needed his rest, pacing the nights away out on the North Atlantic, an old rust bucket under him and the lives of fifty odd men weighing him down and making him older.

Most tales of ships at sea in wartime usually have, about this time, some violent action. A torpedoing, maybe, with men dying in the life boats, a capture by an armed raider, a spy in the crew. But me? Nothing. Day in and day out we slogged along making our eight or nine knots. Bad weather followed bad weather followed in turn by worse weather. We made port and discharged. We sailed back across the Atlantic only to repeat the whole business over again. Voyage after voyage, and although our vigil was maintained and our fears remained, the only enemy encountered was the weather. And a scheming brute it was. Like some cunning animal it lay in wait for us or stalked our trail in the darkness, pouncing when it thought that we had let our guard down. Tearing at hatch tarps, shrieking round the bridge, it sought to destroy us. Trip after trip we were pummeled and mauled, but mile after countless mile rolled under our stern with never a letup in the monotony of being frightened, of being blown out of the water at any minute, of being catapulted from our bunks into the sea without warning.

Upon our return after the first voyage, The First and Second Mates paid off. The Old Man offered me the Mate's berth. At last I was **The** Mate. I'd clean up this tub, by God, or else we'd have a new crew. It took me a long time to realize that this was now wartime, and that a sailor's pride in his ship had disappeared. In my enthusiasm to make her, *Shipshape and Bristol fashion,* I neglected to take into account the mental condition of a new crew just signing on. Many of them were fresh out of Training schools, signing Articles for the first time. The old hands were usually fresh ashore from a sinking. Some of them had had two, three, and even four ships sunk from under them, and they spewed overboard in nothing but their under drawers.

Experiences such as these tended to destroy any sense of permanency. A ship was no longer a home to take pride in, and on which one lavished care and affection. It was a floating bomb which could, in an instant, erupt into a flaming hell. Under these circumstances it was understandable that a sailor's only interest was in getting her there and back. Ships went to wrack and ruin while peacetime Mates like myself tore their hair out and ranted and raved at a lazy crew. We did, that is, until we started to feel the same way. Then it was wheel and lookout, take care of the cargo handling gear and the life boats and the hell with the rest of the ship.

After that first voyage, a surprising thing happened. The Captain was transferred to a new ship then being built in a shipyard. The new Skipper was a replica of the old one. He, too, had spent his career on tankers and was retired. At once, he and I hit it off, and quickly became close friends. This was a great boon to me. I enjoyed his full backing. Well do I remember my first trip with him. He had retired four or five years before the war. He was very set in his ways and testy by nature. He had one obsession. He hated all Limeys. He blamed them for getting us into the war. Anything and everything that could go wrong, the English were at the bottom of it.

After we finished loading we sailed in a small convoy to Halifax, which was the main port of departure for Eastbound convoys. We came to anchor in Bedford Basin. The next day he was summoned ashore for his first convoy conference. When he came back, he made a bee line for the chart room, me right on his tail. Upending a bulging brief case, he said,

"Look at all this foolish stuff. Some Limey spent all afternoon going over and over this junk. Stow it away, someplace, or read it if you like. If you can make anything out of it, let me know. I'm going down to supper."

I went down to supper and slid in alongside of His Nibs

"Well, did you learn anything?"

"Yep, we're suppose to sail in an hour."

"I know that. I've already told the Chief Engineer. Eat your supper. If you hurry, you can get it down before you go forward to hoist the anchor. Anything else?"

"Well, Captain, it would seem that a dozen or so ships will be sailing with us out of here with a temporary Commodore. We're supposed to steam Easterly. Then two days or so out we're to meet up with a big convoy coming up from New York. Their Commodore will then become our Commodore, too. We have been assigned the position of last ship in the starboard, outside column."

"Fancy that, Mister. Why don't they just give us the compass course and leave it to us to keep in sight of each other?"

He had me driven half crazy. The war was non-existent to him.

Right on schedule, out we steamed. The Commodore was hoisting one flag hoist after another: *Speed, five knots. Take up your proper station. Close up.* The Skipper was racing from one side of the bridge to the other. On his way through the wheel house he'd shout new steering orders to the man at the wheel, then bellow down through the engine room phone, *Faster! Slow down!"* More often or not he'd run headlong into the Navy signal man coming with yet another flag signal from *that damned Limey.* All ships were blacked out. Night had come on. All we had to steer by was the blue stern light of the ship ahead.

The next day things were no better. Ships were all over the ocean. Out of station, out of column, steaming in between columns. The old coal burners were belching clouds of black smoke. It was chaos. And there were only a dozen of us.

At noon the Old Man got a pretty fair sun sight. He had his officer's cap on backward while he peered through his sextant. I was in the chart room marking his chronometer time. In he came. Carefully putting his sextant back in its case, he grabbed my time slip and started working out his noon position. He leaned over the chart and carefully marked a small cross.

"I make her to be just about there, Mister. Now let's see, we've got to advance the clocks to our LAT." (Local Apparent Time.)

Now, if ever, I had to be diplomatic.

"Captain for the last few years all ships have been sailing on Zone Time."

"What in hell is that? Something that the Limeys dreamed up?" (It was.)

"Each fifteen degrees of Longitude East or West of Greenwich is one hour ahead of, or behind Greenwich Civil Time (GCT), and as long as a vessel is in that Zone, she keeps that Zone Time. When she crosses the boundary of that Zone, she advances or retards her clocks by one hour. In that way, all vessels in one Zone are on the same time."

"Not on this ship, Mister. I've been sailing all over these oceans for a good many years on Local Apparent Time with no problems. Now set the clocks ahead." (I've forgotten how many minutes, but the result was that now our clocks were ahead of all the other ships.)

That night the fog came down upon us. It was so thick that we couldn't see the bow, let alone the ship ahead. Sparks came in with a message to stream fog buoys, a wooden contraption towed from the stern. It was so constructed that it jumped around in the water and made a big wake. The idea was that the bow lookout on the ship astern would watch it and keep his bridge advised. We hung it over the stern where it promptly disappeared. Same for the one ahead of us. We never did see it. To make matters worse, all Merchant ships in those days had magnetic compasses. The day of the wonderful Gyro compasses, perfectly accurate, was far in the future. A gadget that raised hell with our compasses was *DeGaussing,* a great electric cable completely encircling the ship just inside of the hull. It was supposed to neutralize the natural magnetic effect of a steel hull, and thus render impotent the new magnetic mines so favored by the Germans.

Because of all this, all ships were probably steaming on slightly different courses. This didn't matter in clear weather. We would just follow the ship ahead. Now, though, in thick fog it was a different story. Vessels were gradually getting closer, farther apart, falling astern, or forging ahead. Some mess! Like a herd of blind elephants. *Things couldn't be worse, I* thought. Oh, yes they could, and very shortly, too.

At noontime, the Old Man again had the Second Mate advance the clocks based on our dead reckoning position. All ships had to observe radio silence but the Commodore could and did transmit, in code. Right after supper Sparks handed the Skipper a message.

"Mister, you go into my office and decode this. The code book is in the safe. It's unlocked."

Decoding is a tedious business. A page full of numbers might yield a sentence. I waded through the job and brought the message out to him. It was from the Commodore of the main convoy and said that they expected to join up with us between 2200 and 2300 hours. At 2300 hours all ships were to change course forty degrees to port. Holy Moses! That meant that forty odd ships would be helling along right into us twelve, and we were stone blind in the fog. The big convoy was obviously in clear weather and didn't realize that the fog was up ahead of them. Now the Old Man's stubbornness caught up with him. Our clocks were two days Easting ahead of all the other ships. That meant that we would be going hard a'port before them.

The Old Man finished reading the message in the dim light from the binnacle.

"Mister, what the hell is this 2200, 2300 hours mean?"

"Captain, all ships are now using twenty-four hour time. It means ten PM, eleven PM."

"By God, Mister, why don't they say so? I'll bet that this is another Limey invention. They're not content with dragging us into their miserable war; now they're trying to take over our ships."

He sure was death on the English.

Long about ten o'clock we could hear ships hooting their fog whistles all around us in the fog. The main convoy had arrived. We were in some jam, all right. We could even smell them. The stink of big diesel motor ships, the acrid scent of the old coal burners.

The wheel house clock rang six bells. The Captain promptly told the man at the wheel to come left forty degrees. Dear God, here we go, ploughing through forty odd ships. How we ever missed colliding with one of them, I'll never know, but miss 'em we did. I kept the whistle going. *The International Rules of the Road specifically state that in fog, mist, falling snow, heavy rain, or whenever visibility is impaired, vessels shall sound a long blast on their whistle every two minutes.* I confess, I was blowing it almost constantly. After awhile the only whistle we heard was our own. Daylight came, the fog lifted, and we were all soul alone on the ocean.

"Mister, where the hell is the convoy?"

"Well, Captain, you know that we changed course much sooner than they did so I guess that we are lost."

Not for long, though. Up over the horizon heaved a Canadian corvette, her blinker light flashing furiously, *Follow me.* Obediently, we fell in behind her and rejoined the convoy.

From that incident on, the Captain learned very, very fast the changes that the war at sea had brought.

As Mate of that ship, the Skipper and I made voyage after voyage. The crew changed almost to a man each time we returned. Second and Third Mates came and went. So did the engineers, those strange people who were seen only at mealtimes, and then they seemed to be ill at ease, eating their food absent mindedly, caring little what it was or how it was cooked. Their eyes were fixed on their plates but they were seeing engine, pumps, boilers, condensers, and all the other things that could go wrong, leaving a ship wallowing helplessly, sure prey for the submarines that followed the convoy. We made fun of the black gang but they had courage. It was bad enough up on deck but down there below the waterline they were trapped. At least we could see but all they could do was listen and hope and wait while the minute hand of the big brass engine room clock dragged slowly around until the long four hours were past. Every half hour I used to whistle down the speaking tube and give the First Assistant a brief picture of what things topside were. *The convoy was well bunched and the destroyer escorts were patrolling on all sides, astern and ahead. Or, we had just executed an emergency turn to port. The escorts were converging, flying the black pennant which means, in Navy language,*

WE HAVE DETECTED AN UNDERWATER OBJECT

Fancy way of saying that they were charging down on a submerged submarine, depth charges at the ready. Then I would tell the First to stand by for the underwater explosions that were coming. Up on deck the explosion of a depth charge has a muted rumbling sound, but down deep in the engine room and fire room it sounds as if end of the world had come. Sound travels much faster in water than in air and a depth charge exploding nearby creates the effect of a gigantic hammer blow on the ship's hull. I have been down below when one went off and unless one is forewarned, the experience is nerve shattering.

A tremendous crashing thump, the ship lurches, all the lights flicker and some of them go out, shattered by the sound waves. I can imagine the feelings of those poor brave souls down there when a depth charge suddenly exploded. *The ship must surely have been torpedoed up forward. Are we going down? Should we shut the plant down and jump for the ladders? Can't do that. The telegraph is still on, Full Ahead. We'll stick around for a few minutes and see what happens. They can't all be dead up there on the bridge.* That's why I used to keep the First Assistant informed of what was going on. It was the least that I could do. The hell of waiting, wondering, guessing, down there in the dimly lit, steamy bowels of a freighter would be more than I could stand. And we ridiculed *Those People*, the black gang. The deck and engine room will never, in a thousand years, see eye to eye, me included, but they must be given their due credit. They were brave patient men. And they died by the hundreds, never seen, never heard, carried down to a watery grave while the fortunate deck crews escaped on a life raft only to die of cold or starvation. *Gone Missing*, as they say.

All of this sounds sort of morbid, pessimistic, as if we on the freighters were defeatists. That because of our circumstances we couldn't win; that we were licked, knocked over like sitting ducks, lacking the means of defense or escape. We were men of a peculiar breed. Man always has hope and man always has his dreams.

We never believed for an instant that our ship would get it, nor did the men of all the ships that did go down. That's why all of us kept going, trip after trip, year after year. I suppose that the same thing was true of our enemy, for they were men, too. I like to think that even though many of them were as good, as tenacious, as patient, as hopeful as we were, there were more of us better than they. Or maybe we just outlived them. Being just a sailor, I can't say.

As the war spread, so did our voyages. For a long time our destination was always the British Isles. Then came the Allied invasion of North Africa. Our old tramp followed trouble like a hound tracking a rabbit and soon we were cautiously steaming in and out of the Straits of Gibraltar. Like an old faithful ferry boat, back and forth we steamed.

The Western approaches to Great Britain had become the graveyard of hundreds of ships. So had our Eastern seaboard. So, in fact, had the whole Western Ocean. But not us. The convoy system had by then been brought to a high degree of perfection, and the building program of new tonnage was beginning to catch up with the awful losses. Many ships had been torpedoed and sunk while sailing in company with us but our luck was holding.

Usually a ship would get it at dusk, although to the Germans, any time was a good time. When the pale wintry sun was dipping low, the escorts would commence their prowling on our flanks. They were constantly signaling, *Close up, close up. Regain your proper station. Enemy underwater craft are in the vicinity.* The Navy signalman on our bridge would repeat the message in a monotone. Word went through the ship, *Blackout. Check your portholes. No lights.*

The Naval escorts were not unlike sheep dogs. Their blinker lights substituting for the yapping of the dogs as they nipped at the heels of their docile charges, urging them to bunch up for the night.

When full dark came our senses became more alert. It was a tricky business keeping station in a low powered convoy. Ships were deep laden and their engines overworked. With a bit of a beam sea running, the columns of ships tended to set to leeward, some faster than others. Then would come the windward lookout shrieking, *Ship close on the port beam.* A quick glance to starboard through the night glasses showed our starboard companion maybe a dozen ship lengths off. **Right wheel. Ease the helm. Steady, steady.** While we were easing to starboard the ship in our wake kept steadily on, not knowing or caring what we were up to. We had to get back in our column, but how? The ship astern had speeded up having lost sight of our stern, and was now occupying our station while we were steaming right in the middle of two columns of ships.

In convoy we never used the engine room telegraph. Speed had to be so carefully maintained that it was done by voice down the speaking tube to the engine room. *Up two revolutions, First, that should do it.* Or, *Down ten, First. We are right on top of the ship ahead.*

My watch as Mate was the four to eight so I got both dawn and dusk and more than my share of the black hours. At the very first sight of dawn when the blackness was imperceptibly turning to gray, the ships of the convoy gradually emerged. As the sky brightened, more and more of them came into sight, stretched all over the sea. Columns were crooked, ships out of position, some far behind, and some mornings some of them would be missing. Our signalman would gam by blinker light with our neighbors. *What happened to the Dutch tanker? What about the Canadian?* Most times, we never heard. In some convoys the Commodore would announce by signal to all ships that two ships had straggled and were presumed lost. In the early days it was almost certain death to break down. Naval escort vessels were so few that each convoy was inadequately protected. None of them could be spared to stand by a straggler. It was the many versus the few and the many were too important to leave unprotected. It was a heartbreaking experience to see a ship break down. The way would fall off of her as she swung out of column. Two black balls, signifying, **NOT UNDER COMMAND,** would appear on her signal halyards. Ship after ship would steam past her until it was our turn. Our Old Man would raise his clasped hands over his head in the manner of a prize fighter. The Old Man on the disabled ship would wave, their signalman would jauntily blink

**British Armed Escort Trawler used early
in the War**

North Atlantic convoy photographed by a U.S.S. Albermarle (AV-5) plane. Most of the ships are tankers.

Convoy scattering

A destroyer escort (DE) operating with an Escort Carrier, 1944

Bad weather as usual. A Russian Transport passes astern.

farewell as she dropped swiftly astern. And all of us, escorts included, kept steadily on while the crippled ship vanished astern. Certain death and tough to swallow. We were so damned helpless...

Slowly, gradually, it got better. Instead of queer looking little wooden cockleshells for escorts, there appeared a new type of vessel, the DEs, or Destroyer Escorts. They were built for the job and a fine job they did. Then, toward the end of the war, or so it seemed to me, the little aircraft carriers came to travel in our midst. Rescue ships patrolled our wake, ready and able to stand by and defend a poor straggler. And if that failed, to rescue her crew. Yes, then we steamed in high style, escorted like princes. But a lot of ships were to be sunk and a host of seamen were to die before all this came to pass.

I remember one time when we were sent into Gibraltar for orders. This was highly irregular. We had been bound for someplace in North Africa, the actual port as yet unannounced.

The Captain fussed around the bridge while I went forward to clear away the anchors.

Once at anchor, there was a great business of British Naval launches coming and going. The Old Man's door remained shut while various and sundry gentlemen in fine fitting uniforms came and went.

After they had all gone, he sent for me.

"Well what do you know. We are to take our cargo of foodstuffs to Malta. Ever hear of it? These Limeys are nuts."

Yes, I had heard of Malta, and recently, too. The Italian and German Air Force were determined to bomb it beneath the sea, for it was a sore British Naval thorn in their sides. This didn't sound too attractive to me. Our luck had been holding up pretty good, so far, so why stretch it? Last voyage several ships had been torpedoed, one right on our beam. Thank God she wasn't loaded with ammo or we wouldn't be here in Gib. No sense growling, you can't lick City Hall—or the British either for that matter.

The following night we got under way.

I wish to have no connection with any ship that does not sail fast.
For I intend to go in harm's way.   *John*
                      John Paul Jones

-23-

A WARTIME TRIP TO MALTA

Even before we poked our nose out of Gib, we were surrounded by British Naval escorts. As I remember, there were only four or five cargo ships. Just as soon as we were clear of the harbor, the escorts herded us close together. There were more escorts than ships. At least one of them was a cruiser. The others appeared to be destroyers.

Our gunnery officer had his twenty-eight gunners at what I called half battle stations. Fourteen of them on the guns day and night. They were manning all the 20 millimeter Orlikons, the three inch anti-aircraft gun on the bow, and the big five incher on the stern. It was all so unreal. The beautiful blue Mediterranean sparkling in the brilliant sunshine. This false sense of security was heightened by the Old Man's absolute conviction that all this war business was way over rated. To him it was business as usual. His lifetime on tankers, plus his New England obstinacy, had completely insulated him from the harsh realities in which we now found ourselves. He blamed the Limeys for the whole mess. He thought that it was a big to do about nothing. His job, as he saw it, was to take his ship from one port to another, discharge, load, and go on. All this business of gun crews, Naval escorts, submarines, convoys, were just obstacles to him, dreamed up by the Limeys. We could be in the midst of the most God-awful conditions, but if he felt that we were on course, making knots, the weather clear, he'd up and go to bed and sleep like a baby. I envied him.

The next morning the Commodore blinked over,

EXPECT LOW FLYING ENEMY AIRCRAFT, NOW!

The Gunnery Officer hit the General Alarm lever. I blew the whistle several times for good measure. Running foot steps pounded throughout the ship. The Old Man came out, blinking at the morning sun, just over the bow.

"What's this all about, Mister? The Limeys making a fuss again?"

Quickly, I told him of the signal.

"Hrumph, I don't see any aeroplanes."

Swoosh! Two Italian torpedo bombers flashed by at masthead height. They were after the cruiser, I guess, for they were gone in an instant. If they dropped their torpedoes, we didn't see them. Frantic signals...

ZIG-ZAG PLAN. EXECUTE NOW!.

Off we went on a thirty degree angle to starboard.

"My God, Mister, did you see those aeroplanes? The damned fools almost ran into our fore mast. Guns, how did you know that they were Eyetalians?"

I have heard people say that the Italians were lousy fighters and soldiers. Maybe so, but some of them sure could fly.

"Ho, Hum," says the Old Man. "I believe that I'll take a little nap before dinner."

Don't mistake me. He was a canny, caring shipmaster, and he would be on the bridge all night.

On we went, slogging along at ten knots, making our Easting. We had no detailed charts of Malta. That afternoon we were ordered to the port of Valletta. The Skipper and I read up on the place in the Sailing Directions and poured over the Mediterranean Chart. We planned as best we could, not that we could do much. We had no choice but to follow the ship ahead. Still, if somehow we got separated from the convoy, we had done what we could.

There came the time when a blinker signal was received ordering us to break off and proceed independently to Valletta. The signal was received just after dusk. The Old Man was not in the least upset, but I was. Malta was no place to be, and certainly not in a lousy Liberty ship that could barely make ten knots. The Captain and I poured over the chart again. He reckoned that we could be off the entrance to Valletta harbor at dawn. He drew the course line, got the compass course from the compass rose on the chart, and told me to haul out of our little convoy on our new course. I did. The man at the wheel, who was no dummy, raised an expressive eyebrow.

"Mind your damned course. How do I know?"

The other ships and the escorts disappeared in the darkness, bound for God knows where. We never saw them again.

The next morning, just at dawn, there was the entrance to Valletta, dead ahead. The Captain had been on the bridge all night. He was out on the bridge wing warming his hands on a mug of my coffee.

"Good navigating, Skipper."

"What did you expect to see, Coney Island?"

Still, I think that he was pleased. A blinker started to wink up ahead of us from what looked to be a big tow boat. As we got closer we saw that a great submarine net was rigged across the entrance. One end was fast to either the shore or a breakwater. The other end of the net was made fast to the tow boat. To open the contraption, the tow boat would steam around, dragging the net. Our signalman told the Old Man that the net was fouled, and they wouldn't be able to let us in for at least two hours. They suggested that we steam back and forth while they made repairs.

I remember that it was a beautiful Sunday morning, with the blue sea like glass. It was all so peaceful. The war seemed like a far away bad dream.

"Now then, Mister, there's no sense steaming around wasting fuel. We'll just slip down the coast and anchor."

"But Captain, this is a bad place. We'd be a sitting duck for those Italian planes."

"Oh, baloney. Those two the other day were just a fluke. You worry too much. In fact, you're starting to sound like those Limeys back in Gib."

Having disposed of me and the Limeys, he leisurely poured himself another mug. I headed for the focsle head to clear away the anchors.

The Old Man took us down the coast a good five miles. I heard him ring the telegraph for Stop. When the way was almost off the ship, he hollered to let go. I swung my sledge and down went the starboard anchor. I grabbed the big, two handled brake and started to brake her. Nothing happened. I wound the brake tighter. Still the chain kept roaring out. At last the chain stopped paying out. By this time the Old Man had the ship going astern to set the hook. I ran over to the side and looked over. I was astonished to see that the chain was still leading straight up and down. By this time the ship was stopped. His 'Nibs' figured that the anchor had taken a'hold. When I pointed my arm up and down, he blasted at me through the bow phone

"Dammit, Mister, you've let out too much chain. We'll have to go astern again."

He rang up, Half Astern again and backwards we went. I kept watching the chain. No good, still straight up and down. We must have backed for half a mile. The Old Man was hopping up and down and yelling at me. Ignoring him, I dropped down the forepeak hatch and peeked into the chain locker. Holy smoke. All the chain was out. The bitter end was shackled to a big ring bolt in the bulkhead. Thank God that it was. In Naval vessels, I have been told that they don't secure the bitter end. Merchant ships do. Now I knew why. Up the ladder I flew and told his Lordship what had happened. Only then did he duck into the chart room and turn on the Fathometer. I guess that there were about a zillion fathoms under us. That's what came of not having a local chart.

It took me quite awhile to get all that chain heaved in. Had to keep stopping. Even though I had the ship's carpenter leaning into the chain locker with a chain hook, the chain kept piling up to the hawse pipe. I was pacing around, a nervous wreck. I expected those planes to take a slam at us at any time. Maybe the Skipper was lulled by the serenity, but not me.

Just about the time that the anchor fetched home, a queer looking

WAR SHIPPING ADMINISTRATION TRAINING ORGANIZATION

United States 🛡 Maritime Service

Designation of Grade

This is to certify that

FRANK FRANCIS FARRAR, (4472-00140)

has this date been designated

Commander (D)

in the UNITED STATES MARITIME SERVICE

Effective August 28 , 19 46

Original enrollment at _____ on _____
(Place) (Date)

Regular enrollment at _____ on _____
(Place) (Date)

Date of issue August 28 , 19 46

_____   W. G. TORPEY
(Signature of enrollee)   Lieutenant, USMS
                                 Personnel Officer

Rhino Barge alongside #4 hatch

Wounded being evacuated from Normandy Beach

launch appeared. Some sort of British patrol boat. Its Skipper shouted over and told us that the harbor submarine net was fixed and for us to proceed into the harbor and anchor. Back we went, with me glancing skyward every two minutes. It wasn't just a fairy tale that this island had been under constant siege from the air.

We crept slowly in through the opening in the net. The Old Man backed and filled, muttering to himself. It was a breathtaking place. Snow white, limestone buildings nestled against the steep hillsides. Once more the command came, **Let Go.** After she fetched up, I left the focsle head and went midships. The gun crews were still at their guns, joking and laughing. They were a new group. I envied their innocence. Just as I was climbing the midships ladder to the boat deck, the Old Man popped out on the bridge deck above me.

"Mister, swing out number one life boat."

"Captain, what for?"

"I'm going to Sunday morning mass, that's what for."

Dear God, he's gone daft. I always knew that he was a devout Catholic, but break out men to lower a boat when practically all hands who were off watch were standing by to help the gun crew? He's the Captain so what he says goes. I climbed up to the boat deck and started to release the gripes on number one. I was down on my hands and knees fiddling with the pelican hook, a quick release device holding the boat secure, when, **Blam!.** By Godfrey, there was a great gout of water shooting up just off our starboard beam. A damned bomb? Funny, I never heard a plane, and our guns were silent. Out came his Nibs, dressed in a black rusty suit and hat.

"What in hell is going on, Mister?"

"That was a big ugly bomb, and I think that it was aimed right for your cabin. Still want this boat?"

"No, I don't. It's probably too late for church. No telling what hours these foreign churches keep. Besides, it's Sunday and you look tuckered out."

Now he's worried about my health! I didn't believe him for a minute. He was finally waking up to the fact that there was a big, nasty war going on, Limeys or not. He was so damned set in his ways. (We later speculated that it was not a bomb but one of those newfangled magnetic mines that just decided to go off.)

I secured the life boat and went below for a mug of coffee. A weaseled faced critter oozed himself into the saloon and inquired for the Chief Officer. One of the Engineers nodded in my direction. In a heavy Brooklyn accent, he asked if he could speak privately with me. I invited him up to my cabin. He settled himself down at my desk. I didn't like the look of him one little bit. He looked and sounded like a cheap gangster in the movies. Without any shame he told me that he had been deported from the States for bootlegging

during Prohibition. Then, says he,

"You are scheduled to commence discharging tonight as soon as it gets dark. You are to discharge several hundred tons of bagged wheat from number five hatch into a lighter on the port side. Instead, if you will discharge into my lighter on the starboard side, this is yours."

He opened a sack and dumped its content on my desk. My God, the desk was covered with old-fashioned yellow backs! Before Roosevelt came to office, the country was on the gold standard, and all bills, twenty dollars and up, were gold colored on one side and green on the other. Also, they were half again bigger than our present currency. I hadn't seen them since I was a kid. He had evidently smuggled them out when he was deported. I must admit, the looks of that big pile of cash was fascinating, however, I then did something that I'm still pretty proud of. Going to the door, I yelled for the Bosun and Carpenter, two big brutes. Turning to rat face, I made a sickening, patriotic speech.

"We've brought this damned cargo half way round the world to feed some brave, starving folks, and it's **not** going into your black market. Bosun, throw this bum off the ship. And I mean, **throw.**

I've never told this story before, but I still feel pretty good about it. Maybe I should have taken his dough. Maybe it was no good, anyway, and couldn't be exchanged. The hell with it. The war was bad enough without making money from hungry Allied friends.

The rest of this story is dull. At dusk, longshoremen came out in small boats. Our cargo was discharged, the anchor was hove up, and we sailed away and joined a Westbound convoy. My luck was still holding.

It is more blessed to give than to receive.
Acts

-24-

BONANZA IN BONE

As a young sailor I was forever wheeling and dealing, but the best score that I ever made took place years later.

I was Mate on a Liberty ship during the war. We had taken a mixed cargo to North Africa. After we finished discharging, we were to be chartered to the British Ministry of War Transport for an indefinite period.

We lay alongside in Bone, a flea bitten dump on the North African coast. The port and the surrounding area were under the control of the British Army. The longshoremen were a Port Battalion who had been recruited from the docks of London, Liverpool, Glasgow, and any other British ports that had *dockers,* as they called them. They were a tough, thieving crew, as longshoremen the world over are.

Christmas day was just another day. All five hatches were discharging full blast. Number three hatch was discharging from the Lower Hold. Truck chassis, jeeps, spare parts, etc. were poring over the side. Up in number three 'tween decks we had a strong room. Actually, it was a big wire cage with a padlocked door. I had the key. It was full of valuable stuff consigned to Naafi in another port. Naafi was the British abbreviation for our Army's PX. We had the usual assortment of tooth brushes, razors, and such, but also in the strong room, which was huge, there was piled up to the deckhead hundreds of cases of Black Horse Canadian Ale. It had the kick of a horse, too.

Right after dinner I was making my rounds of the hatches, checking the cargo handling gear. When I got to number three hatch I leaned over the hatch coaming and looked down into the hold. My God, they were all roaring drunk. Even the winch operators were stinko, and they were hoisting a big truck. Right behind the port winch operator was the big iron door to the mast locker. Inside the locker was a ladder leading down to the 'tween deck. I flung open the door and scrambled down the ladder. What a mess. The strong room door was hanging on one hinge. Cases of Ale were strewn all over the place. Two drunken Limeys from number one hatch were inside hoisting cases on their shoulders. I tried to reason with them but I might just as well have saved my breath. They were getting pretty belligerent so I beat a hasty retreat up the ladder. Damn! The winch operator outside had slammed shut the door and dogged it fast. There I was, locked in, like a rat in a trap. I banged on the door and yelled for them to let me out. All I got back were curses. What to do? Right over my head was the trunk to the ventilator for the hatch. It's a great, cowl shaped affair. Its opening was covered by strong steel mesh. I managed to shinny up inside of it, and got my fingers clutched in the mesh. To anyone on the outside I must have looked like an animal in the zoo, peering out of his cage. My head was on a level with the forward end of the boat deck. There was the Old Man staring down into number three, a look of horror on his puss. "Captain, Captain," I hollered.

He looked all around, trying to locate me.

"I'm up here, Captain."

Thank God he spotted me.

"What the hell are you doing up in that ventilator? Come down out of there at once. These damned longshoremen are all drunk."

"I can't, Captain. They've got me locked in."

"Well damn my soul, no Limeys are going to lock up my Chief Officer. I'll be right down there."

From my vantage point it was like a tragedy unfolding. He brushed by the winch operator and reached for one of the dogs on the door. **Clang!** The winch man swung at his hand with a big hammer, just missing. The Old Man danced up and down, screeching like a little Tom cat. (He only weighed about a hundred and thirty pounds.)

"Captain," I pleaded. "Don't mess with that big ape. Go and get the Bosun."

"Shut up, Mister Mate. I'll handle this."

Damned if he didn't spring on that big soldier's back. They were stumbling and falling over the steam guard paying no attention to me, up there in the ventilator. Thank God, along came the battalion Captain,

"'Ere, 'ere, chaps, what the 'ell is going on 'ere? Canadian Ale is it? Almost as good as Spirits," said he, taking a big swig out of the nearest bottle.

Well, I got out at last with the Old Man chewing me out all the way up the deck. As soon as got I away from him, I went looking for the Army Captain. I made a big speech to him about his men stealing cargo, getting drunk on the job, how the British soldiers in some other port would be deprived of their NAAFI stores, all to no avail. Before the night was over they had cleaned us out. *Well,* I said to myself, *the hell with them. I couldn't stop them, anyhow.* It was a miracle that the Old Man didn't get hurt, but I was very grateful to him for sticking his neck out for me.

For Christmas supper we had turkey that had first been boiled, a sea cooks's clever way of tenderizing an old bird that had probably been frozen back in the thirties. Then it was shoved in the oven for a few minutes to give it a roasted look. Nostalgia was ever present on a ship at Christmas. I remember that our radio officer hooked up the loud speaker in the saloon to his record player. Over pie and coffee, Silent Night, and Bing Crosby singing A White Christmas poured out, making our thoughts even more sad. Our Naval Gunnery Officer, with tears streaming down his cheeks, got in a fight with Sparks, insisting that he shut the damned thing off. I settled the matter by sneaking up to the radio shack and turning it off. Merry Christmas, Hah!

New Year's day rolled around. All the cargo for Bone had been discharged. Just a few hundred tons for another port remained. About noontime a fully loaded British freighter poked her snout through the breakwater. There was no free berth for her so she was tied up to us.

At supper, the saloon and crew's messrooms were deserted. Everybody had gone ashore, even though there wasn't a damned thing of interest. Mates and Engineers to crash the British Officers Club, just a tent out in the desert. The crew and the Naval gunners headed for the enlisted men's NAAFI. God help them. The Old Man and I were left with the Bosun and a couple of A.B.s. He and I sat around the saloon table, gazing morosely into our cups of cold coffee. Long about nine o'clock he decided to turn in. I continued to sit there, feeling sorry for myself. This damned war was going to last forever, or so it seemed.

I came out of my reverie with a start. The wind was howling like a banshee. I ran out on deck right into a snow storm. Yep, snow in North Africa, believe it or not. The wind was gusting pretty high and was blowing us right against the dock. As I was turning to go in, I heard a weird grinding sound. My God, the life boats! I raced out onto the boat deck. All life boats, during the war, were permanently rigged outboard of the ship, ready for instant lowering. When the Limey tied up to us, we had swung our davits inboard. He had done the same with his. Even then, they were almost touching. I found things in a shambles. Their ship, being deep laden, and ours being light and high out of the water, were reacting differently to the swells that were rapidly making up. It was now blowing a gale. Their life boats were made of wood, lap-straked. Ours were metal. One of their boats had ground itself to splinters against our davits, and their other one was fast following suit. Ours were somewhat dented, but the position of our davits had protected them.

I was soaked to the hide, and my teeth were chattering from the cold, and I couldn't see too good in the dark, either, so I ducked into my room for oilskins and a flash light. Out I went again, and jumped over onto the Limey, intending to wake up their Chief Mate. I met him in the alleyway, on his way out. We stood on his boat deck, assessing the damage. There wasn't much that we could do. Neither of us had any fenders big enough, and even if we had them, there was no way to get them between the two big ships which were pressed tightly together by the gale.

While we stood there, we heard a thump from up forward. His mooring lines were made fast to our bitts, and one had just parted. I yelled at

143

him to break out his crew, and I'd round up what men that I could. If the wind shifted and his ship went adrift in this storm, God knows where she'd fetch up. What he said floored me. All his crew were ashore. All he had was one apprentice.

"Well, get him. I'll be right back."

I raced through the crew's quarters and dragged the Bosun out of his bunk. He rounded up a couple of Navy gunners, one cook, an oiler, and two A.B.s. By the time we got back on deck, another line had parted. I sent half of my gang on board the Limey and we went to work. As fast as new lines were made fast, old ones parted. We toiled on in the snow and darkness. The Limey Mate shouted over that he had no more lines. We kept running from forward to aft, using the shipboard end of our lines. We were nearly at the end of our rope, so to speak.

At long last, the wind started to die down, and the crisis was over. I dismissed my faithful volunteers and wearily slumped down on the edge of my bunk. Too damned tired to pull off my wet clothes. A knock came on my door. I opened it, surprised to see the Limey Chief Mate standing there with a wooden case on his shoulder.

"Right, Oh, stand aside, there's a good chap."

Pushing past me, he set the case down. Right behind him came his apprentice with another case. Behind him came one of their cooks.

"There you are, old boy. Shipmates, what? Hands across the sea, hey? Cheerio, we'll be back in a jiff."

I looked down. Dear God, Black and White Scotch whiskey! Back they trouped, dumped their loads and departed. Back and forth they tramped. My room was filling up to the deckhead. My bunk was covered three deep in cases. Back they came, yet again, this time with two cases, each.

"Got to double up, old chap. Daylight's not far away, what?"

"Please stop. What'll I do with all this booze?"

"Drink it of course. You did me some big favor. Besides, this stuff is for NAAFI, and those Army blokes never appreciate good Scotch like us Merchant blokes, right old boy? We'll be back in 'arf a mo."

What to do? If the STO (Sea Transport Officer, the British organization to whom we were chartered.) Officer came aboard after breakfast and saw what filled my room, I'd probably be shot. In desperation I went up and pounded on the Old Man's door.

"Go away, Mister. Take care of your own problems. Let an old man get his rest."

"You've got to come out, Captain, right away."

He opened the door and stood there, blinking, in his under drawers.

"Now what is it, Mister? It had better be good. I don't liked to be awakened in port."

"I haven't time to explain, Captain. You wouldn't believe me, anyway.

The author, Chief Mate, somewhere in the Mediterranean

Come on down to my room."

He padded after me in his bare feet. Dramatically, I flung open my door. *Voila, mon Capitaine.* He peered around my shoulder, his little eyes bugging out like a mongoose's.

"I'll explain later, Captain. We've got to get this booze hidden in your stateroom before breakfast. Fifty-fifty partners? Have we got a deal?"

Wiping the saliva off his chin, he being a Scotsman, he said,

"Done! Carry two, Mister."

We filled his shower and bath chock-a-block full, then used up half or more of his bed room with the rest.

"I'll have to sleep in my office, Mister," he moaned.

"Take my room and I'll sleep on your settee."

"No, that wouldn't look right. The crew would get to talking. Besides, anyone going through my stateroom door will only do so over my dead body."

This little tale has a happy ending. We started shuttling to Italy. There, between the Old Man and me, we made contact with some American fly boys who had money coming out of their ears. They passed the word. A full quart of Black and White Scotch, price $125.00 a quart. Even though the Old Man short changed me two cases, which he kept back for himself, we did very well, indeed.

145

On June 6, 1944, there was only one piece of land and water worth concentrating on; and any soldier, sailor, or airman who could not join in was missing an irretrievable moment of history.

Nicholas Monsarret

-25-
THE NORMANDY INVASION:

THE BEST-KEPT SECRET

It has long been my intention to tell of the role the merchant ships played in the invasion of Normandy in World War II. Tell it, that is, from the very limited perspective of the Chief Mate of a Liberty ship chartered, together with twenty-five other American ships, to the British Ministry of War Transport to carry troops to the beach head. As this undertaking was probably the highpoint in my career, memories of those days are indelibly imprinted on my mind. For me, it all began this way.

I was the Mate of a Liberty ship berthed in Jersey City, New Jersey. We had just come in from a long voyage in the Mediterranean where we had been shuttling between North Africa to Italy, carrying troops and supplies to the Armies fighting their way up the Italian Peninsula. One morning I went up to the Marine Superintendent's office at the head of the pier to see if I could get a few days off to go home to Massachusetts and see my family. The Marine Superintendent, Captain Blackledge, had had a long career with the Company before the War and his natural abilities made him ideal for the important post that he now held. Among these talents was that of a master con artist. Part of his job was finagling with the truth to fill out a crew. He hadn't the slightest scruple about telling a few tall ones. After all, he probably reasoned, there was a War on. Any way, he cooked up what later turned out to be a beaut. Turning on all his charm, he sold me on the story that the ship was scheduled to make a short trip straight to Liverpool and back, and if I'd make this one trip it would be a personal favor, look good on my record, blah, blah, and as soon as we returned home, six weeks at most, I could have a whole month off. I swallowed it hook line and sinker, as he knew I would. Boy, was he good.

Back to the ship I tramped and set about making up my stores list—wire, rope, shackles, paint, all the things needed for still another North Atlantic voyage. My list was fairly short because we would only be gone for six weeks.

Time dragged on. Longshoremen were loading us with the usual war time cargo; trucks, jeeps, spare parts, food stuffs, ammo, you name it, we loaded it. The ship was the usual bedlam. The alleyways were crowded with repair men, salesmen, runners, and God knows who else. Jersey City was nine

146

miles South of nowhere. To get over to New York City took forever on the Tubes. Locally, the only attractions were the Jersey City joints, and I mean dumps, the usual social drink being a double shot and a beer chaser, and this in a dark, smelly, dirty bar. So I and most of the other regular officers stayed on board playing cards, telling lies, and feeling homesick. Most of the crew had paid off when we docked so we were short handed. I had the Bosun, the Carpenter, and two or three A.B.s. And of course I had the Deck Cadet. These Cadets were students at the Kings Point Academy, a fine government school turning out Third Mates and Third Assistant Engineers. They were required to put in six months sea duty. My cadet, Tim Pouch, had been with me on that long voyage in the Mediterranean so his six months and more were up and he was supposed to return to the Academy. However, he was in bad trouble. During their sea time these cadets were required to do considerable studying. They had to complete a *Sea Project,* which involved some difficult tests. I had frequently tried to help Tim. To no avail. He simply wasn't a student. I knew, and he knew, that as soon as he returned to Kings Point he'd be washed out. However, during the long months at sea Tim had turned out to be a natural seaman. He caught on faster than any sailor that I had ever known, and he had become indispensable to me. Right then I decided to pull a Captain Blackledge stunt on the Academy. If Blacky could con me into staying aboard for another trip, I'd do the same thing about Timmy. A day or two later, his examining officer called on me to fill out Tim's fitness report. I really laid it on, stressing all his accomplishments, but I insisted that he needed just a little more sea time. By God, it worked. Reluctantly, his officer agreed to letting him make one more trip, seeing as how it was only to be for six weeks. All during this interview Tim sat over in a corner and, thank God, had the sense to keep his trap shut. When we were alone I landed on him with both feet.

"You'll study this voyage, Mister. By God, I just saved your neck, but now it's up to you."

It didn't work. Even though, before the coming voyage was over, he became the best hand in the ship, he later washed out of the Academy. In spite of that, he sat for his Third Mate's ticket, got it, and went on to become a fine officer and a credit to the Merchant Marine.

A day or two later my deck stores started arriving. The Bosun received them from the Ship Chandler, signed for them, checked them off on a copy of what I had ordered, and stowed them in the fore peak. One afternoon he came up to my cabin and said that there was a whole barge load of stores alongside, tons of them, none of which were on my order list. Up forward I went, and sure enough, there was a big stick lighter laying abreast of number one hatch. Her deck was covered with coils of rope, hawsers, wire netting, and dozens of other items that I couldn't recognize. Some looked like big long punching bags, but were made of concrete. Hollering down to the Lighter Captain, I told him that he had the wrong ship. This was a common occurrence during the War, because the names of ships on bows and sterns, were painted over, supposedly to confuse enemy spies. He asked if this was the *Cyrus H.K. Curtis.* I said that it was. He replied that indeed, he had the right ship. I told him to hold everything and hurried down the gangway, heading for Captain Blackledge's office. I was teed off because every Chief Mate, as a department head, tries to keep his costs down. Such costs are noted in his record and have a bearing on future promotion. Blackie ambled out of his inner sanctum, purring like a sleek Tom cat.

"Something bothering you, Mister?"

Oh, he was slick all right.

"You bet there is. There is a whole lighter load of stores alongside that I didn't order and I'm not accepting them."

"Ahem," says he, butter melting in his mouth. "Those are some special stores consigned to the British Ministry of War Transport. Stow 'em in number one 'tween deck. When you get to Liverpool, they'll take them off your hands."

Right then I should have smelled a rat. That story of his was too pat. These were American stores, and for all of Lend Lease, Chief Mates of American freighters had never lugged deck stores across the Atlantic to store Limey ships. But, orders are orders. Back I went and told the Bosun to hoist the damned stuff aboard and stow it in number one 'tween deck. Still, those stores stuck in the back of my mind all the way across. I should have been able to figure it out, but surprisingly, I didn't stumble onto the obvious fact that Captain Blacky had hornswoggled me again.

The time of departure drew near. The Old Man returned to the ship from his home in Rhode Island.

The next few days were the usual hectic ones before sailing. A new crew was shipped, last minute stores arrived, the new Second and Third Mates reported aboard. The Second Mate was a big, young Norwegian American, Bill Ommendson. The Third Mate was a small intense young bird by the name of Funk. Sailing day finally rolled around. The Captain went ashore for the usual convoy conference. The Shipping Commissioner came on board and signed all hands on Articles. As soon as the Old Man hurried up the gangway, it was hoisted and off we went again. Out through the Narrows. The Statue of Liberty, the Quarantine Station, and Staten Island slid by on our starboard hand. Then it was,

Full Ahead, for the pilot boat out at Ambrose Light Vessel.

It was just coming dusk when we disembarked the pilot and took our departure, course set for Nantucket Light Ship. We were gradually surrounded by dozens of other vessels all forming up into convoy columns. All this was taking place in pitch darkness, not a light showing. This was getting, *Old Hat,* to the Old Man and me. I went about my business of securing for sea. Anchors dogged down, all booms cradled, hatch tarps wedged tight, and life boats swung out and griped so that they could be instantly lowered if we were torpedoed...That is if there were any of us left to lower them.

During the next few days I got better acquainted with the two junior Mates. Before this voyage would be over, Bill Ommendson was to prove himself to be one solid seaman. He could always be counted on. No matter the emergency, he was there. His massive physical strength and absolute steadiness, his coolness and superb seamanship, were a solid anchor to windward.

I remember one night about half way across the Atlantic. Very high seas were running and the ship was rolling heavily. Sometime around three, AM, Bill sent a sailor to wake me and tell me that six drums of lubricating oil had broken adrift from their lashings up on the boat deck. I jumped out of my bunk and ran down to the main deck where I broke out the Bosun and Carpenter. The boat deck was pitch black, and the wind howling around the life boats made it almost impossible to be heard. Bill was waiting for us, having been relieved by the Old Man. He was above us, out on the bridge wing yelling orders to us that we couldn't hear. Even after our eyes had become accustomed to the dark, we could hardly see a thing. We could hear the oil drums rolling and thrashing around and slithering from one side to the other as the ship rolled. Each roll would send them shooting outboard, only to wedge themselves under the two life boats which were hanging out over the side. Then, as the ship righted herself, they would hurtle across the deck and bash against the housing. This had caused one of them to broach, and that thirty weight oil made a skating rink out of the whole boat deck. What to do? I hollered up to the Captain and asked him if he could fall out of our convoy station and head the ship into the wind on a Slow Bell. This he did after some fancy maneuvering to avoid the ships steaming all around us in the blackness. Soon, the motion of the ship lessened. The rolling let up and we were pitching gently. Now was the time. We had determined that one drum had flung itself over the side after staving in one life boat. The others were under the boats right at the edge of the deck. The Bosun and Ommendson had made lassos out of one inch manila. They each slid across the oily deck and under the boats, me right behind them. We each lassoed a drum and slid out on our backsides. Then they were hauled out, stood on end and lashed to the after boat deck railing. While the carpenter and I were lashing, Bill and the Bosun went back for the last drum. A couple of minutes later I heard the Bosun screaming,

"Help, I'm going overboard."

I dove under the boat.

"Bill, what's the matter? Move out of the way. Where is the Bosun?"

"I can't move Mister Mate. I'm lying on my belly and I've got the Bosun by the belt. He's hanging over the side."

I felt around. One of Bill's arms was over the side and the Bosun was firmly clutched in his big paw. God Almighty! I didn't know what to do. Up spoke Bill, calm as you please, and said for me to put a line around him, and then for me and the carpenter to pull like hell.

"What about the Bosun?" I croaked.

"Not to worry, Mister Mate, I'll not let go of him."

All this time the Old Man is screeching at us from the bridge and the Bosun is yelling under us with the black North Atlantic under him. We did just what Bill said and out from under the boat he came, dragging the poor Bosun behind him, safe and sound. We later found out that the Bosun was wearing a wide, heavy belt like truckers wear today. Without it he would have been a goner.

Then there was the young Ordinary Seaman. I've forgotten his name but how he ever shipped out is still a mystery to me. We never found out until much later, and he never told anyone, that he had been in the Navy on a destroyer that was blown out from under him. Anzio, I think it was. He was one of a handful of survivors and he received a total disability discharge as a case of something like shell shock. How he managed to lie his way past the Coast Guard who issued all seamen's papers, through the Union, and aboard our ship, God only knows, but there he was. Ships' crews can sometimes be cruel to someone who has something wrong with him, like stuttering, or being too fat (Fatso), or too thin (Skinny). They soon found out that this kid was a nervous wreck. They'd sneak up behind him and drop a sledge hammer on the steel deck, and then laugh when he would fling himself flat, screaming and crying. I had two old hands on my watch, Angus Collins and Scotty Gillis. They were natives of Prince Edward Island, and both were Scotch Gallic. They were also first cousins. Scotty played the bag pipes until I had to stop him, it was so awful. He'd stand his lookout watch way up in the crow's nest and blow his wild crazy songs on the chanter. That is the part of the pipes that have the finger holes. That wailing and screeching would sound all over the ship, driving all hands crazy. Anyway, Angus and Scotty had been with me for over two years so they were senior members of the focsle. I prevailed on them to stop the rest of the crew from picking on the kid because he was actually mentally sick and belonged in a mental hospital. It didn't work. Scotty got in a fight with a long rangy Texan and lost badly. He came on watch one afternoon with one eye black and closed. Speaking out of puffed lips, he told me to run my own Ward 8, no more for him.

So it went... Another Eastbound voyage on the Great Circle, bound for the Western Approaches to the British Isles where the Kraut U boats concentrated. As we approached these waters the convoy escorts scurried around us more and more. Signals from the Commodore, flying his flag in a British merchant ship at the head of the middle column of ships, became more frantic, urging us to close up, maintain station, sharpen our lookouts, hold our speed.

On our ship, the Old Man and I didn't have to be told. We had sailed a lot of convoys in this long war, Big ones in the Atlantic, little ones in the Mediterranean. Sometimes we had steamed alone, and didn't like it one bit. So he and I were forever hollering down the engine room speaking tube to either increase revolutions or decrease them in order to keep our position in the convoy.

It was at about this time that two more psychos developed. The first was a Greek A.B. who wouldn't go to bed on his watch below, and instead took to roaming the decks at all hours of the day and night, carrying his life jacket. Finally, he got so exhausted that he took to napping, down in the steering engine room, all the way aft under the Navy gunners' quarters. He explained to me in broken English, that ships never got torpedoed in the stern. Crazy as a bed bug, he was. Torpedoes had hit ships from stem to stern time and time again. I couldn't blame him, though. He had had two ships blown out from under him.

The other was the Second Assistant Engineer who stood the twelve to four watch. He, like the Greek, had succumbed to fear. After coming off watch at four AM, he would come up on the bridge with me, lugging his life jacket, his teeth actually chattering. With daylight coming on I was pretty busy getting the ship back into position, trying to get a couple of star sights, trying to anticipate all the fool questions the Old Man would ask when he crawled up on the bridge for a mug of my coffee. Coffee that I had bought and paid for, not the black muck that the Steward called coffee. Where ever I turned, that damned Second was in the way, asking fool questions. *What did that last signal from the destroyer escort say? Submarines? Could he have some of my coffee to keep him awake? No! Go below and go to sleep, you nut.* I tried to be patient, realizing how terrified he was, but finally I got the Chief Engineer to order him off the bridge. I even suggested that he go and sleep with the Greek in the steering engine room. I whispered that ships **never** got it in the stern.

One fine sunny morning we sighted the Southern tip of Ireland and headed Northward up the Irish Sea for the Mersey River and Liverpool. A lot of the convoy kept on going, bound for the Channel Ports and London. Not one ship had been attacked or sunk on this trip. Things were definitely better on the sea lanes. The convoy system had been brought to a high peak of perfection, thanks to the British, who had been successfully convoying ships since the days of Lord Nelson. We picked up a pilot and steamed up the Mersey River to Liverpool, and made fast to a pier over in Birkenhead, on the other side of the river from Liverpool.

Even here, tied up to the dock, the crew were giving me a fit. British Custom officers are known the seas over for being bastards. War or no war, they'd tear a ship to pieces looking for contraband, usually booze and cigarettes. The Carpenter, who hated them, had hidden two rat traps in the drawer under his bunk. He hid them under his skivvies. Sure enough, he caught one.

Damned near took a finger off. The first I knew of it was from the Captain, hollering for me from his office. Up I went, and there he was, pounding on his desk and yelling at the Customs high mucky-muck. Turning on me, he wanted to know what kind of Mate was I that couldn't keep my crew honest, especially in this great port of our dear friends and comrades in arms.

I was starting to burn and was just about to yell right back at him when one of his eyes drooped in an unmistakable wink. *Ah, hah,* says I to myself, *The old Mahoska.* Oh, he was some actor, alright.

They took Chips ashore and locked him up, charged with assault, evading his Majesty's duties, and God knows what else. A couple of days later I had to appear in court on his behalf. What a show those Limeys put on. Here's a poor seaman from an Allied ship, his only crime trying to hide a few cartons of cigarettes to smuggle ashore to get enough dough to have his back straightened out by one of the LIverpool whores, of which there were about a zillion per square block. Anyway, this pompous looking bird, wearing a silly looking white wig, made a long, tiresome speech to Chips, berating his honesty, patriotism—damned near called him a traitor.

"Now just a damned minute, your damned holiness," says I, getting out of my seat. "You're talking about a fine American who"...that's as far as I got.

Two flunkies in monkey suits and brass buttons grabbed me from behind and bingo, I'm in the cooler with Chips. Fine kettle of fish. We're locked up, there's a first class war going on, so who's fighting who?

All this took place in the morning. We sat around in a big tank full of sleazy critters all talking as if their mouths were full of nuts. Sometime in the late afternoon *"Tea"* was announced. We got a thick mug with no handle on it, half full of tea, and two slices of bread smeared with ersatz marmalade. That was the famous Limey supper of *"Tay and Two."* By this time I was getting worried. The Captain must have missed me by now. He had, because in he bustled, wanting to know what the hell I was doing in there, and ordering me to come out at once. I pointed out the obvious; the cage was locked. He snorted and turned to the jailer, or turnkey, or whatever the hell they called him, and delivered a soliloquy that sounded like Daniel Webster addressing Parliament. Damned if it didn't work. The door was unlocked and we were free men again. The Old Man paid our fines, me for contempt, Chips for everything but treason. Back to the ship we tramped. All the way the Old Man never stopped raving. He sounded like a damned preacher.

The next several days were busy ones, discharging all the stuff that we'd brought over. They were also frustrating ones, because no matter how I tried, I couldn't get rid of those stores in number one 'tween deck. I tried the British Ministry of War Transport, first.

"Right oh, says a very proper Limey voice. I'll send a chap round immediately."

152

Next morning a beady eyed *'chap'* arrived at the gangway.

"I sy," say he. "You're having a spot of trouble about some gear shipped over to us, are you? Let's have a look at it, what?"

These birds all talked a weird brand of English. Sort of like a Down Mainer with a sore throat. Up we went to number one hatch and down the ladder into the 'tween deck. I shone my flashlight around while he kicked at the stuff like a buyer kicks the tires of a second hand car. Finally, he pulled a handkerchief out of his sleeve, for God's sake, dusted himself off and says that he is from the STO, the Sea Transport Office, and that we have a problem.

"No we don't," says I. "Just get this stuff off my ship, then it's your problem."

"The problem is transport. Lorries are quite scarce."

"What's a lorry?"

"Why, you chaps call them trucks."

"Well, for God's sake. Why didn't you say so. Lorries!"

As he went down the gangway, he says,

"Tootle Loo. I'll send a lorry soonest."

Soonest! Boy, they sure mangled the King's English.

You guessed it. No lorries ever showed up. Once again there was that big dead rat, and I never got a whiff, not even a sniff.

Our purser was Mr. Kane. He was from New Hampshire; a bit older than most of us and a very proper New Englander, indeed. He was also a very patriotic American. He and his wife had left their sand and gravel business, she to enlist in the WACS, he to Purser's school at Sheepshead Bay. One evening he suggested that we go over to Liverpool and have a decent meal. I was pretty sick of ship's food that the Belly Robber had been shoving at us, so over we went. Mr. Kane had done some inquiring and had heard that a certain hotel on Lime Street did some fancy cooking, and, if the price was right, weren't too fussy about Ration Books. We went in through an ornate lobby to the main dining room. A haughty head waiter, white tie and all, seated us and presented two tiny menus. Here we were in the heart of the British Empire and the menu was in French.

"We'll have it all, whatever it is," says Mr. Kane. "First, though, we'll have two double Scotch and sodas."

"Sorry," said the waiter. "Only two drinks per person are allowed."

"OK," Mr. Kane answered. "Put two in each glass."

The service was superb. The crystal, silver and china magnificent, but not enough food to satisfy a terrier. We polished off what there was, then Mr. Kane called the head waiter over, slipped him ten bob and pleaded with him for something, anything to fill the gap in our innards.

"Sir," said the waiter. "The marrow is very good, and no coupons needed. We both interpreted marrow to be some succulent dish made from bone marrow.

"Fine, Mr. Kane said, "Bring us two orders."

In swooped the waiter with two plates of something very waterery, gray-green in color, and altogether, quite revolting. Only then did we discover that marrow is the British word for summer squash.

We paid the check, and feeling rather gloomy, made our way out onto Lime Street, Liverpool's main thoroughfare. It was still broad daylight, England being on what they called, Double British Summer Time. It was two hours ahead of Standard time, and had been imposed as a coal saving scheme.

There we stood, not knowing what to do with ourselves. I happened to look to my left and here came two Liverpool whores on the prowl. When they caught my eye, they heaved up alongside in a flash. Poor Mr. Kane had led a pretty sheltered life up there in New Hampshire and had absolutely no idea that they were what they were. He swept off his panama hat and bowed, remarking on what a fine evening it was, how charming they looked, chattering away like a damned chipmunk. The two bimbos listened impatiently, anxious to either make a score or be away for greener pastures. Finally, one of them switched her backside and said to Mr. Kane,

"Hey, Jock, do yer want to or dontcha?"

Old Kane reared back as if he'd been stung by a scorpion. Putting his hat back on, he said, very stiffly,

"My dear young ladies, we have an important engagement. We bid you good evening."

Mr. Kane's education was proceeding.

I managed to sneak away from the ship for a day and took the train for Chester. It is reputed to be the oldest habitation in all of England. I roamed around for hours. I was told that the main street was once a river. Then, way back in antiquity the river was diverted and its bed became the main street. Then, years and years later, it was decided to route the river back down the street. Not wanting to move or demolish the buildings, they added a couple of stories and back came the river. Once again, many years passed, and again the river was diverted around the town so the river bed once more became the main street, bordered to this day by peculiar buildings with their main entrances up on the second floors. Sounds like a fairy tale, but the bartender in one of the oldest pubs swore to its truth. The town sure was old, though. The bar in the pub was of solid wood, about two feet thick. In front of the cash drawer it was worn down about a foot from centuries of pennies and 'arf' crowns sliding across it.

Sailing day arrived. We had orders to proceed up the West coast of Scotland to Loch Ewe, which was a tremendous natural anchorage. It was completely sheltered, had good holding ground, and like Bedford Basin in Halifax, it could hold hundreds of ships. It was a main forming up place for Westbound convoys. Good news. We were homeward bound.

Off we went in a small convoy, six or eight ships, no escorts, steaming along practically independent of each other. These were tough waters to navigate in. The chart showed hundreds of islands. All with queer Scottish names. It was just our luck that as soon as we dropped the pilot it started to blow half a gale and the rain came down in torrents. All ships were now on their own. The Captain never left the bridge and I napped on and off on the settee in the chart room trying throughout the night to get an RDF bearing. No good. The canny Limeys had shut the transmitting stations down. No aid to the enemy. Northward we steamed, passing The Little Minches, The North Minches, the Isle of Skye, Isle of Lewis, all of them making up the Hebrides, a Godforsaken part of the world.

This late in the War, age and overwork had taken their toll of the Old Man. Hour after hour. Day after day, pacing the wheel house, wearing him down.

At last, after a harrowing night, we stuck our bows into the entrance to Loch Ewe just at dawn. Tim was on the bridge with the Skipper, and I was on the focsle head standing by to drop the anchor. I, too was half asleep. The Old Man kept maneuvering around and between ships until we wound up out on the edge of the rows of moored vessels. At last he headed the ship into the wind, stopped the engines, and hollered to *Let go*. I belted the big brake handle with a sledge hammer and out she roared. I heard the engine room telegraph jangle for Half Astern to set the anchor. The chain was leading nicely off the starboard bow as she caught the bottom. I pointed my arm in the direction of the chain. The Old Man acknowledged, and I heard the telegraph ring for Stop. It was a cold, gray, misty morning and I huddled under the bulwarks, trying to light a smoke. Faintly, I heard the Cadet yelling from the bridge. As I straightened up, I pretty near fell overboard. The ship was drifting backward, heading right for an anchored freighter. I jumped for the bridge telephone. Tim answered.

"Tim, for God's sake, tell the Captain to come half ahead."

"I can't," he answered. "He's gone to bed!"

"Tim, now do exactly what I tell you. Ring up Half Ahead and come starboard, easy."

Tim never rattled, and between us we got her stopped and then moving ahead. I heaved up the anchor as soon as we were clear. Then I let her go again, and this time she fetched up and held. Just when we finished, the Old Man came bounding out onto the bridge, hollering at Tim, screeching at me over the phone, wanting to know who was the Captain, what the hell's going on, and more, most of it unprintable. It all blew over, though, and he went back to bed and Timmy and I went to breakfast. Tired as we were, the fact that we were bound for home made anything OK.

Well, there we lay in Loch Ewe. Upwards of a week went by. Ships

155

came and departed. We could see the Royal Navy launches scurrying around delivering sailing orders to various ships who would then make steam, weigh anchor, and head out, bound for home. It seemed odd that we were ignored. However, one morning here came the launch. Up the accommodation ladder came two gold braided Britishers. They disappeared into the Old Man's cabin, not to emerge for over an hour. The **Word** passed through the ship like wildfire, **Homeward Bound.** As soon as the Navy had left, the Captain sent for me.

"Mister, heave up the hook. We are on our way."

"Yes, **SIR.**

"Now hold on," says he. "We have orders to proceed by way of Pentland Firth to the port of Leith."

"Leith, Captain. That's on the East coast of Scotland. What in the hell are we going there for? That's **away** from home."

"Don't ask me. All I know is that four or five ships are to sail at once for ports on the East coast of Scotland, and we are going to Leith. Now get up on the focsle head and heave up the anchor."

By God, something was rotten in Denmark. Finally, the rat was beginning to smell. Pretty rank, too.

Off we steamed up the coast to Cape Wrath. Rounding the Cape we headed East into Pentland Firth, a dismal hole between the Northern tip of Scotland and the Orkney Islands, where the tides run ten knots. Once more it was every ship for her self, and I must say, the Old Man did a fine job of conning the ship through the narrow, twisting passage. And he did it in the middle of the night with the rain coming down in buckets.

I had been through these waters years ago as a young seaman on the Hamburg-Bremen run, and knew full well what a dangerous body of water it was. We shot through in fine style and squared away for the long, narrow entrance to Leith.

Once again the Captain had been up all night and was tuckered out. About five in the morning we arrived off the entrance. No sign of a pilot boat. The Skipper slipped into the chart room for a peek at the chart. When he came out there was still no sign of the pilot boat.

"Mister," says he, "We'll not wait any longer for these damned Limeys. I'm taking her in myself. Half Ahead, and mind your helm."

Then he went out on the starboard bridge wing where he could see better. He looked kind of pitiful out there, an old leather jacket, two days growth of whiskers, and an old beat up cap on his head. Right near him was Timmy in full regalia, spotless Kings Point uniform, pink cheeks, the picture of youth and health. In we crept, in strange waters, me hanging out of the wheel house window using the binoculars. The cadet was relaying the Old Man's steering commands to the man at the wheel. Further and further we went until we could see the piers. It was then that I spied a small boat flying the pilot flag. I sang out to the Old Man that the pilot boat was dead ahead. He made no answer, nor did he make a move to slow down. We were coming up on the little boat fast. I went over to our master and inquired if we were going to stop and embark the pilot.

"Why should we," he snarled. "I brought her in, didn't I?"

A little later he relented and told Tim to stop the engines. Up the Jacob's ladder came the pilot He bustled through the wheel house and out onto the bridge. Brushing right by the Old Man, he grabbed the cadet's hand and boomed out,

"Good morning, Captain. You're the picture of good health this fine morning."

Oh, Boy! Timmy was trying to disengage his hand, making furtive motions towards the Skipper. That did it.

"Mister, if this Limey or Scotsman, or whatever the hell he is, opens his trap just once, you will remove him from **my** bridge. No, on second thought, I'll do it myself."

He walked over to the abashed pilot and inquired,

"Now then, what pier are we supposed to dock at?"

Backing away from an irascible, thoroughly aroused Yankee shipmaster, he squeaked, "Quay 8."

"What in the hell is a key? If it's a dock, say so. That's all that I need from you. Get your ass over on the port wing."

Wee, that's telling 'em, Captain.
The American flag was very obviously flying.

Damned if he didn't take her alongside beautifully, just as if we were a twin-screw yacht. As he and I went below he confided,

"Can't let these foreigners tromp on us."

It made me think of our ensign in the early days of our country. It had a picture of a coiled rattle snake on it, and an inscription that read, *Don't Tread On Me.*

Within minutes of docking a horde of shipyard workers came steaming up the gangway. I headed for my cabin. At my door was yet another STO officer. I invited him in and offered him a snort. He tossed back half a glass, belched, and said,

"Your vessel has been chartered by the British Ministry of War Transport, and I am in charge of converting her to an assault troop transport for about six hundred troops, together with their guns and vehicles!"

Holy Smoke! And this was to be a six weeks' voyage. Those *stores* in number one 'tween deck were to be used to disembark troops on some hellish beach.

The days flew by. All the 'tween decks were converted to troop quarters. Latrines were built, hanging over the side. All the cargo winches and heavy lift derricks were overhauled and tested. Things were moving so fast that I didn't know if I was going or coming. During my few quiet hours I speculated on our destination. I finally became absolutely convinced that we were going to invade Norway. I remained steadfast in this conviction right up until we sailed from Southend on June 5, 1944.

One morning the STO officer had his beak stuck in my booze, as usual.

"By the way. Half of your chaps will have to attend gas school for three days, and then the other half."

"Gas school? What for?"

"There's a good chance that Jerry, or whoever, will be giving you a spot of bother with poison gas."

This invasion business was beginning to sound serious. Hell, the Old man and I had had more than our share of Lady Luck, so far, but gas? Off I went with half the crew to gas school. The first thing they did was to give each of us a primitive gas mask. Then they told us that we would have dozens of bags of a neutralizing chemical piled up around the ship. I was told to assign crew members to various parts of the ship and to conduct practice drills. We were supposed to run out with the gas masks on, break open the bags (They contained nothing but lime.) and scatter it everywhere. Great! After the second half of the crew went to the school, I called for a drill. It was a disaster. I ran into the Captain's room, gave him his gas mask and told him that he was in charge.

"OK, Mister, I'll take charge."

Out on the bridge he went, muttering to himself. When he got out on the bridge wing, he flung the gas mask overboard, thumbed his nose at it, and told me to get the crew back to work. End of drill. (We later threw all the bags overboard, too.)

Our stay in Leith was a pleasant one. Every night we went into Edinborough, truly a beautiful place. The Beer was excellent and the Scotch whiskey smooth as silk. I treated myself to a magnificent British sextant, a Huson. It cost me seventeen pounds and was well worth it. I've used it ever since, and have never once had to have it adjusted.

The conversion work was almost finished. The shipyard gang had been at it day and night. On this particular morning a British flying officer stuck his head in my door and introduced himself, his eyes glued to the half bottle of Scotch on my desk. Waving him in, I pored him a big dollop. Gratefully, he dumped it down. Poring him another, I asked him if I could help him.

"Yes, Mister Mate, actually I'm looking for a bit of a favor. You see, I am in charge of an Air Force Training field nearby, and we are training our chaps to fly out over the ocean and cover you chaps coming to our shores. You see, our chaps need to recognize your vessels instantly, and as your ship is a Liberty, and they are coming in such vast numbers, would you please let me bring a group of our flying Cadets and give them a close up look at the type of ship that they will be protecting?"

"Why God bless you, Colonel, or Commander, or Leftenant, I'd be proud to have your boys as my guests."

A date was made for the following morning. I went down to see our *'belly robber,'* of a steward and told him to figure on twenty or thirty guests for dinner. Such language! He would have to pay cooks and messboys overtime, all that extra food, on and on he went. I cut him short.

"Just do it, you mean old bastard. These same guests just might save your worthless hide. And don't you dare scrimp or I'll..."

I never finished my threat because he slid by me into his room and locked the door. Well, piss on him.

The next day down came the Cadets. Our Cadet was in his glory. He appointed himself guide and narrator, and he was great. He took them from bow to stern, bridge to fireroom. He showed them our deck guns, rung in Mr. Blake, our Gunnery Officer, who vied with Timmy in showing off our ship. I hate to admit it, but that damned Steward did himself proud, feeding them in relays while their Commander dined in style with the Skipper and me. Oh yes, there were good days in those dark days.

The next morning it was raining cats and dogs. Right after breakfast one of the hands told me that there was a car at the gangway and the driver was asking for me. Out I went and there at the gangway was a stunning blonde in the blue uniform of a Wren, they being the British Navy's counterpart of the ATs, which were our Wacs. She announced that Commander so and so, our guest of the previous day, wanted to show his appreciation, and had appointed her and chauffeured car as my guide to really see the sights of Edinborough.

"Well now, how very kind of him. If you will give me two minutes to change my clothes, I'll be with you."

Away we went, the rain still pouring down. I soon found out that she was a full Leftenant in the Wrens and didn't usually do this sort of thing. She had, I gathered, an important job at their flying field. My Boston accent seemed to fascinate her, and she kept urging me to talk. And I did. Not long, though, because on the outskirts of the city the car stopped.

"We walk, now."

"In this down pour?"

"Petrol shortage, you know."

Out we got. In an instant my thin top coat was soaked through but off we slogged. Somehow, Limeys never seemed to get wet. This girl was striding along talking a mile a minute, pointing out the famous gardens, buildings, and landmarks. After a couple of hours I'd had it. I suggested that we stop for a drink and lunch.

"Oh, a hot cup of tea is just what you need."

159

Yeah, maybe, but a double hooker would suit me better, I thought, miserably. We went into a small place, no booze, of course, just tea and cookies.

"Well, now," I said, "Thanks so very much for the great tour, but I must get back to my ship."

"Oh, dear no. You must walk the Royal Mile and climb up to Arthur's Seat"

She explained that the Royal Mile was a must for tourists. Up she stood, dry as a bone, while my wet clothes were starting to steam and stink. Grabbing the last of the cookies I followed her out into the rain. These damned Limeys, give 'em a cup of black, rank tea and they can lick the world. Did, too, with some help from us.

Off we went, tramping those hard wet cobblestones up the Royal Mile. When we got to the end I'd had it. I bleated that as much as I hated to cut short such a wonderful day, I just **must** return to my ship.

"But you haven't seen Arthur's Seat."

"Where is it?"

"Why, right up there," said she, pointing up where black cliffs disappeared in the mist.

Not me. I was licked and knew it. Confrontation she wants? That's what she's going to get. Putting my wet, sore foot down, I announced,

"Allies we are. Hands across the seas notwithstanding, I quit."

With a shrug of her perfectly dry shoulders she murmured,

"If you insist, but I do wish that you could have seen jolly old Arthur's seat."

Balls, I muttered to myself. *It could be Arthur's bare backside, for all of me.*

She got me back to the ship just before supper. I just had time to change before the supper bell rang. Sliding in opposite the Old Man I clutched a mug of coffee in shaking hands,

"What's the matter, Mister? You look kind of peaked. I got a look at that Wren that you went off with. She wear you down?"

Yes, Captain, she sure did, but not in the way your evil mind thinks, thought I.

There came the night when it was *All Hands, fore and aft,* let go everything, and out we steamed, bound for London, this time with a proper Coast Pilot aboard. Ships were slipping up and down this East coast nightly in little groups. Most always at night because German planes and E boats had been pretty active, and the darkness of a moonless night was most welcome.

By this time we had run out of American food and had been stored by the British. Boy, oh boy, not even our lousy steward could stomach it. Stomach it we did, though, for the next four months.

160

We sneaked down the coast, protected by the darkness and were soon shoving our rusty snout into the Thames estuary. Up the Thames River we steamed. We were ordered to Tilbury Docks, an enormous complex of piers and warehouses, ten or fifteen miles from London. Just as soon as the gangway went down we were buried in shore workers again. Longshoremen swung out the five ton derricks at numbers one, three, and five hatches. The fifty ton derrick at number two and the fifteen tonner at number four were swung over the side. Immediately amphibious ducks, trucks, jeeps, self propelled guns, and God knows what else started to swing aboard. Numbers two and four lower holds were rapidly filling with the big, heavy stuff, most of them big enough to carry trucks, jeeps, and guns. We were told that when we reached our unknown destination, another freighter would rendezvous with us, carrying a British Army Stevedore Company. The idea was that they would board us and discharge the trucks, guns, and jeeps into the big amphibious ducks. I asked the STO officer what I thought was a sensible question: Why didn't the stevedores travel with us? No satisfactory answer. *Decision of the high command, don't you know.*

The next day we finished loading all the lower holds and the entire deck, fore and aft. The on deck vehicles were secured by means of *Spanish Windlasses*, which were nothing but two parts of wire cable rove through an eye pad welded to the deck, then around the chassis frame of the vehicle. The two ends were clamped together with wire clamps. Then a stout stick was shoved between the two parts and twisted round and round until the cable was drum tight. The ends of the sticks were then tied fast with marlin. Simple and crude but very effective for a short voyage. They could be released in an instant by cutting the marlin. The sticks would then whirl around and away went the vehicle.

The Skipper and I were sitting in the saloon right after dinner, speculating on our destination.

"Norway," I insisted.

"Bunk," he snorted. "South of France. I know what I'm talking about. Every piece of evidence points directly at the South of France."

"What evidence? Nobody in this country will even tell you what day it is."

"Nonsense," he shouted. I know what I'm talking about."

Before we could settle the matter we were interrupted by the entrance of a distinguished looking figure in immaculate British Army uniform.

"Captain McGirr, I presume. I am Colonel Grey, in command of the troops now embarking on your fine ship."

The Old Man shook hands with him and introduced me. We sat down and ordered. Tea, of course, and the Captain, about as subtle as a Sherman tank, started prying about our destination. Real sneaky, he took the indirect route:

161

"South of France, of course, right Colonel?"

No dice. The Colonel deftly fended off our questions with one answer, "All in good time, chaps."

I went out on deck by the gangway. British troops in full battle dress and full packs were streaming up, heading fore and aft. Directing them and roaring out directions was an enormous soldier. As each trooper passed him, he instinctively ducked. I walked over to him and said,

"Hello, Sergeant."

"Sergeant **Major**," he shot back.

"Yes, sir," I squeaked.

He looked and acted just like Victor McGlauglin, only bigger and uglier. I learned later that a Sergeant Major in the British Army was far more important in the scheme of things than a whole squad of Generals.

The troops immediately set to work brewing their infernal tea. They cooked it in their tin hats, using gasoline poured over sand. The decks were strewn with jerry cans of gas, hundreds of them, under the vehicles, all over the place. I worried about fire, but the hell with it. Besides, the soldiers were using up all the fire fighting sand to cook tea.

Late in the afternoon I heard a hell of a commotion coming from the crew's mess. The crew's mess and the Navy gun crew's mess adjoined each other, and they were both packed. Peeking over shoulders I'll be damned if there weren't a Catholic Priest, a Jewish Rabbi, and a Minister, offering their services. Pushing and shoving my way to the front, I demanded to know what was going on. One of them informed me that very probably some of these fine young men were going to die quite soon so they were offering solace, for God's sake! I said, to my shame,

"I'll make this short. This whole crew is scared half to death, including, and especially, me. Now you come aboard and tell us that we're all going to get killed. Well, we're not, and you are just making it worse. I'll give you ten minutes, no more, then beat it."

All the years since, I've felt guilty about that outburst, but not a one of us ever got so much as a scratch. Three of the crew got the Clap, though.

I was sitting in my room after supper when Bill Ommendson, the Second Mate burst in.

"Come quick, Mister Mate. That shell shocked, crazy kid is going to kill the cook."

Out he bounded, with me right behind him. He went clattering down the inside stairway that led to the main deck, midships. At the bottom was a door that opened right by the galley. Bill pushed open the door and then started to back up the stairs. I tried to push him down but he wouldn't budge.

"Bill, move down. What's going on?"

By pushing against his big back I managed to peek over his shoulder.

SUPREME H ADQUARTERS
ALLIED EXPEDITIONARY FORCE

Soldiers, Sailors and Airmen of the Allied Expeditionary Force!

You are about to embark upon the Great Crusade, toward
which we have striven these many months. The eyes of
the world are upon you. The hopes and prayers of liberty-
loving people everywhere march with you. In company with
our brave Allies and brothers-in-arms on other Fronts,
you will bring about the destruction of the German war
machine, the elimination of Nazi tyranny over the oppressed
peoples of Europe, and security for ourselves in a free
world.

Your task will not be an easy one. Your enemy is well
trained, well equipped and battle-hardened. He will
fight savagely.

But this is the year 1944! Much has happened since the
Nazi triumphs of 1940-41. The United Nations have in-
flicted upon the Germans great defeats, in open battle,
man-to-man. Our air offensive has seriously reduced
their strength in the air and their capacity to wage
war on the ground. Our Home Fronts have given us an
overwhelming superiority in weapons and munitions of
war, and placed at our disposal great reserves of trained
fighting men. The tide has turned! The free men of the
world are marching together to Victory!

I have full confidence in your courage, devotion to duty
and skill in battle. We will accept nothing less than
full Victory!

Good Luck! And let us all beseech the blessing of Almighty God upon this great and noble undertaking.

Dwight D Eisenhower

The Normandy Invasion, June 6, 1944

**Signatures of the British officers on our
first trip to Normandy, June 6, 1944**

Dear Suffering Christ! That crazy kid had the biggest automatic pistol that I ever saw shoved into Bill's belly. Just as calm as you please, Bill reached out his hand and said, real low,

"Give me that gun, Sonny."

The kid looked up into Bill's eyes and handed him the gun, butt first. Holy Smoke! Bill and I backed up the stairs and went back to my room. Bill laid the gun on my bunk and leaned against the bulkhead, trembling. I was shaking all over.

"Unload the damned thing, Bill."

"I don't know how to."

"Well, go get Scotty Gillis. He was in the Canadian Army so he'll know how."

Bill returned with Scotty who pulled the clip out of the butt. By God, the gun was empty! It was a German Steyer. I still have it. I went up and told the Old Man the whole story and urged him to get this nut off the ship. If we ever got into action there was no knowing what he would do. He went out on the dock and phoned the War Shipping Administration who came and took the kid away. They were lucky to get into the dock area because it had been sealed off. The longshoremen weren't even allowed to go home. This invasion had to be the best kept secret of the century.

Shortly, a British pilot came aboard, wearing a full uniform. He backed the ship out of her berth and down the Thames we went. When we got to the mouth, we anchored right off the seaside resort town of Southend. We lay there all day, the troops cooking tea and pissing over the side. About dinner time swarms of planes started passing overhead, all flying East. Flying forts they were. Four engined bombers. They passed in the hundreds and still they kept coming. the sky was black with them. All afternoon and far into the night they never stopped. Somebody was sure catching hell, I hoped. Thousands of them passed over.

Colonel Grey was taking his meals with us in the officers' saloon. During supper he announced that he could now tell us what our destination was, and suggested that I summon all the officers. When I returned, the Colonel had set up a large, detailed map of the Bay de la Seine, which stretched from Le Havre on the left to Cherbourg on the right. With a pointer he ticked off the code names of the assault landing beaches, Sword, Gold, Juno, for the British forces. Then, down near Cherburg, Omaha, and Utah, for the American forces. Pointing to a seaside village in the Sword area called Gray Sur Mer, he said,

"That's where we go ashore. You, Captain, will anchor your vessel as close to shore as depth of water permits. I have proper navigational charts for you and your officers to study."

At last we got **The Word**. Norway, South of France, indeed. Weren't we the smart alecks? Then the Colonel got down to details, displaying charts that showed the narrow mine swept channels down the coast of England to a point off the Cliffs of Dover where we would turn to port and head across the Straits of Dover to the French coast, then port again parallel to the French coast to Sword. He emphasized that we would be in company of twenty odd ships in columns of two down to Dover, then in single column going across. This was because the swept channel was very narrow.

"Any questions, gentlemen?"

The British pilot started off. What about the weather? How was the channel marked? Were there any lighted buoys? On and on he went, with the Colonel patiently answering him.

It was a quiet, thoughtful group of men that filed out of the saloon. I sat on the edge of my bunk and pondered about the days ahead. Things looked kind of grim. All of a sudden I jumped half way out of the door. That Limey pilot was due to get off the ship down by the Dumpston buoy, near Dover! And he knew every detail of the invasion of Normandy! I tore up the stairs to the bridge deck where the Colonel was quartered in our one spare cabin. The Colonel let me in and I burst out with my news. He eyed me for a second, then said,

"Did I understand you to say that this chap will be leaving us before we go over? "

"Right, Colonel, and if he talks"...

Very quietly the Colonel interrupted me.

"A slight correction to your statement, Mister Mate. He will **not** be leaving. We will carry the nosey buggar right along with us. Why don't you assign him to some dirty job? I've got it. Put him up in that little round coop on the foremast, the thing that you Yanks call a Crow's Nest."

Hah, God bless the Limeys. They were a stalwart bunch of men. Going back to my cabin, I reflected on all that I had heard. The constant roar of those Flying Forts, still passing over in the hundreds gave me a great deal of comfort.

164

These are the times that try men's souls.
Thomas Paine

-26-

THE NORMANDY INVASION:

WE HIT THE BEACH

Our schedule was such that we were to pass through the Straits of Dover during the dark hours, and arrive off Sword Beach shortly after daylight. This time there was no feeling of elation as I engaged the windlass and heaved home the anchor. Down the coast we steamed in two columns abreast. I assumed that we were all bound for Sword, but I never found out.

I remember watching a ship in the next column through the binoculars. The jerry cans of gas stored on her forward deck were afire. It was blazing all around her deck load of vehicles, and I was kind of worried that their ammo might start blowing. She very quickly dropped out of line and disappeared astern. We never heard what became of her.

Soon enough we were down below Dover and started across in single file. We were being led by a little mine sweeper. There were mine sweepers on each side of us, too, chugging along sweeping as they went. While they had their big sweeps out they couldn't make much speed, so we had to slow down to their speed. Damned if the little, temporary marker buoys didn't have dim lights on them. The Limeys had really done some fine planning for this show.

The slow dark hours crept by and the tension increased. I stayed on the bridge with the Old Man as the watches changed through the night. It being the month of June, dawn came early. Four o'clock in the morning, and the sky was just beginning to lighten. Gradually the light increased. I looked out of the wheel house window, and never have I seen, nor expect to see again, such a sight! From one horizon to the other; in front, astern, and on both beams, the sea was packed with ships, thousands of them. I hadn't realized that our column wasn't the only one. They stretched on both sides of us for miles, all steaming East, each with its minesweeper escorts. We were all dumbfounded as the vast scope of this undertaking at last sunk in. Blinker lights were flashing on every side. It seemed like utter chaos but there was order to it all. Ships's Masters had done their homework well. On and on we steamed. With the coming of daylight, that old feeling of being naked and exposed swept over us. What about enemy planes? E boats? Mines? They were the worst. Hit a mine and your bottom would be blown in. Nothing happened. We turned to port and headed up toward Sword.

Out on the port bridge wing we had a British plane spotter. These men were civilian volunteers. (Ours was a dentist. We called him **Teeth**.) They had gone to a school where they watched films of both Allied and German aircraft. The film was run faster and faster as they became more and more adept. Our guy could catch a split second glimpse of a wing ducking out of a cloud and sing out the type of plane. Teeth was very, very good at his job. The English are to be greatly admired. During those days when their very existence was threatened, every man, woman, and child was doing his share.

During our conversion in Leith, a rather crude sort of radio had been installed on a bulkhead in the wheel house. It had no switches nor knobs. It was on all the time. Over it we were supposed to receive all kinds of orders. It was forever squawking, **Yellow Alert. Expect Red Momentarily. Negative Red. Now Green.** It went on so incessantly that we wound up paying no attention to it. Slowly we crept toward the beach, still following our little minesweeper. At last he swung aside. I was on the bow as usual, standing by the anchors. The Captain was on the bridge conning her in. The Second Mate was in the chart room calling out the depth as shown on the Fathometer. Old faithful Tim was manning the engine room telegraph. Before I expected it, the Old Man hollered, "Let go, Mister."

Down roared the starboard anchor. We were at Sword beach facing a determined enemy. As soon as she fetched up I headed midships. Colonel Grey was waiting for me. I wondered where the stevedore ship was. There were many ships off in the distance, a mile or two. Some were anchored, some still steaming about, but none of them were heading our way.

"Mister Mate, they've got fifteen minutes. If they don't show up, you'll have to offload my chaps and their gear."

Immediately I sent Tim to break out all hands. Assembling them on the forward deck, I made a little speech. I told them that they would all be assigned jobs. The deck crew would handle the winches, two oilers would keep them running. The Second Mate and I would run the winches for the fifty ton derrick at number two hatch from where I could see the forward deck. The Bosun and the Carpenter would handle the fifty ton guy ropes which were rove through snatch blocks to the niggar heads on the anchor windlass. These guys would pull the big derrick out over the side as soon as the lift had cleared the hatch coaming. As I wouldn't be able to see the after deck, with its two hatches, I put Tim in charge of the after deck. Ordinarily this might have caused some resentment, a kid in charge, but it didn't. The whole crew knew that he was as good a seaman as any of them. I felt comfortable with the arrangement, and later events would prove that my judgement and faith in him were justified.

The Colonel then dropped a beaut on me. He announced that he was sending all his troops into the holds where they were to take their places in the vehicles, the same for the vehicles on deck. They would release the lashings and rig the hoisting slings.

"My God, Colonel, you want me to hoist this stuff through the air and over the side with men sitting in them? What if we drop one, or a sling breaks?"

"So what? My men are valuable and I don't want to lose a one, but we've got a job to do over on the beach and we're going to do it."

But Colonel, they'll be sitting in those vehicles for hours with nothing to eat or drink. Let me rig the scramble nets."

"No, besides, a stomach wound on an empty stomach has a far better chance of healing."

This man was one tough critter. Guess that's why he had the job.

First, we had to unload the deck cargo. I was running the topping lift winch and Ommendson was on the starboard hoisting winch. The Limeys had furnished us with tin helmets of the same type that our troops wore in World War One. Bill looked so ridiculous with that silly tin hat perched on his big square head. Mine kept falling down over my eyes so I flung it overboard. First, we hooked onto the big duck abreast of the hatch. Up she swung, with fifteen or more men in her, all loaded down with rifles, grenades, machine guns, and draped all over with belts of ammo. As soon as she cleared the bulwarks I blew my whistle and the Bosun up on the windlass flung three round turns of guy line on the spinning niggar head, and over the side she swung. I stopped my topping lift winch and ran over to the rail where I could see and signaled Bill to lower away. The big duck splashed into the water and away for the beach she went. Troops pushed the next one down the deck, and the whole process was repeated until the forward deck was cleared. The same thing was being repeated on the after deck. Now I found some use for some of those *stores* in the number one 'tween deck. Those big concrete things. They were designed to be hung over the side at number one to act as fenders so the ducks wouldn't drift under the flare of the bow. Same thing back aft at number five.

All the while that this was going on, the poor soldiers were sweating it out down in the lower holds. The Captain was keeping the bridge, hollering orders through a megaphone to Tim and me. We couldn't hear him anyway, so we just kept on going hour after hour. The Belly Robber, bless his mangy soul, kept sending around sandwiches and coffee which we gulped down while the winches were running. At last, late in the night, we could see no more. Darkness had set in and the ship was completely blacked out. I got into a big argument with the Colonel but he finally gave in. I told him that we couldn't see to work, and that it was suicide to continue. It was impossible to see down into the holds while hoisting, and if a lift got caught on a 'tween deck hatch coaming, we'd not only lose the lift and kill his men, we'd also pull the booms down and kill ourselves. Reluctantly he agreed when I assured him that we would resume at first light. Bill and I stretched out on the steam guards and dozed off. It seemed just minutes later when somebody kicked me. I forgot where I was and rolled off the steam guard onto the deck. I looked up and there was the Old Man and the Colonel.

"What in the hell go you think you're doing, lying there on the deck?" growled the Skipper. "Let's get at it. The quicker we get rid of these damned passengers, the quicker we can get away from this damned beach. If we hang around here much longer we could get ourselves killed."

Up spoke the Colonel, with that affected upper class English drawl,

"I say, Mister Mate, I've brought you a spot of tea. Drink it down quickly, there's a good chap, and give it another go."

Wearily, we dragged ourselves back to the winches and resumed hoisting. As the lifts came out of the hatches, the poor soldiers looked wan and gray. I thought to myself, *Here, they should be as fit as fiddles, alert and ready to take on anything that the Germans have to offer. Instead, they were a sleepy, hungry, and bedraggled group of men. We'd be heading back to London, shortly, while their moment of truth was right in front of them.*

There came the time when the last lift went over the side. The Old Man was standing alongside of me.

"Get up forward, Mister and get that anchor heaved up."

"Wait a minute, Captain, we've got to put all the hatch beams back in, put the hatch covers and tarps back on, and secure the booms for sea."

"Bullshit, Mister. You can do all that after we get underway. Heave her up. I'm going to the bridge and I want to hear anchor chain rattling in the chain locker when I get there."

Orders are orders. I started heaving up, and as soon as I signaled that the chain was up and down, he rang for Full Ahead. Up and down means that the anchor has broken clear of the bottom. And there we were, scooting down the coast at full speed. Damn him, if the anchor should catch on a ledge or some other underwater obstacle, it could pull the damned windlass off the deck, or at least part the chain. And our anchors weighed five tons apiece. It was OK, though. The anchor fetched up in the hawse pipe all secure.

Now we had several hours ahead of us battening down. I left all the 'tween deck beams lying in the 'tween decks. and only put in the main deck ones. Hatch covers were put on and the tarps battened down. Then it only remained to square the booms, tighten the guys, and heave snug with the cargo runners. I crawled into the saloon, dog tired and filthy.

"What have you got, Mess? Pot roast? Not me, that damned steward is trying to poison us. I'll have bacon and eggs."

"The steward doesn't like special orders when it is so late."

"He doesn't, huh? If I don't get bacon and eggs, you tell him for me that I'll come into that galley and fry and eat him."

Damn that steward's soul to hell. Back came the messman with a watery mess of powdered eggs and raw chunks of Canadian bacon.

"The steward sends his regrets. We are now on Limey stores."

Oh, the slippery bastard. Some day there'll be a reckoning.

After supper I dragged myself up to the bridge to relieve his holiness who went below. There were ships all over the place. Our signalman had been blinking at them trying to get our orders. A minesweeper answered and told us to fall in behind him, so back across the Straits we went. Pretty soon the Second Mate and the cadet showed up. They each had an armload of tin cans. Heinz Ltd. canned soup, by God! Those clever Limeys had designed a soup can with a little cap on the top. Flip off the cap, drop a match down the hole, which contained Sterno, and Presto, hot soup in thirty seconds. Boy, they were great. Be sure to punch two holes in the top, though,. If you forgot, they'd blow like a hand grenade. We three practically lived on them for several trips. Bill craftily hid them in the flag locker.

Back we went to Tilbury Docks, this time to load Canadian troops. Back and forth we shuttled. The memories get blurred. One trip merges into another. No shore leave, of course. Just load the troops and their vehicles and go again. I remember that after the first or second trip the British lost Sword. It got too hot. We were diverted to Gold and Juno. It made no difference to us. They all looked alike. There was a big improvement, though. After that first trip the Army stevedores showed up. They were living just above the beaches, I guess, because they came out in launches. This substantially reduced our turnaround time, which suited us fine. The quicker we could get away from those beaches, the safer we felt.

Early on, we arrived at one of the beaches just as a piece of bad weather blew in. We were at anchor, well inshore, waiting for the stevedores, who couldn't come out in that gale of wind. The seas were making up pretty good, so the Old Man suggested that I go forward and run out another shot of anchor chain. While I was slacking off, the ship started to pound, badly. By God, we were aground! The Old Man rang up *Full Astern,* and screeched at me to heave up. Thank god that our telegraph was always on, *Stand By,* so we had steam. I got the anchor up and joined his nibs on the bridge. We were slamming up and down on the sandy bottom pretty bad and not moving. Move she did, though, after awhile. We backed well off and anchored again, this time with plenty of scope on the anchor chain. By this time we had been discharging onto a weird contraption called a Rhino Ferry. It was a big, flat steel barge about half the size of a football field. On its back end there were mounted two outboard motors like you have never seen before. They were about six feet high, with tremendous power, but still they were helpless in a heavy seaway. Early next morning one of them appeared drifting down on us. It was pouring and still blowing a gale. There were two bedraggled figures on it, waving frantically. **Bang!** She crashed into us. We threw them a couple of lines and tied them fast. They scrambled up a Jacob's ladder and stood there, shivering. Damned if they weren't two US Coast Guard kids, and had been blown all the way from the American beaches, We fed them and put 'em to bed. When the weather cleared, we moved back to the beach, Rhino and all, and finished discharging. Back we headed for London. The Skipper and I were on the bridge. He had his beak in a can of our soup, having caught us red-handed late one night.

"I'm worried, Mister. We'll have to go into drydock and have a look at our bottom. It won't look too good that we were fool enough to let our ship go aground."

Finishing my last can of soup, I motioned him out on the bridge wing, out of the hearing of the man at the wheel and the signalman.

"Captain, have you written up our grounding in the official log, yet?"

"Nope, planning to do it after we pick up the river pilot."

Didn't it occur to you that we never ran aground at all? Don't you remember that big underwater explosion that went off on my watch that morning? The one that we both thought was a magnetic mine?"

"Now look ahere, there was no explo...Oh, ho, Mister, you'll make a good shipmaster yet. Yes, I'll go below right now and write up the log while that, er, explosion is fresh in my mind."

Sure enough, as soon as we picked up the pilot, we radioed the War Shipping Administration in London, and were ordered to dry dock. The head of the WSA for Northwestern Europe was one rough, mean critter, whose reputation was known throughout the merchant marine. Captain Jones Devlin. He had been Master and Port Captain for the United States Line, the cream of American steamship lines. Now he held the biggest job pertaining to merchant shipping in England. We knew that he would personally inspect, and we were worried. He'd be tough to fool. Sure enough, he arrived just before the dry dock was dry. He went straight to the Old Man's room to read the official log. Pretty soon they came out and the Captain introduced me.

"Let's get down in the dock and have a look at your mine damage," says Captain Devlin.

I trailed along behind the two of them. The Old Man looked decidedly pale. Down we went and crawled under the bottom. Holy Moses! The bottom from the bow to midships was badly set up between every frame. It looked like a gigantic wash board. Captain Devlin, who was no fool, no indeed, looked thoughtfully at the two of us.

"Yes, yes, that was **some** big mine."

He turned abruptly, hurried up the stone steps, and was away for London. The Old Man and I looked at each other and gave the thumbs up sign.

Did Captain Devlin know the truth? At first I was convinced that we had fooled him. Now, I'm not so sure. He was too capable a man to be hornswoggled by us two. Maybe he said to himself, *Fortunes of War.* Long years later when I had come ashore and gone to work for a large Stevedoring firm, headquartered in New York, I would, from time to time, meet up with Captain Devlin, by then a VP for US Lines. Never once did either of us mention the incident. Maybe he didn't even remember it. Or maybe he had stood in our shoes once or twice himself.

That evening I decided to go up to London. It was our first chance since Leith. Soon, I found myself wandering around Piccadilly Circus in the pitch black blackout. All of a sudden there was a terrible spluttering, roaring sound overhead. It sounded like our modern jet planes, but there were no jet planes in those days-or were they? Me and everyone around me dove headlong down the subway stairs, The damned, whatever it was, crashed in the street and blew up. It wasn't until the next day that I found out that it was one of the first German buzz bombs, jet propelled, no pilot, aimed at London. The British nicknamed them Doodle Bugs, and they were something terrible. In the next few weeks they came over by the hundreds. They would just run out of fuel, drop out of the sky, and explode on impact. They had a ton of high explosive in them, and they sure made a mess out of London. Killed a lot of folks, too.

Because of the Doodle Bugs, the British Ministry decided to install a balloon on our after deck. First, they loaded a couple of dozen long gas cylinders on deck. Then they bolted a big spool of piano wire onto the niggar-head of one of the winches at number four hatch. Then they stretched out a great, deflated balloon on number four hatch. I made Bill Ommendson *Balloon Officer.* Just another damned gadget to me.

Next day we headed back down the river again. Bill was back aft, happy as a pig in mud, rigging up the balloon. I looked aft from the bridge just before supper and there she flew, way up in the sky. Well, I tell you, before we ever got back to the beach, that balloon became some pain in the neck. Naval vessels were forever signaling, *Lower your balloon two hundred feet. Raise your balloon. Stow your balloon on deck.* They had me run ragged. This trip we had a load of free Polish troops, and you talk about soldiers! They literally ran up the gangway. They were short, powerful, big boned brutes. They had hatred of the Germans coming right out of their pores. They couldn't wait to come to grips with the bastards that had devastated their homeland. God help the Germans that met up with this crew.

What with fog and changes of orders, by the time we were discharged, I hadn't been to bed for two days. Dirty, cranky, too many cigarettes, gallons of stale coffee. I was draped over the rail trying to keep my eyes open. A launch heaved alongside and up the ladder came a British officer. His uniform was pressed, his cheeks red, his eyes sparkling with good health and plenty of sleep. By Godfrey, if it wasn't still another STO officer.

"I say, do you know where the Chief Officer is?"

Peering at him with red-rimmed eyes, I said,

"You're looking at him."

"Oh, sorry, old chap. Be a good fellow and raise your balloon. It's way too low."

""Why certainly, Sir. At once, Sir."

Back aft I went, released the brake, and came midships again.

"I say, that balloon is now way too high," says Mr. STO.

"You ain't seen nothing yet."

Just about then the spool ran out. As far as I know, the damned thing is still going.

Back and forth--London to the beaches, the beaches to London. We had a few scares. Beaches were shelled. Occasionally a plane dropped magnetic mines. Our gun crew would fire up at it. Once, even the troops were firing BARs, resting the tripods on the bulwarks. I had to tell the gunnery officer to cut it out. They were firing right up through the cargo handling rigging.

Sometimes it all seemed unreal. One Sunday I was eating dinner, right off the beach. Small arms fire was rattling, punctuated by the sharp bark of German 88s. And there was I, dining on roast chicken, snow white table cloth, an attentive messman hovering at my elbow, *More chicken, Sir?* And right outside of the porthole men were dying! Another time a British battleship, the Rodney, I think it was, anchored just outside of us and started shelling inland of the beach. Those great triple snouts would elevate, and then *Crash!* The sound and concussion were fierce. All the inside, wooden doors on our ship had well fitting, heavy brass latches. Every time a salvo went off, every door on the ship would unlatch, fly open, then crash shut. *Weird!*

This terrible barrage went on for the best part of an hour. Then she steamed off and disappeared. All of us went around deaf as stumps for the rest of the day. I took great comfort in the fact that those great, one ton shells must have made life a little easier for some of the troops that we had discharged onto the beach.

One time, back in London, we had just finished loading and were standing by, fore and aft to let go and sail. It was late at night and dark. Our decks were covered as usual with ducks and trucks. We were taking in the mooring lines, me on the bow. The Bosun was spooling a twelve inch manila hawser on the niggarhead of the windlass. All of a sudden we heard the roar of an approaching Doodle Bug. As it got directly overhead, it shut off. *This is it,* I said to myself. Out of the corner of my eye I spied the Bosun racing down the forward deck. Just as I threw myself face down, I saw him launch himself head first under a truck. He didn't quite make it, and went head first right into the bumper. Thank God, the bomb sailed right over our bow, just missing us, and exploded in the next slip. *Whee!* I stood up, shaking like a leaf. I shut off the windlass and hurried down the deck to see about the Bosun. He was sitting down, a big flap of his forehead hanging down over his eyes. He was bleeding like a stuck pig. I helped him to his feet and said,

"What hit you?"

"Shrapnel," he croaked.

"You're a lying bastard, no damned medal for you. I saw you leave me and dive under that truck. Now get back up on the focsle head and get those lines in. We're sailing away from this cursed place. It's safer over on the beach."

"I can't see, Mister Mate."

"Well, if you can't see, feel. I'll stitch you up when we get clear of the dock."

It was on this trip that I got to go ashore on the beach. The Army stevedores that had handled our ship ever since the second trip were the same group that I had met the year before in the North African port of Bone. Then, too, we were under charter to the British Ministry of War Transport, shuttling around from North African ports to Italy.

On this particular voyage to the beach, the stevedores finished discharging early in the day. Their Captain stuck his head in through the saloon door, looking for our Captain.

"Here are your sailing orders," said he, and handed the Old Man an envelope.

"Well now, Mister. Listen to this. We don't sail until sunset. I believe that I will take a little snooze. Call me for supper."

I invited the stevedore Captain to sit down and have coffee and a piece of pie. He gratefully accepted and wolfed down two slabs of apple pie. (Made from canned apples of course.) The British Army has never been noted for its cuisine, so he sure was hungry. Surprisingly, he offered to take me ashore in the launch, show me around, and bring me back about suppertime. I was pretty leery about his offer because in Bone I had had a lot of trouble with both him and his men. They had been stealing a large consignment of NAAFI stores, especially several hundred cases of Canadian Black Horse Ale. There was no love lost between us. However, this time I must say that they had treated me well. Maybe they meant it and had let bygones be bygones.
We would see.

I was as leery as an old coyote. I had it all figured out that they'd get me ashore and work me over. I slipped up to my room and got a jacket. I also slipped a pair of brass knuckles in my hip pocket. **Be Prepared**, as the Boy Scouts say.

I had misjudged him, badly. His scheme was to give me a wartime sightseeing tour and get me back to the ship at suppertime. Then, I'd have to invite him to stay for supper. In that way he'd get the first good meal that he'd had since leaving London.

We climbed down a rope ladder into his launch. He fired up the engine and off we went. In no time at all the little boat ploughed up onto the beach and we transferred to his jeep.

There was fighting going on quite near around the town of Caen. General Montgomery was having a hell of a time trying to take the town away from the Krauts. We had heard that Churchill was raising the roof about the delay. The entire area was devastated. I wasn't at all comfortable. I was a ship person, and had been for most of my life, and didn't at all enjoy riding around and peering into pill boxes and smelling the awful stink of war. Finally, I begged off and suggested that we return to the ship.

"Way too early, old boy."

"Not really, Captain. I've got half a bottle of Black and White that needs nursing."

His response was predictable. He whirled the jeep around and raced for the beach, his tongue hanging out like that of a hound dog.

We sailed that evening for London. Early next morning we were approaching the White Cliffs of Dover when, without any warning, the fog descended. Our little minesweeper disappeared. We had no choice but to anchor. These channels had to be swept every trip. The Doodle Bugs were still swarming over from France. The entire London area and the approaches had been festooned with balloons, and they were proving to be effective. The Bugs would fly into their mooring cables and fall down before they got to the city. We also had heard that the British had formed and trained a squadron of fighter pilots to fly out over the Channel and shoot them down. We were told that these pilots were all Belgians who had escaped to England. As we lay there in thick fog we could hear the Doodle Bugs approaching from the East. Then we would hear the distinctive whine of Spitfires. By God, those Belgians were shooting them down not knowing that we were right under them. Every so often we would hear one splash into the sea and blow up with an awful bang. The Captain and I were hanging out of the wheel house windows.

"Damn it, Mister, I'll be glad to get back to Rhode Island. I'm sick of being tired and, yes I'll admit it, scared, too."

I couldn't have said it better. It was wishful thinking, though. We wouldn't be going home for awhile, yet.

As it always has, the fog lifted, and back to London we steamed. Generally, we were never in port overnight so there was no reason for the Captain to give a *draw,* an advance on a seaman's wages. Consequently, none of us had any money, nor any chance to spend if it we did have any. Damned if the STO leach didn't inform us that we were not due to sail until the next night. I was broke, having shot the works on my new sextant in Leith. Tim and I were drinking coffee turning over ways and means of getting a few pounds. I was about ready to sell one of the anchors. Shore leave really turns a feller on after so many weeks of work, work, and more work. And that with never enough sleep. Plus eating the steward's slop. Our taste buds had rotted off. Food became just fuel. Choke it down and keep going. All of a sudden Timmy exclaimed,

"I've got the answer. Mother and father have friends living in London. He is attached to the American Embassy. We'll go to town, inquire where they live, and put the bite on them."

Things were looking up. In short order the two of us were hurrying down the gangway with just enough dough to pay for the train fare. When we got to London station, Tim phoned the Embassy and got their address. Off we went again, this time in a bus. We knocked on the door and received a warm welcome. They, of course, didn't know the real reason for our call. They assumed that it was purely a social visit and settled down for an evening's reminiscing. Both Tim and I were squirming while the conversation droned on and on. Mutual friends from Staten Island, which was Tim's home, the health of Tim's folks, wasn't the war terrible, on and on they went. The delights of London were fading fast. Tim was watching his chance very closely, though, and during a temporary lull, charged right in with his pitch. Only this one night ashore, no draw, financially embarrassed. Oh, he did a first rate job. I figured on at least fifty pounds, which would just about do the trick. I'll be damned if they didn't advance him five pounds, twenty bucks! And made him sign for it to boot. We beat a hasty retreat. Standing out on the sidewalk we debated what to do. Like real sailormen, we put aside one pound for bus and train fare and drank up the rest. Didn't take too long, either.

So it went all summer, like a damned ferryboat. Or more like the mythical Flying Dutchman, doomed to sail the seas until Eternity.

At the end of one trip the Old Man was summoned to the offices of the War Shipping Administration. This was most unusual because with the exception of drydocking, all of our dealings had been with either the British Ministry of War Transport or the Sea Transport office. We were British in everything but the American flag which still streamed proudly from our taffrail. He was gone a long time. I happened to be out on the boat deck right after dinner when I spied him plodding along the quay. Quay? My God, I was starting to think and talk like a Limey! I hurried down and met him at the head of the gangway. He had a peculiar look on his sour puss. It almost seemed to be a look of suppressed glee.

"Hello, Captain. Nice time in London?"

"Grumph," he grunted and headed toward his room. Sort of casually he flung over his shoulder,

"Come up when it's convenient."

Convenient? Ha! He was never that polite in his life before. I shot up after him into his office. Slumping down on his settee he slowly took off his hat and flung it in a corner. Taking his time, and savoring every minute of it, he said,

"My compliments to the Chief Engineer and tell him to make steam. When he is ready, break out all hands, fore and aft. We're shifting to anchor in the stream."

"Captain, I was sure that you had good news. And all it is that we shift to anchor so that another ship can have our berth. I'm sure let down."

"Mister Mate, maybe I **have** good news but you talk so damned much that I can't get a word in"

Drag it out, you old devil.

"Now, as I was saying, we will go to anchor this afternoon. Tomorrow morning we will bunker from a barge alongside. Then, tomorrow night we will sail for home!"

Dear God, at last. All the while we were having this conversation his door had been shut tight. By the time I reached the main deck, the whole crew were cheering. Homeward bound! The damned bulkheads had ears.

Well before supper we were swinging to the hook out in the middle of the Thames. The Old Man and I were trying to choke down the miserable mess that had been placed before us.

"Better eat it, Mister. That's all you're going to get until we get back to Jersey City."

"Oh, God, I'd give anything for a decent meal. Have you got any money in the safe?"

"Why, yes. Why?"

"Could you let me have fifty bucks? Bill Ommendson and I would like to ashore for a decent meal."

Bill pricked up his ears when he heard that. As big as he was, he could eat a dead skunk and like it.

I ran up to the bridge and told the signalman to hoist the *Launch Wanted* flag, collected the fifty from his Nibs, beat Bill to the showers, and we were off to see the Queen. First, we went to a hotel bar and had about a zillion Scotches. (The Old Man had slipped Bill fifty, too.) Then, by continued bribing with good old Yankee money, we really had a meal. War or no war, American green removed any obstacles. Feeling no pain and as full as two ticks, we ambled out.

Let's get a taxi and go to one of those *private* night clubs that we've heard about," suggested Bill.

"Right, Oh, William. Cabbie, take us to the best joint in town."

"Joint, Sir?"

"Yep. That's Yankee talk. Let's go."

These private clubs were operating all over London. All you needed

Battleship shelling the Normandy Beach

**Discharging from a Coast Guard Transport
onto the Normandy Beach**

APPRECIATION AND THANKS

The Minister of War Transport has requested that the following message from the Admiral Commanding the Allied Naval Expeditionary Force may be communicated to all officers and men of the Allied Merchant Navies :—

On relinquishing his command as Naval Commander, Eastern Task Force, and withdrawing from the Assault Area, Rear Admiral Sir Philip Vian has sent me the following message :—

" I would be grateful if an expression of my appreciation could be conveyed to the officers and men of the Merchant Navy who have been operating with me off the French coast.

" By fine disregard of danger, by adherence to orders and by a ready appreciation of the demands of the varying situations that have arisen, the Merchant Fleet has once again proved the staunch and faithful ally of the Royal Navy."

2. It gives me great pleasure to pass on this expression of appreciation from Rear Admiral Vian, and to endorse it most heartily on my own account.

3. All of us who had been associated with the Merchant Navy in past operations in the Mediterranean and elsewhere were confident that the high standard of courage and devotion to duty previously displayed by the officers and men of our sister Service would be fully maintained during this, the greatest amphibious operation ever planned. We have not been disappointed.

4. I would be grateful if, when conveying to the officers and men of the Merchant Navy, Admiral Vian's message, you would add an expression of my thanks and high appreciation of the great service rendered by them to the Allied cause.

(Signed) B. H. RAMSAY,
Admiral.

1 July, 1944

For Posting on Ships' Notice Boards

(67963) Wt. 8092/2350 15,000 7/44 Hw. G.388/10.

Thanks from the Limeys.

German shell exploding on the morning of "D" Day

Normandy Beach, June 6, 1944

Rhino Ferry lands vehicles on Omaha Beach

to get in was a membership card that the doorman wrote out on the spot. A pound apiece. The taxi pulled up in front of a blank door. Out in front stood the doorman dressed up like a Central American General. Paying our two pounds, in we went. It was bedlam. Smoke so thick that you could cut it with a knife. A colored band thundering out jazz. When we were seated Bill said to the waiter,

"We'll have two Scotches."

"Two, Sir? I suggest that you start off with one."

Then it dawned on us. We had to buy a whole bottle.

We sat there nibbling at the Scotch. Sitting at the table next to us were two young girls. Bill, in a burst of generosity, went over and dragged them back.

"Waiter, two more glasses," boomed Bill.

"Oh, no," says one of them. "That Scotch is too strong. We're drinking Pims Cup."

"What in the devil kind of drink is that? Waiter, Pims Cup for the ladies."

By God, the stuff came in a big pitcher. Tasted somewhat like watered down gin. We had barely settled down when, *Air Raid!* The damned Doodle Bugs, or worse yet, their successors, the VIs. These new rockets were far more deadly. They were launched right up into the stratosphere, traveling faster than sound. If you heard one you were safe. Lights blinked, the band disappeared. One of the girls said why don't we pack up the Scotch and go to her home. Her mother would love to meet two Yanks. Why not? Away we went. They lived in a five story apartment building on the top floor. No elevator, of course, so we trudged up the five flights. There, we met the girl's old lady. Boy, she could really soak up the Scotch. *Air Raid!* The old lady hollered,

"Everybody grab a mattress and down to the cellar."

Down the five flights we stumbled, lugging a mattress apiece, into a dark cellar, dimly lit by a few flashlights. The Limeys call them torches. By the time we got down there, the folks from the lower floors had all the good spaces occupied. We had to wedge the mattresses in between a chimney foundation and the wall. In we crept. There wasn't room enough to stretch out so there we sat, with our knees against our chins. *All Clear!* Pick up the damned mattresses and up the five flights. We would just get the Scotch going when, *Air Raid!* Down the five flights again, mattresses and all. The third time this happened, Bill balked.

"They can blow this damned building to hell and gone. I'm not going down in that cellar again."

Nor did we. At dawn's early light, out we stumbled and headed back for the launch, arriving on board just in time for powdered eggs and tea. The coffee had all been used up.

Going up to my room something dawned on me. I had left my nice top coat up on the fifth floor. Just then the Captain stuck his head in.

"No more shore leave, Mister."

How in the hell was I going to get my coat back? Spying Tim out on deck, I told him to sneak up onto the bridge and hoist the *Launch Wanted* flag, and for God's sake, don't let the Captain see him. I gave him the last of my money and off he went. Thank God the Old Man was occupied in his office and saw nothing.

Time went by. No sign of Tim. After dinner the Old Man sent for me.

"Mister, all of our bunkers are aboard. Why don't we just heave up the anchor and go down the river real slow. Then we will be able to drop the pilot just at dark and be on our way."

I felt like a rat in a trap.

"We can't, Captain."

"What the hell do you mean, we can't? Who's running this here ship?"

"Well, you see, sir, the Cadet is still ashore."

To my everlasting shame I lied and hid behind Tim.

"What the hell is he doing ashore? Didn't I tell you No Shore Leave?"

"I don't know why he went, Captain, but I hear the launch coming now."

Out we went. There was Tim, standing up in the launch, his bright blue uniform sparkling in the sun. My brown coat draped over his arm looked strange.

"Get aboard this ship," snarled the Old Man. "What are you doing with that coat?"

"I found it on the train," lied Tim, God bless him.

The Captain chewed him out good, and he never flinched. I have been very grateful to him ever since. It's a wonder that the Old Man didn't recognize my coat. I'd been ashore with him a dozen times wearing it. Maybe he did.

At last! Down the Thames for the last time. Coming out of Southend we were joined by several ships, one of whom blinked over that he was the convoy Commodore. As we proceeded down the coast, more and more ships fell into column. By the time we reached the Lizard we were a full sized convoy complete with plenty of escort vessels. We took our departure with the Lizard abeam, seven miles off, and headed Southwest on course 277 degrees, true, toward the Azores and the Southern route home.

The Bosun and the deck crew were busy dismantling and dumping overboard the on deck latrines and all the debris left behind by God knows how many poor, brave soldiers that we had transported to an uncertain future.

It is sort of an anticlimax to say that we arrived safely home. I finally got my vacation; five days! Another voyage chronicled in the Log Book. It was a real pisser, though.

-27-

The Chief Mate

American cargo ships usually carry three Mates, a Third Mate, a Second Mate, and a first, or Chief Mate. Passenger ships frequently carry a Fourth Mate, or a Junior Third Mate, and a First and Chief Mate. British ships always refer to them as Officer rather than the term Mate. That is, Chief Officer, Second Officer, etc.

The Chief Mate is the second in command, and has complete authority over all departments under the Captain. He compares to the Executive Officer in the Navy. By tradition he sticks his nose into all departments. He will, however, have learned from bitter experience, to tread very softly where the engine room department is concerned. Soft talk with the Chief Engineer is the only way to go. All Engineers are a temperamental, touchy, clannish lot, and they will defend to the death any interference from the Deck department.

The Second Mate is usually referred to as the Navigating Officer, a term that is somewhat misleading. He doesn't do the navigating, the Captain does. He does take care of the navigating equipment such as the Gyro Compass, the Radar, RDF, etc. He also keeps all the charts in order and updates all publications such as Light Lists, Notices to Mariners, and chart corrections. He stands the twelve to four watch, and, if he's on the ball, gets up early enough to shoot a morning sun line with the Old Man, as well as the traditional noon sight for Latitude.

The Third Mate stands the eight to twelve watch. In my opinion he has the cushiest job on the ship. His watch allows him to sleep straight through from midnight to 7:20 AM, when he is called for breakfast. His sphere of responsibility is the fire and safety equipment on board. Topping that list are the life boats. A good Third Mate will spend many an afternoon at sea checking over the lifeboat contents. He makes sure that the water breakers are always full, that the food containers have not been broached, that all emergency flares are dry and in good order, that the engine, if the boat has one, is in good working order, and ready for instant starting. He will frequently check the lowering gear. If this is motorized, he ensures that the wire falls are greased, and that the lowering tracks are free and clean.

The Chief Mate stands the four to eight watch. During the War, I hated it because in the North Atlantic in the wintertime it got dark by 4:OOPM, and didn't get light until 7:30AM. This meant that most of the watch was stood in darkness. In a convoy, trying to keep proper station in the pitch dark was often impossible. When I came off watch at eight in the morning, my eye balls felt as if they were falling out, they were so strained from using those big 7X50 binoculars for so many hours.

In peacetime, though, it's the finest watch. You get to see the beautiful sunsets and sunrises. The Third Mate relieves you for supper, which breaks the monotony. During the morning watch, you get the coffee percolator bubbling at 4:30. As soon as dawn breaks, the sailor on bow lookout comes up on the bridge to mop out the wheel house and shine the brass. I can still smell that pungent ammonia smell of the polish. Then the Bosun comes up to get his orders for the day. A great way to make a living, right? Well, most times, anyway.

The Mate becomes sort of a father figure as soon as he takes the job. No matter that he's a young man, or that it is his first trip as Mate; he gets the unpleasant task of father confessor. Sailors seek out his counsel. They pour out their troubles expecting an immediate solution. Every bit of gossip eventually reaches his ears. A wise Mate will, in turn, take counsel with his Captain. After all, he has been down that road before him. Most Mates, me included, glory in their job. Seven days a week they are up at 3:30 in the morning and don't get to bed until 9:00 at night. Sounds rigorous, but they seem to thrive on such a schedule.

All three Mates have to take an examination before the U. S. Coast guard before they are issued their 'ticket.'

The Third Mate's exam leans heavily on fire and safety. The part dealing with navigation is somewhat rudimentary. He must, of course, be well grounded in the Rules of the Road, both International and Inland. The Second Mate's exam leans more heavily on celestial navigation and chart plotting. The Chief Mate's exam is a whole new kettle of fish. In addition to all that he had gone through in his two previous exams, he is exhaustively grilled in cargo stowage and seamanship. He is given intricate problems in the proper stowage of different cargos having different stowage factors. He must stow them properly, having due regard to the fore and aft draft of the vessel. He must also take into account the stability of the ship. If, for example, he should stow heavy, dense cargo such as steel and copper ingots high in the ship's hold, and light bulky cargo such as cartons, vehicles and such, in the lower holds, the ship's stability would be destroyed. In other words, she would be top heavy. In a seaway, she could roll over and sink.

Seamanship--Now there's a beaut for you. How do you study for such an exhaustive subject? This isn't a case of tying a bow line or rigging a handy billy. Nope. Those inspectors can really dream up some dillies. When I sat for my Mate's ticket, seamanship was the last subject. Up to then, I had sailed through in a breeze. Now, though, they had me over a barrel. The first two

S.S. Sandwich, aground in the Cape Cod Canal after colliding with a pleasure craft

S.S. Boston

or three questions on the subject had been a cinch. I read over the question again and shook my head. They had me in a bind...

Here's the question:

Your ship has run aground bow first. From her bow back to number one hatch, she is buried in sand and mud. How would you unship the anchors, carry them well aft of the ship, one on either side, shackle them to the anchor chains, and by means of the windlass, heave the ship backward into deep water?

Boy, this was something! All of us seamen have poured over dozens of books on seamanship. Most of them were long out of date, and were written, or updated around the turn of the century. In one or two, this very same problem and it's solution was described. The trouble was that in those days they were writing about sailing ships and sailing ship anchors. Here's what they told you to do. Launch two life boats. Row them under the bow of the ship. There, two strong backs, usually 6X6 timbers were lowered and lashed athwartship across the two boats with a space in between them. Then, the anchor was to be lowered in between them, and the cross part of the anchor shank was lashed to the timbers. Then the two boats were rowed out. While this was going on, the men on the bow would be slacking off on the anchor chain, or rope, as it usually was in those days. When the boats were in position, the lashings were cut and down went the anchor. Back on the ship men heaved away on the windlass and presto, pulled the ship free. The trouble with this fine scheme is that a steel cargo ship has anchors weighing five to ten tons apiece. Also, they have no cross piece on the ends of their shafts which could be lashed to the strong backs. And last, their great weight would undoubtedly sink the life boats. Well, I had to write something, but what?

Back in the dim recesses of my memory a thought stirred itself. I forced it back. Too crazy to even consider. Forget it. But yet, what could I lose?

Here it is: Back in the early thirties I was an A.B. on a ship running to the East Coast of South America. The depression was in full swing, and steamship companies were fighting for the few scraps of cargo that were offering. When we reached Buenos Aires, the Southernmost port of call, the Chief Mate announced that the ship would not be following her regular route, which was to proceed back up the coast, picking up cargo in several Brazilian ports. Instead, we were to load a full cargo in Buenos Aires, and go direct back to the States. He didn't consider it necessary to tell us the obvious, that there was no cargo offering in Brazil, nor did he say what our cargo was to be. A soon as our cargo was discharged, the ship was shifted to an open pier. Piled up on it was a mountain of empty oil drums. They were to be our cargo. In short order, all the holds were filled with them. Then, both the forward and after well decks were covered with them, up to the height of the boat deck. The Mate still wasn't satisfied, so the midships deck was loaded with them. Still not satisfied, the outside midships alleyways were loaded. Even the poop deck was buried with them! We were kept busy lashing them down, not the easiest of jobs, crawling around on top of those drums, passing the lashing wires. Eventually we sailed, arrived home, and discharged without incident.

Getting back to my problem with the Inspector, I started to write. I filled sheet after sheet with my cramped, printing style of writing. Here was my answer. I launched two life boats, lashed them together with the strongbacks, and positioned them under the Starboard anchor. The anchor was lowered and secured between the strongbacks. Don't ask me how; miracles can be accomplished with a pencil. Next the anchor chain was unshackled from the anchor. Now each link in the chain was almost a foot long and was very heavy. Sharpening my pencil, I was ready for the oil drums with which this fictitious ship was loaded. A third and fourth boat was launched. The third boat took on board the end of the anchor chain and made it fast. Meanwhile, the first two boats were slowly rowing out in back of the ship. When they got into position, they waited, anchor and all. Back on the ship, the chain was slowly lowered. As number three boat slowly pulled away, the men in number four boat were busy lashing empty oil drums to the chain, one right after the other. Number three boat finally reached the two boats with the anchor. Behind them stretched a continuous line of bobbing oil drums. The end of the chain was shackled back onto the anchor. Number three boat followed the floating chain back to the ship, cutting the drums adrift as they went. When all was ready, the anchor lashings were cut and down she went, right where they wanted it to be.

With my magical pencil, I repeated the whole process with the port anchor. All four boats were hoisted back on board, and a full head of steam was fed to the anchor windlass. Low and behold, the ship slid off the mud bank just as slick as a greased pig. That is, it did on the last page of my paper. In actual practice, that heavy anchor would have swamped both boats, and the chain was far too heavy to have been kept afloat by those oil drums. No matter. I had done it with my trusty pencil, so who was to deny it?

By the time I finished my masterpiece it was late afternoon. Thrusting the sheaf of papers into the Inspector's hand, I slunk back to my seat. This question was the last question that I was to be asked, but I didn't know that.

Furtively, I watched him. First he squirmed in his seat. Then, every couple of minutes he would snort. Over and over I could see him shaking his head. After what seemed to be an age, he beckoned me to come forward. He looked up at me for the longest time.

"Mister, I have been sitting at this desk for twenty-two years. In that time, I have read the most incredible, the most ludicrous, and the most outlandish answers ever dreamed up by man, but you take the cake. Here, go get your license!"

I turned to leave.

"You are wasting your time floating around the world in a rusty old ship. You would do far better writing fiction."

Little did he know that years later, that's just what I'd be doing.

-28-

A DIFFERENT KIND OF SHIPMASTER

Ninety nine out of a hundred shipmasters got there by just one of two routes. The first, by working their way up from Able Seaman, usually referred to as, *He came up through the hawse pipe.* The second, by graduating from one of the State Nautical Schools, or The United States Merchant Marine Academy, commonly referred to as Kings Point. Generally, this holds true of foreign countries. England, though, leans heavily on the Company Cadet program.

There remains that one percent. These are the real specialists, rare birds indeed. This story is about one of them.

I met this man under rather unusual circumstances. It was during World War II. I was the Chief Mate of a cargo ship. We were discharging a mixed cargo of War material in a godforsaken North African port. It was going painfully slow. The British Army was in the process of recruiting native Arabs as longshoremen. They were pitiful. Most of them were undernourished and weak. This, coupled with the heat, had slowed discharging to a crawl.

One morning, before breakfast, I made my way aft to number five hatch. Heavy trucks were to be discharged that morning. They weighed five tons apiece. This was the maximum safe working load of our booms and running gear, so I wanted to make sure that all the guys and cargo runners were in good shape, and not frayed nor worn. We had 7/8 inch runners so they were more than adequate. I checked them over carefully and found that they were in good condition. The Bosun joined me. He had found that the burton runner at number four hatch was badly worn from being dragged over the hatch coaming. We unshackled it from the hook and ran it off the winch, being careful to run a heaving line from the bitter end up through the head block on the boom. It was to be used to pull the new runner through the block and back to the winch. This job we left to the Arabs.

We had just turned to go 'midships for breakfast when the Bosun said,
"Mister Mate, here comes the damnedest looking ship that I ever saw."

I looked out over our stern. A ship was just docking. She was flying the red duster of the British Merchant Navy. And, yes, she was the damnedest ship that I, too, had ever seen. She was of medium size, somewhat smaller than our ship, which was a Liberty. The strange thing about her was her cargo handling gear. On both her forward and after decks were the biggest heavy lift derricks that I had ever seen. I found out later that the after derrick had a safe working load of seventy-five tons, and the one on the forward deck of one hundred tons!

Another peculiar thing about her was the location of her winches. They were perched up on platforms about fifteen feet above the deck. There were four of them; one for the topping lift, one for the lift, and two for the guys. The topping lifts and the lift were rigged with massive, five part blocks through which were woven heavy wire cables. Both guys were rigged with wire and triple blocks. *By Godfrey,* I thought, *An automated heavy lift ship. But what was she used for?*

What with running around all morning trying to keep the Arabs from wrecking our gear and killing themselves, I forgot about our new neighbor docked astern. It was shortly before noon when a horrible accident occurred, back at number five hatch. They were hoisting out big, heavy boxes. Each one of them contained two truck chassis. Because it was number five, the burton, or over the side boom, didn't reach over to the pier. The flare of the ship, back there, was such that at both numbers one and five hatches, this condition existed. To overcome this problem, the signal man would attach two heaving lines to the box, and throw the ends out onto the pier. There, four or five Arabs would tail onto them, and by alternating pulling and slacking off, would set the box to swinging. When the signal man, up on deck, judged that it had reached it's maximum swing, and was over the pier, he would signal the burton winchman to slack off. If he had judged right, the box would land on the pier with a crash before swinging back towards the ship. The signal man at each hatch was a British Army soldier. I had just made my way aft to number five when the tragedy happened. I saw it all, and to this day, it haunts me.

The signal man's job was to signal the winchmen to heave away, lower away, or stop. The winchmen could not see down the hatch or over the side, hence they took all their orders from the signalman. In this case, the box had been lowered over the side, and was hanging in mid air. The Arabs out on the pier were pulling on the heaving lines, setting the lift to swinging. As the lift swung towards the pier, one of the heaving lines became unhooked. An Arab scurried under the box, and was attempting to hook it up, again. At that very instant, the signal man signaled *Lower Away!* The heavy box crashed onto the pier, crushing the native like a bug! Without any hesitation the signal man signaled to raise the lift.

"Pull the gook out from under," he shouted.

This was done, and the work went on as though nothing had happened. Life was cheap in those days. Maybe it still is.

Right after dinner, I decided to take a look at that strange ship berthed astern of us. Cargo handling gear on ships has always been of great interest to me. I can still remember that whenever we were at sea in convoy, I used to spend hours studying the rigging of nearby ships through our big 7X50 binoculars.

I walked down the pier and stood gawking up at those massive derricks. I noticed a giant of a man up on the boat deck.

"I say, Yank, come aboard," he roared.

By the time that I had reached the head of the gangway, he was there waiting for me. He wore the four stripes of a Captain in the British Merchant Navy. Brilliant white teeth gleamed from a heavy, flaming red beard.

"Welcome aboard. By the look of you, you're the Chief Officer of yonder Yonkee ship."

His accent was pure, unadulterated Scottish. I found out, later, that he was a native of Glasgow, a city that had produced thousands of the best ships' officers that ever manned the deep water ships that roam the seven seas.

He was some good host. He escorted me to his quarters, which were small but comfortable and offered me a snort. Good Scotch, of course. I must have asked him a million questions about his ship. He patiently answered them all. I found out that his ship had been especially built for her task, which was the salvaging of the cargos of bombed or torpedoed ships. Early in the War she had been employed in the waters around the British Isles. Now, she had been sent to the new theater of the War, the Mediterranean. I found out that in addition to her wonderful deck machinery, she had Port and Starboard ballast tanks that filled and emptied automatically to correct the ship's list when hoisting heavy lifts. It became obvious that a tremendous amount of planning had gone into the design of this vessel.

The conversation turned to him and his background. In his younger life he had been a Company Cadet on a British ship. He had worked his way up to Chief Officer. He held his Master's ticket, but had yet to get his first command. It developed that, like me, his number one interest had always been cargo handling. About this time he had gotten married. Very quickly, the relationship between him and his wife became strained. It was the age-old problem that had confronted seamen and their women for centuries--the prolonged separations brought about by the nature of his job. He decided to do something about it. All during his next trip, he wrote letters to various companies, seeking employment. His ship put into Capetown for bunkers. There, he received mail that had been forwarded to him. One letter was of great interest. It was from a firm that specialized in heavy lifts. It was a company very similar to Merritt, Chapman, Scott, which operated all over our East and Gulf ports. They had floating heavy lift cranes. They not only did considerable salvage work, but were employed, daily, in the loading of heavy lifts on ships. This British company offered him employment on one of their larger rigs. He immediately cabled them, accepting the job. Just as soon as his ship returned to England, he paid off and took up his new duties.

His rise in the ranks was rapid. In a very few years he had risen to Operating Manager. He enjoyed an excellent reputation throughout the shipping industry. Then the War came along. The powers that be decided to build a ship instead of a conventional barge for wartime salvage work. The British Ministry of War Transport and the Admiralty fought and argued over who would operate the ship. The Admiralty wanted her under the control of the British Navy. The Ministry wanted her under their control, which was civilian. The Ministry won, and preconstruction planning commenced. My new friend was appointed her Master, and was immediately plunged into her planning and construction. When the ship was commissioned, she was, in many ways, his brain child. When she was delivered to the Ministry, she had very few faults.

So here he was, on the North African coast. His next assignment was a British cargo ship aground a few miles down the coast. She had been severely bombed. Her Master had made a run for the coast and ran her aground, where she was abandoned. She had been the Commodore's ship, and therefore had been carrying a box full of secret documents, codes, destinations, and the like. These boxes were weighted with lead, and were meant to be thrown overboard in the event of an attack. In their haste to abandon ship, the Commodore's staff had neglected to throw it overboard. Maybe they didn't have time. My friend's task was to retrieve the box.

Next, he gave me a tour of the ship. Boy, she was something! Long before she slid down the ways, he had recruited her crew. Without exception, they came from his old company, and were specialists. Even the Steward's department came from his heavy lift barges, where good food was at the top of the list. Not that they were eating too good right now. The War had required many sacrifices, and ships' Stewards had to make do. When I heard this, I invited him and his Chief Engineer to take supper on our ship. They accepted with alacrity. They were both big men, and obviously liked their groceries.

I met them at our gangway and escorted them to the dining saloon. Our Captain was seated in his usual place at the deck officers table. I introduced my guests to him, whereupon he unceremoniously banished the Second and Third Mates to another table. Quite by coincidence, the Steward had prepared an excellent meal for a change. Our guests fell to like a couple of starving animals. Their plates were scraped clean in a matter of minutes. Seconds were urged upon them. When hot apple pie with a big dollop of ice cream appeared, they positively drooled. It was a pleasure to see two big healthy men enjoy their food. When coffee was served our Captain started firing questions at them. Just before the war, he had been a supervising rigger in a shipyard, so his interest in their ship paralleled mine. He asked a million questions, most of them were the same ones that I had asked before. They answered them patiently and thoroughly. It was a fine evening that we had. A welcome interlude in the business of fighting a global war far away from home.

When the meal was finished, we all adjourned to the Captain's cabin. He rummaged around in a cabinet and unearthed a bottle of Scotch. Glasses were filled and refilled. Ten o'clock rolled around only too soon, and our guests upended their glasses for the last time.

"A good night to you, laddies 'twas a fine evening. We sail at dawn. Would you, two, like to go with us? We'll be back before dark."

"Would we ever!"

The Captain accepted like a shot, and we promised to board their ship the following morning at 4:30 AM.

I went to my cabin and flung off my clothes. I was having second thoughts about tomorrow. After all, there was a first class War raging, and here us two were going off on an all day pleasure cruise. What if we had an air raid? Suppose the ship was ordered out of the harbor to disperse? It had happened to us before, when we had been ordered out of one of these ports in a hurry. I tossed and turned the remainder of the night. A little after three I got up, pulled my clothes back on, and took my trusty percolator down to the saloon. I went in through the pantry and charged up the pot with fresh grounds and water. I was just plugging it in when I heard a snore. Tiptoeing into the saloon, I snapped on the lights. There was the Third Mate, who had the night watch, stretched out on the settee sound asleep! Well, now! I sneaked up to him and gently rolled him off onto the deck. He came awake with a howl of rage.

"Get your ass out on deck, or up on the bridge," I hissed. "You can thank your lucky stars that I found you instead of the Old Man. He's due in here any minute. Git!"

He had no more than gotten out when the Old Man crawled in. I plunked a fresh cup of coffee down in front of him. He sat there with his head between his hands. He had some hangover.

"Mister," he moaned. "What's the matter with us damned fools, sitting up half the night swilling whiskey instead of getting our rest."

"Drink your coffee, Captain. It will wear off. It always has before."

It was pitch black out on deck. We stumbled down the gangway and set off up the pier. He was still muttering about the evils of strong drink. I kept reassuring him that he would live.

The Chief Engineer met us at the gangway. He said that the Captain was on the bridge and that we should join him. I begged off and went roaming around the ship. I was still having strong misgivings about going on this joy ride. Of course, I wanted to see all this wonderful equipment in operation, but a heavy lift ship wasn't needed to retrieve a lead box. Too late to get out of it, now, so what the hell.

As I poked around the deck, the ship was getting under way. There was little fuss about it. One minute we were alongside. The next, we were swinging around and heading out through the breakwater. As the first signs of dawn appeared, I noticed that all the guns were manned by DEMS men. These were the British counterparts of our U. S. Naval Armed Guard. DEMS was the acronym for Defense, Merchant Ships. I walked over to one of the forty millimeter antiaircraft guns and asked how come? Were they expecting an air raid?

"Standard operating procedure when entering or departing from port."

These Limeys had been in a long War, and had learned from bitter experience, to never let their guard down.

Soon, we were steaming down the coast, keeping about five miles off. About an hour later I was up on the focsle head chatting with the gun crew manning the forward gun. They were sprawled out on the deck drinking strong, black tea out of thick mugs. They gave me one. Boy, oh boy, it would take the enamel off your teeth! Funny, though, it perked you up like a double hooker of booze.

Loud speakers blared out all over the ship.

BOAT CREW AND BOARDING PARTY TO THE STARBOARD MOTOR LAUNCH. YANKEE CHIEF MATE INVITED TO ACCOMPANY.

I looked out over the bow. Just off to Starboard was the stranded ship. Only her bridge and smoke stack were above water. Her stack was hanging over at a drunken angle. Her bridge structure was all varnished wood, a style much favored by British merchant ships.

I hurried up to the boat deck and jumped into the boat. The Chief Mate, still another Scotsman, was in charge. The falls were slacked off, and we hit the water with a splash. The falls were unhooked, the engine fired up, and off we putted. I got the strangest feeling that we were pirates, off to plunder a helpless victim.

We pulled up right alongside the port bridge wing and climbed out. These guys were real professionals. No verbal orders were given. Two coxswains and two DEMS gunners stayed in the boat. They were fully armed. This crew were very well trained, indeed. It was so obvious that they had been hand picked, and each man knew his job. No shouting of useless orders was needed.

The Mate and I picked our way into the wheel house. It was pretty badly smashed up. Two DEMS gunners went into the chart room, just aft of the wheel house. I peeked in. There, on the deck, in plain sight, was the box that they were looking for. It was dragged out and stowed in the launch.

"Time to go," said the Mate.

He took one last look around, paused, and stooped over and picked up a pair of binoculars. He looked at them for a moment, then handed them to me.

188

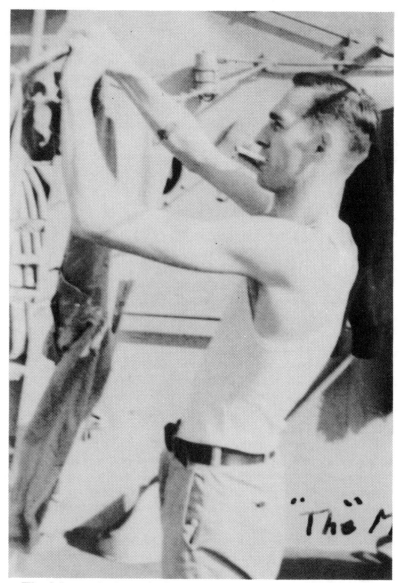

The Mate, clothes pin in mouth, somewhere in the Med

"Here you are, Mister. A souvenir from the British Merchant Navy."

I looked through them. One lens had a scale etched into it. They were used by gunners to establish their range. Some unknown DEMS gunner had dropped them in his haste to abandon ship. I still have them. They're 6X35 power, and not very good, but they bring back some memories.

Back we went to the mother ship, which immediately got under way. I joined the two Captains on the bridge. I took a peek into the compass, and noted that we were steaming due North.

"Strange, I wonder why?"

The Second Mate was operating the depth finder, and calling out the depth, which was increasing, rapidly. The Captain went out onto the bridge wing, leaned over and yelled,

"Over the side with it. Heave."

The two DEMS ratings who had retrieved the box, pushed it over the side, where it immediately sank. The Captain came back into the wheel house and said to the Second Mate,

"Plot a course back to the harbor and steer it. How about a spot of lunch, gentlemen?"

All through the meal, he and his Chief Officer reminisced about their many salvage jobs. They were both good story tellers. I could have listened to them for hours. I watched my chance, and interrupted them.

"Captain, why did you throw that box overboard?"

"I'll tell you why, Mister. Red Tape! If I had brought it back, I'd be a week filling out forms and another week trying to find someone to take it off my hands. My log book says it couldn't be found, and must have been jettisoned as per instructions."

All too soon, we were back and tied up to the pier. They sailed to an unknown destination the next day.

I am the better for having known them.

189

The Show Must Go On.
Old Broadway saying

-29-

A BOB HOPE SHOW THAT WE MISSED

At the time that this incident took place, I was the Chief Mate of a Liberty ship shuttling around the Mediterranean. We were chartered to the British Ministry of War Transport. Our job was ferrying British troops and supplies from North African ports to Italy during the invasion of that country. We'd been at it for a long time, and were heartily sick of it. Watch on, watch off. Load in a day. Join a small convoy. Dock or anchor out in some dismal hole like Taranto or Brindisi. Dump off our troops and cargo, then back to some equally dismal hole in North Africa and repeat the whole damned process over again. Shore leave was out of the question. Every port that we went to, either in North Africa or Italy had been bombed or fought over until there was practically nothing left but ruins.

On one of these trips we were bound for some dump in Italy. We had on board the usual assortment of war material plus about a hundred and forty soldiers. There were only four or five ships in the convoy, and we had the usual escort of British Naval vessels zipping around.

Right after dinner one afternoon I was hanging around the bridge with the Old Man and the Second mate. The conversation was the usual belly aching about how it seemed that we were doomed to stay in the Med forever. These damned Limeys that controlled us seemed to think that we were robots, or made of iron. Their soldiers and sailors were forever getting sent off on R & R, but did they ever think of us? Never! Why, they were even stingy with their bunker fuel oil, doling it out each trip like it was champagne.

As I remember, we were steaming along in two columns, in sight of the North African coast, somewheres off Tunis. A flurry of signal flags appeared on the boss escort ship. Our signal man came running in from the bridge wing. "Captain, all ships are to reduce speed to four knots. Execute at once."
"Now what," the Old Man snorted. "Maybe that Navy bloke is going to invite us over for a few hands of bridge."
Another flutter of flags went up on the escort's halyards.
"There he goes again. What is it this time, Flags."
"Captain, all ships are to form a single column and proceed on course such and such to the port of Bizerte."
At least I think that was the port.

190

"Flags, ask them why?"

Flags used the blinker light. He was clacking away for quite a while. "Captain, we just got told in a polite way to obey orders and don't ask a lot of useless questions. However, their signal man told me on the QT that there is a hell of a battle going on somewhere up ahead of us, so they have to leave us and go and assist. Another convoy is sure catching hell."

After considerable shuffling around, we got ourselves into a single column. Our Skipper had cleverly outmaneuvered the others, so we wound up the lead ship. He called for full speed, and off we went on our new course. The escorts vanished hell bent over the horizon. We approached the harbor at full speed. No pilot boat was in sight so the Old Man took her right in. He had Flags run up, a signal that we would anchor where we were, and that the other ships should give us plenty of room when they anchored.

I went forward to stand by the anchors. Soon, the Old Man went half astern, and hollered for me to let go, which I did. When she fetched up I rejoined him on the bridge. Flags had just received a blinker message from shore that we were to lay at anchor overnight, and to get under way at first light the next morning. Escorts would meet us outside the harbor.

The Captain went below. My watch had just started, so I made myself busy and took two or three anchor bearings and noted them in the rough log and on the wheel house blackboard. I could hear Flags clacking away out on the bridge wing. These Navy signal men were a close knit fraternity. They got all the latest gossip, most of which was usually wrong or greatly exaggerated.

Flags came into the wheel house with a smug look on his puss.

"Out with it, Flags. What's the latest from the fighting front?"

"I don't hear nothing from the fighting front, Mr. Mate, but I got something from that Limey escort, over there that is more important."

"Spill it, Flags. Let's hear it."

"Well, it seems that the USO has arranged to have the Bob Hope show appear here. They have built an enormous outdoor amphitheater some where outside the town. The whole Hope gang will be on stage. Jerry Colonna, Frances Langford, the whole bunch!"

The policy of the USO had always been a thorn in the sides of us merchant seamen. They wouldn't admit us. During the War they had a USO in every major city in the country as well as overseas. Talk about discrimination! They would admit black soldiers, but not us. We were resentful, and the feeling ran deep.

The word ran around the ship like wild fire. Our Navy Gunnery Officer contacted the Navy ashore and arranged a launch to take one half of his men ashore so that they could go to the show. Just before supper our Purser came up to my room with an amazing proposition. He proposed that he and I put on a pair of dungarees, a blue work shirt, a sailors white hat, and crash the show! I jumped out of my chair and shouted at him,

191

"Not by a damn sight, Mister. That no good USO can stick their show up... " On and on I raved.

"I'd rather jump over the side than be found dead in one of their facilities. "

When I ran out of breath, he moved in. And I must say that our Purser was some persuasive critter. He finally won me over when he very cleverly suggested that we compose a thank you letter and hand it to one of their flunkies on the way out. I made a deal with the Third Mate to stand the rest of my watch and went back aft to the gun crew's quarters to borrow a white hat.

I got the Bosun to lower the accommodation ladder. We were all set for the festivities.

In spite of my prejudices, I was looking forward to the evening. Like every other seaman, I was a great fan of Bob Hope. All these years later, he still is the best. He has devoted years and years of his life entertaining our Armed Forces who are stuck overseas at Christmas time. The launch showed up right on time and we all piled in. I spotted a watertender and an oiler all rigged out in white hats. Evidently the Purser was not the only one to think up a scheme to crash the show.

When we got to the launch landing, a Chief Petty Officer told us how to get there. We had to walk, and it was going to be a long one. Full blackout was being observed. The Purser and I quickly found ourselves alone. On shore, sailors are always uncomfortable in the company of officers. I know; I used to be one.

We quickly got out of town and were trudging along a sandy road. It was so dark that we could barely see the horizon line. Suddenly we heard a vehicle coming. It was a jeep, it's headlights blacked out to little slits. It slowed to a stop and the driver hollered,

"Air Raid. Get off the road. Take cover in the ditch!"

"Purser, how do we take cover in a ditch? Jump in and pull it over us?"

There was a fairly deep ditch on either side of the road. While we stood there thinking it over, we heard the distant drone of planes. At the same time a line of vehicles came towards us, their little headlights piercing the darkness. It was no time to be standing around on that exposed road. I took a nose dive right into the ditch, the Purser right beside me.

"Mr. Mate, move over. you're laying right on my leg. "

We could hear the vehicles stopping, and the sound of many voices as they, too, dove into the ditch. Somebody landed right on top of me, damn near squashing me.

"Hey, get off of me, you big bum, " I shouted.

He only grunted and rolled over on top of the Purser. The Purser, too, cursed him, and pushed him back on top of me. The sound of the planes grew louder, and then, with a roar, they swept over and were gone! From both sides

Another of the endless convoys forms up. The box-like object in the foreground is a life raft on the deck of the British cargo ship from which this photo was taken.

of the road we could hear voices as men crawled out of the ditch. Flashlights winked on. By their light, I got a good look at the guy that had jumped on top of me. By God, it was Jerry Colonna! No mistaking him and that big walrus mustache.

"Thanks, pal. You damned near smothered me. How about an autograph?"

That was me, trying to be nonchalant. He did shake hands, though, before climbing back into his jeep. As they raced off in the darkness, one of the drivers shouted back,

"The Bob Hope show is postponed until tomorrow."

Back to the launch landing we hiked. I got back on board in time for a couple hours sleep before heaving up the anchor.

So ended that day, as the log book says.

-30-

AT THE MOVIES

Sometime, early in the war, I was Mate of a Liberty ship. She was berthed at the Company's piers in Jersey City. We had come in from yet another miserable voyage across the North Atlantic. The ship was loading around the clock. The usual stuff--tanks, guns, ammo, foodstuffs, topped off by planes on deck.

Most of the crew had paid off and left upon arrival. Even the Second and Third Mates had quit, as had all the Engineers except the Chief. Thank God we still had the Chief Steward and a couple of cooks. The Saloon messman also had departed, so what few of us that were left were waiting on ourselves and washing our own dishes. The officers' bedroom steward was still with us so I tried to enlist him to work in the saloon on overtime. No dice. He had a good thing going with just the Chief Engineer and me to take care of.

The Old Man had gone home to New England. I was supposed to let him know when sailing day drew near. It was not far off. All the lower holds were full, and the "tween decks were not far behind. It was time to call him, which I did. He arrived back the next morning. The night before sailing he invited me to go over to New York to see a movie that he had heard about. So, after supper, away we went. On the way over he said that we should enjoy this picture because it was about a Liberty ship just like ours.

When we got to the theater, we stood gawking up at the lights which proclaimed, **"ACTION IN THE NORTH ATLANTIC"**, starring Humphrey Bogart as the Chief Mate, and Raymond Massey as the Captain. In we went. Almost every seat was taken, the two stars being very popular. We squeezed our way past several people and found two seats in the middle of a row.

Settling himself down, the Old Man nudged me, and in a hoarse whisper, heard several rows away, said,

"Well, let's see some of the action."

Oh, it was awful!

We who had been sailing these lousy ships could see and abhor what Hollywood had concocted. I suppose that as propaganda for the War effort it served a purpose, but to us bonifide Merchant Seamen, it stunk. They had cast the Deck Cadet as the hero who manned the five inch gun all alone after all the

194

Navy gunners got killed, and shot down the enemy plane, getting himself killed in the process. About there the Old Man stood up in the darkness, and in a loud, bridge to focsle head voice proclaimed,

"Mister, this stinks. Let's get out of here."

So, with everyone hissing at us, we crawled over peoples' knees and headed back for Jersey City. All the way back he muttered about Bogart. In the film, the Captain hurt himself; fell off a ladder or something. So the Mate took over command. He even conducted the burial service at sea for the Cadet and the gunners. A real phony tear jerker. We would have brought the bodies home in the freezer. Just as we were going up the gangway, the Old Man stopped abruptly and said,

"Do you ever read the Bible?"

"Not much," I confessed. "Why?"

"Well, see if you can find that burial service. We might need it."

Don't you know, I spent hours during the following months pawing through both the Old and the New Testament for that service, the one that ends,

"We commit this body to the deep."

It was years later before I found out that it isn't in the Bible at all. It's in It's in the Episcopal Prayer Book. No matter, I never had to use it.

195

-31-
THE NAVY AT ITS BEST

In spite of the bad blood that has existed for years between the Merchant Men and the Navy men, I must give credit to Naval seamanship, which, on this occasion, was superb.

We were in the Mediterranean during World War II. I was Mate on a Liberty ship. The Second Mate, Joe Bandoni, and I had been shipmates before the war—A.B.s on the same ship. The deck cadet, Tim Pouch, was rotating between watches, and was at the time, on Bandoni's watch, the twelve to four. The Old Man had relieved the Third Mate from duty and confined him to his room, so the Skipper and I were sharing his eight to twelve watch. That meant that I was on the bridge from four to ten, twice a day, the Old Man taking the bridge from ten to twelve, morning and night.

We were somewhere in the Eastern Mediterranean, steaming West in a small convoy. For many weary months we had been slogging around carrying cargo and troops for the British. The long hours and the work were taking their toll on me. I had become cranky irritable, and short tempered.

One morning I crawled up the ladders to the bridge to relieve the Second Mate at four AM. Full blackout was being observed and, with no moon, it was pitch black. I entered the lee side door to the wheel house and fell flat over the prostrate body of the Second Mate. Before I could get up, Tim came in from the opposite side, called the engine room on the phone and said,

"Down four revolutions. That should do it."

Then he looked into the binnacle and said to the man at the wheel,

"Come left five degrees."

"What the hell is going on here? The Second Mate asleep on the deck and the cadet in full charge. Get up, you lazy bastard."

"Mister, he isn't asleep. He's sick. He just keeled over."

A fine kettle of fish. I risked using my flash light, shading it through my fingers. His eyes were open and looking right up at me.

"I can't get up. Every joint in my body is on fire."

I blew my whistle for the lookout and the standby man, and they carried him down to his room. There didn't seem to be much sense in calling the Captain. He was old and needed his rest. When he showed up after breakfast, he was in high spirits.

"Mister, Sparks just received a message for us. We are to break off from the convoy and go into Augusta, Sicily, and you know what that means."

196

Indeed, I did. Augusta was one of those great natural anchorages, and was used to form up homeward bound convoys. I told him about the Second Mate, but he just pooh poohed it.

"Probably over tired, although God knows why. He just stands up here drinking coffee eight hours a day. Have a look at him. Mister, we just might be going home."

I left the bridge and went down to have a look at Bandoni. No question about it he was **sick,** and in big pain. The working of the ship, even though we were in fairly good weather, was excruciating. His joints, from head to foot were killing him. I got extra pillows and wedged him in against the bulkhead. Then I filled him full of aspirin, and made arrangements with the saloon messman to bring him his meals.

In the meantime, the Old Man had swung us out of the convoy and set course for Augusta. I grabbed a quick bite of breakfast and headed back for the bridge. The Skipper was in the chart room studying the chart for Augusta.

"A perfect place to anchor, Mister. We'll just ease along inside, drop the pick and be snug as bugs."

"Fine, Captain but if we get orders to go home, or even if we don't, there's just you and me."

"You're a worry wart, Mister. Bandoni will be up and around in no time. Now stop worrying and get forward and clear way the anchors."

The next day I decided to launch our motor life boat. I called it *Boat Drill.* Actually, I wanted to take a little cruise around this beautiful harbor. I rounded up the Bosun, Carpenter, two Navy gunners' mates, a couple of A.B.s, and off we went. We had a full tank of gas and not a care in the world. Sort of like, *School's Out.* We had spent so many months being scared and tired, with practically no chance or desire to go ashore, that we were like colts let out to pasture.

One of the men called my attention to the fact that several ships were making steam. Their funnels were belching smoke and we could hear their anchor chains clanking over the windlass. What the hell! We were a long ways from our ship. I put the tiller over and opened the throttle wide. We swung around under the falls. Right above us, the Old Man was dancing up and down on the boat deck, screeching like a maniac. He had the boat falls all rigged to the winches, and the very minute we hooked on, he hollered, *Heave Away,* and up we went, still in the boat. As soon as we came even with the deck, the Skipper told me to jump out and get my ass forward and heave up the anchor, fast.

"What's going on, Captain?"

"Air raid, that's what. All ships are to get underway."

I raced up to the focsle head thinking, *some short vacation.* The Carpenter and I got the anchor aweigh. She was just coming into the hawse pipe when I heard the phone ringing. Signaling Chips to shut off the windlass, I answered.

"Let the God damned anchor go, Mister. No air raid."

I kept looking in on the Second Mate as often as I could. If anything, he was worse. Couldn't get up to go to the head. No bedpans on these ships. He had to make do with a bucket. He didn't want to eat, and was starting to moan and cry. The poor guy was in bad shape, and we couldn't even figure out what was the matter with him.

The day came. Up came the old hook, and it was, Slow Ahead. Out we steamed, ships ahead and astern. We formed up into columns like the old veterans that we were. As I wearily climbed up to the bridge I allowed as how we had earned a stripe or two.

We were in good company. Instead of British escorts, we were being herded by DEs and destroyers of the good old US Navy. The convoy was steaming due West for the Straits of Gibraltar and the Atlantic. When we reached the Straits, more ships came out from Gibraltar and joined us. By the time we felt the first long swells of the open Atlantic, we were a full fledged, first class convoy.

Our ship, being light, not even any ballast except sea water in any double bottom fuel tanks that were empty, commenced to thrash around. There was a full Westerly gale blowing, and we were pitching badly. The Saloon messman came up to the bridge and begged me to come down and look in on the Second Mate. I got the Old Man to relieve me and followed him down. Joe was screaming with pain. The pitching of the ship was tearing him apart. I patted him on the back and raced for the bridge.

"Flags, blink over to that destroyer and ask them if they have a doctor."

They blinked back in the affirmative. I scribbled a message describing Joe's symptoms as best as I could. Back came a question, *How old is the patient?* Then a few more questions about his condition. Finally,

YOUR PATIENT EXHIBITS DEFINITE SIGNS OF REUHMATICFEVER. ADMINISTER ONE FOURTH GRAIN MORPHINE SULFATE TWICE A DAY. WHEN THE WEATHER MODERATES, WE WILL ATTEMPT TRANSFERRING PATIENT TO THIS VESSEL.

I got the Skipper to open the safe where the narcotics were kept. We had never used any. The Morphine pills were very tiny, and just fit, one on top of the other, in a glass bottle the diameter of a straw. We shook one out, then had to cut it in half, they being one half grain. The Old Man pulled out a big form and laboriously filled it out. Every crumb of this hellish stuff had to be accounted for. Back down to Joe I went, clutching the wee little pill It seemed so tiny that I wondered if it would do him any good. I pushed it down his throat and settled back to wait. Nothing. He went right on crying and moaning. *Humph, maybe they are stale. They've been in the safe ever since the ship was built.* Then, very slowly, he quieted down and slipped off to sleep. *Wow! This stuff is strong.* This went on for two or three days, with me dragging my weary carcass from the bridge to Joe, to the saloon, to bed for two hours and back to the damned bridge. The Old Man and I were now standing all the watches, or rather he was standing the eight to twelve and I was standing the other sixteen hours.

After four days, it was still blowing a gale. Every day I gammed with the doctor by blinker light. Joe was getting worse again. The effect of the Morphine was either wearing off or he was tolerating it better. We could hear him yelling way up on the bridge. I reported this to the doctor. He blinked back and asked if we had any Codeine Sulphate? If so switch—same dosage. Sure enough, way in the back of the safe was another little glass bottle. I started feeding them to Joe, hoping for the best. They worked for a day and a half, then the yelling started up again. I was ready to start yelling, myself. Sixteen hours on the bridge, trying to bring my inventory books up to date, wrangling with the Bosun about what work the crew should be doing, playing nursemaid to poor Joe who, I was convinced, was dying.

I had Flags blink over the bad news. The weather had moderated somewhat. There was some delay before a lengthy message came back.

FALL OUT OF STATION TO PORT. STEER 270 DEGREES, TRUE. MAINTAIN EXACT SPEED, EIGHT KNOTS. WE WILL STEAM PARALLEL TO YOU ON YOUR PORT SIDE. WE WILL FIRE LYLE GUN WITH MESSENGER LINE ACROSS YOUR AFTER DECK. YOU WILL PULL ABOARD OUR LINE, MAKING IT FAST TO YOUR NUMBER FOUR HATCH CRADLED BOOMS. WE WILL SEND OVER BREECHES BUOY TROLLEY TO WHICH YOU WILL SECURE STOKES BASKET WITH PATIENT SECURELY LASHED IN. HE WILL WEAR A LIFE PRESERVER. ACKNOWLEDGE YOUR COMPLETE UNDERSTANDING. ENDS.

We acknowledged, and things started to move. The Bosun and his crew were sent to stand by on the after deck. I went down to get Joe ready. The messman helped me dress him in his warmest clothes and tied a life jacket on him. Then we lashed him in the Stokes Basket and carried him out to the after deck.

All during this time I was regretting this scheme of the Navy. With the trolley line made fast to the two ships, what if both ships rolled away from each other at the same time? The line would part like a piece of thread and Joe would be drowned. It all seemed foolhardy, yet something had to be done. In my anxiety, I had underestimated the US Navy.

When we got down to the after deck, there was the destroyer, close on our port beam. The Old Man was carefully conning our ship, maintaining course and speed. The Bosun had rigged up a four legged bridle which he shackled to the rails of the stretcher. We were ready. **Blam!** Their Lyle gun fired. The messenger sailed right over our number four booms. The Bosun and Chips pounced on it and pulled in their big line and the trolley line and block. The line was made fast to the port boom. A round turn and two half hitches, with the bitter end married to the standing part and secured with a piece of marlin. The trolley block was made fast. Looking over at the destroyer, their plan became clear. They had fastened a snatch block well up on their midships structure. Their end of the line was rove through it. About twenty sailors were tailed onto its end. As the ships alternately rolled towards and away from each other, they would run up and down the deck, keeping a constant tension on the line and preventing it from parting.

By God, I thought, *they have one clever Chief Boatswain's Mate over there.*

We lifted Joe and the stretcher up onto the bulwarks. Poor Joe looked me in the eye and whispered,

"I always knew that you didn't like me, but this is a hell of a way to get rid of me."

He was wrong but there was no time to answer. I waved to the destroyer, and away he went. The Navy sailors moved up and down the deck according to directions from their Chief. Others were heaving smartly on the trolley line. Joe was sailing along through the air for all the world like he was on a ski lift. As he neared the destroyer, a heavy swell swept up under him just as the line was being slacked off. By God, he sailed right through that big wave. Then willing hands snatched him aboard.

My hat is off to them. They were **real** seamen. We released their gear and resumed our station in the convoy. The destroyer hauled way out on our beam to resume her escort duties.

After that, we had an uneventful Westbound passage on the Southern Route for low powered steamers. Rough, rotten weather all the way to New

The author at the tiller of #1 Life Boat
off Scilly, 1943

York. I heard months later, that Joe recovered, but permanent damage had been done to his heart by the Rheumatic Fever. His seagoing days had come to an end. As the log book says, So ends this day.

When the ship goes 'wop' (with a wiggle between). And the steward falls in the soup tureen. Why, then you know (if you haven't guessed.) You're Fifty North and Forty West.
Rudyard Kipling

-32-

WARTIME GADGETS ON MERCHANT SHIPS
(BAD ONES)

In the early days of the war, the German submarines took a fearful toll on our merchant ships. Our East Coast from Maine to the Caribbean was the graveyard for hundreds of ships, many of them tankers coming and going from Gulf ports or the Caribbean. Southbound ships were diverted from their regular route, Hatteras to the Northern tip of the Bahamas, outside of the North setting Gulf Stream, to inside of the Stream, right along the coast in shoal water. Northbound vessels continued to ride the Gulf Stream from Key West to Cape Hatteras. It was the thinking that they'd be safer closer to shore. Not so. Tankers were blowing up and sinking every night. From Hatteras South, their masts were sticking out of the water like telephone poles. People sunning themselves on the beach at Miami had a ringside seat. Ships were being torpedoed right in front of them. Men were being burned alive and drowning while they watched in the balmy sunshine.

The same thing was taking place on the tanker route from Venezuela and the Aruba refineries to the Florida Straits. The North Atlantic from Nova Scotia to the Western approaches to the British Isles was equally bad. Hundreds of thousands of tons of shipping were being sent to the bottom every month. It was a fearsome, black period in the war at sea.

Then, first a trickle, then a torrent of new ships were sliding down the ways. Shipyards on both coasts and the Gulf were launching them daily. Foremost among them were the Liberty ships. These slow, ugly tubs saved our necks. I sailed on seven of them, four of them as Master. I came to know them as the palm of my hand. I had first hand experience with their many good points and their very many bad points. Their major fault, far and away worse than all the others was their lack of power. They were equipped with an old fashioned triple expansion engine of only twenty-five hundred horse power. Steam turbines were much more efficient and powerful, but they were all ear marked for the mammoth construction program under way for Naval vessels. So a deliberate decision was taken by the Planners for new construction. They took a British hull design and modified it by placing three hatches forward of the midships housing and two aft. The triple expansion engine, with its three cylinders and relative ease of operation and maintenance, was, of necessity, the only choice. The ship, as finally designed, was of 10,500 Deadweight tons, meaning that the combined weight of stores, fuel, and cargo would actually weigh 10,500 long tons. This translated into up to 9,500 tons of actual cargo, provided the cargo was dense enough to fit into 475,000 cubic feet of actual cargo space. The Planners tried to take into account the fact that these ships would be coming home empty, with none or very little ballast. For this reason, they made the entire bottom double hulled, called double bottoms for the fuel oil. This placed the center of gravity very low and consequently they were very stiff. *Stiff*, meaning that the ship had tremendous righting ability. They could and did, roll thirty-five degrees with no danger. The pendulum effect of the low center of gravity would snap her right back upright. This made them good ships in a seaway, but they sure were uncomfortable. It was said of them, *They'd roll in a heavy dew.*

As the submarine sinkings intensified, and as more and more ships were launched and thrown into the breech, so did the Planners intensify their efforts to combat the attacks. A slew of contraptions began to make their appearance on the Libertys. I had the misfortune to be shipmates with several of them.

The first of these nightmares to come my way was Mark 29. An innocuous name for a full blown disaster.

I was assigned to a Liberty then being built at the South Portland shipyard in Maine. After the usual sea trials, we sailed her South to Boston. The usual complement of twenty-eight Naval gunners reported aboard. The Gunnery Officer told us that he would shortly have several ratings reporting aboard, and that they would be specially trained to handle the Mark 29 gear which was going to be installed. He had no idea what this new device was, but said that he expected further instructions.

The next morning a horde of civilian Navy Yard workmen came aboard and set to work on the forward deck. Right up on the bows, on either side, they welded a weird looking pair of frameworks hanging above the bulwarks. I didn't know it then, but they were similar to those installed on minesweepers. Then, on both sides of the forward deck they welded enormous reels. They were probably eight feet in diameter. Fair leads and chocks were burned into the bulwarks. Wire cables were running all over the place. The whole apparatus was utterly confusing.

All this work took a couple of days. The third day a big Navy barge came alongside. The first things hoisted aboard from it were two strange things called Paravanes. One was suspended from each of the frames hanging over each bow. Then came great rubberized cables, five inches in diameter. These were wound round and round the big reels, filling them completely.

That afternoon back came the Gunnery Officer with his additional men. He and I sat in the saloon after supper and as best he could, explained the working of this diabolical assembly. It went something like this: The Paravanes would be launched from both bows. Because of their construction, fins or something, they would swim straight out from each bow at right angles to the ship. They would be tethered on a long stout cable. In some unknown way the Gunnery Officer could set the depth at which they would swim. All this was to be accomplished while the ship was in the open sea, going full speed ahead. Then, the big rubber cables were to be hauled out and one end made fast to the tethers holding the two Paravanes. When it was all rigged there would be four of the big rubber cables on each side of the ship, parallel to the ship and as long as the ship. The whole business would swim along just under the waves. This sounded to me like an impossibility to do under winter seas conditions. Then he hit me with the clincher. The outer cable was full of sensitive microphones. The next two were full of high explosives, and those nearest the ship were to act as stabilizers to keep the whole mess in place just under the water. Whoever dreamed up this monstrosity had never sailed the North Atlantic in the winter. In fact, it's safe to say they never, ever saw salt water.

The idea was that a torpedo would pass close to the outside cable. The microphones would hear it, and in some way, arm or cock the trigger on the next two cables. Then when the torpedo passed near the first one, it would explode, blowing up the torpedo, thus saving the ship! The second explosive cable was supposed to do the same for a **second** torpedo!

I sat there, speechless.

"Lieutenant, is this your first trip to sea?"

"Why yes, I was a school teacher in Ohio."

"You've got your hands full this time. That contraption is a full fledged disaster in the making."

"I wouldn't be too hasty in your condemnation. The Navy has assured me that it has been thoroughly tested, and will definitely protect us from four torpedoes."

The following day we sailed for Halifax, as usual. We slipped up the coast with a few ships and came to anchor in Bedford Basin to await the formation of a convoy to the United Kingdom. In due time we got our sailing orders. We and another Liberty, also equipped with Mark 29 were assigned to *coffin corner*, the last ship in the outside column. I think that the Planners were hoping that a submarine would take a shot at us just to see if the damned thing would work.

The following morning we got underway. It was a bitter cold wintry day. As soon as the convoy was settled down, we got the inevitable signal from the commanding escort, *STREAM MARK 29.* The Gunnery Officer was running frantically from one side of the forward deck to the other. Under his arm was a thick, bound note book. Every few minutes he would consult it, then race around spouting more orders. His crew had run our cargo runners off the winches and were rigging up their own cables to them. Steam hissed, winches clattered, the Paravanes went over the side—more yelling, Navy kids boiling all over the place. What a performance!

At last the whole mess was overboard. The Old Man and I stayed clear of the whole show. We were up on the flying bridge making uncomplimentary remarks, deliberately letting the Navy signalman overhear us. He'd spread the word the minute he went below.

We had been so intent on watching the action that the Skipper hadn't been paying too much attention to keeping proper station in the convoy. By God, we were a mile astern of the convoy! He flew into the wheel house, grabbed the engine room phone and chewed out the engineer on watch.

"What the hell's the matter down there? Get back on, Full Ahead."

When the engineer could finally get a word in, he shouted back,

"We are going Full Ahead, sixty-six revolutions."

The light dawned. Those damned rubber cables had cut our speed through the water and we were fast falling astern. Sure enough, here came an escort vessel blinking at us and shouting through his bull horn.

REGAIN STATION. CLOSE UP IMMEDIATELY.

More cursing and yelling between the bridge and the engine room. Right on cue, up came the poor Gunnery Officer, dirty grease all over his fine uniform. The Old Man immediately turned his wrath on him. The whole crew, mine and Navy were eating it up. Right in the middle of this confrontation the signalman said to the Gunnery Officer,

"Sir, look over the side."

We all peered over. My God, all those big black cables were slithering along the top of the water like long black sea serpents. The Gunnery Officer was off like a shot. He went racing up the fore deck. More yelling, twisting dials, and snapping switches in the black box. It was no use. They refused to sink. By this time it was sunset, or would have been if there was any sun. The sky was a dirty gray, the wind was making up out of the Northwest, and the ship was starting to roll and pitch. We were in for another North Atlantic winter gale.

Black night came on. The wind commenced to moan in the rigging. We were sure in for it. There we were, all alone, the convoy up ahead, some-where. It wasn't a good feeling. I came off watch at eight o'clock. Before going below, I took a turn around the decks, checking the hatch tarps, lashings, and the life boats. Feeling uneasy, I went into the saloon for coffee. The Gunnery Officer was in there poring over his Mark 29 book. He looked so forlorn.

"I can't find the reason, Mister Mate. Those cables should be slipping along well beneath the surface."

"Cheer up, Lieutenant, it will come to you."

The uneasiness persisted. I sat on my bunk thinking, *There must be a better way to make a living.*

Fully clothed, I dozed off. A furious pounding on my door brought me to my feet. The Second Mate burst in, his oilskins streaming.

"Better come and look at the port life boats. And you'll need your oilskins. It's howling a full gale."

Struggling into my oilskins, I lurched out on the starboard side of the boat deck. The ship was rolling something fierce. I crawled aft on the boat deck. Coming around the corner, the full force of the gale fair took my breath away. It was as black as the inside of a sheep's stomach. (What nut ever said that?) I crawled along, hanging onto the railing welded to the midships house. Right abreast of the port boats I bumped into the Second Mate.

"What in the hell is the matter, Mister?"

"Well I'd better let the Gunnery Officer tell you."

"What happened, Lieutenant? What's the matter?"

"It's difficult to explain why but all four cables have been washed aboard and are draped over the two life boats. There is no reason to be alarmed, though. I'm pretty sure that they are disarmed. I pushed all the correct buttons."

A dim form bashed into me. The Old Man!

"Now then , Mister, get those things off those boats. Quickly now."

"But Captain, those things are full of high explosives."

"Hm, quite so. Lieutenant, **you** get them off. We'll be over on the lee side in case they blow up and kill you."

Give the Gunnery Officer his due. He and his men toiled until daylight. No good. Those cables were too heavy and too wound up in the boats and the davits. When dawn broke, gray and gloomy, we were all alone on the sea. Not a mast in sight. The shrieking gale was whisking the tops of the waves off into scud.

The Old Man was on the bridge with me.

"Mister, we're in some hell of a mess. If this storm ever blows itself out, some damn fool of a German is going to come along in a submarine and sink us to hell and gone. Send for the Lieutenant."

Up crawled the Lieutenant. He was not only tired and discouraged. He was also very seasick.

"Now, Guns," says the Old Man, surprisingly in a gentle voice.

"It's not your fault. You just have a jerk for a boss. Right now he is probably sucking up martinis in some plush Admiral's club. Now I don't care how you do it, but I want those cables jettisoned at once. Go!"

Guns was half way down the ladder before the Old Man finished. He backed up the ladder and said, sheepishly,

"Please, Captain, what does jettison mean?"

"Throw the damned things overboard, landlubber."

How he did it, I'll never know, but do it he did. They used sledge hammers and cold chisels. At last the whole mess was cut adrift and sunk forever.

With the loss of that drag we were able to make knots. The convoy finally appeared over the horizon, and we resumed our old spot in coffin corner. When we reached England, British Naval demolition experts came aboard and untangled the mess on the port life boats. Good riddance!

TORPEDO NETS

These unholy inventions were a little improvement over Mark 29, but not much. They were supposed to work like this:

In addition to the regular cargo booms which were cradled two to a hatch, the Planners installed four more booms, two adjacent to the fore mast and two more back aft at the mizzen mast. On these Liberty ships the masts were massive steel things. Way up on the top of them, running thwartships, they were capped by well braced cross trees. These new booms were pinned to the deck on either side of the masts. They stuck up vertically, way above the cross trees, and were secured to the cross trees in big iron collars welded to the ends of the cross trees. These additional booms were much longer and heavier than our cargo booms, which were big enough. Topping lifts were attached to the top of them and led down to our cargo winches. Stowed on each side of the fore deck was a big pile of steel netting.

To rig this nightmare, or, *Stream Torpedo Nets,* in Navy parlance, a man in each cross tree would release the collars, give the boom a push with his feet while sitting down and holding on for dear life. If he timed it just right, when the ship rolled, and the man on the winch slacked off right with him, the boom would commence lowering over the side. When it was horizontal another winch on the forward deck would hoist up the netting and pull it out to the end of the boom. The next step, according to the Planners' script, was to start heaving on a winch back on the after deck. This would draw the net along a cable stretched between the two booms. **Presto!** there we were, safe and sound, steaming along, protected on both sides by the two nets, which hung down well below the surface. Or so the Planners said in their instruction book. *This sad tale ain't over yet.*

Let us suppose that the ship is steaming along with the nets rigged out. A submarine comes along. A nasty torpedo leaps out of its tube and heads directly for the ship. It strikes the net and is entangled in it. The torpedo doesn't explode, being set for impact. What next? On page six, paragraph five of the Planners manual, they neatly solve the problem. Welded to each boom within easy reach, are long levers. Just pull them and away go the nets to the bottom with the torpedo still in it. Pretty slick, huh? The catch was that it didn't always work out that way. I have been told that more than one ship made port with a live torpedo still hanging in her net. She wasn't too welcome, either, and was usually banished to a remote anchorage while the experts gingerly extracted the torpedo.

I had a little different experience with this gadget. Our ship was equipped with it, but for some unknown reason, we weren't ordered to use it on our outbound trip to North Africa. However, homeward bound, just as soon as we cleared the Straits of Gibraltar, the convoy Commodore blinked over and ordered us to, *Stream Torpedo Nets*. We got them overboard, alright, but just as with the Mark 29, we couldn't keep up with the convoy. Just before dark an escort came back and told us to, *Retrieve Nets*. We couldn't. The wind and sea had freshened considerably, We were in ballast and rolling heavily. The ends of the booms were dipping under the waves. Back to the Planners' book. Hah, there was the answer, sort of an afterthought, a minor footnote. *Torpedo Booms should **not** be streamed nor retrieved if the vessel's roll exceeds so many degrees.* As we were already exceeding the limit, we were stuck. If we tried to hoist them, when we got them half way up and the ship rolled, they would crash against the crosstrees, possibly flinging the man up there overboard or crush him to death. I neatly solved that one without the Planners. We gave a good yank on those long levers and away went the nets to Davey Jones' locker. It was three days later before we could hoist the booms.

Maybe this invention saved a few ships, I don't know, but I sure **do** know that they were hell to handle.

SUBMARINE DETECTING GEAR

This one was a real beaut. The way I figure it, the Planners cooked this one up without really trying, sort of with one hand tied behind them. Just wanted to keep their hand in, or maybe they had a quota to meet, and were desperate.

Two big microphones were welded into the ship's hull, one on each side, forward of midships. They were placed well below the waterline. Wires ran from them to a fancy control box up in the wheel house. Two great gongs were installed, one on the port bulkhead of the wheel house and one on the starboard.

The way it was supposed to work sounded great. The port side microphone would pick up the sound of an approaching torpedo. The portside gong would go off with a sound that would wake the dead. Whereupon the Mate on watch would take *Evasive Action,* for God's sake! What should he do? Turn to port? Starboard? Mess his drawers? The trouble was, the damned thing was too sensitive. The Bosun could drop a sledge hammer on the deck and off both

Liberty ship with torpedo nets

British Liberty ship with torpedo nets deployed

All Alone in the North Atlantic

gongs would go off. The Planners had allowed for this. There was a sensitivity dial on the box for just such a problem. It never worked. We fixed it by plucking a hand full of wires out of the black box.

Now, if those Planners had the sense of a hen, they'd have given us sensible gadgets. Like a good Gyro compass, or that greatest of all contraptions, the greatest since the Chinese invented the compass, Radar! Then there would have been no more poor ships wandering off course, slamming ashore with good seamen drowned and good cargoes lost. And they wouldn't have gone bashing into each other in fogbound convoys.

Sometimes I wonder how we ever won the war. I wonder, too, what kind of jobs those Planners returned to. Probably driving cabs in Brooklyn. Even then they're over rated.

-33-

WARTIME GADGETS ON MERCHANT SHIPS (GOOD ONES)

I've done more than my share of scoffing at the many crazy gadgets tried out on the wartime Liberty ships. Now it's time to tell of two gadgets that, when used together, were, and are, absolutely the greatest aids to navigation since the magnetic compass, the marine sextant, and the chronometer:

RADAR AND THE GYRO COMPASS!

Late in the war, I was assigned as Mate to a Victory ship then being built in the shipyard at Baltimore. These Victorys, now just coming off the ways, were a great improvement over the Liberty. Although they both had the same basic hull design, dead weight, and cargo capacity, there the similarity ended. First, they had a raised focsle head which tended to make them dryer. They had steel Pontoon hatch covers on the forward deck which made them safer. They had modern, powerful, fast, electric powered cargo winches which made cargo handling more efficient. And last, God bless them, they had a 6500 horse power steam turbine which could scoot them along at better than sixteen knots. Now here was a ship.

I spent every day during her construction on board learning every thing that I could about her. At last she was launched, the SS Smith Victory. We went out on her sea trials, and after those Libertys, she performed like a yacht. Now this was more like it. We would go to sea like bloody oriental potentates. The very next day after she was turned over to the company, we received peculiar orders. We were to proceed in ballast to Savannah, Georgia, there to be converted to a troop transport capable of carrying 2500 troops. I wondered why this wasn't done while she was being built, and only realized, much later, that the war in Europe was fast coming to an end, and we were being converted to carry troops from Europe to the Far East for the invasion of Japan.

Off we went, down Chesapeake Bay, out the Virginia Capes to the Lightship and headed South for Hatteras and Savannah. There was just one small fly in the chowder. We still had the magnetic compass. I would have thought that on such a fine modern ship the Planners would have given us a Gyro. No dice.

We arrived at the Savannah Lightship, picked up a pilot and proceeded up the Savannah River to Mingledorf's shipyard. We immediately went into drydock where we remained for about two months. Once more, shipyard workers descended upon us, and just about tore the ship apart. All the lower holds were converted to troop quarters. In the 'tween decks, great kitchens were built, a hospital, doctor and nurses quarters, officers quarters, and quarters for the twenty-seven permanent Army staff. They even put a piano aboard.

We all had a fine time in Savannah, swimming at Tybee Beach, eating all that marvelous Southern cooking. It was a welcome interlude after all those North Atlantic convoys.

It seemed to me that the conversion work was proceeding too slowly. Then one fine day the war in Europe was over. The work force was doubled, three shifts were put on, and things started to fly. One morning the Second Mate said that there were a bunch of workmen installing something up on the bridge.

"That's odd," I muttered. "We don't need any changes up there to carry troops. Let's go up and have a look."

Glory be to God! They were installing a Gyro compass. The Master compass would be in the chart room, a repeater on each bridge wing, and another repeater at the wheel for the quartermaster. I was so happy that I felt like dancing.

A couple of days later, the Second Mate remarked that still another gadget was being installed in the wheel house. Up we went again. Just to the left of the wheel was a large, strange looking machine. It had a round glass face set into it and numerous switches and dials.

"Say, Mr. Foreman, what's that thing?"

"Why, Mister Mate, I'm surprised at you. This here is the latest model Radar.

By God, I thought, *another damned useless gadget.* I had heard, vaguely, about Radar that the Navy had, but had never seen one or even talked with anyone who had. In my ignorance, I pooh poohed it as just another useless gadget dreamed up by those mysterious Planners in their ivory towers. Dope that I was, I studiously stayed away from the bridge. Even when the Second Mate announced that the manufacturer's representative would come to the ship the next morning to instruct us in its use, I snorted,

"You go listen to him. Not me."

Sailing day arrived. We had orders to proceed at best speed to Le havre, there to load 2500 troops for the Orient via the Panama Canal. We had a compass adjuster aboard. Because of the extensive alterations to the ship. the magnetic compasses would have to be readjusted. This was a common proce-dure, and would be accomplished by slowly steaming in a circle around the Savannah Lightship. A Mate would be stationed out on the bridge wing at the

Pelorus, which was a dummy compass surmounted by sight vanes (Only this time the sight vanes would be mounted directly on the Gyro repeater.) As the ship slowly steamed around the Lightship, the Mate would call out its bearings to the adjuster stationed at the magnetic Master compass. Then he would add or subtract magnets stored in the base of the binnacle. A straight forward, simple piece of business.

Pretty soon we raised the lightship and started our circling. Before we got half way around, the sky got as black as night, and we were hit by one of those fierce summer thunder storms. The poor Third Mate, out on the bridge wing was soaked to the hide in an instant. The compass adjuster suggested that I call him into the wheel house.

"No way. He won't melt."

"No, but he can't get proper bearings. He can't even see the Lightship. I'll just flip on this Radar, here, and use it to take the bearings."

"You'll what? Use that gadget? This I've got to see."

Well, I saw. My eyes pretty near popped out of my head. Built into the Radar scope was still another Gyro repeater, so he was getting true bearings of the Lightship all the time. Each time the lighted sweep revolved, it left a lingering blip on the scope. The circumference of the scope was the Gyro repeater from which a true bearing was obtained. There was even a little crank which, when turned, propelled a tiny white light out along the sweep. When the light reached the blip, a glance at the indicator above the crank gave the distance off in yards, and it was accurate to the yard! Wow! Was I ever converted to the true faith. This was no gadget. It was a miracle come to rest on the bridge of this fine ship.

The storm passed. The adjuster and the pilot left and we headed for the Great Circle route to Bishop's Rock, the Southern entrance to the English channel. I spent the whole trip camped at that Radar set. Every day, every night, I was looking for ships to take bearings on. We made Bishop's Rock ahead of schedule, and I got a good bearing. Then the fog set in. We couldn't see beyond the bow. No matter, we had the gadget to end all gadgets, and away we went at sixteen knots. A radio message informed us to anchor inside the Goodwin Sands for orders. The Goodwin Sands, in the English Channel has the same dismal reputation that Nantucket Shoals and Diamond Shoals at Hatteras has a graveyard of ships. We did ourselves proud, though. We crept into a perfect anchorage, thanks to Radar.

This story was about Radar and the Gyro compass, but just to finish this voyage, we loaded 2500 troops at Le Havre and headed for the Panama Canal. Half way there, the atom bombs were dropped on Japan and hostilities were at long last, at an end. We were rerouted to New York to disembark the troops, which we did.

The previous experience had an undesirable after effect. I had become so dependent on my new toy that I became lax in the exercise of good seamanship. I came to rely too much on a mechanical device. My snoot was constantly stuck in the Radar hood to the almost complete exclusion of ever looking out of the pilot house windows. It almost proved my undoing.

Peace had come and I had been promoted to Master, this time back on a Liberty.

We had just finished discharging grain in a North European port. Orders were received to proceed to Fowey, England, there to load a part cargo of china clay for Philadelphia. I had never been there before. It is a small yachting town in Cornwall, on the Southeast coast. Off we went. The weather was lousy, but usual for the English Channel. Rainy, misty, poor visibility. We were going along on dead reckoning, heading in for the mouth of the Fowey River. As usual, I was camped on a stool peering at the Radar scope. Nothing was showing. No coast line, no ships, nothing. The Mate came into the wheel house and dolefully announced that visibility was zero.

"No problem, Mister, this little beauty can see for twenty miles. I'm right now expecting to pick up the pilot boat any minute."

The sweep kept rotating round and round. Nothing showed. I thought, *Everything's ok, though. Can't fool this gadget.* The Mate burst in shouting, "Captain, you'd better go Full Astern. The shore is just ahead."

Full Astern we went, and thank God, in time. That damned Radar looked as if it was working but it wasn't. I learned my lesson fast. There will never be a substitute for careful plotting and prudent seamanship.

-34-

THE LIBERTY SHIP AT HER BEST

One time during the war I made a *Pier head jump.* That's seagoing lingo for a last minute, emergency personnel replacement on a ship about to sail. I had just paid off a ship as Chief Mate and gone home. The day after I arrived, the phone rang. It was my nemesis, or better, my keeper, the Marine Superintendent. He turned on his usual persuasive charm. A ship was laying in Baltimore fully loaded and ready to sail. The Mate had either gotten sick or disappeared, I've forgotten which. I was ordered to catch the earliest train out of Boston and join the ship. This guy was something. He had worked this stunt on me before, and I have no doubt that he was working it on other officers, daily. That's probably why he was so good at it.

Damn it to hell. My two kids were growing up without me. I had become practically a visitor in my own home. But, as you have probably guessed, off I went, bound for Baltimore and still another lousy Liberty ship.

Rattling along in a day coach, I tried to take stock of myself. I was making good money. With overtime, I frequently made more than the Skipper, so, financially, I was in pretty good shape. My health was excellent. I had also been very, very lucky. A lot of my friends and shipmates were dead, either bombed, mined, or torpedoed. A lot of my childhood friends who had either enlisted or been drafted in the other Armed Forces had been killed, reported MIA, or maimed. Still, I was paying a price insofar as my personal life was concerned, but, I rationalized, so were millions of other young men. And a lot of them, unlike me, were dead.

Putting all this philosophy and speculation aside, I staggered out into the Baltimore railroad station. I flung my suitcase, sea bag, and sextant into a cab and directed the driver to the Western Maryland piers, down on the waterfront.

The cab wasn't allowed inside the gates so down the pier I walked, all loaded down with my luggage. Up ahead I spotted my new home. Just another tired old Liberty. They all looked alike, rusty peas in a pod. Something about her seemed odd. Instead of the accommodation ladder leading down to the pier, a short brow led from the pier **down** to the ship. My God, had she sprung a leak and was resting on the bottom? There was no sign of life about her decks. No watch on the gangway; she seemed to be deserted. I spotted one of the Navy Armed Guard boys meandering down the deck.

214

Hey, where is everybody?" I hollered.

"We're due to ship the merchant crew tomorrow. What few that are left are ashore, I guess."

"Where's the gangway watch?"

"Right here. I am."

"Is your officer aboard?"

"Yessir, he's asleep."

What kind of ship is this, I fumed. I stumbled down the brow to the midships deck and found my way up to the Mate's room. It was empty. Dumping my stuff on the bunk, I went looking for the Gunnery Officer. Sure enough, he was sprawled out on his bunk asleep.

"Wake up, Guns." He slowly came to life.

Who are you?"

"I'm the new Mate. Where is everybody? Where's the Old Man? What kind of cargo is in this ship? Is she overloaded or resting on the bottom?"

"Well, Mister, since the old Mate left, the crew, what few there are, come and go as they please. The Captain is staying at the Lord Baltimore Hotel. He has company, if you know what I mean."

This last was said with a leer.

"Guns, lend me your flashlight."

"Sure, it's over there on the desk."

The Armed Guard was equipped with dandy flashlights that you could stick underwater. Armed with his flashlight, I headed back to the gangway.

All ships are marked on each side, amidships, with what is known as the ship's Plimsoll Mark, named for an Englishman who devised this universal mark to show the legal limit to which a ship could be loaded. Every ship in the world is so marked, and God help the person, or persons, who loaded deeper than the allowable mark. First, the hull and cargo insurance could be declared null and void, and second, her Master and anyone else involved could be heavily fined and lose their tickets.

When the war came along, all ships were painted gray, and they deliberately painted over the Plimsoll Mark. Some nonsense about giving aid to the enemy. That didn't matter, though, because when the ship was built, the shipyard had chiseled the Mark right into the steel hull.

I went out on the dock and lay down on my stomach. I knew right where the Plimsoll Mark was located, right opposite the second porthole of the crew's mess room. The water was pretty dirty but that couldn't be helped. I rolled up my sleeves and stuck my arm under the water. I started looking just under the surface, feeling with my other hand for the chisel marks. By God, I got down way over my elbow before I found it.

This Plimsoll Mark had been cleverly contrived. There is a Winter, North Atlantic mark a Winter mark, a Summer mark, a Tropical mark, and

215

uppermost, a Fresh Water mark for loading in fresh water. The lowest mark is the WNA mark, Winter, North Atlantic, which was where we were going. Somebody was guilty as hell, but it wasn't going to be me that took the rap.

I went back uptown to the Coast Guard headquarters. Since the War began the Coast Guard had taken over all the functions of the Steamboat Inspection Service, administered by the Department of Commerce. They ruled the roost as far as merchant ships were concerned. By the time I got there I was steaming. No sleep on the train, no breakfast, and now it was way past dinner. I was shunted from one office to another. Each time that I launched into my complaint they'd cut me off and send me to Lieutenant so and so. Finally, I arrived in an office where he heard me out. He looked like a high school kid; dead white skin, delicate pale hands, all poured into a beautifully fitting, tailor-made uniform. It seemed unreal for a kid to be wearing one and a half stripes.

"Now then, Mister Mate," says he, looking down from his great height of supreme authority,

"Maybe you have overlooked the obvious fact that there is a great war raging out there. In wartime we always take calculated risks and some that aren't calculated."

My safety valve blew off with a roar.

"Me, you little pipsqueak! Why, I've been booting these rotten ships across the oceans ever since 1931. When 1939 came along, and you guys took over, things started to get hairy. Who convoyed us? You and your outfit? No Sir. The British and Canadians took care of us, some of us at least. I'm one of the lucky ones. I'm still here. Where were you? In grammar school, that's where. Your damned eternal inspections, your nit-picking insistence on, *Regulations*. It was us that took care of the cargo handling gear and the life boats. It was our engineers that kept the plant going. Not you, Mister. What about your damned regulations, now? You're willing to sweep them all under the rug and send a ship into the North Atlantic in the middle of the winter, dangerously over loaded. I'll be on that ship, Junior, and some seventy odd more souls. And where will you be? Parked behind that desk on your skinny backside telling some other poor dope that, *There's a war on, don't you know?*"

Oh, I poured it on. All the frustrations that I had hoarded came rushing out. I really made an ass of myself, especially as I was talking to myself. This young squirt was probably as dedicated, in his way, as I thought that I was.

Anyway, he terminated our discussion by saying that I could see Commander so and so. *Now,* I thought, *I'll get somewhere. Go right to the top. A Commander will certainly see things my way.* Shortly, I was ushered into the august presence. God Almighty! He was younger than the Lieutenant. But he was slicker, though.

216

"Mister Mate, I'll send an inspection team down at once. We do not, repeat, <u>do not</u>, send ships to sea in an unseaworthy condition, war or no war."

"Fine, Commander. When can I expect them?"

"First thing in the morning. 0800 hours suit you?"

I left, feeling somewhat mollified, and returned to the ship. As I boarded the ship it dawned on me that I had forgotten an important step in reading the Plimsoll Mark. The marks are on both sides of the ship. Should the ship have a list, the reading on one side would be different from that on the other side. Proper procedure called for a stage to be rigged on the offshore side and the Mark read and averaged with the other side. As soon as I got aboard, I got the Gunnery Officer to loan me a couple of his kids, and we rigged a painting stage over the offshore side. Armed with my trusty flashlight, over the side I went. I'll be damned if the ship wasn't on an even keel. Both sides read the same. Wow! Were we ever overloaded. I went up to my room to see of I could find a cargo manifest or a loading plan. Sure enough the loading plan was laying on the desk. I unfolded it and started studying it hatch by hatch. By God, we were loaded with solid iron. Several thousand tons of steel railroad rails, hundreds of tons of rail spikes, splice plates, rail car wheels and axles, spare parts for locomotives. Godfrey, we were a floating railroad. A fine cargo to go thrashing across the Western Ocean in mid winter.

Wearily I refolded the cargo plan. Now for some supper. I was starved. Entering the saloon, I met the saloon messman. He looked half drunk, or hung over, or both.

"What's for supper, Mess?"

"Fried eggs and potatoes. Are you the new Mate?"

"Damned right I am, and if you don't have a clean white coat on by breakfast, I'll fry you right down the gangway, and tell the Steward that goes for him, too, if he ever shows up."

I was half through my eggs when a man walked through the door.

"Are you the Mate?"

"Yep. Who are you?"

"I'm the Captain of the tow boat alongside. We are shifting you over to Cottman's heavy lift pier."

"Now, just a minute. We don't have steam up and I don't even have a crew to take the lines in.'

"I know. Your Agent has sent a shore gang to handle your lines, and I have a second tow boat on the way."

"Why are we shifting, Captain?"

"Damned if I know. Maybe they need this berth."

And shift we did.

I felt foolish parading around on the bridge of a dead ship while the tow boats pushed us over to a long open pier over which two enormous heavy lift cranes towered. In no time we were tied up. I checked our moorings carefully, because as deeply laden as we were, if a sudden wind broke us adrift, it would be difficult to stop her. There was nothing more that I could do so I hit the hay. I could use the rest.

The next morning things seemed to be close to normal. The whole steward's department was back on board. The black gang was down below getting ready for sailing day. Most of the deck gang had trickled down from the Union hiring hall. I set the Bosun to work lowering the booms and battening down the hatches for sea. I wondered where the Skipper was, then put him out of my head. I had a lot to do. We hadn't received our sailing orders, yet, but for all I knew, the Old Man could be on his way to the ship with them. Stores to check. Meet with the Purser, assign watches—where the hell were the Second and Third Mates? Some well organized ship!

About mid morning I stopped for coffee. In the saloon I met the Chief Engineer and the First Assistant. During a lull in the conversation, I heard some sort of commotion out on the forward deck. Looking out of one of the port holes, I was astounded to see one of the shore cranes hoisting aboard a draft of twelve by twelve timbers. Now what? Up forward I went. A gang of men were laying out the timbers on both sides of the deck.. Four welders were welding big pad eyes to the deck. Up over the side came a great sling load of big turnbuckles and lengths of chain.

"Who is the boss here? What's going on?"

My voice was drowned out by the rumble of a locomotive pulling a string of flat cars out onto the pier. Each car had either a locomotive or tender on it. *It can't be. Not on this ship!*

Just then an Army Captain bustled onto the scene, shouting orders and waving a sheaf of papers.

"Captain, what's going on?" I demanded

"Out of my way. We're loading four locomotives on the forward deck and four tenders on the after deck."

"Oh, no, you're not," I snarled. "This damned ship is almost under water, now."

By God, where was that Coast Guard Inspection team? Down the gangway I flew, heading for the nearest phone. Furiously, I dialed the Coast Guard.

"Give me Commander so and so."

"Sorry, he is out in the field and won't be available for the rest of the week"

"Out in what field. I am the one that's out in the field...left field. Let me talk with that Lieutenant, his assistant."

"Sorry, but he is with the Commander."

I was hopping up and down with rage and frustration. I slammed the phone back on the hook and stormed out of the booth—and ran right smack into a blinding apparition, dripping with gold braid. Four stripes on his shoulder boards, scrambled eggs all over the visor of his cap. Hah, at last, the Old Man. Only he wasn't so old. Probably about my own age. Quickly I spilled out my tale of woe.

"Captain, we've got to do something. We'll be going to sea like a damned submarine."

Nothing I said seemed to faze him.

"Oh, we'll be all right, Mister. Besides, it's too late. We're sailing just as soon as the deck load is secured."

Right then, I threw in the towel. If I could have done so without losing face, I would have packed my bags and quit. Maybe that's what the previous Mate had done.

All four locomotives were landed on the fore deck and were secured by chains and the big turnbuckles which, in turn, were shackled to the pad eyes welded to the deck. The same thing took place with the four tenders on the after deck. We were so deep in the water, that you could just step overboard. We resembled a loaded tanker, the only difference being that tankers were supposed to set low in the water when loaded.

We were ready to sail. The lashers were all ashore, a tow boat was alongside, and the Bay pilot was on the bridge. I was just about to give the order to take in the brow when the Army Captain jumped out of a jeep and hurried aboard. He had a big, loose-leafed book under his arm about as thick as a phone book.

"Here you are, Mister Mate. These are the lubricating instructions for your deck cargo. Several pails and drums have been secured on your after deck. This schedule of daily greasing **must** be adhered to exactly. We wouldn't want these locos to arrive in anything but perfect condition, would we?"

"Oh, dearie me, no, Captain. Where are the diving suits?"

"I don't understand."

"Listen and listen good, Captain. Once we get to sea, the entire forward deck will be taking green water aboard. The same goes for the after deck. It will be a miracle if all the deck load doesn't go overboard long before we get to wherever we're going."

He looked kind of crestfallen.

"Cheer up, Captain. It's not your fault. If they do go over the side, just send the bill to Commander so and so, care of the Coast Guard. So long and give my very best to all the Generals.

All hands, fore and aft, the old familiar cry echoed through the ship. I went forward to take in the lines, the Bosun at my heels. While we were waiting, I gave him some strict orders.

"Bosun, this ship is loaded way too deep, and a lot of water is going to come over our bows. I want all the mooring lines stowed below. Take off all the hatch ventilators and lash them between the winches. Strip all the cargo booms of their guy tackles. Stow them below, too. Don't swing out the boats. Leave them in their chocks and put round turn lashings on them. Put extra lashings on both accommodation ladders. Cement shut both hawse pipes and make sure that the turnbuckles on the devil claws are snugged up. Clear the boat deck of any miscellaneous stores. I'll want life lines rigged on both the forward and after decks. We have about twenty hours down to the Virginia Capes, so keep all hands at it. After you have finished and sent the hands below, call me, and you and I will start on the focsle head and work our way aft to the poop, making damned sure that we are battened down and secure. This is going to be a wet voyage. Can do?"

He shifted his chew and said, "Aye, Mister." He'd do.

And so we sailed. The ship was slow and sluggish. I went to the bridge to stand the rest of my watch. The Old Man was toasting his shins against the wheel house radiator and chewing the fat with the pilot.

"How goes it, Mister? Getting everything lashed down?"

"Yes, Captain. I've got all hands working so we'll be all set before we stick our snoot outside."

"No need for that, Mister. We're going down to Lynhaven Roads and anchor to wait for a convoy."

Now he tells me, after I had authorized a fortune in overtime.

The next day we dropped anchor in Lynhaven Roads, a fine natural anchorage just inside of Cape Henry. There were dozens of ships anchored all around us, all waiting to join an Eastbound convoy. The deck gang were kept busy checking all the lashings. I had the other two Mates at it, too. I know that they all thought that I was being an old woman, but I kept them at it. I had a very healthy respect for the Western Ocean in the wintertime. I warned the Steward and Chief Engineer to make sure that there was no loose gear that could go shooting around, smashing things up.

The next day we got a blinker message for the Old Man to go ashore to the convoy conference. I had Flags hoist the *Launch wanted* flag, and away he went, dripping gold braid as usual. I swear, he slept in full uniform.

He returned late in the afternoon, loaded down with the usual stack of instructions—Convoy signals, zig-zag diagrams, radio listening schedules, etc. Both he and I were *Old Timers,* and it was all too familiar. I was very pleased that he and I were hitting it off so well. We had never met before, but we had many mutual acquaintances in the Company. We had both been with the Line for some time. Him longer than me. In fact, he had started as a company cadet. This steamship company had been one of the few that had had a peacetime policy of carrying their own cadets, so he had served his time well, and was a good seaman.

Late that afternoon up came the anchor, and off we steamed out between Cape Charles and Cape Henry, bound for Southern France, Quickly, we fell back into the routine of convoy life--maintain station, strict blackout at sundown, me, as usual studying the other ships through the binoculars, comparing their rig to ours.

We were headed Northeast, up towards the Great Circle route. After the first day, the winter seas started to make up, and as we gradually bore more toward the Eastward, the Northwest winds hurled the seas against our port quarter. They were also breaking green over our bows, and as I had predicted, were flooding down the forward deck waist high.

The first thing to carry away was the box containing the lubricants for the locos. Over the side the whole shooting match went. Good riddance. Nobody could live on the forward deck, anyway. Back aft, it was just as bad, if not worse. I worried about the gun crew who were quartered all the way aft, under the poop. They were a young, green, devil may care bunch, and were forever running back and forth, not using the life lines. It had become a game with them to see if they could outrun a broaching wave. I kept after the Gunnery Officer to stop them. He tried, but never did succeed, entirely.

We were about two days South and East of Newfoundland, as I remember it. The weather had moderated, temporarily. I was in the wheel house standing my usual four to eight watch. It was about four-thirty in the morning and black as pitch, no moon and overcast. You couldn't see two ship lengths. My eyes were getting tired searching for the ship ahead. The windward wheel house door opened, and in came the dim form of Flags.

"Mister Mate, would you step outside? I'm hearing a strange noise."

I followed him out onto the port bridge wing, and crawled after him into the twenty millimeter gun tub. The gale had died down considerably. By God, I've never heard such a noise, sort of a loud screeching. It sounded as if a giant hand was scratching a blackboard. It fair tore my ears off, and it seemed to rise and fall as the ship rolled and pitched. The pair of us were hanging over the splinter shield, trying to locate where it was coming from. It definitely was coming from the forward deck. We crossed over to the starboard side and listened again. Nothing. It came only from the port side. Maybe it was one of the locomotives coming adrift. I thought, *If we're lucky, it will hurl itself over the side and we won't have to get half drowned or squashed securing it.*

Dawn comes late in the wintertime, and I was busy getting the ship back onto her proper station. Flag signals were coming from the Commodore.

CLOSE UP. TAKE PROPER STATION. TRUE
COURSE TO BE MAINTAINED.

It was the same every morning in every convoy. I was so occupied that I didn't notice the Old Man out on the port wing. He came running into the wheel house, shouting,

"Mister, don't you hear that noise?"

"Sure, Captain. I've been listening to it for the last two hours"

"Well, you'd better come out here and look."

We crawled into the gun tub, again. Oh, my God! The bulwark was cracked wide open and was opening and closing as the ship worked. The ungodly noise continued unabated.

After the war, we all heard tales of Liberty ships breaking in two. Various theories were put forth. One seemed to prove that the steel used in their construction had either too much, or too little manganese in it, and this caused the metal to crystalize and fracture in cold weather or cold water. Another held that they were driven too hard in heavy weather, trying to keep up with the convoy being more important than prudent seamanship. I don't think, though, that overloading was ever advanced as a possible cause. Needless to say, I have my own theory.

But, at the time that it was happening to us, we were unaware of Libertys breaking up at sea. I sailed in several of them and always felt, and still do, that they were ruggedly constructed and very seaworthy.

The Skipper scribbled out a message for Flags to blink over to the Commodore, telling him of our trouble. I asked the Old Man to relieve me and raced for the crew's messroom. **All Hands. Bosun, unlash the life boats. Uncover them and swing them outboard. Make sure the plugs are in. Rig the boat ropes. Remove the heavy weather lashings from the life rafts. Tell the steward to get any men off watch out of their bunks. All hands to keep their life jackets with them. Have all hands put extra warm clothing on. The deck gang to wear oilskins.** Then I roused out both Mates and told them to check the contents of the boats, especially water.

Back to the bridge I went and reported all this to the Captain.

"Guess what, Mister. The Commodore wants to know if we are seaworthy. How the hell do I know? Do you?"

"No, Sir, but at least the crack hasn't gotten any worse."

Flags came into the wheel house with another message from the Commodore.

FALL OUT OF CONVOY AND PROCEED, BEST POSSIBLE SPEED, INDEPENDENTLY TO HALIFAX. ESCORT WILL MEET YOU.

The Old Man almost had a stroke.

"Best possible speed," he spluttered. "What the hell does that mean? Damn his Limey soul. Quartermaster, come left, easy. Half Speed Ahead.

Here we go, Mister. "

We fell out of the convoy which soon disappeared over the horizon. A terrible, desolate feeling came over all of us. We were so alone. And making less than five knots. Talk about a sitting duck. I pulled the lookout down from the crow's nest and stationed him on the bridge wing. The Third Mate took the wheel, allowing the helmsman to act as an additional lookout. Guns had all his men at battle stations, and they, too, were on the lookout. If a sub ever spotted us we were cooked.

Then a strange thing happened. The crack stopped opening and closing. Both the Old Man and I were both of the opinion that the reduction in speed had done the trick. We breathed easier—but not much. I was scared to death and I wasn't the only one.

We went along like that all the way to Halifax. Nobody went to bed, just napped in our clothes wherever we happened to be. The weather, for the first time in a thousand years remained perfect. Slight seas and just a light breeze. Unheard of in the Western Ocean in midwinter. It wasn't until we raised land that a Canadian corvette came out to meet us. They blinked over,

WELCOME. FOLLOW ME.

And we did, right into Bedford Basin where we dropped the hook. Safe and sound at last. It sure was a great feeling.

The steward did himself proud that night. A turkey supper with all the fixings, even mince pie.

I was awakened before daylight by the crash of something colliding with us. It was the first time in a long while that I had taken off my clothes and really let go. Still in a stupor, I managed to drag my clothes on and stumble out on deck. It was freezing cold and dark. My first thought was that some ship had dragged her anchor and drifted down on us. I had visions of smashed life boats, propeller and rudder gone, holed below the waterline. I had become the consummate pessimist. That's the way my head was working back in those bleak days.

Hearing voices up forward, I slid down the ladder to the fore deck. There was some sort of large craft tied up on the port side. Men were running around on her deck throwing heaving lines up onto our deck. I bumped into the Third Mate.

"What's going on, Mister?" (He had the anchor watch.)

"Mister Mate, that's a floating heavy lift derrick, here to remove the locos. "

"Well, God bless me, Mister, that's the best news that I've had since I arrived in Baltimore. In fact, it's the only good news. Good riddance. They never should have been loaded in the first place. "

Well, now, things were looking up. I went back midships to the saloon. The messman was dozing in the Captain's seat.

"Mess, where's the coffee?"

"Right in front of you. Help yourself."

One of these days, I thought, *I'll fix this bird's clock. That is if he doesn't poison me, first.* And he would, too, in a minute. I wasn't too well liked on this cruise ship. No matter. The big thing was that we were getting rid of those locomotives.

"What's for breakfast, mess?"

"The usual."

I should know better.

The Skipper appeared for breakfast, and he, too, was overjoyed when I gave him the news.

"Mister, without the deck cargo, and if we don't have serious structural damage. we shouldn't be here too long. What's for breakfast?"

"Don't ask," I muttered.

Right after breakfast I went back to the forward deck. Canadian workers were releasing all the turnbuckles holding the locos down. Others were rigging hoisting slings. In short order the hoisting engine huffed to life and the first monster swung out over the side. The derrick barge was shifted forward, abreast of number one hatch, and the second one went over the side.

I felt a tap on my shoulder. It was the Old Man. He had two civilians with him. He introduced them. One was from the American Bureau of Shipping. The second one was from some Canadian Government Agency.

"Mister, if you will open number three hatch, these gentlemen want to assess the extent of our damage."

I blew my whistle for the Bosun and told him to open up the after end of number three. When it was open, we all piled down the ladder into the 'tween deck. The Bosun sent down a couple of cluster lights. Our guests prowled around for a long time, constantly making notes. I, too, stuck my nose between every frame, studying both the frames and the shell plating for signs of fracturing. They were a very thorough pair. They scraped every weld clean. After what seemed to be a long time, up the ladder they went. Nosey me, I asked them what the verdict was. They answered that they would be in touch with us as soon as they had made their conclusions. And off they went in their launch. There was nothing to do except wait it out. I put in the rest of the day prowling around the ship, sticking my snoot into everyone's business but my own. To tell the truth, I was uneasy. I didn't subscribe to premonitions, but I had a big one. About what? I didn't know. I only knew that I had a strong feeling about something ominous. Best to put it aside. Easier said than done.

At supper my appetite deserted me. The Old Man sat down opposite me and polished off a huge meal. Belching contentedly, he leaned forward and

Her maiden voyage

peered at me.

"Out with it, Mister. Something is bugging you. What is it?"

"Captain, I wish that I knew."

"Cheer up. We are going to get a clean bill of health. Things looked pretty good to me, down there in number three.

"Yeah, they did to me, too, but I just can't shake this feeling."

"I've got just the cure for you. Come on up to my room. I've got half a bottle of good Rye."

My heart wasn't in it, but I went along. We had two or three good snorts, but I was poor company.

"Good night, Skipper. Thanks for the good booze, and thanks, too for your concern."

The next morning I was up forward as usual. A gang of longshoremen had topped number three hatch booms and were shifting cargo in the 'tween deck away from the port side shell plating. Our guests of the previous day were down in the 'tween deck again. About mid morning a gang of ship repair men arrived in their work boat. They proceeded to hoist aboard the biggest turnbuckles that I had ever seen. They were as big in diameter as a five gallon pail, and three or four feet long. Welders were welding enormous pad eyes on deck abreast of number three hatch. The same thing was going on down in the 'tween deck, on the port side. When all the turnbuckles were in place, straddling the cracked area, they were simultaneously tightened by pneumatic wrenches. Believe it or not, little by little, the ship was dragged together. Heavy stiffeners were welded in place. Some fine piece of work.

While this was going on, I noticed that the heavy lift barge, with the two locomotives, was still alongside. I went looking for the superintendent.

"Say, when are you going to remove the two locos from the starboard side, and the four tenders from the after deck?"

"We're not removing anything. As soon as the welders finish, and the work is approved by the ABS man, we'll be hoisting the two locos back aboard."

"Well, I'll be damned to hell and gone. Here we almost broke in two, out there, now we are right back where we started."

I moaned and ranted to everyone that would listen to me. I practically got down on my hands and knees to the Old Man.

"Mister, we'll be OK. These people are experts. Trust them."

I have never been so frustrated in my life. One voice crying in the wilderness.

Well, they did it anyway. Hoisted the damned things aboard, chained them down and away we went, in another convoy. I hate to admit it but we crossed the Atlantic without incident, steamed through the Straits of Gibraltar to Marseilles where we discharged our floating railroad. Then we steamed back home where I promptly paid off.

My luck had held, in spite of my pessimism and dire predictions. It was still holding, for the ship sailed on her next voyage to Murmansk with another Mate, and was torpedoed and sunk.

-35-

FANCY NAVIGATING

One time early in the War I was Mate on a new Liberty ship. The Old Man was a cantankerous, irascible, tired old New Englander, but he and I were good friends, though. I guess it was mainly because we were both *peacetime* sailors, men who had been sailing before the war.

We had just returned from yet another North Atlantic trip. A lousy, miserable trip like they all were becoming. Fearful storms all the way home, made bearable by the solace that the submarines lurking in our path found it just as intolerable.

Most of the crew had paid off and had gone seeking greener pastures, of which there weren't any. I had called the Union hiring hall for replacements, and was now draped over the bulwarks at the gangway waiting for them. From bitter experience, I had not ordered a Bosun. Instead, it was my intention to look over the A.B.s and make my own choice. A good Bosun was prized above gold, and could make life more bearable for a tired, harassed Chief Mate.

The sound of steps on the gangway aroused me from my musings. A snow white officer's cap appeared, then a gorgeous, tailor made, form fitting uniform. One and a half gold stripes glittered in the sunshine. The face under the cap matched the uniform. Perfect features, blinding white, even teeth, a pencil thin mustache. By Godfrey, he looked just like Errol Flynn!

Painfully conscious of my wrinkled old khakis and battered, salt stained cap, I straightened up.

Good morning. I'm the new Second Mate. Is the Captain aboard?"

"He sure is. I'm the Mate."

We shook hands, after which I showed him his cabin and escorted him up to the Old Man's quarters. The Captain answered my knock clad in nothing but a tattered old bath robe.

"Well, Mister Mate, what have we here, an actor?"

Knowing the old devil pretty good by now, things weren't starting too well for our new Second Mate.

"Well, don't just stand there, come in. You, too, Mister."

He flopped down at his desk and motioned us to the settee.

"Now then, you're our new Second Officer, are you? Tell me, what experience have you had?"

The Second had to reluctantly admit that this was his first job as an officer. Both the Old Man and I were completely ignorant of what he then told us. It seemed that the new ship construction was sliding off the ways so fast that crews couldn't be found for them. There were just so many of us pre war men, and that number had been substantially reduced by the German submarines. Therefore, the US Maritime Commission had opened schools for both officers and seamen. They had also cut in half the time required for an original license. Where, before the war, an Able Seaman had to show three years discharges to sit for a Third Mate's ticket, now he only needed eighteen months. And by showing two and a half years instead of five, he could sit for a Second Mate, Original ticket, which this man had done.

He told us that the school was in New London, Connecticut. The number one priority of the school was to turn out graduates **fast**. Never mind all those tedious logarithms, solving spherical triangles, and astronomy, etc. Just teach them how to use a sextant, and how to use a new book of tables called Ageton's. It could be assumed that the students were already capable seamen, and they were.

The Old Man ran out of questions and dismissed us. When we got outside the Second asked me where the ship's sextant was kept.

"Ship's sextant? I never heard of such a thing. Mine's up in the chart room, right alongside of the Old Man's."

"Strange, they told us at school that the Government was supplying each new ship with a Navy Mark something or other, because you can't buy one anymore."

"Well I'll be damned. Let me ask his Lordship."

I banged on his door again. This time all he had on was his skivvies.

"What is it this time?" he snarled.

"Captain, do we have a ship's sextant?"

"Who wants to know?"

"The new Second Mate."

I explained what the Second had just told me.

"Well, yes we do, as a matter of fact. It's over there in the bookcase. You tell that young squirt that I'll skin him alive if anything happens to that sextant."

Boy, oh boy. The poor Second Mate sure was starting off on the wrong foot. And his fancy uniform only made matters worse. In peacetime ship's officers only wore a uniform cap with the Company's house flag as its insignia. This poor guy looked like Lord Nelson to the Old Man, who only had one rusty brown suit to his name. Me, too.

In all the hustle and bustle of loading cargo, shipping a new crew, storing the ship, the Second and Third Mates were farthest from my mind. I had the Third Mate checking all the life boat gear, the life rafts, fire extinguishers, making sure that every man in the crew had his life jacket and that he knew where his Fire and Abandon Ship station was. I put the Second Mate to work rearranging all of our charts, and we had drawers full. In wartime you never knew where you might be going, so the Captain had really stocked up. This was a big mistake, as I soon was to find out. The Old Man had stuffed them into the chart table drawers helter skelter, and only he knew where to find them.

I popped into the chart room one morning, and was pleasantly surprised. The charts had all been sorted and neat, typewritten labels were affixed to each drawer, listing its contents.

"Damned good work, Second. Now we can put our hands on any chart in the world, practically at a minute's notice. That's a job that needed doing. Now I tell you what. I've asked the Gunnery Officer to stop at the Hydrographic Office while he's ashore today, and pick up all the latest Notices to Mariners. Then you can use them to bring up to date our Light List and charts."

In due time the ship was fully loaded. I had picked a middle aged Norwegian as Bosun, and he was proving out well. As soon as the longshoremen finished loading a hatch, and had dropped the main deck hatch beams in place, he was right there with his crew, spreading the three tarpaulins wedging the battens tight, securing the cross hatch battens, and lowering the booms. I had posted the sailing time at the gangway and in the messrooms. Sea watches were set, and we were waiting for the deck cargo to be secured. The Bosun had two men at the gangway, ready to pull it up as soon as the last carpenter went ashore and the Captain, Gunnery Officer, and Sparks returned from the convoy conference. The Third Mate had tested the telegraph, steering gear, whistle, and was out on the dock reading the ship's draft.

At last the Old Man and his entourage came striding down the pier in strict order of rank. Sparks, of course, was last. Believe it or not, there is a rigid, unwritten protocol that governs life on a merchant ship. We don't have any written rules like the Navy, but what we have are forged in steel and never, never broken, as you will soon see. Being unwritten and never spoken about one would wonder how we learned them. I guess that was by some sort of osmosis, absorbed through the pores. For example, if an A.B. had to go up to the bridge, he would pause with his head just above the top step of the lee ladder. Unlike the Navy man who would then say, *Permission to come on the bridge, Sir,* Our man would remain silent. The Mate on watch would, of course, immediately spot him, and growl,

"Well, come up. Speak up. What do you want this time?"

Frequently he would be deflated when the A.B. would drawl,

"The messman just made fresh coffee. Want a cup?"

Back to the business of getting underway. The Captain, the pilot, the

Third Mate, and the quartermaster would be on the bridge. I was on the bow with half of the deck gang, the Second Mate on the stern with the other half.

"Single up, Mister," shouted the Captain.

Turning aft, he repeated the order. We pounced on the offshore lines, flinging them off the bitts. Three round turns on the windlass niggar head. Finally, only two lines held us to the dock. The command came to let go. We were off on another voyage to God knows where.

The Skipper would remain on the bridge until the pilot was dropped, and the convoy formed up. Frequently this took several hours.

The Captain stood the Second Mate's first midnight to four AM watch with him. It wasn't a question of not trusting him. He just didn't know him, and being the prudent shipmaster that he was, had to be shown.

It was heartening to me when I relieved the Second, and he had gone below to write up the log, to hear the Old Man remark,

"Kid seems to know what he's doing. Where the hell did he learn?"

"Well, Captain, you have to remember that he has been an A.B. for a long time, and he has stood many a wheel watch in convoy, and he has sharp ears and eyes."

"Mmm, maybe you are right, but does he have to wear that fool uniform in the middle of the night? You would think that he's going to a wedding or something."

As tactfully as I could, I reminded him of an inflexible rule that existed before the war, and that had now gone by the wayside. No matter how crummy a tub it was, the rule held that all officers, both deck and engine, always wore a jacket in the saloon. They were khaki drill jackets, bought and worn only for one purpose. They were never seen anywhere except in the saloons of freighters. They didn't have lapels like present day uniforms. Instead, they had little stand up collars, two breast pockets, and brass buttons. An Engineer, coming straight from a sooty boiler, stripped to the waist and plastered with sweat would no more go into the saloon for the noonday meal without slipping into his jacket, than he would go down the gangway stark naked. No matter that he was filthy and stank like a pole cat. It was the rule.

"Well, Mister, you have a point, but he's so young. I'm going to bed. An old man needs his rest."

Balls! I've seen him keep the bridge for days, his head nodding on his chest while the convoy escorts raced back and forth, trying to keep us afloat and alive. I thought that the Second Mate was out of the woods but it was not to be.

Sailing in convoy had become a way of life. Slogging on alone back in peacetime days was but a dim memory. Now, it was second nature. All hands on the bridge always had one eye on the Commodore's ship. Invariably, he was a British Admiral, dragged out of retirement to do his bit. I shouldn't say dragged. Knowing the British like I do, it's safe to say that these old

Admirals leaped at the chance. And they sure knew their business. Thirty or forty years under the white ensign couldn't help but produce superlative seamen. He was charged with the internal organization of the convoy and always travelled in the lead ship of the center column. He would be accompanied by a large staff of British Navy signal men, radio operators, and navigators. All orders emanated from him. In the daytime by flag hoist or blinker light. At night by hooded Aldis Lamp, colored lights, and occasionally by radio. He was the boss.

It was the Commodore's habit, in all convoys, to hoist his noon position. As soon as his flags fluttered out, every ship in the convoy hoisted its position. There was intense rivalry throughout the convoy to see how quickly their position was hoisted. I rather think that there was some mild cheating going on. A scene stealing Master would have his binoculars trained on the Commodore's bridge. The second that he read the Commodore's flags, he would subtract a minute or two, and up would go his position. Small satisfaction, not to be stooped to by our doughty Skipper. The trouble was, though, that both he and I were struggling with five decimal place logarithms, out of Bowditch. The result was that we were usually amongst the last to hoist our position. I know that it was rankling in the Old Man's mind, as it was in mine. Now came the poor Second Mate's Waterloo. I mean that he was struck down in the flower of his youth, never to rise again. It all came about because of another of those age old, unwritten protocols. On most ships the shooting of the noonday sun was a solemn, nay, hallowed, tradition. Present would be the Captain, always the Second Mate, most times the Third Mate, and sometimes the Chief Mate. They would all gather out on the lee bridge wing with their sextants in hand. In measured order they would reverse their caps so that the visors wouldn't interfere. A certain amount of fussing with the sextant shades would then take place. (Totally unnecessary. Everyone had his own favorite shade.) Then the sighting. The Old Man would peer intently into his scope. He might grunt, *Good, sharp horizon.* Ever so carefully they followed the sun on its journey up to the Zenith. In unison their hands stopped turning the verniers. The sun was *'hanging'* for just a few seconds before starting down toward the West. The Old Man would mutter, *Local Apparent Time, Gentlemen.* Then they would all parade into the chart room in descending order of rank. By virtue of their superior rank, the Captain and the Mate would drape themselves over the chart room table. Lesser ranks had to make do on the settee. They would all set to work reducing their sextant sights to the sought after result—Latitude. The Bowditch tables were exchanged, again, in strict order of rank. Now comes the tricky part. Always, but always, the Old Man marked his position first. No matter that one of the Mates had finished his computations well before him. Rank ruled. One by one, first the Mate, then the Second, and last, the Third Mate would put their position on the chart.

There was method as well as tradition in this exercise. Anyone, even his Holiness, the Master, can make a mistake. If all the positions were clustered close together, the Skipper's was noted in the log book. If, and it has happened, his position was way away from the others, he, with good grace, picked one of the others as the official noon position. Usually, just to save a little face, he would mutter something like, *Must have been a little dirt on my horizon mirror,* or some such nonsense, and hurry below for dinner, The important thing about this is that the Captain's position is marked **first**.

Our second day out dawned bright and clear. After I came off watch at eight, I had a good breakfast and made the rounds with the Bosun. We peered into all the living quarters, inspected the gun crew's quarters back aft, and while there, checked the steering engine room. All OK. Next came the life boats. That took considerable time, and we didn't miss a thing. Those frail looking boats could be very important to us some dark night, or day, too. I happened to glance up at the bridge, and there was our new Second Mate, cap on backward, peering through the Navy sextant. All of a sudden he started walking toward the wheel house and chart room. By God, he was reciting poetry aloud. I heard, *One chimpanzee, two chimpanzees, three chimpanzees.* Oh, ho, he's counting seconds from the time of his sight until he could reach the ship's chronometers. **Smart boy.** He must have picked that up from some Mate while standing wheel watch. *This kid is going to be all right,* I mused,

"Well, Bosun, let's check the deck cargo lashings."

We finished up well before noon, so I decided to join his Nibs in the time honored ritual of the Noon Sight. Later, I wished that I hadn't. That time bomb that would blast that poor young Second Mate to smithereens was ticking loud and clear, but I didn't hear it.

The Third Mate didn't have a sextant so he was relieved and went below. The three of us paraded out onto the bridge. The Second broke tradition by leaving his cap in the chart room, but no matter. The reversing of caps rule was a minor rule. The performance began. Up, up, slowly, hang. The Old Man lowered his sextant and squinted at the Second Mate's back, already disappearing into the chart room.

"Mister, that boy seems to be too eager, wouldn't you agree?"

Not wanting to take sides I only grunted. When we got to the Chart room there was the Second, sprawled over the chart table. Bad form! A slight chill crept into the air. The Skipper busied himself putting his sextant back in its box. I was doing the same. The Old Man laid his little slip of paper with his sextant altitude on it on the Chart table and reached for the Nautical Almanac. He couldn't reach it. The Second was in his way.

"Excuse me, Mister."

"Just a second, Cap."

Cap?? The countdown was approaching blast off.

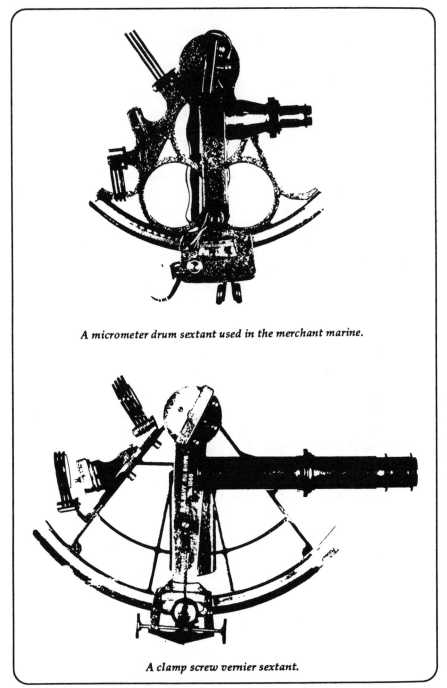

A micrometer drum sextant used in the merchant marine.

A clamp screw vernier sextant.

Two of the many types of sextants that have been developed over the years. The one at the top is just like the one I used in these stories. I bought the clamp screw vernier model before I got the dough to buy the other one.

"I make her to be right there, Cap," said he, snapping shut a little black book.

"You do, do you? And how did you arrive at that position, may I ask?"

"Nothing to it, Cap. This little book does all the work. It is called Ageton. I think that Ageton was a Naval officer, and he put these tables together just to save us all that work that you are about to do."

The countdown reached zero.

"A Navy man you say? Those overdressed dopes couldn't find their way out of the shower room. Let me see that book."

Ignition—Blast off! The Old Man picked up the little book by thumb and fore finger. Holding it well away from him in an exaggerated parody of carrying a dead skunk, he walked to the port hole, undogged it, and flung the book into the sea. Turning to me, he said,

"Mister Mate. It's time for dinner. Coming?"

The whole, sad episode was really a tragedy. That young man was most able, and showed all the promise of becoming a fine deck officer. The Captain, however, was bound tightly by a lifetime of inflexible tradition. It was the new generation taking over from the old. And take over they did.

The rest of the voyage was uncomfortable, to say the least. The poor Second Mate's navigation activities were at a standstill. Ageton was all that he knew. He stood his watches well, kept the ship exactly in her proper station and was absolutely correct in all his dealings with the Captain. It was all for naught. The Captain remained distant and cold towards him, and except for necessary ship's business, ignored him.

When I would relieve the Second, he would rehash the whole business. "Where did I go wrong? How can I make amends?"

My sympathies were all for him, but I had to tell him the brutal truth.

"The Old Man is what he is. He's never going to change, and that is sad. But he is the Master of this vessel. You have only one course open to you. When we get back, pay off and get another ship."

That's just what he did. I never saw or heard from him again, but I know that he did well.

As for me, the very day we docked I slipped ashore and bought an Ageton. The next voyage the Old Man caught me using it. The following day, I caught him using it.

Drawing on my fine command of language, I said nothing.
Robert Benchley

-36-

MURDER IN LE HAVRE

His name was Stanislaus Balnewik, and he was a Pole.
And he was, moreover, a stalwart man.
When I first met him, he was an A.B. on a Liberty ship. I was the Mate. It was wartime, and ships were being manned by many nationalities. In fact, we would take anybody who could tie a bowline, and quite a few who couldn't.
The Bosun had assigned Stan to my watch, the four to eight, and I gradually got to know him. I don't think that he knew more than twenty words of English—Yes, No, Starboard, Good, Bad, and of course, OK. He was learning fast, though. He had to or starve in the crew's mess.
Little by little during the dark hours when he was on the wheel, I came to know him and learn of his horrible past. Physically, he was typically Polish. Short, broad, extremely powerful. His hair was bright yellow. His face was wide and flat. His eyes were china blue, and quite without expression. When he looked at you, those blank staring eyes would give you the creeps. Well they might. He had lived an extraordinary life in his twenty-five, or so, years.
I had been kicking around the seas for several years before the war came along and spoiled things. In my wanderings in many ports and many countries, I had become quite adept at Pidgin English. Real basic stuff like, *Baby, you go along me? Me hungry. You ketchem fried eggs?* I could also cuss pretty good in Spanish, French, German, and my Arabic was fluent in consequentials such as, *Effendi, salaam. Arrest not me.* I had even learned a little Chinese from child beggars. *Please, no got mama, papa, no place to sleep.* Perfect Yangste River dialect. But no Polish. Sailors always manage to communicate, though, and gradually, as Stan came to accept and trust me, his story came out. Or as much of it as he would tell me.
When the Germans poured across the Polish border, Stan was home with his family: mother, father, and two sisters. He was a messboy on a Polish ship sailing out of Danzig. He and a young shipmate who he had brought home with him were out walking around the small farm that his father operated. Hearing the sound of loud voices, they sneaked up to the back of the house and cautiously peeked in the kitchen window. Both his father and mother were lying on the floor in a welter of blood. They were both dead, bayoneted.
His teen aged sisters were stripped naked, and were being fondled by

German soldiers. They heard enough to realize that the two girls would be taken to a German Army field brothel. Quickly they crawled back through the bushes and hid. They could hear the soldiers getting back into their truck. As they drove away, the two boys heard the crackle of flames as fire consumed the house and barn.

What to do? Those two kids were both terrified and stunned. Stan vaguely realized that Poland had been invaded. They decided to hole up by day and travel West by night. Their flight was an incredible story of pure luck. What food that they managed to scrounge came from kitchen gardens, raw turnips and the like. This went on for two weeks. Half starved, their clothes in tatters, their condition was desperate. Stan remembers that the only thing that kept him going was a vast, all consuming hatred of the Germans. Night and day his only thought was, *Keep going, Some day I kill Germans.*

Then came the night that they arrived on the bank of a good sized stream. Now what? They talked it over and decided to swim across. With their shoes hung around their necks, they struck out in the darkness. Only Stan made it. He never saw his friend again. He crawled up and down the bank until daylight, but in vain. Now sorrow mingled with his hatred, but on he went, night after night.

God only knows how, but he finally arrived safely in France. Kind people took him in, fed him, and sent him on his way. His goal was London. He had no idea of the vast scope of Hitler's ambition, but instinctively knew that he would find safe haven in England. France had not yet been overrun so he travelled safely to the Channel coast and bummed a ride on a cross-channel ferry to Dover.

By stages, he made his way towards London. He didn't speak a word of English, so it was inevitable that he was picked up and detained. All of England was apprehensive, and a foreigner jabbering in Polish was a prime suspect.

The police sent him under guard to London. Finally, realizing that he was a Pole, an interpreter set matters straight. Through the good offices of the Polish Legation, he was issued temporary British seaman's papers and found himself Ordinary Seaman on a British steamer. He made several trips across the Atlantic before his ship was torpedoed off the coast of Ireland. He was washed ashore half drowned and repatriated to England where he promptly shipped out in another freighter.

Bad luck again. Approaching Newfoundland in mid winter, his ship was torpedoed again. His luck was holding, though, and he was picked up by a Canadian Corvette and landed in Halifax.

Just about this time shipping companies in the States were experiencing difficulties in filling out crews. Pearl Harbor had come and gone and we, too, were at war. The seamens' unions, Immigration, and the Coast Guard, all gave a little, and Aliens, if qualified, were allowed to sail on our vessels. That's how I won Stan.

In spite of the gulf existing between focsle and bridge, he and I became good friends and shipmates. During those long hours when he was on the wheel, I helped him with his English, and he learned fast. Still, there was a mysterious gulf. I think that he regretted telling me what had happened in Poland, preferring to nurse his hate in private.

The time came when I was transferred to another ship. I managed, in spite of the Union hiring system, to take Stan with me, and promoted him to Bosun. Then, late in the war I got a fine new Victory ship built to carry 2500 troops. The only job open for Stan was ship's carpenter, so carpenter he became.

This trooper was the softest job that I ever had. She rated four Mates, so as Chief Mate, I didn't have to stand a watch. There was no cargo handling gear to maintain. All I had to do every day was to stroll around and look wise. We had twenty-seven permanent Army personnel attached to the ship—cooks, nurses, a doctor, and an entertainment staff. The Skipper, Captain Paul Mahoney was an old friend, and we got along like brothers.

Off we went, bound for Le Havre to load troops. The trip across the Atlantic was a joy. Slight seas, good food, plenty of sleep and getting paid to boot.

When we got to Le Havre the troops hadn't been completely assembled so we were to lay over an extra day. That morning I sent for Stan and asked him if he could make me a wooden grating for my shower. The tiles were slippery.

"Where will I get the wood, Mister Mate?"

That posed a problem. He had me stumped.

"Ho, Stan, I've got it. Down in number two 'tween decks are all those great ovens for feeding the troops. There are also several warming ovens that have wooden racks in them. Those Army cooks will all be ashore, so you just slip down there and swipe one of those racks. Why, you'll only have to cut it to size."

"You think good, Mister Mate. I go."

I guess that it is just as well that I didn't know what was going to happen down in that deserted 'tween deck. Nobody saw what happened so I can only speculate, especially as I was the first on the scene, or, to be more precise, I was the first after the participants.

About an hour later, I was sitting at my desk writing a letter to my son. God knows when he'd get it, but just writing it made me feel as if I was talking to him. A shadow fell across the page. I looked up. To my astonishment, there stood Stan. He had come in like a big, silent cat. His blank blue eyes were glittering like cold ice, and his big, powerful paws were clenching and unclenching like two vices.

"Stan, didn't you ever hear of knocking before entering? What's the matter with you? What are you trembling for?"

All I got was a stream of Polish.

"Slow down. Speak English."

His voice rose to a scream.

"I kill German. Dirty dog is dead. I kill him good."

"Where? Why? When? God Almighty, Stan, do you mean it?"

"Yes, Mister Mate. Now I need friend. I reach in oven for wood. Catch leg. German hiding there. I pull him out and kill him so."

And he raised those big hands and crushed them together,

Oh my God! What to do?

Stan, show me."

And down we went. The decks, thank God, were deserted. There he lay, his face all swollen up and contorted.

"Stan, I never saw this. You understand? Stuff him back in the oven. Never mind about the shower rack—and stay out of my sight and keep your mouth shut. Not a word to a single soul. Do you understand?"

When I returned to my room, the enormity of what I had seen, and how I had become an accomplice to murder overwhelmed me. Well, the die was cast. I'd sit tight and hope that Stan did the same.

I didn't sleep too good that night. I felt, in my bones that we were both in for big trouble. I have always been one of those dopes who had never gotten away with anything in my life. And I was the world's worst liar. Every time that I told a lie, my face would turn crimson, even my ears.

In the morning the ship was humming with activity. Two wide gangways had been rigged and troops were pouring up each of them. Army staff were racing around waving clip boards frantically, as they directed the soldiers to their proper hatches. I skipped breakfast and tried to make myself as inconspicuous as possible. Sometime about mid morning the saloon messman found me and told me that the Old Man wanted to see me. **Here it comes.** With dread in my heart I mounted the stairs to his office.

"Come in, Mister, you know Captain so and so, our Special Services Officer. And this is his Chief Cook, Sergeant so and so"

I nodded and backed into a corner.

"Now then, Mister. We have a problem. The cooks found a dead man in one of the warming ovens. Know anything about it?"

"News to me, Captain."

He peered at me out of his shrewd, down Maine eyes. He, too, had sailed for many years as Chief Mate, and knew very well that all Chief Mates knew about **everything** that went on. Every whisper of gossip or rumor found its way to the Mate's sharp ears.

"Hmm, well anyway, I've sent for some shore blokes. Meet them at the gangway and handle things. Make sure they take the body away. These here cooks just might fricassee him for supper. Hah!"

Sick Maine humor, I said to myself as I beat it out on deck.

As I approached the forward gangway, the Army sentry said,

"Mister Mate, a couple of men just came aboard. Told me that if I saw you, they'd like to see you in number two 'tween decks."

Boy oh boy, I said to myself. *Here it comes. Keep your big trap shut. Remember the old Army rule, never volunteer for anything.*

I made my way down through the hatch. Two officers were standing by the oven. A pair of feet, clad in broken, worn out shoes were sticking out. They introduced themselves, Army Intelligence.

"Now, Mister, what do you know about this, ah, incident?"

"Nothing, only what the Captain told me."

"And what was that, please?"

"That the Army Chief Cook told him that there was a dead man in the warming oven.

"And this was the first that you heard anything?"

"Yes."

"Well, it's all pretty straightforward. Obviously, there were two of them. Stowaways. Only one would fit in the oven. They fought. This one lost, and the other one is still hiding on this ship."

"Sounds reasonable to me," I said. (Oh Yeah?) "I'll have the ship searched immediately for the missing German."

"German, Mister? Why German?"

I had slipped up badly.

"Well, I just assumed..."

"We never assume. In our business it is always facts. And my men will search the ship."

"Yes, Sir. Anything you say."

And out I went. *There were two of them, and they fought. Phooy!*

They sent for a bunch of soldiers and searched from the double bottoms to the crow's nest. From the bow to the fantail. Nothing. Late in the day I saw the body being carried ashore.

After they had held up our sailing time for six hours, they quit. I met the two spooks at the gangway. They were dirty, tired, dusty, and discouraged. They gave me strict orders that if the missing stowaway turned up, to radio London. Then, just as they turned away, one of them turned back, and what he said just about floored me.

"By the way, we searched the body. He was an Estonian. They are stateless, you know. They are wandering all over the continent. Poor devils. They're harmless, you know."

An Estonian! Stan had strangled an innocent man. His hatred for

238

Germans had led him to the wrong conclusion. This affair had turned so tragic. What should I do? I paced the deck the whole night through. I tried to put myself in Stan's shoes, to think like he did. I couldn't. I, too, had been through a long war. I, too, hated the Germans, but not personally, like him. To me they were faceless, impersonal people, far away. Either under the water in their murderous submarines, or a speck in the sky, the sun glinting off their wings as they rolled over and went into their bombing dive. Who should I tell? Or should I tell anyone? It was so tempting to wake up Captain Mahoney, spill the whole story, and let him decide what to do, but I didn't. I've kept it all to myself, all these years until now.

We never heard another word. Death had become commonplace in Europe, even after the war ended. The Underground in France, for instance. Communist resistance fighters were butchering their erstwhile, Non-Communist brothers for control of France. Corpses were being fished out of the Seine, daily.

On the trip Westward toward the Panama Canal and the Orient, the two atom bombs were dropped on Japan and the war was at long last over. We received orders to divert to New York and discharge the troops.

I found myself avoiding Stan. The night before we docked I called him to my room and told him to quit when we paid off. He looked at me with tears running down his cheeks.

"You fire me, Mister Mate?"

"No, Stan, I just think it best that we part."

I never saw him again. I did hear, through the seamens' union, that he had quit the sea, applied for American citizenship, got it, married a Polish-American girl, and opened a Polish bakery. I hope he has learned to live with his awful past.

(Stan's name has been changed in this story.)

239

CAPTAIN PAUL MAHONEY

A HARDROCK, DOWN MAINE SKIPPER

Captain Mahoney was a good friend and shipmate of mine. I sailed with him as his Chief Mate, and from him learned a great deal.

He and I went ashore together, and at sea, we were in daily contact. He was a master story teller, and as we relaxed on the settee in his quarters, he would tell me fascinating stories of his lifetime at sea. They remain very vivid in my memory, and I'd like to share some of them with you.

Captain Paul, as we referred to him, was a native of Portland, Maine. He was born with the sea in his blood. Back in the early twenties he shipped out with the Eastern Steamship line. Eastern was a Coastwise Company that was headquartered in Boston. She carried both passengers and freight to every port on the coast from Baltimore and Norfolk to Bath, Maine, and Yarmouth, Nova Scotia. As a small boy, Captain Paul had watched their steamers round Portland Head and steam to their berth in downtown Portland.

Advancement, back in those days was a slow, arduous process. Only the best made it. Every one of their Masters and Mates were expert Pilots. They did all of their own piloting in and out of every port. They never engaged the services of tow boats, and docked and undocked in all kinds of weather.

Captain Paul slowly made his way up the ladder to Master. For several ears he served as Second Pilot and First Pilot on the overnight Passenger ships unning between New York and Boston. On these ships they didn't carry Mates. Instead they carried Second and First Pilots. Actually they were Mates and did all the piloting under the direction of the Master.

At last he made the final jump to Master of his own ship. He was given command of a tiny four hatch coastal cargo steamer, the S.S. Sandwich. By today's standards she was a midget. She was powered by a small triple expansion engine. Her boilers were coal fired. Her top speed never exceeded eight knots. Most of the time it was nearer seven. She ran up and down the coast winter and summer wherever cargo offered.

One cold winter day she was Northbound for Portland. Captain Paul kept calling for more speed. With any luck she would make port the day before Christmas. Most of the crew were down Mainers, and they, too, were anxious to spend Christmas at home. The coal passers turned to with a will, and the firemen shoveled furiously. Black smoke poured from her tall, skinny stack, and the whole little ship vibrated. Captain Paul figured that she was doing eight and a half, at least.

Course was changed to run in on Cape Cod Light. Without any warning a full Northeast gale pounced on them. It roared in on the starboard beam and layed her over until the gunnels were awash. Captain Paul went sailing across the wheel house until his big belly wedged him against the engine room telegraph. He shouted to the man on the wheel to come starboard twenty degrees. The little ship shook herself like a water spaniel, and, as she answered the helm, she slowly came back on an even keel. Now, though, it was even worse. In these coastal waters the depth is fairly shallow. This allowed the seas to make up quickly. And make up they did. The ship's cargo was mostly light and bulky stuff--cartons, barrels, bales, etc., so she was riding light. She immediately commenced pitching badly. Up and up and up her bow would go. Then she would roar down the back of the wave only to bury herself in green water all the way back to the bridge. Captain Paul realized that something had to be done, and that the only thing he could do was to slow her down and jog, an expression used by the New England trawler men. It meant that the ship wasn't going anywhere, just holding her own. Actually, she was hove to. This state of affairs didn't suit him one little bit. Portland he was bound for and by Godfrey, to Portland he would go! Back in those days, advancement in Eastern was so slow that all the Masters and Mates became intimately familiar with their ships. They knew how much weather they could take. They knew exactly how their ships would react in any kind of weather. They were superb seamen and ship handlers. Captain Paul was no exception. He could be sitting in his cramped stateroom, and the feeling coming up from his feet on the deck would tell him what the ship was doing--making leeway, her speed over the ground, and how she was taking the weather.

Now he commenced a series of maneuvers that on the surface seemed quite commonplace. He had to get the ship hauled around in the direction of Cape Cod without having her swamped by the huge seas making up from the Northeast. Little by little he reduced her speed until the seat of his pants told him that he could start easing her to port. The weather turned squally. One minute the gale would howl around the wheel house with the snow obscuring visibility to zero. Then the wind would die down and the snow would lift. Each time this occurred he would bear off to Port only to have to head her back into the wind whenever another squall hit. By repeating this over and over the ship was gradually approaching the Cape, or so Captain Paul hoped. His instinct told him that he should be sighting the light. Still another squall passed, and there she was, fine on the Port bow. Course was changed to Starboard so as to pass about five miles off. Unfortunately, the wind increased, reaching gale force again. The Captain intended to get a bow and beam bearing of the Cape which would give him the distance off when she was abeam. To explain: A

241

bearing would be taken when the light bore 45 degrees off the Port bow and again when the light was abeam, or 90 degrees off the bow. How so? If you will draw a line from the ship to the light when she bore 45 degrees, and then draw another when she bore 90 degrees, you will have created an isosceles right triangle in which the sides opposite equal angles are equal. This translates into the distance run between bearings equals the distance off when the ship is abeam of the light.

The little ship struggled all through the night, alternating between jogging, and then falling off to port whenever the weather permitted. Four different times the Mate got a good four point bearing, only to have the ship haul back to Starboard and commence jogging again. Finally, twelve hours late, she weathered the Cape and course was set for Portland Light. The weather was still bad, and the temperature was dropping. By the time she rounded Portland Head and entered the harbor, she was completely iced up. It was Christmas morning. Captain Paul ordered all hands and the ship's cook to turn to and chop off the ice. All four hatches were frozen fast in ice. The booms were frozen in their cradles, and the winches were covered in a sheath of hard ice. Even though it was Christmas morning, longshoremen were standing by on the dock when the ship tied up. They came aboard and pitched in with axes. It was estimated that four hours would see all the cargo discharged. They had counted on finishing by noontime. Alas, they didn't finish until supper time. Captain Paul and the entire crew never got a chance to leave the ship. Christmas dinner consisted of pea soup and bread.

At four P.M. watches were again set, nevertheless, all hands were kept on deck, battening down the hatches and securing for sea. At six-thirty Stand By on the engine was rung up, the lines were let go, and the little ship backed out of her berth and headed out.

As the ship rounded Portland Head, Captain Paul was again in his favorite position, big belly wedged firmly against the engine room telegraph. Course was set to the Northeast, direct to Yarmouth, Nova Scotia. The Captain heaved a big sigh and remarked to the man at the wheel,

"There's gotta be a better way to make a living," a remark that Skippers have been making ever since man first set sail in a log canoe.

-38-

CAPTAIN PAUL AT HIS PHLEGMATIC BEST

This story about Captain Paul was told to me by a fellow shipmaster and friend. At the time of the story, he was a quartermaster, or helmsman, on the S.S. Boston. The Boston was one of Eastern's crack passenger ships on the Boston-New York run. Mahoney was her Master, having been promoted, at long last, after several years on the little coastwise steamer, the S.S. Sandwich. One night the ship left New York, bound via the East River, Long Island Sound, and the Cape Cod canal for Boston. There were two ships on this run. The other ship, the S.S. New York, left Boston at the same time, 5 P. M. They were due in at 8 A. M.

These ships carried upwards of a thousand passengers and a fair amount of cargo. It was a killer of a run. Heavy fog, bad tides, heavy traffic, all took their toll of those hardy skippers. Two of them that I know of committed suicide from the strain. One of them went back aft of a Sunday morning, stepped up on the rudder quadrant, threw a rope over the awning spreader, tied it around his neck and stepped off! To maintain their schedule and dock on time, they had to make knots regardless of fog or traffic. Either that or be fired.

Eastern had a peculiar custom. It wasn't mandatory or anything like that. It was just an in-house custom. The Radio Officer took all the RDF bearings instead of the Mate on watch. The RDF, or radio direction finder, was located in the chart room, just aft of the wheel house. It consisted of a radio set with a loop directional antenna, which was rotated by a hand wheel under the set. A dummy compass was mounted on the face of the set. To operate it the dummy compass would be rotated and set to the ship's course, magnetic. A large arrow rotated around the dummy compass as the antenna wheel was turned. The operator would put on a pair of earphones and tune in to the station on which he wanted a bearing. All the lightships and most of the major lighthouses had transmitting sets, each with it's own distinctive call sign. He would then rotate the antenna, listening for the call sign. When he got it, he would continue to slowly turn the antenna back and forth, listening for the "null", the place where the signal faded out. At that point he would read the bearing from the dummy compass. This bearing was only as good as the course that the man on the wheel was steering. If he was off course three or four degrees, then the bearing would be in error by the same amount. It was for this

243

reason that the RDF operator was forever hollering into the wheel house,

"How are you now?"

"Right on, Sir," or,

"Two degrees to the right, Sir."

What with the operator trying to estimate the null just at the moment that the ship was exactly on course, it was nigh on to impossible to get a bearing closer than two degrees, and everyone knew this.

The Radio Officer on the Boston was a crackerjack man. He was also a first class practical joker. I know, for many years later, I sailed with him, too. His name was Dinty Moore.

These Eastern skippers were a hard case group. They had nerves of iron. Night after night, helling through the East River, Hell's Gate, Long Island Sound, and Buzzard's Bay in all kinds of weather. Threading their way through the Cape Cod Canal and Massachusetts Bay. Their responsibility was awesome. They were equal to it, though. Most of them were either Down Easters or Nova Scotians--phlegmatic, dour, but, oh, so able. I sailed for several years for Eastern as Mate and Master, and came to know and admire them. It was said, and not as a joke, that during Eastern's long years in the coastwise trade, that her vessels had collided with everything but the Bourne Bridge, spanning the Cape Cod Canal. My old boss, Marine Superintendent, Captain Roland Litchfield corrected that one night when he was Skipper of the Acadia, the flag ship of the Company. He rammed into the abutment of the bridge, backed off, and away he went for Boston. Docked on time, too.

One thing these hell for leather skippers never neglected to do, though. They sighted or heard every buoy or light ship. If they couldn't see or hear it, they stopped or circled until they did. Without exception, they identified each aid to navigation on their route. They were drivers and tough, but never foolhardy. They never forgot that they had several million dollars worth of ship and a thousand souls on their conscience.

Back to the tale about Captain Paul. The ship was racing along doing eighteen knots. Thick fog set in. They couldn't see the bow. It was late October, the worst month for fog in these waters. Night had come on and they were due to pick up a Lightship. I've forgotten which one. Captain Mahoney sent for the Radio Officer.

"Dinty, get me a good bearing on the lightship."

"Yes sir, Captain, right away."

Then came the usual,

"How are you now?"

"Right on, right on. Two degrees right. Right on."

Now clown Dinty appears. He came into the wheel house and with a straight face announced,

"Lightship bearing twenty-seven and one half, Captain."

His idea of an in house joke. To get a bearing correct to one half of

244

Another T2 tanker

a degree is, of course, an impossibility. Captain Paul pulled his head in from the window, shook the water off his head, and played along with Dinty's joke.

"Quartermaster, steer twenty-seven and a half."

The quartermaster, an old hand and now my friend, played along, too. "Twenty-seven and one half, sir, right on."

And of course, it is also an impossibility to steer closer than two degrees of the course, even in a flat calm. Everyone chuckled silently. Good joke. Shortly afterwards, there came an ungodly crash. The ship had sideswiped the lightship! Captain Paul pulled his head in from the window, again, and drawled,

"Damned good bearing, Dinty."

After circling the lightship and ascertaining that both vessels were seaworthy, with no serious damage, off they streaked. Got to make Boston on time.

CAPTAIN PAUL THE GOSPEL PREACHER

When I was shipmates with Dinty Moore, he told this story about Captain Paul. This incident also happened on the S.S. Boston.

The ship had two big focsles up in the bow, one for men and one for women. For the price of a ticket one could use them and save the cost of a room. The Captain received a strong letter from the office that a bunch of whores were booking passage every night and plying their trade. They, of course, never used the focsles. Complaints had been received from several straight-laced passengers and he was instructed to stop the practice at once.

This was right up his alley. He professed to be a strict moralist and would bore his officers with interminable sermons about how the country was going to hell. To listen to him, sex out of wedlock was the most grievous sin. The whole country was spending all it's time drinking and whoring instead of working hard and going to church twice on Sunday.

He took to roaming the public rooms and the dining saloon at all hours of the night. The trouble was, he didn't know how to spot them. Twice he accosted ladies that seemed to him to fit the bill, only to find out that they were respectable married women travelling with their husbands. What to do? Finally, he hit upon a scheme that seemed foolproof. He summoned all the bedroom stewards and delivered a rousing sermon. He knew that these stewards had more contact with the passengers than anyone else.

He urged them to come forward and help him banish these heathens from the ship. Not one of them said a word. Disappointed, he decided that he would roam the ship from bow to stern each night just before sailing. Maybe his shrewd, down Maine eyes, plus an assist from the Lord, would divulge the sinners.

His nightly searches produced absolutely nothing. Frustrated and cranky, he sat in his cabin one afternoon trying to think of a way out of his dilemma. A timid knock on his door roused him out of his reverie.

"Come in, he boomed."

The woman that entered was an Amazon. She was also the boss of the cleaning crew of women that cleaned all the staterooms, changed the bed linen, towels, etc.

"Well, Tessie, what is it that brings you up here?"

"Captain, I know where those, er, ladies that you are hunting for hide each time you make your afternoon search. If I tell you, you must never let on

246

S.S. Arcadia, flagship of the fleet

that it was I that told you. They tip the stewards pretty good, so they would kill me if ever they found out that I told you. Will you promise?"

"I promise, Tessie. Now tell me."

After Tessie left, the Captain rubbed his hands with glee.

"This time I've got'em," he chortled.

Promptly at four-thirty he went below to the main deck. As arranged, he met Tessie.

"Tessie, I want you to come with me. We are going to inspect the public bath rooms."

On these old ships, few, if any of the cabins had a bath. All they had was a big pitcher of water and a wash basin. Consequently, these public bath houses were large and commodious.

Down the alleyway they went, Captain Paul's big belly leading the way. They entered the first bath house. It was deserted. Not a single soul was in there. He peered around. Something wasn't just right. At first he couldn't put his finger on it. Suddenly, like a flash of lightening, it came to him. Every stall door was shut! He walked over to them and peered under the doors. He fully expected to see pairs of feminine feet. Nothing. No feet. He turned away, disappointed.

"Let's go, Tessie. We'll try the next one."

Suddenly he turned around, walked over to the doors, again, and one by one, flung them open. By God, there, standing on the johns, was a whole row of over dressed ladies of the evening! They looked like a row of hens perched on the roost for the night.

He had them escorted forward to the female focsle where they were promptly locked in. He and Tessie continued their search. By the time they were finished, they had flushed out another dozen.

As soon as they docked, they were carted off to jail. Captain Paul went back aboard well contented. What he didn't know was that they were all released by noon for lack of evidence. The first thing they did upon being released was to go back to the wharf and book passage on the Boston, due to sail that evening!

CAPTAIN PAUL AND HIS DISCIPLE (ME)

Years after these escapades, Captain Paul and I became shipmates. He was master of a large troop ship, and I was his Chief Mate. It was the best job that I ever had. The ship carried four Mates so I didn't even have to stand a watch. She didn't carry any cargo so I had no worries about either the cargo or the cargo handling gear. The ship had twentyseven permanent Army staff assigned to her; cooks, bakers, security personnel. We even had a Commissioned Officer whose title was Special Services Officer. That meant that he was in charge of entertainment. We even had a piano! We had a doctor and three Army nurses. All I had to do was stroll around and look wise. Some job! And I got paid for it, to boot.

In due time we shot across the Atlantic and loaded a full load of troops, twenty-five hundred of them. Among them was a contingent of WACS. These were female members of the U. S. Army.

A few days after we had got to sea, Captain Paul sent for me.

"Mister, we have a serious problem on this here ship."

"Is that so, Captain? And what might it be?"

"I'm trying to tell you, and I will if you will stop interrupting. There is fornicating going on, on this ship. Now, Mister, they can fornicate on the poop deck--they can fornicate on the focsle head--they can even fornicate down in the engine room, but by God, Mister, they will not fornicate on the bridge of my ship!"

"Why, Captain, that's impossible."

"No it isn't, Mister. They're up on the flying bridge all hours of the day and night. I repeat, Mister. It will stop, and you will stop it. Got it?"

"Yes sir, Captain, right away."

I had better explain that we were using the lower, main bridge. Up on top of it was the flying bridge. It consisted of a deck covered with a wooden grating. It was about ten feet square and contained a steering wheel, the master compass, an engine room telegraph, and a ship's telephone. Oh yes, and a General Alarm lever and another lever to blow the whistle. It was surrounded by a waist high canvas wind dodger. The Captain refused to use it. Claimed it was too cold and windy. I agreed wholeheartedly. As a sailor I have stood wheel watches on those old prewar Hog Islanders, and they had an open bridge. There you were soaking wet or freezing up there, completely exposed to the winter gales.

Typical Victory ship

Another Victory ship

Now Preacher Paul's problem had become my problem. What to do.
Should I dump it onto the Special Services Officer? That went against my
grain. It was up to me, but how? I thought and thought. At last the solution
hit me. It was so simple that I marveled that it took me so long to solve it.
I waited until the flying bridge was unoccupied, which wasn't often. Then I
went up and unlashed the canvas wind dodger, and threw it overboard. If
anybody took his pants off, now, he'd freeze to death.
The next morning I slid into my seat in the saloon. The Captain was already
there polishing off a stack of flapjacks.

"Well, Mister?"

"Yes, Captain. About that small problem up on the flying bridge. I
took care of it."

"You did? How?"

"Very simple. I just made the atmosphere untenable up there."

"What in hell does that mean. Never mind, never mind. I'll take your
word for it. Try the flapjacks."

And, as the log book says, "So ends this day."

-41-

PREACHER PAUL ALMOST GETS CAUGHT

Captain Mahoney and I were still shipmates; he as Master, me as his Mate. We had just docked at Savannah, Georgia and were ordered to dry dock for extensive work. The crew were paid off. Just six of us were kept on, Mahoney, the famous Dinty Moore, the Chief Steward, the Chief Engineer, the Purser, and myself.

1We weren't all needed. Why keep the Steward when the ship wasn't feeding? And of what use was Dinty, the radio operator? Or the Purser? Or of any of us, for that matter? I like to think that it was the Company's way of insuring that their key men stayed with them. It made us all feel very loyal. A good Company to work for, I'd say.

The Steward managed to cook breakfast for us. He even washed the dishes. The other two meals we all took together at a Morrisons cafeteria. The food was great and reasonable.

The days dragged by and boredom set in. The summer heat was fierce. The coolest place on the ship was the officers' saloon. We would spend most of the day there, telling stories and drinking coffee. Dinty was at his very best, but after a couple of weeks even he ran out. The Purser and I took to going out to Tybee Beach in the afternoon. At least we could keep cool submerged up to our necks in the tepid water.

One night at supper Captain Mahoney dropped a bomb. He announced that a lady friend of his was coming down for a visit. She worked in the Company's office in Boston. We had heard faint rumors about her and the Captain, but that's all they were--rumors. Now, though, they were coming home to roost. Speculation ran rife. Wonder what she looks like? All of this gossip, naturally, was behind the Old Man's back, but it was juicy stuff. We couldn't wait to get a look at her. The biggest thing, though, was that after all his preaching, he was flesh and blood, after all. And doesn't the Bible say, *The flesh is weak?*

A ship is like a little world of it's own, and something as scandalous as this only happened once in a lifetime. I swear we were worse than a bunch of old women.

A couple of days later Captain Paul appeared at breakfast all rigged out in full uniform. Four stripes on his shoulder boards and scrambled eggs on his cap visor.

250

"Have to meet a train," he announced.

We all leered at each other.

That's the last we saw of him that day until he came sailing into Morrison's with *her* on his arm. He bowed graciously to us, but made no attempt to join us. We watched closely as he pulled up at a table across the room. He pulled out her chair and seated her.

"Oh, boy, he's working the perfect gentleman stunt," whispered Dinty.

We got so engrossed watching the sinners that we forgot to eat.

My recollection of her is vague. I'm sure that had she been a raving beauty, I would have remembered. She must have been average looking, averagely dressed--someone that you would pass in the street without a second thought. I think it was in all our thoughts; what did she have? What was her attraction for the Captain? I guess it is summed up best in the age old adage, *Beauty is in the eye of the beholder.*

For the next few days we saw very little of the Old Man. One morning all five of us were in the saloon drinking coffee and speculating, lewdly, on what he was up to. The door opened and in he walked. He looked awful! Pale, drawn, almost sick looking.

"Morning, Captain. Have some coffee."

"Thanks, I believe I will. Gentlemen, I'm in big trouble. I have just come from the Agent's office. There was a telegram for me. My wife is arriving on this morning's train! What am I going to do?"

We were astounded. Dinty was the first to speak. His nasal, down Maine twang pierced the gloom that hung over us.

"Captain, here's what I'd do... "

"Dinty, you've never even been married. What in the hell do you know about this kind of a mess?"

Dinty collapsed into silence.

"Well, gents, what's the solution? Mr. Mate, you've been married for some time. What would you do?"

"Captain, I don't know. I think that my first thought would be to flee--like to some South Sea island, but that's not the answer. I just don't know."

"Chief, what would you do?"

"Captain, I'd introduce them and take them both out to supper. Feed 'em good and they'll get along like two bugs in a rug.

"Chief, you're worse than Dinty. You just take care of your engines. Purser, any ideas?"

"Yes, Captain, I think I have your solution, but it will all depend on how good an actor you are, and it will take a lot of sustained nerve. Should you break before it's over, you just might as well jump overboard."

"Get on with it. I've got nerves of steel. Acting? That I don't know.

251

Let's hear it."

"Go and meet the train. Act as if you are absolutely delighted that she came down to keep you company. Take her to a good hotel, but make sure that it's not near to the one where Miss Whoosits is staying. Then you tell both of them that on Company's orders, you have to stay on board every other night. The ship is so torn up that they couldn't possibly come aboard. If that works, and there is no reason it shouldn't, you work any stunt you can think of to get rid of one or both of them. There's just one catch, though."

"That sounds just fine purser. I know that I can pull it off. Wait a minute. What's the catch?"

"Well, Captain it's going to be quite a strain on you."

"Baloney, I just told you that I have nerves of steel."

"I don't mean your nerves, Captain. I mean it will be quite a strain on that, er, I mean, that is on your, er... that thing between your legs!"

By Godfrey if he didn't pull it off! We would see him every night, waddling into Morrisons; one night with one of them, the next night with the other one. We would all bow and wave, and he would wave back. One night he even winked at us with the eye on the side away from his companion.

I was worried stiff that some fine night the dame who was *'off'* that night would take it in her head to dine at Morrisons. I mentioned it to the Captain one day.

"Not to worry, Mister Mate. I've told them to eat their supper in the hotel. What with all the soldiers wandering the streets, a decent woman isn't safe."

So much for that.

Big mouth Dinty, never known for his tact, said to him one morning,

"Captain, you don't look too good. You've lost weight, you're pale, and your eyes are starting to sag like a bloodhound's."

That did it.

"Dinty, you look like a half starved weasel, yourself. You just tend to your damned radios."

A week or ten days went by. Captain Paul did look awful. The strain was beginning to get him down, and he knew it. One morning he announced to us that the ship would be sailing in two days.

"That's good news, Captain, we're all sick of this town."

That was Dinty, again.

"Now wait a minute. We're not really sailing. I'm just telling my, er, companions that. One's taking the train this morning, and the other one leaves tomorrow."

And that's just what happened. He had pulled it off! It left it's mark on him, though. Ever afterwards, whenever someone would bring up the subject of women, which was often, Captain Paul would fling down his napkin

Typical T2 Tanker

and storm out of the saloon, muttering to himself.

I used to listen, entranced, to Dinty Moore and Captain Paul telling stories. Their inimitable Down Maine twang made them hilarious. One night they got to talking about fog. Captain Paul started off by saying,

"Naow, this here fog weren't no every day pea soup fog where a man couldn't see the focsle head from the pilot house. Nosiree, this here fog was so thick that a dog had to back up to bark."

Dinty, who was a great tea drinker, once drawled,

"This here tea is so strong that a man could float a horse shoe in it."

-42-

MAKING IT THE HARD WAY

I have been through the Cape Cod Canal many times. It is fairly simple. It is a short passage.

There are no alarming currents. Traffic is strictly one way, a blessing. There was one time, though, that was definitely the exception. I was the Chief Mate of a Liberty ship, the S.S. Robert Treat, commanded by Captain Moulton. The time was about midway of World War II. The Canal played a crucial role during hostilities. It provided a safe, protected passage for vessels bound to and from East Coast ports. The alternative was to go outside Cape Cod and Nantucket Shoals, where the German submarines lurked.

We were Northbound from New York via Long Island Sound, thence through the Canal to Boston. Coming into Buzzard's Bay, our steering gear failed. The engines were stopped while the Chief Engineer worked frantically to discover the cause, and hopefully, to make repairs.

I was in my room when I heard the engines stop. I made my way out onto the forward boat deck. I had mistakenly assumed that we had stopped to allow Southbound vessels to exit the Canal. There were none in sight, and the green lights were lit, meaning that ships could enter.

Something fishy, here, I thought, making my way up to the bridge where I joined the Old Man and the Pilot. The Chief Engineer was fussing around the Telemotor. The linkage between the ship's steering wheel and the throttle of the big steering engine, all the way back aft, is hydraulic. This is a very ingenious hook up because, in some mysterious way, the man on the wheel can *'feel'* the ship right through the hydraulic piping. It has been in use virtually since steamships first appeared. Now it had gone Kaput. Luckily, it was a balmy summer day, so the ship was in no danger. I ran up two black balls on the signal halyards, the International signal for, *'Not Under Command.'* There we lay. What to do?

The Chief went back to the steering engine room. When he returned, about a half hour later, he reported,

"Can't be fixed, Captain. The steering engine is OK, so there has to be a busted hydraulic line somewheres between the wheel and the steering engine throttle. The break must be down in either number four or five hatch."

The Skipper and I talked it over. We had no solution. Just then, the Navy Gunnery Officer wandered in. The Old Man took one look at him, walloped me on the back, and shouted,

"I've got it, Mister! Guns, I want you to rig up two sets of your sound powered head phones. One here in the wheel house, and the other back on the poop deck by the emergency steering wheel. Jump!"

The Navy gun crew had these phones at every gun tub and on the bridge. They were for the Gunnery officer to direct fire power in the event of an enemy attack.

The Captain was doing some good thinking. There was an emergency steering wheel way back on the poop, complete with it's own compass and binnacle. Although it looked like a ship's steering wheel, it was actually an extension of the steering engine's throttle. However, it's worst draw back was it's location. Being so very far aft, the ship's head could swing thirty degrees before that aft compass responded. Then too, the man at the wheel couldn't see the ship's head. No way could the ship be conned from back there. Hence the Skipper's brilliant idea.

"Mister Mate, you get back on the poop, put on those head phones. I'll be wearing the other set up here. You listen carefully, and do **exactly** what I tell you. Get going!"

Before I could get out of the wheel house, the pilot spoke up.

"Captain, I can't permit this. You are putting the whole Canal at risk. That waterway is absolutely vital to the War effort. If you lose control in there, or run her aground, they'll have to close the Canal. I'm going to send a signal to shore to that effect. Then we'll move out of the channel and anchor."

By God, the Old Man came on like the thoroughbred that he was. "Mister pilot, I am the master of this ship. You are on board in the capacity of advisor to the master on local conditions. It's my responsibility and I fully accept it. This ship is an Eastern Steamship Line vessel, and their ships have been going through this Canal ever since it was dug. Now, you will keep out of my way. Should I need your advice, rest assured, I'll ask for it."

Wow, that's telling it like it is! As I headed aft, I was thankful that in those days pilots didn't carry VHF radios like they do, now. The Bosun went forward to heave up the anchor.

Back aft, I put on the headphones.

"Testing, testing, do you read me, Captain?"

"Loud and clear, Mister. Come Right, easy... ease the wheel. Meet her, her... steady, steady, just a touch of left wheel. Steady as she goes."

Thank God that we had a couple of miles to go before we entered the Canal. At first we were all over the fairway. Gradually, though, the Old Man and I were getting the hang of it. For the first time in my life I was steering with my ears instead of my eyes. Then I noticed something.

"Captain, for God's sake, have the Second Mate pull down those two black balls! If the Canal authorities see them, we'll all be in jail or shot."

They came down on the run in two seconds, flat.

And so we sailed through the Canal like a bloody cruiser. Sounds like boasting, but Captain Moulton and his Chief Mate made a pretty fair team.

Long years after the War, I read somewheres, that a ship did get out of control in the Canal and went aground, blocking all traffic. Wars being what they are, some big dredges were dispatched to the scene. They dug a great hole in the side of the Canal and pushed her in. She's there yet, for all I know.

Just to end this story: Captain Moulton and I had become close friends. We were near the same age and were compatible. As soon as we tied up in Boston, he went ashore to the home office. When he returned, he called me up to his office and told me that the ship was ordered to the West coast for service in the Pacific. He asked me to go with him. It didn't take me long to make up my mind.

"Thanks, but no, Captain. That's just too far from home. I'll stick to the Atlantic and the Med."

As things turned out, I had made a wise decision. After the War, I learned that the 'authorities' lost the ship out there. I don't mean that she was sunk. She was just forgotten, mislaid, sort of. And there she lay at anchor in some God forsaken Far East island until the end of hostilities. Sure, all hands paid off with a big bundle, but I'll bet that some of them were prime candidates for the funny farm.

I find the medicine worse than the malady.
John Fletcher

-43-

A SHIP'S MEDICINE CHEST

Way back before World War II, medical treatment at sea was pretty crude. I remember one Chief Mate saying that he had only two remedies, Iodine for the outside, Epsom's Salts for the inside.

While still in my teens, I had developed some bad cavities in my back molars, brought on by neglect. For over a week I suffered. First one tooth would ache, then another. In desperation, I sought help from the Captain. I didn't dare see the Mate, fearing that he would try to pull them out with a pair of pliers, and they'd break off. The Old Man peered into my mouth and muttered,

"Had the same thing when I was your age. Now, you just sit still. I'll be right back."

Back he came with a small, brown bottle with a glass rod in it. I didn't know it until later, but the bottle contained Sulfuric Acid.

"Now then, we'll just give those two gnashers on the right a drop of this."

There was a pretty good sea running, and the ship was pitching. Just as he poked the glass rod into my mouth, the ship lurched, and the drop fell off the rod in between the tooth and my cheek. Holy Smoke! It felt as if he had thrown a lighted match into my mouth. I was hollering and dancing up and down with pain. Quick as a snake, he flung his arm around my neck and dropped acid onto the bad teeth.

"Come back tomorrow and we'll repeat," says he.

After the third day the teeth were gone, eaten away by the acid, and I had a burned yap. Rough, brutal, but effective.

Another time we were making our approach to New York. It was February, and snowing and blowing a gale. I was on the eight to twelve watch, and was on the wheel. About eight-thirty at night, the Old Man heard the horn on Ambrose Lightship. He was bound and determined to find the pilot vessel and pick up a pilot, even though he knew in his heart, that no small pilot boat could possibly be launched in such weather. He decided to steam back and forth between the Ambrose Lightship and Fire Island Lightship while waiting for the pilot boat. He told the Third Mate to get the pilot ladder and boat rope rigged out on the port side, it then being the lee side. The Third Mate blew his whistle for Charlie Ennis, my watch partner. Charlie left his post as bow lookout and reported to the bridge. He was given his orders—rig pilot ladder and boat rope

257

on the port side of the forward deck. Down he went in the pitch darkness and the snow, and set to work. Shortly, the Old Man pulled his head in out of the pilot house window, and grunted with satisfaction. He had just heard the horn on the Fire Island Lightship. Peering into the binnacle, he ordered me to come hard starboard. We changed course one hundred and eighty degrees, heading back for Ambrose. I guess that it never entered his head that Charlie, down there in the dark was now trying to rig the ladder on what now was the weather side. Green water was now bursting over the forward well deck, on the port side. We didn't know it at the time but a boarding wave picked Charlie up and slammed him into the forward shelter deck bulkhead, splitting his forehead wide open. He didn't know it, either. He was a *Hard Case* seaman and pain never seemed to bother him.

The lee side pilot house door slid open and in came Charlie, streaming water.

"Mister Mate, I can't rig the ladder in this weather."

The Third Mate turned his flashlight on Charlie. My God A'mighty! His scalp was hanging down over his eyes, and he was bleeding something awful. He had unbuttoned his oil skins, and the blood had run down his wet clothes until he looked like a real Red Skin.

The Old Man took one look at him and told the Third Mate to go get the Chief Mate. Up he came, the famous Mister Bang, of the Cape Horners, and a marvel with palm and needle. He told Charlie to go down to his room and for God's sake, take a towel. He didn't want blood dripping all over his room.

"Not to worry, Captain. I'll have him stitched up in a jiffy."

Sometime later he came back up, rubbing his hands.

"Did a first rate job on him, Captain. I put in some real fancy stitching.   "I sent him below, Slim, so you're stuck on the wheel until midnight."

When I got relieved by the twelve to four man, I hurried back aft to the focsle. There was Charlie, sitting on the edge of his bunk, smoking. He was also half drunk. I asked him how he felt.

"I'm all right, but my head aches something fierce. Old Bang is OK, though. He gave me a full mug of rum before he went to work on me."

I took a look at his bandage. It was slipping down over his eyes and was pretty bloody.

"Charlie, I'm going to change that bandage. It's a mess."

I had two rolls of gauze in my locker. I wrung out a towel in cold water, took off the bandage, and swabbed off his forehead. Dear God! That damned Mate had put in cross stitches like you see on a baseball. And he had done it with a sail needle. These needles aren't round like a sewing needle. They are triangular in shape, and the needle had made holes in Charlie's forehead bigger by far than the coarse black thread he had used. Charlie was

Little Joe and Charlie Ennis, he with the
baseball stitches in his forehead.

back working the next day, but from that day to this, if he is still living, he is walking around with a perpetual frown on his big ugly mug and a row of *Fancy Stitching* across his forehead.

A cargo ship, in those days, was no place to get sick. Every man had to pull his weight, and just one man laid up, and not able to stand his watch, put a strain on the rest of us.

THE NAVY FLOPS

Some few years after the war, I was Master of a ship laying in the port of Dahousie, New Brunswick, Canada, loading a full cargo of newsprint for New Orleans. We had come in around the Gaspé Peninsula and up the Restigouch River. The Second Mate and I were lolling over the chart table discussing our Southbound route. We were scheduled to put into Halifax for bunkers. In those days there was a narrow, natural passage between Nova Scotia and Cape Breton Island, called The Gut of Canso. It has since been filled in and a causeway built. Back then, though, it was available to deep water ships, and it would save us many miles compared to going way around the island and out of the Saint Lawrence estuary by way of Cabot Strait. Should we take the short route? If the fog caught us in the Gut, we would have our hands full. However, I reasoned that it was August, and a few clear days could be expected.

"OK, Mister, we'll go through the Gut. We will have Sparks keep close track of the weather, and if fog threatens before we get to the Gut, we'll just haul off and take the long route."

My decision was challenging to me, and I derived great satisfaction from cutting corners if the risk was reasonable. I always figured that part of my obligation to my owners was to always take the shortest route, *Having due regard for existing conditions and circumstances,* as the International Rules of the Road so aptly put it.

Shortly after leaving Dalhousie, Sparks commenced feeding me weather reports. Without exception they were good. Good all the way to the Gut, through the Gut, and around to the entrance to Halifax, where we picked up a pilot. When he came up to the bridge, he asked where we were from. When I told him, he asked where the pilot was. I was rather puzzled. I told him that we didn't have any pilot. He seemed quite shocked, and told me that although it was not mandatory, all vessels running through the Gut always hired a pilot. This was news to me. Now, though, I hadn't hired a pilot and still made a successful passage. I felt pretty smug.

It took us several hours to bunker. As soon as the fuel hose was uncoupled, we sailed. Just before we left, the Chief Engineer told me that he had a young oiler who was sick.

"What's the matter with him?"

"I don't know but he won't get out of his bunk."

I had wished the thankless job of ship's medicine man on Mister Butler, the Second Mate.

"Mister Butler, slip down and have a look at that oiler."

Then I promptly forgot all about him. Later, I wished that I hadn't.

Day after day we steamed along in fine style, making our usual ten plus knots. The weather was sunny and fine, and the ship, even though she had a homogenous cargo, was taking the mild seas most kindly.

As I remember, we were about down to the latitude of New York, or a bit South. I was hanging around the bridge shooting the breeze with Mister Butler.

"Captain, I'm worried about our sick oiler."

"Why, what seems to be the matter with him?"

"I don't know, but he's much worse. He has lost a lot of weight, he's too weak to get up, and he won't eat. Says that his throat is too sore to swallow."

"Well, as soon as the Mate relieves you, we'll go and have a look at him."

Just as soon as the Mate came up, down we went. I felt like Doctor Kildare. I didn't have a little black bag, though. I knew as much about medicine as a quahog clam.

By God, this boy looks awful, I thought. He could only whisper. I peered down his throat. The inside of his gullet looked sort of grayish, instead of a healthy red. He hadn't eaten for over two days. The inside of his throat was terribly swollen, too. He was taking water through a straw, and that was all. Wouldn't even suck up soup. Said it burned his throat.

"Mister Butler, come up to my room. I've got a medical book left over from the war. It describes every illness known to man; symptoms, causes, and cures."

I dug out the book and we started with A and worked down through B and C, and got to D. Bingo! We found it. Diphtheria! Every symptom matched the boy's. Swollen throat, white tissues. Holy Smoke! An infectious disease and me with a very young crew. I made up my mind in a hurry, and rushed up to the radio shack.

"Sparks, call up NSS, Annapolis, and tell them that we need medical advice. Call me when you get through."

He didn't get through. Something was wrong with his transmitter.

"Fix it, Sparks. Keep me advised."

The next day Mister Butler came piling into my room.

"He's worse. He can't get his wind. I guess his throat is swelling shut."

Dear God, I've got to do something. Back to the radio shack. Sparks had got his transmitter fixed. He had just made contact with the Navy in Annapolis. All radio traffic in those days was by key, not voice. NSS sent that a Navy medical doctor was standing by and for us to transmit the patient's symptoms. As I wrote them, Sparks tapped them out on his key. I told Sparks to stress that the boy was almost suffocating from lack of oxygen. Back cameaquestion.

DO YOU HAVE AN OBA ON BOARD?

Yes we have two. OBA means Oxygen Breathing Apparatus, and consists of a mask into which oxygen could be fed from a small cylinder. The device was meant to be used in fighting a fire in an enclosed space. Message from NSS:

DO YOU HAVE ANY CATHETERS IN YOUR HOSPITAL?

"Mister Butler, what the hell is a catheter?"
"I know what they are. I'll go and look."
These old Liberty ships had a room set aside as a hospital. During the war it was well stocked with a full line of elaborate hospital equipment. It was presided over by a combination Purser/Pharmacist who supposedly had a smattering of medical education from a quick crash course. Now, though, Pursers were long gone.
Back came the Second Mate with a handful of slithery rubber tubes, just about the diameter of a piece of spaghetti, and just as limp.
"Sparks, send,

YES, WE HAVE.

While we were waiting, I asked Mister Butler what they were used for. He gave me the creeps when he told me that when a man couldn't pee, a catheter would be shoved up his dink into his bladder to let the urine out. What in blazes did this doctor have in mind? Sparks held up his hand for silence. NSS coming in again. We waited. He copied the message directly onto his typewriter. Ripping the copy out of his machine, he handed it to me.
"This job's for you, Captain."
I read the message out loud.
"Come on, Mister Butler, and for God's sake bring those damned catheters."
We raced down to the main deck. I grabbed one of the OBA suitcases out of its rack near the galley and hurried to the oiler's room.
"Now then Mister Butler, open up that suitcase and disconnect the

262

oxygen bottle."

This bottle, or cylinder was about six or seven inches long and three or four inches in diameter. God only knows how much pressure the oxygen was under.

"Now let me read this message again.

PUSH THE CATHETER UP HIS NOSE AND DOWN HIS THROAT. THEN TAPE THE OTHER END OF THE CATHETER TO THE VALVE ON THE OXYGEN BOTTLE. CRACK THE VALVE SLIGHTLY.

"Got that Mister Butler?"

"Captain, I'm getting sick to my stomach. You'll have to do it."

Try as I might, I couldn't get the damned catheter up his nose. It was just too floppy. I kept at it but it was futile. It wouldn't go. The poor oiler was feebly pushing at my hands and trying to whisper. I gave up and raced back up to the radio shack.

"Sparks, get NSS again tell them that it's no go. We can't carry out the doctor's suggestion. And tell him that things are desperate, here."

Sparks started clicking away again. Presently:

STAND BY.

Then a message started coming through. Message:

A NAVY DESTROYER WITH A DOCTOR ON BOARD IS PRESENTLY ENROUTE, HAVANA TO CHARLESTON, SOUTH CAROLINA. PLEASE RADIO YOUR PRESENT POSITION

I ran over to the chart room, grabbed the parallel ruler, advanced my morning sights by our course and speed, and marked our present position on the chart. I copied off the latitude and longitude on a scrap of paper and dashed back to the radio shack. Sparks sent it off.

STAND BY.

Back came the order.

STEAM SUCH AND SUCH A COURSE. YOU SHOULD RENDEZVOUS WITH THE DESTROYER AT 1500 HOURS.

Right after dinner I went back to the bridge. Mister Butler was fussing around in the chart room. Butler was a big, heavy set man with a loud, raucous voice. There has always been an intense rivalry between the Navy and the Merchant Service. They both thought that they were the better seamen. In fact, it was more than rivalry. They disliked each other, and on any occasion, said so. Whenever they met ashore, bar room battles occurred, inevitably.

I told Butler to whistle up the Bosun and have him strip number one life boat of all unnecessary junk, swing it outboard, rig a boat rope and have four men to crew it, and two men to stand by to lower it.

"Yes, sir, we'll show those Navy jerks how it should be done."

At about two-thirty, right on schedule, the destroyer poked her nose over the horizon, dead ahead.

"Stop engines, Mister Butler, and come hard Left. We'll make a lee on our starboard side."

Up swooped the US Navy, whoop-whooping on her siren. Her blinker light was clacking furiously.

"What's he saying, Mister?"

"He says,

HEAVE TO. MAKE A LEE ON THE PORT SIDE. WE WILL SEND BOAT WITH DOCTOR.

"No way, Mister. Tell him we are sending our boat."

The destroyer approached almost alongside, her rail lined with sailors, gawking at us. An officer started yelling through a bull horn.

"We are launching boat. Make a lee."

The Second Mate was all ready to roar back some insulting remark. I stopped him.

"Keep quiet, Mister Butler. We are looking for help from them. Slow Ahead, hard starboard, Stop, engines. There, let them send their damned boat."

We watched them swing their boat outboard, four crew sitting in it. The Bosun's pipe twittered, **Lower Away.** Dear God. One of the boat falls hung up. The other one lowered away, and there was the boat, hanging on end. Two of the boat's crew fell off into the drink. The other two were hanging onto the thwarts.

"Haw, Haw," roared Butler. "Look at 'em. Seamen, huh? Balls! Haw, haw."

"For God's sake, shut up. We need them."

The Navy finally got their boat squared away. Oars lifted and fell, and they heaved alongside. Up to the bridge came their doctor and their Executive Officer. Introductions were exchanged.

"Mister Butler, please escort the doctor down to the patient."

"Commander, it was too bad about your boat launching," said I, slipping the old knife in.

He winced, taking the blow bravely. He drew a shuddering breath.

"It was pretty awful, wasn't it?"

"Sure was, but it could have been worse. The boat could have sunk. Or your men drowned."

Oh, this was one for the book. The poor Exec was as red as a beet.

"Those bastards think that they're getting shore leave in Charleston. Well, I'll keep 'em on board until they're ready for retirement!"

Fortunately, the poor guy was spared further torture by the appearance of the doctor, followed by two of his crew carrying our poor oiler in a Stokes basket. We will take good care of him. So long."

As soon as their boat was clear, I rang up Full Ahead, and we swung back on course. I found out much later that my diagnosis was dead wrong. The oiler had septicemia of the throat. With proper treatment in a Charleston hospital, he made a swift and complete recovery. However, my mind remains unchanged. Don't ever get sick on a freighter at sea. The cure is always worse than the ailment.

All the world's a stage. And all the people actors.
Shakespeare

-45-

CAPTAIN LOUIS BRECKENRIDGE

A REAL MASTER MARINER

Captain Breckenridge had attained command in 1925, when I was eleven years old. I know this because he was a member of the Boston Marine Society, and I am, too. The requirements for membership were that a candidate had to have served at least one year as master of an ocean going vessel, and to be of good character. It is the oldest such Society in the world, and it was a high hono to be proposed for membership. At the time he was admitted, he was in command of the S.S. Boston, the same ship that Captain Mahoney had commanded when he was admitted to membership. Of course, I never knew him back in those days. I first met him during the War. He had gone into business for himself as a Coast Pilot, taking ships up and down the coast from Norfolk to Maine. A big shipyard had been developed in South Portland, Maine. They were turning out Liberty ships like hot cakes. A large part of his work consisted of taking these new ships South to Boston, New York, or to wherever they were to load. That's when I first met him.

Physically, Captain Breckenridge was the opposite of Captain Mahoney. Where Mahoney was a huge bear of a man with a big belly, Breckenridge was a little shrimp of a man. He was about five feet, four inches tall and probably didn't weigh more than about a hundred and thirty pounds. He was extremely soft spoken; never raised his voice, but make no mistake about it, he was the boss. He was probably the best that Eastern ever had, and they had some of the best in the business. This opinion of him was shared by all hands in the Company. Not only that, thousands of regular passengers felt the same way. It was said that some of them would deliberately postpone a business trip in order to sail on his ship. From some of the tales I have heard about him, he must have been born with the ability to conn a ship. He never gave an incorrect order.

Being only human, he was fully aware of this reputation that he had acquired. Another talent that he had was that of a first rate actor. During docking and undocking he was on stage. He knew that dozens of passengers would be gathered on the foredeck, just beneath the bridge. From there they could hear him barking out his orders in a crisp, nasal voice. He was one in a million.

266

Here's just one anecdote to illustrate: These ships docked in the early days at pier 18, North River in New York. They never used the services of a tow boat. The Skipper brought her in himself, regardless of the wind and tide. And get this. They had to back her in! The North River is actually the lower part of the Hudson River.

To back a big ship into a pier under those conditions took some doing. The tide in the river ebbs and flows at a high rate. Winter gales against the high sides of a passenger ship can unlay the plans of the best of men. Not Captain Breckenridge, though. He always got his ship in and out without damage. There were days when other ships attempting to dock tore up their piers, pilings and all. And they had one and sometimes two tow boats.

When the Captain's ship had past through the East River and rounded the Battery, she headed up the North River towards her berth. The Captain took center stage on the bridge. His eyes never stopped roving, checking the traffic, the wind, the tide. He would stroll back and forth as if he didn't have a care in the world. If the truth be known, he was wound up like a fine watch. Back and forth he would stroll. Judging his timing to the second, he would swing the ship left, just off the pier. Then, using both engines and rudder, he would get her going astern. When the time was just right, and the ship going just where he wanted her to go, he would pull out an enormous cigar and carefully light it. Then he would head for the companionway and descend to the main deck. From there he would proceed down the inside passageway, bowing graciously to his large audience. On he went, fragrant cigar smoke billowing around him. He had this walk timed to a T. Out he would pop onto the stern docking station. One look around, then, *Stop Engines, Dead Slow Astern. Stop Engines. Heaving lines ashore, please.*

In a matter of minutes the ship would be alongside, all tied up. The side port would open, and the gangway would rumble out.

Finished with Engines.

Yes indeed, this seafarer was a giant amongst his peers who were no slouches themselves. The times that he acted as pilot I felt that I was in good hands. If it was from Boston to New York via the Cape Cod Canal I always stayed on the bridge with him listening to him reminisce. We would stop the ship in Buzzard's Bay for him to disembark into his launch. Just before leaving, he would press a fifty dollar bill into my hand. I would protest, but he would insist.

As soon as his launch was clear, I would ring up Full Ahead and swing the ship around on a course which would take me outside of Block Island. I didn't have the pilot endorsement which would have permitted me to proceed via Long Island Sound, but no matter. I had just left a friend.

Captain Louis Breckenridge died in Winthrop, Mass. in 1986. He was ninety eight years old.

Let the lower lights be burning. Send a gleam across the wave.
Old hymn

-46-

LIGHTSHIPS AND LIGHTHOUSES-
GOD BLESS 'EM

An entry in one of my log books reads:

EIGHT PM. THICK SNOW. IMPOSSIBLE TO SEE BE-
YOND THE WHEEL HOUSE. ON COURSE, PROCEED-
ING UP THE BRISTOL CHANNEL FOR BREAKSEA
LIGHTSHIP.
EIGHT THIRTY-FIVE PM. ANCHORED IN ELEVEN FA-
THOMS AWAITING FAVORABLE WEATHER.

In between those lines there lies a tale of luck that I didn't deserve. It happened this way:

Once I was Master of a fine new ship. A cargo ship again, but with every modern convenience and superbly equipped with every aid to navigation. After discharging in a North European port, we were bound for Newport Mons. It is located at the head of the Bristol Channel in Wales, England. It was winter time, late January, and night came early.

Heading down the English Channel I was reassured by the faint yellow gleam of the Eddystone Light, on the starboard bow. The Eddystone, as it is called by seafarers. I have read somewhere that the Eddystone is the oldest, constantly maintained light in the world. For centuries it has cast its gleam seaward. Sometimes feeble, sometimes too late, and good ships and brave men have foundered and been lost. Whenever I hear the sailors' hymn, *Let the lower lights be burning,* I think of the Eddystone.

Tonight, as the Mate busied himself with getting a bearing of the light, I felt that I was among friends. All down the Channel they had appeared. By day as small fingers, gradually changing to fat, stubby fingers, each with its distinctive marking. At night, first as a dim orange glimmer, then as a sweep across the black horizon; finally bursting as occulting or flashing sentinels, clear and unmistakable. On course and all's well. Signposts of the sea.

Engine trouble plagued us most of the night and the next day, and what with the Chief Engineer having to stop several times, it was evening before we came up to Lundys Island and squared away up the Bristol Channel.

The Mate and I were comfortably toasting our shins against the pilot

268

house radiator discussing the stowage of the cargo we were to load the next day.

Because of the delays caused by the engines, we were already twenty-four hours behind schedule and, as we would lose another day bunkering in Swansea, I was most anxious to hurry along. That was why, when the Mate remarked that it was starting to snow, I grunted, *keep her going,* knowing that his next observation would be a suggestion to slow her down. Bad judgement but my owners expected me to keep our schedule, didn't they? And wasn't I known throughout the company as, **Drive her, Johnny, drive her,** after the famous sea chantey? Overconfidence won over common sense and drive we did into a pitch black night with the snow pelting against the windows making visibility zero.

The watches changed at eight o'clock and the Third Mate relieved the Mate who, after writing up his log in the chart room, returned to the wheel house.

For the past two hours we had been trying in vain to pick up the Breaksea Lightship on our Radio Direction Finder. It should have been coming in loud and clear, yet we hadn't heard her signal once. I couldn't understand it and wondered if there was something wrong with the receiver. Sparks looked it over and reported it in apparent good order. Entering the chart room I put the ear phones on and tried again. Not a peep. On other frequencies I could hear, far away, other lighthouses and lightships but from Breaksea there was dead silence. Snapping off the DF I stepped back into the wheel house. Snow had obscured the windows. The Third Mate, as was proper, was out on the lee bridge listening, or trying to, with the gale blowing snow in his ears and eyes. A premonition of danger made me uneasy. I opened a window and peered out. Snow stung my face and the howl of the wind in the rigging went up and down the scale as the ship rolled from leeward to windward.

"Mister, this doesn't look too good. By our reckoning we should be coming up to Breaksea. Can't raise her on the DF. I think that we'll just back off the starboard anchor nice and easy and steam to it for the night. or until it clears. There is quite a tide here and the water is too deep for the pick to hold us in this wind, so if you will go forward and back out the anchor, we will use the engines on a slow bell to keep her from dragging. Better get some warm clothes first, and give me a shout when you're ready.

The Mate was evidently a lot more worried than I was, for in a very few minutes he phoned from the focsle head that he and the carpenter had the anchor cleared for lowering. The Third Mate put the telegraph on Stop.

Having plenty of sea room I didn't back her to take the way off but let her coast along until, by the feel of her roll, all headway had been lost. The Mate then backed off the chain, link by link, it being too deep to let her go on the run.

While we talked and considered, the darkness gradually changed to

The last lightship in U.S. waters at Nantucket Shoels,
the "graveyard of ships."

gray. Dawn had come, and with it the snow was letting up. We decided to wait for full daylight before getting under way. Pretty soon it was light enough to see the fore deck and then the bow. The snow was now coming down only in flurries driven by the wind. Suddenly the sailor on the bow shouted and we could see him frantically waving his arm ahead. There, not a half ship's length dead ahead, lay the Breaksea Lightship.

"God almighty," the Mate breathed. "A few more minutes last night and we'd have cut her in two. We're lucky, Skipper."

And lucky we were to be spared a disaster after having used such bad judgement in holding on in a blizzard, not knowing for sure where we were.

Now we knew that the lookouts were not imagining hearing a horn when every now and then, through the night, one of them had reported hearing a deep whistle somewhere ahead.

The anchor was hove home and we got under way, sure of our position, thanks to our floating sign post of the sea, the Breaksea Lightship.

* * *

There was another time when these friends were not so welcome. I remember one time we were clawing off a lee shore, the West coast of Norway, it was, in a hard Westerly gale. It was wintertime again, and we were in ballast heading North. For two days, try as we might, the ship was being forced Eastward. A wicked beam sea was running, and the ship, being light, was rolling her bulwarks under. I had reckoned that if we could weather the next Cape, we would have licked the gale. Of course, we had the alternative of heaving to, steaming to the West, into the wind, but our destination was to the Northward.

A little after midnight the Second Mate picked up a faint glimmer ahead. *Must be a fisherman,* I thought. The wind was still blowing as hard as ever but the visibility was excellent. The stars were shining and the horizon like dark velvet. It was freezing cold, though.

In a short while the dim light, fine on the starboard bow brightened and then disappeared. When the ship rose on the next wave the light was flashing brightly and unmistakably. It was a lighthouse. As it was almost dead ahead, it was all too obvious that we would not weather the land. My disappointment was hard to swallow. It was one of the only times that I cursed my owners, for it was they who had refused to spend the money for a pilot to go inside the Sharagard, the belt of islands that completely encloses the entire West coast of Norway. Inside of these islands there is a fine, deep water passage all the way from the Southern tip of Norway to the North Cape. It is protected from all winds and a ship can steam along safely in all kinds of weather. It was especially favored by ships in ballast as we were, but our owners felt that the pilotage was an unnecessary expense. They didn't realize that a ship in ballast in the dead of winter off the West coast of Norway was well nigh unmanageable in a gale. It was not only the high sides of the ship exposed to the winds. The propeller and rudder were thrown clear out of the water with each sea so she wouldn't answer the helm. When this happened, as it was happening to us, the stern would kick up out of the water, the wind would smash against our weather side, the helmsman would put the wheel hard up, but inexorably the bow would fall off, paying to leeward of our course. And there we would lay, four or five points to leeward of our course, until the propeller and rudder again buried themselves deep enough to bring her head back again. Sometimes this took half an hour. And all the while we were being set toward the coast.

There was nothing to do but to head out to sea and weather it out. The ship's head was hauled around to the West, into the wind, and we commenced climbing up the face of the big, vicious seas. First the bow would dip down. Then the stern would toss up clear of the water, and the propeller would race madly until the engineer standing throttle watch would cut the steam. After an hour it became apparent that we couldn't keep on. The engines would shake themselves to pieces or the forward end would have the rivets pounded out. What to do? The glass was still falling which only confirmed the latest weather report—winds of gale force continuing for another forty-eight hours.

The Chief Engineer, the First Assistant, the Mate and I held a pow-wow in the saloon. We finally decided to slow the engines down to half speed and see if the ship's motion and laboring eased any. If it didn't we would ballast the after holds with sea water, something only attempted in a dire emergency.

Returning to the bridge, the Mate and I watched as the engineer signaled on the engine room telegraph that he was slowing to half speed. The noise of the wind howling around the wheel house dropped down from a high whistle to a low pitched muttering. The violent pitching diminished appreciably.

"Well, now," I remarked. "This is more like it. She's riding like a gull."

Just then, through the port side wheel house door, which had been open, poured a mighty gust of wind.

Watch your helm," I bellowed to the quartermaster. "She's falling off to starboard."

And fall off she did, faster and faster until she was broadside to. The wheel was hard to port but she wouldn't answer, just laid there, wallowing like a crippled whale. Full speed was rung up and slowly her head came back to the sea.

Now we were faced with a serious maneuver. The effect of a large amount of water in a ship can be disastrous unless the water completely fills the compartment it is in. If only partially filled, it will shift from side to side as the ship rolls and create havoc with the ship's stability, even to the extent of capsizing her.

The after holds of our ship were bisected, fore and aft by the shaft

271

tunnel. We all were of the opinion that they could be safely flooded to the top of the shaft tunnel without too much danger, feeling that the shaft tunnel would act as a barrier to the motion of the water as the vessel's motion in a seaway tended to slosh it back and forth.

The Chief arranged to let sea water into the holds by the use of fire hoses led down from the deck. In a short time the water was pouring in. Fortunately, the holds had been thoroughly cleaned, so there was no debris to hamper pumping out later on.

The Mate stationed a man in each 'tween deck with a flashlight to watch the water as it rose. When it reached the top of the tunnel they notified the engine room to shut off the fire pump. All this took only a few hours, all during which we were pitching badly. Gradually, though, as the weight of water in the holds increased, the stern settled deeper in the water. The rudder began to take hold and the propeller ceased its thrashing. We hauled back on our Northerly course and the rolling started again. But this time it was different. In spite of the rolling, we were holding our course.

And so, by a difficult maneuver, executed in time, thanks to the gleam of a lighthouse seen from the crest of a wave, another voyage was completed, another log book filed away in the archives, and a little more experience was tucked under my belt.

And a woman is only a woman, but a cigar is a good smoke.

Rudyard Kipling

-47-

WOMEN ON A SHIP—BAD LUCK!

As long as ships have been sailing the sea lanes, sailors have been saying that women on a ship are bad luck. I've said it, too Only once did I have the misfortune to be on a ship with them, and they *were* bad luck, in more ways than one.

The War was over and things on the sea lanes were back to normal. The convoys, the escort vessels, the fears, were all behind us. We were, at long last, back in the business of carrying the world's commerce. It was a good feeling. The nightmares were over and buried in the past.

I was Master of a tired old Liberty ship. She had been spruced up. All the guns and gun mounts were gone. The wartime battleship gray was painted over. The hull gleamed with peacetime black, the deck houses sparkled white, and the masts and booms were sporting their fresh buff color. Our fancy Maritime Administration uniforms disappeared. Only the cap remained, its insignia now a replica of the company's house flag. Mine, however, still had the *scrambled eggs* on the visor. I guess that I was just vain enough to keep this one visible sign of Master, a title that I was very proud of and had worked hard to attain.

We finished loading in an East coast port and took our departure for Marseilles, France. It was full summer, and for once the North Atlantic was behaving. All the way to Gibraltar the weather remained fine. Day after day the Log Book entries hardly varied.

SEA SLIGHT. LIGHT BREEZE FROM THE WEST.

A real pleasure cruise. I lolled around the bridge day after day. Celestial navigation was a hobby of mine, so I was forever taking sights. Stars morning and night, and sun sights all through the day. I know that it annoyed the Mates that I spent so much time up there, but I'd had too many years of winter gales, convoys, and submarines, so I was taking full advantage of this pleasant interlude.

Another thing that contributed to the joy of this voyage was the food. It was marvelous! This was an Eastern Steamship Company ship. For many years before the war Eastern operated a coastwise passenger service, and they were renowned for their cuisine. On this ship I had inherited a complete Steward's department from one of the passenger ships. They were all black,

273

second generation men from the Caribbean Islands. What cooks they were! If you ordered fried eggs for breakfast, they were fried right on your plate. The Chief Steward, Hudson, was Lord and Master, but they loved him. They were a close knit group, always sailing together. In port they didn't get drunk. Instead, after supper, they would sit out on number four hatch and sing negro spirituals and gospel hymns. Many a night I was lulled to sleep by their soft, deep voices singing in perfect harmony. Yeah, man, this was some cruise.

We were approaching the Straits of Gibraltar so it was time to put the sextant away.

Early the next morning there was Gib, dead ahead. The Chief Mate was busy taking bearings on the Pelorus. I slipped below to have another look at the chart. *Cape Trafalga, Tarifa, Punta Carneo, Europa Point.* How familiar those words were. And what memories of the war they brought back. Scurrying through the Straits under cover of darkness. Or slipping into Gibraltar harbor for orders, usually to some stinking hole in North Africa. Or later, to Italy or the Persian Gulf. Now it was different. Steaming along in the bright sunshine like a blooming cruise ship. How sweet it was.

As I write these words, I have before me my private course and distance book in which I had carefully kept different routes ever since I was a young Third Mate. Part of the mystique of being a ship's Captain was the act of being all-knowing. I was no exception to this bit of play acting. In fact, I had become quite adept at it. None of the Mates knew that I had this book, so prior to making a course change or landfall, I'd bone up, stroll into the wheel house and observe that when such and such a lighthouse was bearing so and so, course should be changed to such and such. The Mate on watch would scratch his head and mutter to the man at the wheel,

"Now how does he know that? He hasn't been in the chart room for two days."

Sometimes, just to impress them, I would order that no course lines be drawn on the chart. Then I'd peek in my little book, pop out and change the course. They thought that I had it all in my head and were suitably impressed, or so I hoped. Vanity at its worst. Anyway, here I sit, stumped at what I am reading in my little book.

EUROPA POINT AND PUNTA ALMINA ABEAM, STEER COURSE 099 T, 114 MILES TO CAPE TRES FORCAS ABEAM, DISTANCE OFF 15 MILES. CHANGE COURSE TO 060 T, 114 MILES TO POINT ABUJA ABEAM, DISTANCE OFF, 4 MILES. CHANGE COURSE TO 060 T, 95 MILES TO CAPE TENEZ

ABEAM, BEARING 112, DISTANCE OFF, 17 MILES. CHANGE COURSE TO 054 T, 27 MILES TO POINT PH. CHANGE COURSE TO 000 T, 196 MILES TO POINT PJ. CHANGE COURSE TO 330 T, 32 MILES TO POSITION 1. CHANGE COURSE TO 007 T, TEN MILES TO POSITION 2. CHANGE COURSE TO 072 T, 3 1/2 MILES TO POSITION 3. NORTH TO ANCHORAGE. NOTE: POINT PH-Latitude 39-20N LONGITUDE 5-40E. POINT PJ-LATITUDE 42-30N LONGITUDE 5-40E. POINT PK-LATITUDE 42-58N LONGITUDE 5-20E.

What all this means is that when Europa Point and Punta Almina are abeam, the vessel is through the Straits and has entered the Mediterranean, Eastbound. So far so good. But according to my book I should steam Easterly 128 miles until Point Abuja is abeam to starboard, four miles off. Abuja is the port of Oran in North Africa. What in the hell would I be doing four miles off the coast of North Africa, on the Southern side of the Med when I was bound for Marseilles, on the Northern coast of the Med? And what does PH, PJ, PK, mean? And Positions 1,2,3,? I have racked my brain but it remains blank. The only thing that comes to mind is that for several years after the war, ships had to follow specific routes, particularly in the English Channel and the North Sea, because there were still hundreds of mines that hadn't been swept up yet. Maybe the same procedure was being practiced in the waters around Southern France. Any of my colleagues from those days remember? Me and my fancy navigation!

Nevertheless, we did reach Marseilles and pick up a pilot at the anchorage. A short time later we were alongside, ready to discharge. I rang up, *Finished with Engines* and hurried below to the saloon. It was Sunday, and ever since we got our new Steward's department, Sunday night was steak night. Porterhouse grilled to your taste. Mine was charred on the outside, red on the inside. Fairly drooling, I fell to. I couldn't believe our good luck. We hadn't eaten like this for five years. That steak was so good that I almost growled at it like a dog. It's odd that I can remember the taste of that steak and not remember why we steamed the courses that we did to get there.

Belching with contentment, I leaned back and beamed at the Mates.

"Some ship, hey? Make a note of it, Mister. These days are too good to last."

The saloon door opened and in came a diminutive Frenchman. He was all dressed up in a suit. He even had a velvet vest on, for God's sake. As he approached our table we were enveloped in a cloud of French perfume.

"Le Chief Mate, s'il vous plait," he says. "Je suis votre stevedore, Messieurs."

Stevedore? He looked and smelled more like a queer. He and the Mate got into a discussion about discharging our cargo—number of gangs, tons per hour, estimated time of finish, etc. He smelled too powerful for me so I left.

As the days past, I found out that things were much different in Marseilles than they were in New York or Baltimore. My first evening ashore I sauntered up the main drag, Rue Canibierre. There were dozens of fancy cafes. Slipping into one, I ordered a drink and looked around. My God! There were several ladies of the evening sipping pernod. But what floored me was their appearance. They were very stylishly dressed, but their hair! One had kelly green hair, another purple, another bright canary yellow. Still another had flaming orange. That's not all. They each had a full sized French poodle dog dyed the same color as her hair. There sat those damned mutts, each as big as a police dog, squatting on their backsides. Ah, but the food. That's where the French put us to shame, even our Steward. It has been said that the French can make an old crow taste like pheasant, and it is true.

A few days later I was summoned to the Agent's office. They had received a cable from our owners setting forth our sailing orders. Upon completion of discharge, we were to proceed to Oran, Beni-Saf, and possibly Nemours to load for the States. Then the Agent dropped the boom right on my noggin. Two female passengers would board the next day for passage to the States. He told me what little he knew about them. They were White Russians emigrating to the States. An elderly mother and her middle aged spinster daughter. Oh, God! And this was to have been the most pleasant voyage of my life.

Sure enough, the next noon they arrived at the gangway, loaded with suitcases and boxes. And homely! Wow! They looked like two old black buzzards.

The steward assigned them to the cadet's room, up on the bridge deck on the port side. My quarters and the chart room occupied the starboard side. The only other person on this deck was the Radio Officer. The next deck below was for the Mates and Engineers who shared a common shower and john. There was no bathroom on the bridge deck except my private one.

I was busy all afternoon clearing the ship and settling accounts with the Agent. The Mate had the deck crew lowering the booms, battening down the hatches, and securing for sea. By the time I returned, watches had been set, the lines were singled up, and the Third Mate had tested the steering gear, telegraph, whistle, and had read the draft. As soon as I came up the gangway, the Bosun sang out, *All Hands, fore and aft.* Up came the gangway. I made my way up to the bridge, shook hands with the pilot, and off we went, presumably through PK, PJ, etc.

Somehow or other, I found my way over to Oran. As soon as we docked, the Agent came aboard. He informed me that we were to bunker and then proceed up the coast to Nemours, there to load for Savannah. When it came time for him to leave, he very kindly invited me to have supper with him and his wife.

Ever since we had left Marseilles, I hadn't laid eyes on the two passengers. I had spent the entire trip on the bridge, eating from a tray. Now, however, my troubles began.

I was in the saloon having coffee with the Chief Engineer. He fiddled with his spoon, cleared his throat a couple of times, all the while peering at me kind of sly like.

"Out with it, Chief. What's bugging you?"

I settled back all prepared to suffer through a long tirade against the Seamen's Union, the lousy engines in these old Libertys, what a rotten hole Marseilles was, and God knows what else.

"Well, Captain, it's about these passengers."

"What about them? They're too homely even for you and you've never been too particular. Why, I remember one night you and I went ashore"...

"No, dammit, no. I don't mean in that way. See, they've been using the Engineer's wash room. The Second went in there to take a leak. They were in there and started screeching bloody murder. And this was at four-thirty in the morning."

"Well, for God's sake, what do you want me to do about it? They sure as hell can't piss over the side. Tell you what, Chief. You're either in the engine room or sitting on your ass, here in the saloon. Let 'em use your bathroom.

I will not!. And you'd better do something. This has been a happy ship, but it won't be for long."

"OK, OK, I'll do something about it tomorrow. I've got to go up and take a shower and change my clothes. I'm having supper ashore with the Agent and his wife."

The Captain's quarters on a Liberty ship run fore and aft from the chart room. First, is his office, then his stateroom and bath. To get into the stateroom you first have to pass through his office. Oh, there's a second door opening from his stateroom to the alleyway but it was always locked. I didn't even have a key for it.

When I got to the bridge deck, damned if my office door wasn't closed and locked. I never closed or locked that door except when I was going ashore. And the key was inside on my desk. Something pretty fishy here. Then I heard my shower running. *Oh that dirty skunk of a Chief Engineer.* I banged on the door and was met with a flood of Russian.

"Open this damned door," I roared.

No answer. In desperation I belted out the kick-out panel with my foot. During the war, all ships had these panels on every door except the watertight ones. They even had them set into the partitions between staterooms. Their function was to enable an occupant to escape after a torpedo hit had warped the door frame. I got down on my hands and knees and crawled through the hole. Before I could get up, my unabridged edition of Bowditch bounced off the side of my head. I rolled over, covering my head. There was that old witch of a mother with a book in each hand. Big ones: Farwell's Rules of the Road, and my old Duttons. Damn her, she was winding up to let me have another one, all the while screeching in Russian.

"Me, I am Captain," I croaked in my best pidgin english.

"What in the hell are you doing in here?"

"Oh, very nice Engineer say OK."

"He did, hey? Well, these are my quarters. Get out."

"No, my daughter, she is in the water, there," pointing to the door leading to my stateroom.

"Well, get her out. I've got to change my clothes and go ashore."

She fired off a stream of Rusky at the door.

"Two minutes, Captain."

Twenty minutes later the daughter came out, looking as if she had died a month ago. They went off, down the alleyway, like two spooks. I looked into my shower. What a mess. Wet towels all over the deck. Not a dry one left. Damn their souls! They'd not get in here again. I changed into my shore clothes and hurried down the gangway where the Agent and his wife were waiting in a tiny, beat up French car. Somehow I folded myself into the back seat, which wasn't a back seat at all, just a storage compartment. With considerable coughing and spitting, we clanked out of the dock area.

We went to a fine looking restaurant where the cooking was half and half. Half French and half Arabic. I should have stayed aboard. Steward Hudson's cooking made this stuff pale by comparison.

Still feeling hungry, we parted company. I thanked them sincerely. It was kind of them to think of me, even though I knew that the cost of the evening would be cleverly hidden when he rendered the ship's account.

I took a taxi back to the ship. As I went up the gangway, I thought to slip into the saloon. I was still hungry and there just might be some night lunch left. Also, the Chief might be in there and I had a score to settle with him. Sure enough, he was in there, just finishing up the last of the cold cuts, damn his scheming soul.

The next morning I was having breakfast with the Chief Mate.

Something had been nagging at me all the way across the Atlantic.

"Say, Mister, have you noticed anything funny about the saloon messman?"

"Can't say that I have, Captain. Why?"

"Well, watch this."

I had finished my first cup of coffee and flagged down the messman.

"Yes, sir, Captain. What will it be this morning?"

"The usual, mess."

"And what would that be, sir?"

"What I have every morning, bacon and eggs."

As soon as he headed for the galley, I said,

"See, Mister. Every morning of my life I have the same. I never vary. Now watch what happens."

In sailed the messman and plunked down a stack of flap jacks.

"There we are, Captain. A dash of syrup?"

"See," I hissed. "He never fails. There is something screwy about this bird. He's as neat as a pin. Can't be booze. His eyes are as clear as ice but his head is way off."

What with the business of getting underway, I put the messman, the passengers, and my revenge on the Chief, out of my mind for later. We were bound for Nemours, just up the coast, to load some kind of ore.

Soon we were heading in. A little pilot cutter was waiting for us well off the entrance, and we hove to for him to board. The Med is a beautiful place in the summer. Sparkling blue, too blue to be true. Just a trace of slight sea. The ship hardly rolled at all. This still could be the best trip of my life. Doubts were creeping in, though. But it could be.

All the years that I went to sea, the ship was the thing. Sure, I went ashore and raised some hell, but ships were my life. How to sail them, work them, take care of them, navigate them. I was never lonely at sea. There was too much to learn, too many stories to listen to, too many questions to be asked. I memorized things about ships like some people memorize poetry. How many fire extinguishers, their location. The size and safe working load of all the running gear. The capacity of all cargo holds. All the myriad bits and pieces that, when added together, make for a seaman. They were all filed away, ready to be remembered years later when the need arose.

We docked at a sort of bulk cargo pier. There was a big gantry crane mounted on wide railroad tracks running the length of the pier. Because our gangway would be in the way of the crane, the Mate had rigged the pilot ladder to get ashore. It was only a rope ladder with wooden steps, hanging down the ship's high side. It would have to suffice for the two or three days that we would be in port.

As soon as we were tied up, I headed for my room. The two passengers were waiting for me. What now? Broken English spilled out of the old one. The gist of it was that they just had to have the use of my bathroom. My arguments were pretty feeble. They did have a point. They couldn't be expected to share the Engineers' john, could they? Against my better judgement, I relented. I set time limits, though. They could use it from eight to ten in the morning and six to eight in the evenings. I'd be on the bridge anyway, during those hours. That settled it—or so I thought.

The next afternoon I was sprawled out on my settee writing a letter to my boy. The sound of the Second Mate bellowing out on the fore deck interrupted my thoughts. The roaring of the big crane prevented me from understanding what he was yelling about, so I just ignored it. Not for long, though. He burst into my office all out of breath.

"Captain, there has been an accident."

"Yeah, what happened?"

"The saloon messman just fell off the pilot ladder. He got all the way to the top, and was climbing over the bulwarks, when over he went, right down to the dock. They just took him away."

"Took him where? Is he dead?"

"No, he isn't dead, at least I don't think so."

I pulled on a shirt and climbed down the ladder, looking for the boss stevedore. I found him holed up in a little tin shack, sound asleep. I got him awake and asked where the hospital was, and told him what had happened. He offered to drive me. Shortly we pulled up in front of a little, dirty, one storied building. It looked more like a garage than a hospital. I made inquiry of a dull eyed native clerk. He pointed a limp finger at a door. I went in, and there was the messman, sitting on a stool. Two men were just putting the finishing touches on an enormous plaster cast.

"How do you feel, mess?"

"Kind of weak, Captain. Busted my shoulder."

"My God, it's a miracle that you're not dead. Have you been drinking some of this North African rot gut?"

"No, I don't drink. Just lost my balance."

One of the men spoke up. As it turned out, he was the doctor.

"You can take him back to the ship now"

"Doc, I can't do that. We're sailing tomorrow. I haven't got anyone to take care of him. He'll have to stay here and catch another ship when he is cured."

The doctor patiently explained that this was only a small clinic, and that they had no facilities to care for him. He must go with us. I knew when I was licked so the stevedore boss and I crammed him into the little car and back to the ship we rattled. How to get him aboard? He couldn't climb the ladder with that big cast on him. We solved it by dumping him into the big ore bucket hanging from the end of the gantry crane. Up he sailed, for all the world like, *Rub a Dub Dub. One Messman in a Tub.*

I was so anxious to get shut of the land and back to sea. Away from dirty little ports, the heat and the bugs, the noise and confusion. I couldn't wait to drop the pilot and have a clean sea breeze. The Bosun and a couple of the hands would break out the big, black wash down hose. The engine room would give them a hundred and twenty-five pounds of water pressure, and clean sea water would blast away all the dirt and debris. The old ship would be clean and quiet again. She'd roll easily, and all would be well. A comfortable, old shoe tranquility would enfold us.

Well, it came to pass, except for those two women. We slipped through the Straits of Gibraltar and out into the Atlantic, headed for Savannah, again. Savannah was one of my favorite ports and I looked forward to a pleasant end to the voyage. I settled down to the comfortable rhythm of life at sea. Before dawn I would join the Mate on the bridge. We were old friends, and there was very little formality between us. We would gab about ship's business, and drink coffee. Then, when the first signs of dawn appeared behind us, I'd go into the chart room and get my sextant for dawn star sights. On most ships all the Mates and the Skipper kept their sextants in the chart room. My sextant, though, was a British beauty that I had bought in Scotland during the war. I jealously kept it in my office. I didn't want any young squirt of a Third Mate fiddling with it.

The first morning out I finished my second mug of coffee and went for my sextant. On the way I stopped in the chart room. The previous evening I had calculated our dead reckoning position at the time of dawn and figured out the altitudes and azimuths of three stars. I picked up these notes and felt in my pocket to make sure that I had my stop watch. By God, my office door was locked again! I hammered on the door. No answer.

"Open this door, you crazy Russians. I've got to get in there."

I could hear water running again, and my radio was blaring out Arabic music from Morocco. Sparks poked his head out and said,

"Captain, I was just coming out of the radio shack when I saw them going in. I tried to stop them, but they just slammed the door and locked it."

Back I trudged to the bridge, cursing like a wild man. The Mate tried to console me by offering me the loan of his sextant, but no. There is an unwritten law of the sea that an officer never borrows, loans, or parts with his sextant and his razor. It is always respected. It holds that you must have a razor to look presentable enough to get a berth. Then, if you are fortunate enough to get the berth, you must have a sextant in order to do your job.

The next day the Second Mate came up and asked me to come have a look at the saloon messman. I followed him down to the main deck. The Messman's room was right next to the saloon on the starboard side. We ducked into his room. I stared, aghast, at him. He was sitting on the edge of his bunk. His face was emaciated and the color of putty. Sweat streamed down his face. His hands and legs were trembling something awful. And he smelled, too.

281

"Mess, for God's sake. What's the matter with you?"

He just moaned and pointed to his suitcase. The Second Mate opened it up.

"Look what's in here, Captain. I found these this morning. This guy's a hop head."

I looked. A hypodermic syringe, needles, a bottle of alcohol, and a vial of morphine sulphate pills.

"I'll just throw this stuff overboard, huh?"

The messman was wailing and pleading. He got so loud that you could hear him all over the main deck.

"Mister, give him the God damned stuff. We can't have him screeching all the way to Savannah."

"He can't stick the needle into himself because of the cast."

"Well then, you stick it into him. I'll not have him going bananas on us. It's bad enough that he can't work and we all have to carry our grub from the galley and make our own coffee. Why, I've even got the Third Mate cleaning the pantry."

Damn my soul! And this was going to be the most pleasant voyage of my life. Spoiled, ruined by those two women and the dope head messman. I knew that there was something screwy about him but I never suspected dope. Then the passengers. Two or three days later, the old one came up on the bridge during the Second Mate's watch and accused him of trying to rape her daughter. The daughter had complained of a sprained back, so I had asked the Second to have a look at her. Now, the Second had never been too particular, at least by reputation, but even he wouldn't go so far. I had to take the wheel myself while the quartermaster dragged the old woman off the bridge.

The beautiful summer days slipped by unnoticed. I was reduced to using the Mates' head and shower. My sextant was in the chart room. I timed my meals so as to avoid those two witches. I would find myself furtively peeking into the saloon. If they were in there, I'd sneak away.

My high hopes had been so thoroughly dashed that, even today, so many years later, it is distasteful to write about it.

At last we sighted the Savannah Lightship and the pilot boat. We picked up our pilot, an old acquaintance, and steamed up the river to our berth. After the formalities of Customs and Immigration had been completed, we got rid of the two witches and the saloon messman. The witches to a destination unknown, the messman to the US Public Health Hospital. Good riddance!

When you come to a fork in the road, take it.
Yogi Berra

-48-

PILOTING ON CHESAPEAKE BAY

After World War II, finally ground to a halt, I found myself master of a ship carrying coal to devastated Northern Europe. Our usual run was to load coal in either Norfolk or Baltimore; then deliver it to a Scandinavian port, and then load Swedish iron ore in Narvik, Norway in the winter, and Lulea, Sweden, in the summer. Back and forth we sailed, with very little time in port. We could load almost ten thousand tons of coal in less than a day. It became somewhat monotonous, other than the never ending battle against the North Atlantic weather. I cast around in my mind for some project to occupy me. One day I came up with the answer. I would study and sit for a Pilotage Endorsement to my master's license, for the waters of Chesapeake Bay. Norfolk is at the mouth of the Bay, and Baltimore is at it's headwaters. It is one of the longest pilotages in the country; something over two hundred miles.

Maybe I had better explain just what an endorsement is. All foreign flagged vessels entering or leaving an American port are required by law to engage a pilot and pay a substantial pilotage fee, based on the draft of the vessel. As far as American vessels are concerned, if they are running coastwise, and are under *'Enrollment,'* a Customs term, and if the master has an Endorsement for a particular waterway, he may act as Pilot and avoid payment of the pilotage fee. However, if the ship is under *'Registry,'* that is, running to or from a foreign port, the master holding the proper Endorsement may act as Pilot, but the ship is still liable for the pilotage fee. Sounds complicated, I know, but that's bureaucracy. As we were always under registry, and running foreign, I wouldn't save my company any money. The only advantage was the half hour or so, saved stopping to pick up or disembark a pilot. It was simply a matter of pride with me. I have seen masters' tickets completely covered with Endorsements. Those Skippers were sort of elite. Those Endorsements were actually written in longhand, right across the face of the license.

While I was scheming up my latest project, we were bound for Baltimore to discharge a full load of iron ore. Right on schedule we picked up the Chesapeake Lightship and headed in for the area where the pilot boat was stationed. And there she was, right where she was supposed to be. The *'Pilot Wanted'* flag was flying from our signal halyards. I rang up *Stop Engines* on the engine room telegraph and made a lee for the small boat dancing over the waves towards us. She pulled alongside, and the pilot swung onto our Jacob's ladder. As soon as he reached the bridge, I rang up *Full Ahead,* and we started the long haul up the Bay to Baltimore. I stayed on the bridge all night with the pilot, plying him with questions about navigating on the Bay. Evidently my questions puzzled him, because he asked my why I was asking so many. I told him of my idea. I don't think that he thought too much of my idea. After all, any time that I might act as pilot, it was one regular pilot that wouldn't be needed.

The pilots in every U. S. port are organized into Associations, which are really Co-operatives. They have existed for many years, and are very close knit bodies. They each operate a most comprehensive apprentice program. Almost invariably the apprentices are sons of pilots. Outsiders have very little chance of gaining admittance. When they have served their time they become *Light Draft* pilots. Gradually, as they become more proficient and gain experience, they are raised, foot by foot to deeper draft vessels. These Associations own their own boats. After all expenses for operations, boat maintenance, fuel, insurance, office expenses, etc., are deducted, the net profit is shared among the members on a sliding scale, depending on their draft status. In any busy port these men do very well, indeed.

This pilot gave me the name of a private navigation school in Baltimore, and suggested that I go and see them.

The next day we arrived at the Quarantine anchorage. As soon as we were cleared by Quarantine and Immigration, a tow boat came along side, and we proceeded to the Sparrows Point piers of the Bethlehem Steel Corp. As soon as the Bosun had lowered the gangway, I set off for the Agent's office. Once there, I turned over all my voyage reports for mailing to our home office in Boston. Then we made arrangements for the U. S. Shipping Commissioner to come down to the ship the following afternoon to pay off the crew and sign them off Articles. The Agent very kindly invited me to lunch with him at Millers, a world famous seafood restaurant. What food! Raw oysters, followed by Crab Imperial, made with Chesapeake Bay blue crabs. Food fit for a king, and doubly good after a steady diet of ship's food.

From the restaurant I headed for the navigation school. There, I met the owner, a real old time shipmaster. I told him what I had in mind.

"No problem," he said." "Classes will be three nights a week, or three days a week. Take your choice."

I explained that I couldn't do that because we would be sailing the following day.

"Couldn't you put together some sort of correspondence course?"

He allowed that he could, and that he would have it ready the next morning.

He was as good as his word. When I called by the next morning, he had it ready; all in a neat, loose-leafed folder. I was in a hurry so I stuffed it into my briefcase without glancing at it.

"How much do I owe you, Captain?"

"How does fifty dollars strike you? I've given you everything you need to know to pass the exam. Stop in when you return and we'll have a dry run before you sit."

"You have been very kind, and I appreciate it. So long."

I set out for the ship, again. I'd be lucky to make it in time for dinner. I did, though. The Commissioner had arrived early. Those birds could smell a free meal a mile off. There he was, in the saloon, helping himself to seconds. I joined him for a quick bite. Afterwards I invited him up to my quarters for a quick snort. I always tried to stay on the right side of *officials*. You could never beat them so why not join them, right?

He polished off two big ones, patted his big belly and said,

"Let's pay them off."

I followed him with a brief case full of cash. The Radio Officer had everything ready in the saloon. Discharges piled upon one side, the payroll on the other. We were all set. The Bosun poked his head in the doorway.

"Send'em in, Bosun."

An hour later the last man had filed through. The ship was off Articles!

There was just time for a quick shower and a short snooze before supper. Sleep was impossible, though. The big cranes yanking our iron ore out of the hatches made it out of the question.

Well," I mused, *I'll just take a look at my study course.*

I sprawled out on the settee and opened the cover to the first page. I couldn't believe my eyes! All the courses were magnetic. And what was worse, they were given in points, half points, quarter points, and yes, even in eighths! For example:

> *Chesapeake Light Vessel to Cape Henry Buoy--West, 3/8 South, Distance, 12.7 miles.*
> *Cape Henry Buoy to Buoy MG#lO--North-west, 1/8 North, Distance 14.1 miles.*

This was crazy! All these courses were Magnetic, which made matters worse. Now that the War was over, all ships were equipped with Gyro compasses, which read in degrees and were True. Gyros pointed to the true, geographic, North Pole. Further, as long ago as 1931, courses and bearings were always expressed in degrees, never in points and quarter points. As for eighth points, I had never even heard of them!

What all this meant was that in actual practice, I would have to memo-

285

rize dozens of courses and bearings expressed in Magnetic points, half points, quarter points and eighth points; then mentally convert them to degrees, Magnetic, apply the local variation to arrive at a true course or bearing. This was, obviously, an impossibility.

Still baffled, I went down to supper. The only thing that I could imagine was that I had been sold an ancient, long out of date, study course. Having arrived at that conclusion, I felt that I had been taken by that kindly old shipmaster. Well, I'd straighten him out just as soon as I could get up to his school.

I went through his door like a Northeast gale. He had a small class studying. I marched myself up to his desk, flung the course down, and demanded an explanation. What he told me was beyond belief. It was obvious, though, that he was telling the truth. In fact, what he told me, I knew all along; that change comes very slowly, indeed, concerning anything in the maritime field. In the by-gone days of sail, points, quarter points, magnetic compasses, and such were the way of life; so, modern technology notwithstanding, why change?

I would have to memorize all those courses and bearings one way for the examiners, and another way for actual use. Well, so be it. There being no time like the present, I sat in my room until long after midnight, trying to memorize a lot of useless information.

The next morning discharging was completed, and we shifted to a Baltimore coal pier for loading. The crew was filled out from the Union hiring hall and Articles were signed again.

The time came when it was, *All Hands, Fore and Aft,* and we were off again, this time bound for Sweden. Again, I picked the pilot's brain. He confirmed what I had been told; pass the exam one way, pilot the ship another. He told me that all the time that he was an apprentice, he was schooled in the *old way.* Then, when he started boarding ships, accompanied by a licensed pilot, he got educated in the *right way.* Some fine kettle of fish, but that's the way it had to be.

These Bay pilots didn't have it too easy. When they disembarked down at the Virginia Capes, they had to jump from a swaying rope ladder into a small launch. One false move meant, at best, a dunking in winter waters; at worst, death. Then they boarded the pilot boat, a large seaworthy vessel. Often, if shipping was heavy, they turned right around and boarded another inbound ship for a second night without sleep.

This pilot was a senior man, because we were deeply laden, right down to our winter marks. He gave me some good advice.

"Get as familiar as possible with the Bay's landmarks. The headlands, bays, inlets, etc. Commit to absolute memory all bearings of shore lights and ranges. Have a clear picture of every buoy in the Bay, together with it's day

286

markings and the sequence and color of it's light.

The tide wasn't a serious problem; it either ran with the ship or against it. He stressed over and over again, *When in thick weather, or if you have any doubts about your position, STOP AND ANCHOR!*

All his advice was prudent seamanship which had been inculcated in me for many years, and would be followed,

The next morning he left us, and we hauled around on the Rhumb Line course to a point off Newfoundland, where we would commence our Great Circle course. The weather remained fine and settled, so I had plenty of time to study. I had always found it easier to memorize by writing the subject. Now, I would kill two birds with one stone. I was trying to teach myself to type. The only typewriter on the ship was the one in the radio shack. It had a disadvantage, though. It only had capital letters, but I'd make do.

I arranged my schedule so as not to interfere with Spark's listening times. That old, mechanical typewriter was a pain, but I soon got used to it. Over and over, hour after hour, and day after day, I doggedly pounded away.

At first I concentrated on courses and distances, feeling that they were the most difficult. Then I switched to lights, beacons, and buoys. Wow! They were worse. here's a few.

CAPE HENRY LIGHTHOUSE GP. FL. 3 EV. 20 SEC.
RED SECTOR, 155-233 DEGREES, COVERS SHOALS
OUTSIDE CAPE CHARLES AND MIDDLE GROUND,
INSIDE THE CAPE. DIAPHONE, 2 EV. 20 SEC.
DIRECTIONAL, 077-333 RADIO BEACON, 290 KC, 'K'
OCTAGONAL TOWER, BLACK AND WHITE

YORK SPIT GP. FL. RED, EV 3 SEC.
2 WHITE SECTORS; 107-116, 145-163 DEGREES
DIAPHONE, ONE BLAST EV. 20 SEC.
(ONE BELL EV. 10 SEC.)
WHITE HEXAGONAL TOWER

OLD PLANTATION FLATS FL. EV. 3 SEC.
RED SECTOR COVERS MIDDLE GROUND, 343-022
DEGREES DIAPHONE, ONE BLAST EV. 15 SEC.
(ONE BELL EV. 15 SEC.) WHITE SQUARE TOWER

And dozens more, just as difficult to memorize. I stuck to it like glue, though. Gradually, almost imperceptibly, it was becoming imprinted on my mind. For a change of pace, I turned to another part of the exam: The Inland Rules of the Road, and in particular, the Pilot Rules, which involved vessels meeting, crossing, and passing. The old Captain had stressed that this was an important part of the test, and would weigh heavily on my score. He had also told me to pay particular attention to the lights required to be displayed by towing vessels and their tows.

There is one thing that I have neglected to mention: The requirements layed down for sitting for an endorsement. They are brief but strict. A candidate must have made at least three round trips over the waterway for which he is sitting. And here's the clincher--at least two of the round trips must have taken place in the twelve months preceding the exam.

While all this studying was going on, I was expanding my goal. I would still sit for my Chesapeake Bay Endorsement, but now it would be only a stepping stone to my new goal--Pilot for the Panama Canal! Yep, that's what I would go for. The Canal pilots were the creme de la creme of the seagoing fraternity. Here's why. The United States is one of the few countries in the world that has the apprentice system for pilots. They have never been to sea, yet they were superb ship handlers. Most other countries had the prime qualification that a pilot had to have been a qualified shipmaster, first. England, a first rate maritime country, has their Trinity House, the organization that controls all pilotage in the British Isles. Their members had all been licensed shipmasters. Our Panama Canal has the same system. You had to hold an unlimited master's license to apply. If accepted, you then had to serve a long, tough apprenticeship. However, if you made it, you were at the very top of the profession. And the pay and living allowances were 'way above anything we could dream of. Look out, Panama, here I come!

Back and forth we sailed across the Atlantic. There seemed some diabolical force at work to prevent me from reaching my goal. I just couldn't get the two round trips within twelve months. Twice, I came close. The first time, my second trip up the Chesapeake was within reach. Alas, we returned to the States in ballast and loaded in Norfolk. The second time, we went into Southern England for a load of china clay consigned to Philadelphia, and again loaded in Norfolk. The last time, the ship came home in ballast to New York, and the ship was laid up. The coal business was finished. And all those months I was studying. I felt that the Chesapeake Bay was branded on my brain.

It was all for naught. Never did I get my Endorsement, nor did I ever get to Panama. Dreams and hopes die hard, but die they did.

288

-49-

JUST ANOTHER VOYAGE

Once again we were bound for a Scandinavian port with a full load of coal. It seemed as though Northern Europe had an insatiable appetite for coal, once the war was over. I had been running back and forth for the last couple of years, Norfolk or Baltimore to either Sweden or Denmark. Then back to Baltimore with a full load of iron ore from Narvik, Norway in the winter, and Lulea, Sweden in the summer. Each trip, both East and Westbound, we transited Pentland Firth, between the North coast of Scotland and the Orkney Islands. A lousy place but it saved a day's run. Every trip, up until now, I had struck the Firth just right, clear weather and a slack tide. This time it wasn't to be.

I have my log book of that voyage in front of me. The entries are unusually sparse. Well they might be. It took me three damned days to get through. Fog had finally caught up with me.

> *AUGUST 18-0100 GREENWICH TIME.*
> *CAPE WRATH BEARING 180° TRUE.*
> *COURSE 090° TRUE. SPEED, 10 knots.*
> *0500 GREENWICH TIME. THICK FOG.*
> *STEAMING 090°-270° TRUE BETWEEN*
> *STRATHEN AND DUNNET. SPEED,*
> *SLOW.*

The weather had started to worsen when we came up to Cape Wrath, but we heard her horn. Sparks had reported intermittent fog forecast for the area, but this was thick. We couldn't see the focsle head. *Well,* I consoled myself, *this will clear up shortly. Besides, there is no wind, sea calm, just a temporary delay.* So I thought. The long, slow hours crept by. All day, all night, and all day again. I prowled the bridge like a caged animal. *It has got to clear soon.* I was driving poor Sparks nuts asking for more and more weather reports. I should have known better. This Godforsaken part of the world always had fog, with once in awhile a clear day or two. I had had better luck than I deserved, the past two years. What to do? We were coming up to the third day. Cold sandwiches and gallons of coffee were finally letting me down. My legs were trembling, my feet were so swollen that I had taken to padding around in my stocking feet. I was just about at the end of my rope. The Mate and I were poring over the British chart of the area. Poor bottom, too deep to anchor—damn! Then the Mate nudged me and stuck the dividers into a spot to the Northeast. By God, there was a tiny little spot with a sandy bottom. It was no more than a few ship's lengths in diameter and not quite as deep as the surrounding water.

"Mister, we'll get a good RDF bearing of Sule Skerry, the Second Mate will be on the Fathometer. Then, when we're right over the spot, just creeping along, you will back off the starboard anchor, nice and easy, and Presto—I'll get a couple of hours sleep."

And it came to pass. There we were, all ten thousand tons of us, at anchor practically out in the North Atlantic Ocean.

"Mister. I am going to collapse on the Chart room settee. If the sea starts to make up, get me up if you have to use a club."

Sounds crazy, I know, but I had no choice. I had reached the end of my rope. My last thought before passing out was, *My God. What will the crew think? Anchored in bad water and thick fog, and he goes to sleep.*

Three hours later, the Mate grabbed me by the shoulders and sat me upright.

"It's clearing, Captain. The carpenter has got the anchor coming up."

It is amazing what three hours sleep will do for a man. I hobbled out on the bridge and away we sailed. I must say, though, that damned Pentland Firth showed me who was the boss.

We shot through the Firth in fine style and squared away for the Skaw. Sparks brought me a message from our Charterers nominating Oxelsund, Sweden as our port of discharge. It is located just South of Stockholm. The Sailing Directions indicated that it was a small port, and fairly easy to enter.

Down the Kattegat we slogged, making our usual ten and a half knots. The sea was calm and the air was balmy. When we got down near Copenhagen we damn near collided with a ferry boat running from Malmo, Sweden to Copenhagen. Those ferries run day and night, and act just like the Staten Island ferries in New York harbor—like they own the seas. I guess that all ships stand clear of them because they sure don't give way.

Soon enough we picked up a pilot and threaded our way through the countless islands to the port of Oxelsund. It's a tricky business navigating through these islands. These waters freeze solid almost every winter, so removing thousands of buoys each fall, and then setting them out again in the spring was too big an undertaking.

The Swedes solve that problem by just setting out a few buoys and fill in the rest of the channels with saplings. Yep, that's right. Small trees, anchored. Not too bad in clear weather, but they must be hell at night. No lights on them, of course. It gets pretty confusing because side channels are forever branching off, and the saplings all look alike.

On the way in, the pilot very kindly invited me to supper at his home. After we tied up, he waited for me while I changed into my shoregoing suit. Down the gangway we went and my education to the Socialist government of Sweden began.

He walked over to a very classy looking car, unlocked it and motioned me in. As we drove out of the docks, I complimented him on his fine car. He just shrugged. I remarked that Oxelsund was such a small port, that he must have plenty of leisure time. Again a shrug. I asked him if he had another job during the long winter when the port was frozen in. He looked at me in surprise.

"My job is a Federal one, and it pays me a very adequate salary until retirement whether there are any ships to pilot or not."

Some job! Handle a dozen or so ships a year. He pointed out his home just coming into view. It was magnificent. All natural wood, and hanging out over the water on a high, wooded point. By this time I was envious. Once inside, he introduced me to his wife and three daughters. All three of them had braces on their teeth.

"The dentists must keep you broke," I observed.

"Not at all. No Swede pays anything for dental or medical care."

"Who does pay for the Doctors and dentists?"

"The King, or government."

Socialism has serious drawbacks, but I sure envied him. Their kitchen was right out of a magazine. All stainless steel, with all the latest gadgets. And this was back in the late forties.

After a fine supper, served right out over the water, I reluctantly announced that I had better get back to my ship. The Swedes sure seem to have things going for them. And stayed out of two wars to boot.

The next morning the Chief Engineer laid a beaut on me.

"Skipper, tomorrow is Sunday. Let's put the motor life boat in the water and have a picnic on one of the islands. We'll get the Steward to put up a lunch. Of course we'll have to invite the belly robbing bastard, but at least he won't be able to poison us, seeing as how he'll have to eat it himself. How about it?"

"Chief, that's the first good idea that you've had this trip. Who should we invite?"

"Well, there'll be you and me and the Steward. How about the First Assistant Engineer?"

"And the Chief Mate," I countered. "And Sparks. That's enough."

"Great," says he. "We'll get underway at nine o'clock, right after breakfast. That will give the Steward time to put up a fine lunch. We both leaned back, beaming at each other. A fine prospect. Then an ugly thought intruded.

291

"Now just a damned minute, Chief. Tomorrow's Sunday. We'll have to pay the Bosun and a couple of sailors overtime to rig up the falls to the winches, and you know that old skinflint Norton, (The company Comptroller.) will have a fit, and make me pay for it."

"Phooey, Captain. You are a poor schemer. Charge it up to securing life boats during heavy weather. Your education has been sadly neglected."

He had such a smug look on his puss that I felt like dunking him in his oatmeal. Only engineers would eat the damned stuff, anyway. But, the die was cast. The Steward went for the idea and promised a fine feast. The others were discretely invited and accepted with alacrity Everything was set for tomorrow.

Way before breakfast, the Mate had all the surplus junk out of the boat and piled on deck. During breakfast, the Steward was loading the boat with food enough to feed an army. He even had an enormous fresh salad, made with Swedish vegetables, bought the day before. Swedish meat balls, yet, and lots more. The Mate told the Bosun that as soon as we had lowered the boat, to rig the falls to number three and four hatch winches, ready for hoisting upon our return The plug was screwed in, the bow painter rigged forward, and we all got aboard. The Mate yelled for the Bosun to lower away, and down we went. The falls were unhooked. I spun the crank and she fired on the second try. The painter was cast off, the clutch engaged, and away we chugged. I headed for the entrance to the harbor and started following the saplings. Two or three times we sidetracked up side channels. It was a beautiful Sunday morning, cool, and bright sunshine. There I sat with one arm draped over the tiller, Lord and Master of all I surveyed.

"Say, Captain, there is a likely looking island right over the port bow. There is even a little white beach where we can eat."

"Right, Chief, coming port easy.

Then I did one of the most foolish things of my life. I put the helm over and cut inside of one of the saplings. My feeble mind reasoned that they were for ships, not little life boats. Crunch! The boat lurched and we were hard and fast aground. These Liberty boats were made of tin or aluminum, riveted with tiny rivets at the seams.

"She's leaking. We're sinking, and I can't swim," screeched the Chief.

"Shut up. The water is only six inches deep."

He was stamping his feet on a split seam through which water was pouring. Before I could stop him, he ripped off his shirt and stuffed it into the broken seam. Dear God! We had enough talent in that boat to sail the Queen Elizabeth around the world. Both the Mate and I held unlimited Master's tickets. Both the Chief and the First Assistant held unlimited Chief's tickets, and Sparks held a first class commercial radio operator's certificate. It was my fault, though. What a disgrace. All thoughts of a picnic were abandoned and we started back with the Chief firmly planted on the leak, his big feet holding his shirt in place.

Now the coverup began. We were all sworn to secrecy before we got back to the ship. The boat would be hoisted aboard and not a word about her ruptured bottom would be said. Then, maybe on the way home, when we hit some bad weather, log book entries would be made to the effect that during a gale, number one life boat pounded on her chocks and split a seam. The trouble with lying is that inevitably one must tell more lies to justify the first one. So it was, here. All the way home we had good weather, so, desperation, we resorted to making false weather notations, building up over three days to a full gale. If only I could do it over again, I would tell the truth and the only damage would be to my damned pride. A sorry piece of business, indeed. I paid a high price for a picnic that never took place and never should have. That big, fat Engineer did look so damned funny, though, trying to stuff his shirt in the hole in the boat with his feet.

The next day I received word from the ship's Agent that upon completion of discharge, we were to proceed to Stockholm for bunkers, thence to Lulea, (pronounced Lulo) there to load a full cargo of Swedish iron ore for Baltimore.

It was only a short distance from Oxelsund to the pilot station outside of the Sharragard, the deep belt of islands that protect the entire coast of Sweden. The Stockholm pilot boarded us for the somewhat longer trip through the islands to Stockholm. The scenery was beyond words. All those islands, rocky shores, wooded, hundreds and hundreds of pleasure boats, all of them finished in natural varnished wood. Not like boats in the States which are mostly white.

We tied up at the oil docks where I was told that there would be a delay in bunkering. It was a major holiday. No pump men were available. Sweden has more holidays than working days. Some country!

The pilot said that he would stay aboard over night and take us out on the following noon. The Mate and I decided to take a look at the town. We went on a long walking tour of the cleanest city that I have ever been in. The streets, the buildings, everything was spotless. Feeling the need of a little refreshment, we popped into a nice place and ordered two Scotch and sodas. The waiter explained that Sweden had a sort of prohibition. A drink could only be ordered with a meal.

"But we're not hungry. We just ate on our ship."

"Not to worry. I'll be right back, gents."

Back he came with the two drinks and two plates on which were lamb chops, mashed potatoes, and green peas.

"Waiter, we told you. We are not hungry."

He picked up the plates, and with a flourish, turned them upside down. The food stayed right on the plates. It was all made of wood, cleverly painted.

"There," he said. "That covers the law. You are now having a drink with your food."

So much for the law.

The next morning we finished bunkering. The lines were let go and we headed out through the islands again. The holiday was still on and there were even more sailing yachts than before. Hundreds of them going every which way.

The Rules of the Road have recently been changed to give deep water vessels traveling in a restricted channel the right of way over pleasure boats. Back then, though, a sailing vessel always had the right of way over a steam vessel. Shortly, a large yawl was seen on our port bow heading to cross in front of us. All her sails were set and she was making knots.

"Pilot, how are we going to avoid her? Is there enough water?"

"No, we have got to hold course. If we don't, we'll run aground."

And hold on we did. It was obvious that the big sail boat was trying to pass ahead of us. And it was also too obvious that she wasn't going to make it. She swept under our bow. What her foolhardy Skipper hadn't realized was that our high sides would kill her wind. We were light and high out of the water. All in an instant her sails went slack. Her momentum carried her just beyond our stem but when she came in sight, under our starboard bow, she was capsized with her masts and sails lying in the water. We could see at least six people, either clinging to her cockpit or her rigging as we swept by.

"We can't stop, Captain. They will be all right. There are plenty of boats coming to her rescue."

"My God, pilot, we can't just leave them."

"Yes, we can. This isn't the first time that this has happened. Maybe some day they will learn to stop playing chicken, as you Americans say."

I made a full report by radio to our Swedish Agents, our owners, and gave a written report to the pilot for him to give to the Swedish Coast Guard, or whoever he thought should get it. What is surprising is that from that day to this, I never heard a word. Not even from my own owners. I often think, though, that if we had hit that yawl broadside with our stem, it would have been a tragedy. They would have, undoubtedly, all been killed.

As soon as we got outside of the last of the islands, our pilot left us. I rang up, *Full Ahead* and we squared away up the Gulf of Bothnia for Lulea.

This body of water is practically landlocked, and in this good summer weather, was just as flat as a lake. Being light, our propeller was half out of water, and made a big, thrashing wake that stretched for miles astern. We were following the usual sapling buoys, relieved every four or five miles by a proper, lighted buoy. The lights weren't needed, though. In these Latitudes, it was daylight all night. The sun never sets in the summertime.

I was spending all my time sitting in my high chair out on the windward bridge wing. It was so peaceful, except that those ships, when light and going full ahead, vibrated something fierce. The smoke stack stays and the mast shrouds were flapping and humming like the strings on a big fiddle. You could feel it through your feet, in your bunk, everywhere. The plates in the dining saloon would creep right into your lap if you didn't keep one hand on them. It was a nice feeling, though, because we were making knots instead of bucking the weather.

Our bunkering in Stockholm had been carefully calculated, right to the barrel. As soon as the war was over, Chief Engineers reverted to their old practice of hiding oil, *Up their sleeve.* Our Marine Superintendent, Captain Litchfield, a very canny bird, and more than a match for a whole room full of Chiefs, had come down hard on them. He had sent each of them a letter, which they were required to acknowledge, telling them bluntly that the practice would stop or they would be on the beach. You see, for every ton of oil that they had hidden, we sacrificed a ton of cargo, which represented a sizable loss of income to the company. I even heard of one Chief who, by poring over the ship's blue prints, had found a void space underneath the fireroom bulkhead between it and the double bottom under number three hold. He had drilled holes and ran pipes himself. In it he could hide thirty or forty tons of oil, and did. They were like damned squirrels hiding nuts. Captain Litchfield was too smart for them, though. He had patiently worked through the Log Abstracts from every ship in the fleet. Thus, he established the average fuel consumption for each ship, in good weather and bad, loaded, half loaded, or light. Then he would calculate the fuel requirements for each voyage, allowing, of course, a twenty percent surplus, an insurance requirement, which is what any prudent seaman would be content with. By the same process he told each Chief Mate and Master exactly how many tons of cargo they would be expected to load. Our particular ship had a pretty steady consumption rate of .7 of a barrel per mile. so we knew, to the ton, how many tons of ore that we could load in Lulea. On my first trip to Lulea, I was puzzled by the absence of any reference to pilotage in the Sailing Directions. I found out, after steaming around for a couple of hours, that they didn't board until after the ship entered the harbor. This voyage I steamed boldly right in. There was the pilot, sitting in his little boat, smoking his pipe and reading a newspaper. Leisurely stuffing his pipe in his pocket, he fired up his engine and came alongside. Tying his boat to the ladder, up he came, all business.

"Morning, Captain, *Hard Left and Half Ahead,* if you please."

In no time at all we were alongside, all fast. The Mate had opened the hatches before coming alongside, so in a matter of minutes the loading chutes were swung aboard and ore commenced roaring down into the lower holds. Me, I was off for town. And what transportation! The ship's Chandler was a widow and what a character. She would meet the ship on an ancient bicycle. She had gotten the Steward's order for fresh milk, bread, vegetables, and what not. Now I was perched on the rear luggage carrier, trying to keep my feet from dragging in the dust of the dirt road. I don't know if other Skippers felt it beneath their dignity, but I loved it. There I was, cruising along listening to broken English or broken Swedish, as the case might be. I felt like a kid again.

The town of Lulea is the soul of informality. No going to the Customs House to enter and clear the ship. What few formalities there were took place at shipside and were brief. On my first trip to Lulea, I was told that we were the first Allied ship since the war began to enter the port. It was a great experience. They damned near gave me the town.

Lulea is located almost on the border between Sweden and Finland. Lapland is just to the North. Some of the inhabitants reflect their proximity to Lapland by their slant eyes and broad, flat faces.

Loading proceeded at a fantastic pace. I only had time for one meal ashore, and time to buy my son a *Kick Sled,* a strange sled by our standards. Two long, flexible runners extend way out in back of a little single seat. The operator stands on the runners and by shifting balance, steers it. I was told that all through the snowy winter months, they are the principle means of transportation.

So much for sightseeing. We were loaded deep with almost ten thousand tons of heavy, dense Swedish iron ore destined for the gigantic Bethleham Steel Company's Sparrow's Point steel mill. Just outside of Baltimore, it is the largest tidewater steel mill in the world.

The crew was busy replacing hatch beams and battening down for sea. We would have to creep out of the harbor at dead slow speed because there would only be twelve inches of water under our keel. The Chief Mate had loaded every last pound that the ship could lift. He didn't want Captain Litchfield breathing down his neck.

Back down the Gulf we wallowed. Homeward bound. A great feeling. We steamed out of the Gulf, up the Kattegat, across the Skaggarack, back through that cursed Pentland Firth, this time in good weather, and stuck our rusty snout into the North Atlantic. Bound on the Great Circle route for the States.

After an uneventful passage, we arrived at the Virginia Capes, bound up the Chesapeake Bay for Baltimore. When I first picked up the flashing lights of Cape Charles and Cape Henry in my binoculars, it was pouring rain. The night was black, but in spite of the rain, visibility was good. I put the ship on a slow bell and kept sweeping the horizon looking for the blue light that would identify the pilot boat. Twice I had the Third Mate set off a blue flare, signifying, *I NEED A PILOT.* At last I spotted a dim blue light.

"There she is, Mister, Half Ahead."

The rain was coming down harder than ever. All I had on was a pair of pants and a khaki shirt, so I was staying nice and dry in the wheel house. Slowly we approached the pilot vessel. As we got closer, her blinker started signaling.

"Mister," I hollered at our very young, very new, Third Mate. "Get out there on the light and see what he has to say."

"Captain, I'm not sure that I can read blinker."

Damn. All of us who had just gone through a long war had, of necessity, become somewhat adept at flapping the lamp. In convoy, messages were being flashed throughout the convoy all day long. Sort of a sea going party line. Out I dashed, switched on our big signal light and acknowledged.

WHAT SHIP, AND WHERE BOUND?
SS THEODORE PARKER, BALTIMORE.

I answered.

WE DO NOT HAVE A PILOT AT PRESENT.
FOLLOW ME AND ANCHOR WHEN WE SIGNAL.
WE WILL HAVE A PILOT BOARD YOU FROM
THE NEXT OUTBOUND VESSEL.

Back into the wheel house I sloshed, soaked to the hide.

"Mister," I said through chattering teeth. "My compliments to the Chief Mate. Have him get the anchor lights ready, then stand by to anchor. And you, Mister, better go back to school. One of the requirements of a deck officer is that he be proficient in the use of the signaling lamp. Move it!"

I admit that I was rough on him, but, hell, I was so cold and wet that I could have killed him.

We were still creeping along in the downpour, following the dim blue light. The Mate phoned from the focsle head and said that the anchor lights were hoisted, all ready to be plugged in, and both anchors were clear for running. This Chief Mate of mine was a very efficient man. He had drilled the Bosun and carpenter in the anchoring procedure as if we were a battle ship. Both anchor lights were hoisted, one on the fore stay, the other back aft. The Bosun would stand by the forward light, the carpenter the after one. The minute that they heard the anchor chain running out, they would plug the lights into deck receptacles. The Third Mate would snap off the running lights, and we would be at anchor.

Just about then, the pilot boat started blinking again. I ran out and acknowledged.

ANCHOR WHERE YOU ARE.

The old faithful of World War II

"Stop engines, Mister. Let go the starboard anchor."

The anchor roared out The Third Mate snapped off the running lights. Damn! No anchor lights came on. I phone the bow.

"Get those anchor lights on, Mister."

"Can't, Captain. The plugs are shorted out by the rain."

Just then something made me look aft. Dear suffering Christ! There was a ship heading right for us, her red and green side lights gleaming brightly. Her range lights were right in line. And us with no lights on at all. I raced into the wheel house, snapped on our running lights, and blew the danger signal on the whistle. I dashed back out on the port bridge wing to watch helplessly as the unknown ship went full astern, her bows slicing by us. Whew! She sheared to starboard, missing us by less than a ship's length. I could see that she was one of those big self unloading coal colliers, running in for Norfolk. Those coastwise coal boats did all their own piloting. While all this was going on, the anchor lights blazed on. And us at anchor with the running lights still on.

"Mister," I said to the Third Mate. "Get some anchor bearings on the Capes. I'm going below to change into some dry clothes.

When I came back, he was plotting our position on the chart. Peeking over his shoulder, the enormity of what had just happened bore down upon me. First, we had come to anchor without displaying any anchor lights. Second, I had snapped back on our running lights while at anchor. Third the anchor lights had come back on while the running lights were still burning. Forth, I had blown the danger signal, which is allowable only in Inland Waters. Now our anchor bearings showed that we were **outside** of Inland Waters. The dividing line between Inland and International waters was a line drawn from Cape Charles to Cape Henry, and we were outside of that line. I had, in the space of minutes, violated God knows how many Rules of the Road. If that collier had hit us, the Inspectors would have buried me for a thousand years. I wearily straightened up and pondered, *Am I in the wrong business? Maybe I should go ashore and raise chickens.*

As we lay at anchor, waiting for a pilot, I reflected on the voyage now ending. Ripped the bottom out of the motor life boat, swamped and capsized a sail boat full of people, and now, damn near got sunk while at anchor. What little egotism that I ever had leaked out of me forever more.

Shortly after dawn an outbound vessel dropped off her Chesapeake Bay pilot and he boarded us for the trip up the Bay. He started moaning about being over worked, no sleep, a hell of a way to make a living. On and on he went.

"Oh, for God's sake, shut up," I said, unfeelingly. "Do you think that you're the only one that has troubles with these lousy old ships? Move over, chum!"

Some are weatherwise. Some are otherwise.
Benjamin Franklin

-50-

TROUBLES IN COPENHAGEN

Once I made a trip to beautiful Copenhagen that I could have done without.

It was midwinter, bitterly cold and miserable the day we docked at the Langelinie Piers, just up the way from Copenhagen's most famous statue, The Little Mermaid, perched on a rock in the inner harbor.

Prior to docking, the Mate, Chief Engineer, and I had made the usual search for contraband, and appropriate entries were made in the Official Log Book. We had a full load of coal.

Immediately after docking, longshoremen were aboard, rigging the booms and opening the hatches. Our Agent, Axel Petersen, and I were having coffee in the saloon. The Chief Mate, Mister French, came slamming through the door.

"Captain, about fifteen Customs men have just come aboard, all loaded down with shovels. They have chased all the longshoremen ashore and are down in number three hatch digging in the coal."

Mr. Petersen and I immediately headed for number three. There, the head honcho of the Customs service was leaning over the hatch coaming, yelling at his men. Petersen nudged me to keep quiet and engaged the Customs boss in conversation. Finally turning to me, he translated.

"Captain, he claims to have received a tip that there is considerable contraband hidden on your ship."

"Baloney. We searched the ship thoroughly before we docked. Of course we couldn't paw through ten thousand tons of coal."

Just then, there was a commotion down in the hatch. We peered down through the coal dust. By God! They were lifting out case after case of cartons of cigarettes. Here was big trouble. It is practically universal that whenever undeclared contraband is discovered, the fine is double the value plus confiscation of the goods, and further, if the guilty party is not apprehended, the fine is levied against the ship. And as the Master is the legal representative of the ship, that meant me.

Boy, oh boy. I had better move fast. My Owners, being very proper, conservative Bostonians, would never pick up the tab. They would dump the whole matter right back in my lap, and out of my pocket it would come.

Rounding up the Mate, he and I sat down and worded a strong notice

299

to be posted in the crew's mess and the saloon.

*GUILTY PARTY OR PARTIES MUST COME FORWARD
AT ONCE. SEVERE DISCIPLINARY ACTION WILL BE
TAKEN UNLESS, ETC.,ETC.*

The Mate was too optimistic.
"I'll catch the bastards, Captain. Leave it to me. I've got ways."
"Now wait a damned minute, Mister. This is a strong union crew, and
I don't want any of your rough stuff. You start any of that and the Union will
hang us when we get home. We've got to work with the head instead of the
strong arm. Put on that notice that the guilty ones have twenty-four hours to
own up. After that, don't be surprised at anything. That will start 'em
squealing on each other."
Or so I thought.
The next morning Mr. Petersen came aboard with bad news. I was
required to appear at the Customs House before noon and pay a fine which
amounted to $670.00 in American money. He was prepared to advance me the
amount in Danish kroners, charging it to the ship's account. Then I could re-
imburse the ship upon arrival home. I had no choice, so uptown we went and
paid His Majesty's Danish Government the 670.00 clams.
On the way back to the ship I was getting madder and madder. Even
started talking to myself.
*Some crew I've got. The ungrateful bastards. But I'll fix 'em. I'll
catch the guilty snakes if it's the last thing that I ever do.*
When I got back, the Mate was waiting for me at the gangway.
"Captain, we've got trouble The longshoremen are threatening to go
on strike."
"Come on up to my room where we can talk without the damned crew
eavesdropping, and fill me in."
These Liberty ships had been designed to carry a Naval gun crew of
twenty-seven men and one commissioned officer. Complete quarters for the
enlisted men had been built all the way aft, complete with showers and heads.
After the war, there was no further use for them, so the pipes had all been
drained to prevent freezing, and the doors padlocked. Now, it seemed, the
longshoremen had broken the locks and were using the latrines (No water to
flush them.), and more of them had taken over the living quarters, eating and
drinking and smoking during the frequent discharging delays, waiting for loaded
lighters to be towed away and empty ones brought alongside. All hatches were
discharging offshore into lighters.
Mr. Petersen, the Mate, and I headed back aft to look the situation
over. What a mess. And what a stink.
"Mister, put new locks on these doors. If necessary, have the First

300

Assistant weld them shut. Mr. Petersen, tell these apes that they have got five minutes to get their asses out of these quarters."

The next thing I knew, Mr. Petersen and two loutish looking Danes were hollering and yelling at each other to beat the band. Mr. P told me that they were the stevedore superintendent and the union representative. They insisted that I make the gun crew quarters available to them or they would strike the ship. Their argument was that the ship was berthed at an open pier with no sheds on it, and it was an unusually cold winter. The men had to have shelter. I countered by pointing out that they had never even asked, just broke in and took over. And made a terrible mess, to boot. Off they walked, and there we lay, strike bound. What next?

At supper, I spelled out my strategy to the Mate for catching the smugglers. By law, whenever a ship is in a safe harbor, the Master must open the Slop Chest once a week to allow the crew to buy tobacco and cigarettes.

"Well, now, Mister, we are just going to break that law. No more smokes until somebody owns up. That will fix the buggars. Put up a notice to that effect."

Wow! The next morning all three ship union shop stewards were banging on my door.

"Ah, gentlemen, what's bothering you?"

They ranted and raved and threatened. They would black ball the ship when we got home. They would black ball me. No union man would step foot on a ship if I was its Master. On and on they went. When they finally ran out of breath, I told them that when we got home they could do their damnedest and be damned to them, but here in Copenhagen, I was the boss. Then, just to rub it in, I observed that maybe they were raising such a stink because they were the guilty ones. And well they might have been. Anyway, I said that this was only the beginning. Tomorrow I would be taking another step.

I was in some pickle. The ship on strike, and my Owners would raise hell about that when they heard about it, and me out 670 bucks. To make matters worse, Mr, P showed up the next morning with a copy of Copenhagen's leading newspaper. There we were on the front page. He was reluctant to translate it, saying only that it was most uncomplimentary towards me. I stormed up to my office and dashed off a rebuttal, and insisted that Mr. P take it to the offices of the newspaper. Sure enough, they printed it the next day.

Now for the damned smugglers. Another law says that whenever a ship is in port over twenty-four hours, the crew shall be given a *Draw* on their wages, not to exceed one half of what they have earned to date.

"Mister, put up another notice. *No draw until the guilty party or parties come forward.* That will fix them, but good. Copenhagen is one of the best liberty ports in Europe."

"Captain, you can't! We'll have a mutiny on our hands, and this time the union will crucify us."

"Put it up, Mister, I have reached the point of no return."

For two days we were at a stand off. The crew was wild. No smokes, no money. The longshoremen were parading out on the dock flinging curses at me whenever I appeared on deck, puffing on a cigarette just to torment the crew. This stalemate showed no signs of breaking. Mr. Petersen was holding daily meetings with the longshoremen's union, and I was hiding out in my room, refusing to talk to the crew's delegates. It got so bad that I was afraid the steward would poison me with his slop that wasn't fit to eat anyway. I took to going ashore every afternoon. I would amble up to the Hotel d'Angleterre, where they had a nice bar. There, I'd dump a few and have a leisurely supper.

Two days after the *no draw,* I told the Mate to pull in the gangway. No more shore leave. Boy, my neck was out a mile this time. The storm that had raged over the *no slop chest and no draw,* was nothing compared to the wrath that now descended upon me. I had to stop parading around puffing smoke at the crew. I was honestly afraid that they would try to dump me overboard. The poor Mate was wringing his hands and pleading for me to give in. I sympathized with him. He was in a terrible position. He had a good rapport with the crew and they really put out for him. Now he as well as I were the enemy.

That afternoon I was sitting in the bar in the d'Angleterre idly thumbing through a copy of a Time magazine that the bartender had loaned me. In through the door came a most attractive dame. She took a stool a little ways from me and ordered an aperitif. I, of course, was looking her over out of the corner of my eye. Very stylishly dressed, and obviously not on the make. She had on a fashionable little hat with a black veil covering the upper part of her face. While I watched, she took out a cigarette stuck it through the veil, and touched a match to it. Pfft! In an instant the veil flashed into flame which streaked up her face and into her hat and hair. Quick as a mongoose I swatted her with the magazine, and by good fortune, put the fire out. The place was bedlam. The bartender flung a pitcher of water at her, soaking me, instead. The poor thing was on the verge of hysterics. Between the bartender and me, we got a hooker of brandy into her, and she quieted down, somewhat. Then she got a look at herself in the back-bar mirror, and off she went, again. All the hair on the front of her head had burned off. That took a couple of more brandies.

At last she quieted down and we got to talking. She spoke excellent English but with a heavy Polish accent. It developed that she was a concert pianist, and was in Copenhagen to give a concert. However, her Agent had got his wires crossed, and the event was scheduled for three days hence. So here she was, checked into the hotel and nothing to do but wait until the concert hall was available. Figuring that Dame fortune was smiling on me, I asked her to

302

have supper with me. She accepted. Off we went to Copenhagen's finest, Wivex. What a place! It is rated at the very top in Northern Europe. The prices reflected it. They were astronomical. But what the hell—nothing ventured, nothing gained. We must have waded through a month's pay. Then on to a posh night club. Winding our way back to the d'Angleterre, I suggested (like a fool) a repeat performance the next night. She accepted. Going up in the elevator, I congratulated myself on being such a Lothario. She unlocked her door and **Clang** went the door. As I heard the bolt and chain latch into place, back down to earth I came with a resounding thud.

Walking back to the ship, half frozen and broke, I resolved that some way, somehow, I had to get out of the next night. Before I went to sleep I had the answer.

Our young Third Mate was a super lover boy. If you didn't believe it, just ask him. His incessant boasting about his conquests were enough to make you sick. I had listened to so much of it at the dining table that I was thinking of banishing him to the Engineer's table. To make it worse, he was more good looking than any man had a right to be. Black curly hair, a little black mustache, tall and lean. Oh, he had it all. The trouble was that he wouldn't shut up about it. Now I was about to fix him, good.

Very casually, at breakfast I told just parts of the events of the previous evening. Of course I stressed her beauty and charm, and of how amenable to any suggestions she was. I could see his eyes start to glisten. Then I let it drop that I was tuckered out and was coming down with a cold, and that I wished that I didn't have to go out tonight. He snapped up the bait like a starving shark.

"Captain, if you would like, I'll fill in for you. I'm not doing anything tonight."

"That's very kind of you, Mister, because she is expecting to go out. Matter of fact she said that she would buy a new dress for the occasion. Now here's how we'll handle it. I am supposed to meet her in the bar at the d'Anglererre at five-thirty. At exactly five forty-five, you come flying into the bar and say that there is an emergency on the ship and the Mate wants me right away. I'll introduce you, duck out, and you're on your own."

By God, it worked like a charm. He showed up right on time and put on a great show about the *emergency* back on the ship. The next morning at breakfast I sneaked a look at him. He had a face on him that would sour milk.

"Nice evening, Mister? Hope that you went to Wivex. Marvelous place."

"Aah," he snarled, flung down his napkin and stormed out. The Mate said,

"What's the matter with lover boy?"

I told him the whole story.

Alongside, Copenhagen

New Year's Eve, Copenhagen at the home of
the ship's Agent. Author on extreme right.

Entering harbor
of Copenhagen

Discharging offshore at Oxelsund

Looking back at the entrance
to Copenhagen

"Captain, we've had a pretty discouraging, gloomy week, but this sure is like a ray of sunshine."

"You said it, Mister. Remember that song, *Into each life some rain must fall, but too much has fallen in mine?*"

That same day Mr. Petersen reached a compromise with the longshoremen's union. We would let them use the navy quarters but not theheads and showers. Also, I came to realize that we were not going to catch the smugglers. I opened the slop chest, gave a draw, and put the gangway down again.

This little story still has a sad end to it, though. On our next trip we were ordered to AAhus and Kosoer, in Denmark for discharging. Both are just small towns. When we docked at Aahus, there was old faithful Mr. Petersen. He came into my office beaming. With a flourish, he plunked down a bottle of good Danish Aquavit and said,

"Two large glasses, my good Captain. I have good news."

We each had a snort, and then, grinning from ear to ear, he reached into his brief case and slapped down a big handful of Danish kroners.

"How about that. I was able to pull a few strings at the Custom House and got your fine reduced by two thirds. It's all yours."

"That sure is good news, Mr. Pete, but what am I going to do with all that Danish money? This port and the next one have little to offer."

We mulled over the matter while having a couple more belts of Aquavit.

"I've got it," I shouted. "Give the money to Mrs. Petersen. she's got good taste. Have her invest it in Royal Copenhagen china. Then next trip, we will surely hit Copenhagen. I'll hide it real good and smuggle it ashore in the States."

He agreed and stuffed the dough back into his brief case. Now for the sad part. From that day to this, I have never been back to Denmark. By now, that beautiful Royal Copenhagen china has reached the antique stage and is probably resting in the china closet of one of Mr. Petersen's daughters.

An eye for an eye, a tooth for a tooth.
Matthew v, 38

-51-

ONE BAD APPLE

Some little time after the war, I was Master of a liberty ship that at some time had been converted to an assault troop carrier, and then later, switched back to a cargo carrier. Her elaborate hospital and medical facilities had been left intact, and we inherited them.

As a run of the mill tramp steamer, all these elaborate facilities were of little importance to us, and went unused. The rooms remained locked. Once in awhile our Second Mate, the unhappy holder of the title, *Ship's Medical Officer,* might get the key from me for such minor items as aspirin, iodine, or a band aid. It remained almost a forgotten part of the ship.

In due time we went on loading berth and loaded for the Mediterranean. Sailing day arrived. By the time that I got back from the Customs House, the Mate had the ship battened down for sea and the lines singled up. I joined the pilot on the bridge, and it was, **Let go, forward. Let go, aft.** The pilot backed her out of the berth, swung her around, and off we went, out through the Narrows, outward bound for the pilot station, at Ambrose Lightship.

As soon as the pilot went down the Jacob's ladder, the Mate came up to the bridge and announced that the three shop stewards wanted to meet with me. Each department, Deck, Engine, and Steward's usually elected a spokesman. Coming at the very outset of the voyage, it struck me as unusual that they wanted to see me. Ordinarily, they would go to the Chief Mate, the Chief Engineer, or the Steward with departmental beefs.

"Mister, tell them that I will see them in my office just as soon as we get squared away on our course and clear of incoming traffic. And you be there, too."

I rang up, **Full Ahead,** on the engine room telegraph and hauled around on a course for the Nantucket Lightship. A quick look around the horizon. All clear.

"She's all yours, Mister. I'll be in my room if you need me."

I slipped down the ladder and headed for my office. The Mate and the three delegates were waiting. I opened the door and ushered them in.

"Sit down, gents. What's on your minds?"

One of them, the ship's carpenter, stepped forward and commenced a loud, belligerent tirade. The gist of his yelling was that he had been elected chief delegate, and would speak for all departments. He announced that he was

305

going to run a proper union ship. I interrupted him and quietly said that he was mistaken.   I would run the ship, that we were on the high seas, and that he and everyone else on board were under Articles and subject to **my** orders until such time as the vessel returned to a US port and the crew signed off.

"Let us not have any misunderstanding about it, Chips. Any and all beefs will be listened to. If I can mediate them, I will. If not, they will be settled upon our return."

He ranted and raved that he would have me black-balled; on and on he went. I had enough.

"There's the door, Chips. Get out."

He stormed out, still screeching threats.

"Well, Mister, looks as if we have got ourselves a beaut in this bird. Can you keep him busy?"

"That's a tough one, Captain. Usually, the carpenter works along with the Bosun, but not this critter. He pulls the union agreement on me, daily. Won't do a thing if it's not involved with wood."

"Here's a thought, Mister. It worked for me a few years ago when I was Mate. Have the Bosun hoist a big draft of dunnage out of number one 'tween deck. Make sure that he dumps it on the windward side of the fore deck where the spray comes aboard. Make sure that the lumber is all hard wood, it's tougher to saw. Then tell Chips that you have a big project planned, and that you will need at least five hundred pieces of dunnage, each a foot long. Tell him to sharpen his saw and go to work, eight to five, each day. That should chill him down. Then, each night when you come off watch, slip up forward and throw his day's work overboard. **Rejects.**

Boy, oh boy. Did we have a tiger by the tail. Chips sawed away all that first day. When he went forward the next day, all evidence of his work had disappeared. He was no dummy, and figured out what the Mate was up to. I was on the bridge with the Third Mate. I could hear Chips yelling at the Mate down below, somewhere. Then he burst onto the bridge yelling at me. I tried to adopt a lofty air.

"Quiet down. I'll have no yelling on this bridge. If you have a union beef, I will be most happy to attempt a settlement. Meanwhile, go back to work."

Wow! I thought that he'd bust a gut.

"That's all, Chips. Get off of this bridge or I will have you dragged off."

He was such a miserable looking critter. Thin to the point of emaciation, undersized, with a pinched face that resembled a ferret's. Off he stormed. I watched him making his way forward. By God, he started heaving the dunnage overboard. I sent for the Mate and pointed out what Chips was doing.

"Mister, get up there and tell that carpenter that his pay will be docked for every stick of ship's property that he throws over the side."

I watched intently from the pilot house as the Mate made his way up the spray drenched deck. I could see Chips waving his arms like crazy at the Mate. Turning around, I caught the man at the wheel trying to wipe a big grin off of his puss. I grinned back.

"Captain, I'll deny that I ever said it, but that guy's a real nut. I'm a good union man, but all he wants is trouble. The whole crew is fed up with him."

"Thanks, sailor. I didn't hear a word that you said."

But I did, and took heart from it.

As the days went by, Chips' campaign continued. The Mate had to discontinue the wood sawing project. The weather had worsened, and as we were deeply ladened, green water was coming aboard, and Chips was in some danger of being washed overboard. Not a bad idea, at that.

A few mornings later the Chief Engineer, the Mate, and the Steward came to see me. They were at their wit's end with the beefs streaming from the carpenter. All three of them, like me had been sailing long before the war, and we were all well aware of the abuses, privations, and starvation wages of those bleak times. None of us ever wanted those conditions to prevail again. All the unions, the MNU, the SIU, the MEBA, and the MM&P had all been successful in bringing about changes for the better. In fact, we had participated in it. But, and it was a big but, here we had on our hands a zealot who had been blinded. What to do? The Chief finally suggested that I have a private meeting with Chips and try to reason with him; to point out that we, too, had sailed in focsles much worse than this young squirt could ever imagine.

"Chief, why me? As Master I represent everything that he hates. I haven't got a chance in hell of getting through to him. Why don't we be patient and hope that the crew will clean their own house?"

No dice. They prevailed, and I said that I would try.

The next day was Sunday, a no work day for Chips. I was on the bridge before daylight for star sights and coffee with the Mate. Peeking into the compass, I asked the man at the wheel to tell Chips that I wanted to see him at ten o'clock.

Promptly at ten I heard a hammering on my door. I opened it and there stood Chips.

"Come in. I'd like a word with you."

"Captain, if you want to talk to me, I want two hours overtime."

"You do, do you? Last Sunday you woke me up with yet another one of your phoney beefs. Did you get overtime then? Not likely, but I'll tell you what I'll do. I will give you your two hours overtime, but in return I will expect you to listen to my beef without interruption. Deal?"

307

He nodded and slouched through the door. I pointed to the settee and said,

"Take off your cap. You are in my home."

He flung his cap at my feet. Boy, this is going to be some session. He was so full of hate and defiance that I knew that it was a lost cause. But I had to try.

I noticed that his hands were shaking as he lit a cigarette, and he looked worse than ever. Now, I had been sailing these ships for a lot of years and had become pretty good at reading signs, especially where sailors were concerned.

"Chips, do you drink a lot?"

"None of your fucking business."

"Fair enough, but you look awful. You should take better care of yourself. You're starting to look like a dead man."

Diplomacy at its worst, huh?

With that bad beginning, I waded in. I reviewed the whole union movement, starting with the Wobblies, the IWW, communist to the core. I told of their recruiting efforts; how they would get up on a stool in the focsle and make fiery speeches and pass out literature which always had a cartoon of the shipowner in a tall hat, swallow tailed coat, striped pants, and a big fat cigar. I told him about some of the worst Lines, the Morgan Line cherries, which were stewed prunes, fed day after day. Of some Lines that were paying twenty-nine dollars a month for Able Seamen, good ones. And of one of the worst, the Luckenbach Line, a big intracoastal outfit. Their ships had a forest of booms that had to be topped and lowered at each port. And of how they instituted two watches, six on and six off. They always carried several workaways, out of work seamen wanting to get back to the East or West coast, and were signed on for one penny a month. It was said, and I believe it, that things were so bad that the Luckenbach Mates were even firing the workaways!

The Munson Line, one of the worst. How any self respecting sailor could sign on one of their hell ships, was beyond me. But they did. Anything to get off the beach, bunking in flop houses and living on soup, for which they had to listen to a religious sermon, first, at the Sailors' Haven, Latitude and Longitude duly inscribed on the door.

I described the rotten food that we had to eat, the cold, dank focsles that we lived in, all six A.B.s, two Ordinaries, and one or two Deck Boys. I finally wound up by pointing out that through bitter strikes and too much violence, things got better. One watch to a room, overtime, better pay, and a host of other benefits.

"But, Chips, don't push your luck too far. The War is over, and the foreign flagged vessels are out to bury us. (I didn't know, then, how prophetic some of my remarks were.)

The only thing good that I can say about this misguided little rat is that he did hear me out. When I finally finished, he defiantly threw a lighted

308

cigarette on my nice carpeting, stubbed it out with his foot, and left, slamming the door as hard as he could swing it. Two hours overtime right down the drain.

At supper that night I told the Chief and the Mate of my efforts. *I tried but failed. In fact, I have the idea that he will be worse than ever.*

That night the weather worsened. The seas mounted and the wind started to moan in the shrouds and around the wheel house. The ship was laboring pretty badly so I reduced speed to fifty revolutions. By daylight we had a full gale on our hands. so I reduced speed again. I didn't want our cargo to get smashed up, and the ship was pitching badly, and taking some heavy seas aboard.

I slipped below for a quick breakfast. A bleary eyed Second Mate was poking at his eggs. He stood the midnight to four AM watch, but always dragged himself out of his bunk for a morning sun line.

"Mister, you'll not get a peek at the sun this morning, but, being as how you're up, why don't you accompany the Mate when he comes off watch, and make sure that everything is lashed down. And you might check our fancy hospital. It is chock-a-block full of all kinds of bottles of God Knows what, and they could make some mess if they got adrift.

An hour or so later both Mates came streaming into the wheel house. Even though they both were wearing oilskins and sea boots, they were soaked through.

"Captain, everything is tied down and holding. However, there is something that you have got to see for yourself. The ship's hospital has been broken into, and whoever did it left some mess. Broken bottles all over the deck, pills and instruments flung around. The deck is awash in iodine, gentian violet, and God knows what else."

The Mate and I went down to have a look. They hadn't exaggerated. We crunched our way through the broken glass. All the cabinet doors were swinging and banging as the ship rolled. Who could have done such a thing?

Just then the Bosun stuck his head in the door, his eyes bugging out as he looked at the mess.

"Excuse me, Mister Mate, I just came to tell you that the carpenter is drunk and won't turn to."

A blinding light hit me.

"Grain alcohol, Mister. That's got to be it. Bosun, where is Chips?"

"In his bunk, Captain. He sure is ossified.

"Let's have a look at him, Mister. Follow me."

He was drunk alright, lying in his bunk muttering and laughing to himself.

"Search the room, Mister. I can smell medicinal alcohol."

A thorough search turned up nothing. The Bosun pointed to the open port hole.

"He must have deep sixed the jug.

The Mate was rummaging around under the bunk. Triumphantly, he pulled out a pair of work shoes. They were soaked with a mixture of iodine and gentian violet.

"Bosun, let me know when he sobers up. I will be on the bridge."

The next day the weather cleared, the seas flattened, and we were back on Full Ahead, making knots toward Gibraltar. The Bosun had sent Chips up to see me. He swore up and down that he didn't break into the hospital. When confronted with the shoes, he told a pisser. Said he heard a noise up on the next deck, went up to investigate, found the hospital door open, and stepped inside. No, he didn't have a flashlight with him so he didn't see the damage or the stuff all over the floor. Where did he get the booze? Said he had it hidden in hie suitcase. My word against his. Circumstantial evidence. He had cleverly slipped out of the noose.

As the days went by I brooded on the matter. *Every dog has his day,* I consoled myself. *My day will come.* The Mate, too, was becoming half cuckoo. Chips had shifted his attack to him, and daily the poor harassed Mate would pour out a litany of the complaints coming from that skinny little bastard.

Then he started on the Steward, which was hitting below the belt, because Stewards belonged to the same union as the crew did. Our Steward, and all other Stewards. were in a tough situation not shared by the Mates and Engineers who had their own unions. He had to be one of the crew, yet above them. Stewards had a tougher road than we did. And they did well. They were on duty seven days a week, at sea or in port. They worked from early morning until the last pot was washed at night. And all he got out of it was a room to himself. Big deal. He was only in it long enough to grab a few winks. Even in port he had to take the place of cooks who got drunk and couldn't work. Then too, he had to take the constant abuse from the entire crew, including me, about the lousy food.

How one man could disrupt an entire ship's company, and make our lives miserable, I'll never know, but that carpenter managed to do it. I kept trying to smooth ruffled feathers with only partial success. The First Assistant grabbed him one day and damned near broke him in two. Fortunately there were no witnesses.

"First," I said, "Don't make that mistake again. You're a big brawny brute, I know, but if there's a next time, he'll get you, and it will mean your ticket. Be patient. He has almost enough rope, now, to hang himself. There are some sensible citizens in the crew, and I am betting that they will take care of him. But you keep those big paws off of him, hear?"

"OK, Captain, but it ain't going to be easy. Maybe I'll get him ashore some night."

310

"Now stop that kind of talk. Time heals all wounds."

"Balls, Captain."

Can't say that I blame him.

Not long after, we transited the Straits of Gibraltar and headed once again for Marseilles, our first port of discharge. After tying up, the Agent informed me that our entire cargo was to be discharged there. That meant six or seven days. Then we could steam right back home and, hopefully, unload the albatross around our necks, Chips.

Marseilles held no attraction for me except the food. The Chief Mate, the Chief Engineer, and I ate supper ashore every night. On the way back to the ship, we always stopped on a street corner where the inevitable push cart vendor held forth, his cart piled high with fresh from the sea, succulent oysters. We would eat them as fast as he could shuck them. Then he would count the shells, divide by two, and that was the bill. Great!

The crew were having the time of their lives. Marseilles was one of the best liberty ports in the world. Full of French whores, all very high class and expensive. They didn't just take you to bed and *So Long*. They pretended to have *un* affaire, dinner, drinks, and then let themselves be seduced. They put on an excellent act, and sailors ate it up. But it *was* expensive. I was giving a draw, daily.

A couple of days before sailing, I received orders to head over to North Africa for a full load of cork. Cork, being very light, we would fill all five hatches and load both the forward and after decks with it. Even then, we would only have about a thousand tons. The Chief agreed to press up all the deep tanks and empty double bottoms with sea water for ballast as soon as we got clear of the harbor and into clean sea water.

The crew all said tearful good byes to their new found lovers, promising to write, pledging their undying love, and other such nonsense that neither they nor the whores believed.

We were one or two days out of yet another stinking North African port, loaded to the hatch beams with bales of cork. It was about seven o'clock of a fine sunny morning. I was, as usual, on the bridge with the Mate. The Bosun came up to get his orders for the day from the Mate. With all the decks covered ten feet high with cork, they agreed that little could be done about the decks so they would concentrate on the crew's quarters; soogey them out and repaint them. The Bosun sidled over to me and said, in a low voice,

"Captain, the carpenter wants to see you privately."

"No way, Bosun. If he wants to see me, my Mate will be present. Tell him to be in my office at ten o'clock. OK with you, Mister?"

Right on the dot, Chips showed up. The minute he came in he took off his cap. Odd, I usually had to order him to take it off.

"What's the beef this time, Chips?"

"I ain't got no beef. This is personal and don't concern the Mate, here."

Well, sailor the Mate's staying. Now what's on your mind?"

"It's personal, Captain."

"Out with it. What's your problem?"

"Well, I think that I've got the Old Joe."

"Ho, ho, syphilis, huh? Drop your pants and let me see your dink."

"Not in front of him, Captain, please."

By God, he was starting to cry.

"Mister, I guess that you can leave and attend to your duties."

After the Mate had left, I turned to Chips. He was absolutely terrified.

"Down with the pants, now, and let me see."

He dropped his pants and pulled out his dink. Sure enough, there was a big hard chancre.

"Chips, you've got the Old Joe, that's for sure."

"Oh my God, Captain. Will I go crazy, or get that Loco thing?"

Obviously, he had heard all the wild tales told in focsles the world over.

"Now, Chips, not to worry. I think that I can cure you. Nowadays we have a miracle drug called penicillin. I think that it will do the job. Come on down to the hospital with me."

I unlocked the door and snapped on the light.

"There's just one hitch, here, Chips. If the unknown burglar smashed the penicillin bottles, you're sunk. By the time we get home, your dink could be eaten off." (Not true, but now it was my turn to twist the screw.)

I started looking through the cabinets. At once I spotted several bottles.

"I don't see any, Chips. They must have gotten smashed." (Just another twist.)

He started moaning and crying, again. Boy, he was pitiful.

"Ah, I found it. Lucky for you."

I never realized that I had such a sadistic streak but there it was. I was actually enjoying myself, And I hadn't even begun, yet.

"Now, Chips, we have to inject massive doses of this stuff in your backside twice a day, every day, all the way home. Down with the pants and shorts, and put your hands on the bulkhead. Better put your head against it, too. Bend over."

I selected the longest, biggest needle that I could find and fitted it to a syringe. (We didn't have disposable syringes, back then.) My God, he was so skinny! His backside looked like two shingles on a slab. I am ashamed to admit it today, but I was positively enjoying myself. I rammed that big needle in, felt it grind against his pelvis bone. He jerked forward, banging his head against the steel bulkhead. Sounded like Big Ben, in London.

Of course he didn't need all the massive doses that I gave him, but I

Stormy weather as usual

figured that they wouldn't do him any harm, either. I rammed that big needle into him twice every single day, all the way home. When one side of his ass got all black and blue, I switched over to the other side. I must have pumped a quart of the stuff into him. He was some mess. Told me that he had to sleep on his stomach. Even his head was sore from clanging it against the bulkhead.

I expected bad trouble when we got home, but not a peep. Chips paid off and disappeared. Never heard from him again, thank God.

I suppose that I should feel more guilt than I do, but I try to rationalize it by saying that it was an even swap. I made him miserable and he made a whole ship's company miserable. Maybe it wasn't such an even swap, after all.

-52-

"SPARKS"

In past stories I have written about Sparks, the ship's radio officer, but only in passing. Now it's time to correct that. He is one of the most important men sailing the ocean-going ships. Unfortunately, his role has been largely ignored, both by his fellow shipmates, and the public. His is a lonely life, cooped up in a cramped radio room, earphones on his head, listening to a flood of dots and dashes hour after hour, with the static wailing in the background. When radios first appeared on ships, shortly before the Titanic disaster, they were crude affairs. They were referred to as *'spark gap'* transmitters. The signal was created by an actual electric spark jumping between two terminals which were hooked up to the ship's antenna. Whenever Sparks would be transmitting, one could hear that raucous sound crackling from the radio shack. Ships were prohibited from transmitting in port because their signal interfered with reception on the thousands of radios then flooding the market of those days.

Right from their inception, ships' radios were considered an important tool for safety at sea. On all ships, of all nationalities, the 550 kilocycles band was reserved for SOS, the universal signal for a grave emergency at sea. It exists to this day, and is never violated.

There was, however, an important thing missing from those early radios. Ships only carried one radio operator, and his hours on duty were governed only by the traffic requirements of the steamship company, such as routine messages of destination changes, cargo matters, etc. Whenever the radio officer of those days was in the radio shack, and not busy with ship's business, he would tune the receiver to 550 kilocycles. This was fine as long as he was in the radio shack and awake. However, the operators of those days frequently acted as the Captain's clerk, doing his payrolls, crew lists, etc. He also ran the ship's slop chest. Then, too, he had to eat and sleep.

The ship's radio shack of those days was aptly named. It was a wooden shack up on the boat deck, aft of the smoke stack. Many of them had been added long after the ship had been built. They were pretty flimsy affairs, and many of them were washed overboard, Sparks and all.

It took the Titanic disaster to wake up the international shipping fraternity to the fact that the 550 kilocycle band was **not** being properly monitored. I remember reading that a cargo ship was only a few miles away from the

314

Titanic when she hit the iceberg and went down. The radio officer on the cargo ship was told by the Titanic's to get off the air, that they had important messages for New York. So he turned off his set and went to bed. The bridge watch later testified that they saw the running lights of the Titanic in the distance, but did not see her distress flares. What an awful tragedy!

As a result of this disaster, it became mandatory for all ships in the world to be equipped with *Auto Alarms*. This device consisted of a big gong installed in Spark's sleeping quarters, usually under his bunk. Whenever he would go off duty, he would throw a switch. Then, if a call came through on 550, the gong would go off. It could be heard all over the midships section of the ship. Better late than never.

One of my radio operators was quite an exceptional young man. He had an unusual nickname, *'Skip.'* He was a ham radio nut, and had both the radio shack and his living quarters crammed full of his own personal short wave equipment. These hams were using short wave exclusively, then. Those short waves went out in two waves. one by line of sight to the horizon, the other by bouncing, or *'skipping,'* off the ionosphere. When they were *'skipping,'* the waves travelled incredible distances, frequently half way around the world. That's how he got his nickname.

Skip had a host of friends in every port. They were all fellow hams. Whenever we docked in a foreign port, inevitably, there would be a half dozen of them on the pier waiting to carry him off and entertain him in fine style. These hams were a close knit, and world-wide fraternity. When Skip returned to the ship the following afternoon, he came up to my quarters and plunked down a heavy parcel on my desk.

"Wait until you see what I've got, Captain."

Carefully he unwrapped it and lifted out two metal canisters. They were almost identical, but not quite. They were of a drab, olive green color. Each of them had several dials and switches on the front. He placed one on top of the other. They fitted perfectly. There were small clamps that secured them to each other. They were not too large; maybe fifteen inches long by eight inches wide and eight inches deep.

"What are they, Skip?"

"Captain, one is a radio receiver; the other is a radio transmitter. They were originally installed in a German tank. One of my ham friends *'liberated'* them. Aren't they beauties?"

"Beauty is in the eye of the beholder, Skip. What are you going to do with them?"

"Well, first, I'm going to completely dismantle them, and then rebuild them. In that way, I'll know what makes them tick."

"Better you than me, Skip."

My interest in radios was limited to receiving good weather reports.

315

I promptly put the entire incident out of my mind.

Some time later we were proceeding up the Norwegian coast, bound for Narvik, 'way up above the Arctic Circle. It was mid winter and the weather was awful. A full gale was howling. Heavy snow was blowing across the decks, making visibility nil. I was hounding Sparks for weather reports. The sooner that we got out of this weather, the better I would feel.

I left the chart room and went over to the radio shack. Sparks was hunched over his dials as usual. To my surprise, he had a microphone in his hand, and was **talking** into it. Invariably, he used a transmitter key, transmitting in code.

"Stand by, please. Captain, I have just made contact with one of my ham friends in Annapolis, Maryland. Is there anyone in that area that you would like to talk to?"

"My God, Skip, you can't mean that in this terrible weather, you're talking to a guy in Annapolis? Do you realize how many thousands of miles away he is?"

"Yes, but by a lucky fluke, I've *'skipped'* to him. I may lose him any minute. However, he has a telephone right alongside of him, so he can hold the phone against his receiver, and you can talk to anybody that you want to."

I thought for a minute. We were to load a full load of iron ore in Narvik, consigned to Baltimore.

Our Agent in Baltimore was the Ramsay Scarlett Company. Their manager, Harry Schneider, was a good friend of mine. Baltimore was only about thirty miles from Annapolis.

"Sparks, tell him to call up our Agent and ask for Harry Schneider."

Sparks fiddled with his dials and muttered into his microphone.

"Stand by, Captain," warned Sparks.

After a minute or two, he handed me the earphones and the microphone. "Any time, Captain. Mr. Schneider is on the phone."

"Hello, Harry. This is Frank Farrar, over."

"Yeah? And I'm the Queen of May. Whoever you are, get off the phone. I'm very busy this morning, over."

"Honest, Harry, it's me, Farrar, over."

"Now you listen to me. Farrar is some where up off the Norwegian coast. Get off this phone and stop bothering me."

And, Bang, he hung up.

Weeks later, after yet another miserable winter crossing of the North Atlantic, we poked our rusty snout into the Virginia Capes and made our way up the Chesapeake Bay to Baltimore. As soon as we were tied up to the Bethlehem Steel Company's pier in Sparrow's Point, I headed uptown for the offices of Ramsay Scarlett. Harry looked up when, I entered, and we shook hands.

"Good to see you, again, Captain. Sit down and have some coffee. By the way, a few weeks ago I got a phone call from some nut that claimed that he was you. He said that he was calling from up above the Arctic Circle. Imagine!"

"Harry, that was me."

From that day to this, Harry Schneider has never believed that it really was me that spoke to him through a little old radio stolen from a German tank. This story has a somber ending. A few trips later, Skip paid off, saying that he needed a vacation. He signed on another ship. The second or third night out, he jumped overboard and was never seen again.

-53-

A BELGIAN SHOOTOUT

A month or two after World War II ended, I was the Master of a Liberty ship. She was loaded with a commercial cargo, the first such cargo since she was built. In the rush to get in on the shipping bonanza, Steamship Companies wasted no time. The gun mounts were removed to enable the ship to load that much more cargo. Still in her wartime gray, she was loaded with a full cargo for Antwerp, Belgium. The whole of Europe was starving, and our cargo was badly needed.

This first voyage under peacetime conditions was a joy. When we dropped the pilot outside the harbor, there were no Navy escort ships to herd us into convoy formation. When darkness came, there were no blackouts. Our running lights burned bright red and green. The midships deck lights were all on, and best of all, we were alone on the ocean. When men came off watch, they could undress, go to bed and sleep soundly. No more sleeping in your clothes with your life jacket for a pillow. It was heaven, except for one thing that definitely had not changed--the weather! The weather in the Western Ocean never changed. It was always bad, or so it seemed.

A course was set to a point off Newfoundland. There we would commence steaming on a Great Circle course to Bishop's Rock, located on the Southern tip of England. From there we would proceed up the English Channel to the West Scheldt River, then up the river to the port of Antwerp.
All the way across we were pummeled and mauled. To make matters worse, the seamens' unions were flexing their muscles. They had been silenced all through the War, but now they were trying to make up for lost time. The ship's union delegates were forever making speeches in the messroom, and there was a constant flow of 'beefs.' However, in spite of weather and beefs, we arrived off the Scheldt River and picked up a pilot. Antwerp is a *locked in* port. That is, ships entering or departing have to pass through locks. These locks keep the depth of water in the port constant. Without them a falling tide would drain the water out of the port, leaving the ships sitting on the bottom.

When the pilot came aboard, down at the mouth of the river, I was surprised to see a double barreled shotgun slung over his shoulder.

"Pilot," I said, "Don't you know that the war is over? Why the shot gun?."

"Captain, things are pretty bad, here. With any luck, I'll show you why I brought the gun."

When we arrived off the entrance to the locks, he cleverly maneuvered our ship into a lock. Mooring lines were put ashore and the big pumps started up, hoisting us up to the level of the harbor.

I noticed the pilot out on the starboard bridge wing. He was staring intently at the ground. His shot gun was still slung over his shoulder. The ground on both sides of the ship was open and flat. It was also covered with a dense growth of weeds. While I was still watching him, he suddenly unslung the gun, flung it to his shoulder, and in rapid succession, fired both barrels! *My God! Snipers?*

"Pilot, what in God's name are you shooting at?"

Without answering me, he rushed by me, flinging the shot gun in my arms. He ran down two decks to the main deck, climbed down the pilot ladder, and raced off through the weeds. What he was after, God only knew. I saw him bend over and reach down into the weeds. He straightened up and triumphantly held up a big rabbit by the ears!

He climbed back aboard and up to the bridge. He was all out of breath, but still had Mr. rabbit clutched firmly by the ears.

"Captain, you may pull in the lines. We are ready to exit the lock."

"Pilot, what are you going to do with that poor, dead rabbit?"

"First, Captain, this isn't a rabbit. It's a Belgian Hare, the finest eating to be found in the world. Second, I have a wife and three kids. Ever since the War began we have had to do some fancy scrounging to keep food on the table.

I manage to get two or three every week. Slow Ahead, please."

I scratched my head. I have heard of the Sultans in India hunting tigers, perched up in a howdah on the back of an elephant, but rabbits from the bridge of a ten thousand ton ship?

319

-54-

SKINFLINT NORTON

I sailed for several years as master for The Eastern Steamship Line, of Boston, Massachusetts.

Eastern had been in business for about a zillion years. It operated in typical New England fashion. It was ultra-conservative, it resisted change, and was inflexible in it's policies. Naturally, all of it's top management reflected the company's long standing conservatism.

Scrooge was a philanthropist compared to Thomas Norton, Comptroller of the company. He ruled the financial affairs of the company with an iron hand. I picture him, like Scrooge, perched on a high stool, paper cuffs pinned to his forearms, green eye shade pulled low over his gimlet eyes. Nothing, but nothing, escaped his long nosed scrutiny. At all times, he knew where every single penny had been spent, and regretted parting with every one of them--nay, he fought to the death to prevent its squandering.

All Captains, Chief engineers, and Chief Stewards were prime suspects. He truly believed that they were milking the company; the Captains in their expense accounts. The Chief Engineers were doubly suspect in the padding and subsequent kick-backs from engine room repairs, and the Stewards for similar shenanigans in the buying of food stores.

It became a deadly game between Skinflint and the seagoing staff to see who could outwit who. Sorry to say, Skinflint **always** won. It was no contest. Skinflint always wrote his correspondence in long hand. He, of course, frowned on telegrams and cables--too expensive. His style of writing was archaic, formal, and smacked of the style popular around the turn of the century. One of his typical letters would begin something like this:

Yours of the penultimate and contents duly noted. May we be so bold as to suggest that your account far exceeds the norm that this establishment subscribes to, in the following respects.

Then he would continue with a red pencil, either eliminating, or substantially reducing almost every item. In closing, he would have the nerve to write,

Your most humble servant, T. N.
Servant???

Early on, he got under my skin. We had arrived at the Sparrows Point piers of the Bethlehem Steel Corp. to load a cargo of steel. As soon as the

320

gangway went down, I went up to the Agent's office in Baltimore, a distance of some fifteen miles. My main purpose in going was to go to the bank and get the cash for the crew payoff scheduled for that afternoon.

After the usual formalities of entering the ship at the U.S. Custom House, the Agent and I went to the bank where I received about $50,000.00 in cash and coin. I just barely managed to cram it into my old brief case. Feeling uneasy about toting so much cash, I elected to take a taxi back to the ship. I had the ship's 38 caliber revolver in the brief case, but had little faith in it.

Our expense accounts were always one voyage behind. Just before sailing, I would mail mine to Skinflint, who would have two or three months before I returned, to chop it to smithereens.

When we returned to the States, sure enough, there was my letter from Skinflint. I opened it, feeling no sense of elation. He didn't disappoint me. My entire account, and it wasn't much, maybe thirty or forty bucks, was covered with his red pencil notations. One in particular galled me, and still does. Footnote number five read as follows:

With regard to your item number five, claiming an expense of $4.85 for taxi fare from Baltimore to Sparrows Point, yours truly has ascertained that parallel public trolley car service is available at a cost of 75 cents. Your claim of $4.85 is therefore disallowed. However, 75 cents is allowed, although it is our understanding that you could have obtained a free ride with the Shipping Commissioner who was enroute to your ship to pay off the crew. In future, please be so kind as to pay more attention to similar wasteful and unnecessary expenses, which are a severe drain on the company's operating expenses. Your most humble servant, etc.

I tell you, this crumb was something! I sprawled out on my settee and cast about in my mind for ways to get even with old Skinflint. I couldn't come up with a thing. He was just too cunning for us.

Sailing day arrived and I went ashore to clear the ship. It stuck in my craw, but I took the trolley car to Baltimore. It was a couple of weeks before Christmas, and all the store windows were dressed up in red ribbons and striped candy canes. I stopped in front of a stationary store, thinking. In I went and bought a box of red pencils. I had the clerk sharpen every one of them to a needle point. I put a card inside, inscribed in big letters,

Merry Christmas, your faithful servant.

The clerk wrapped it in red and white paper, and mailed it off for me.
That'll shake up the old bastard, I thought.

The next day we sailed for yet another miserable Christmas, slogging through the eternal mid-winter storms in the North Atlantic.

After what seemed to be an eternity, we arrived back at an American port. The Agent's runner brought the ship's mail, and I settled down to read it. A large, ornate *'Thank You'* card caught my eye. Upon opening it, I was surprised to see my expense account for the previous voyage folded up inside the card. It was practically covered with red pencil notations. On the card, Skinflint had neatly printed

Your most thoughtful gift at hand. You will be pleased to note that one of your pencils was used to 'correct' your attached statement, and you must further agree that it does a far better job than the ones that I had been using.

And he had the nerve to sign it, *Your most grateful servant, T. N.!*

That did it! The gauntlet had been thrown down and I picked it up. War was declared. I went rushing down to the Chief Engineer's room, and unceremoniously burst in. The Chief was sitting at his desk pounding on it with both fists. His face was mottled purple with rage. Seeing me, he picked up his expense account and flung it in my face.

"Look at that," he roared. "Nothing but red pencil marks. And he has the nerve to say that the pencils were a gift from you! Whose side are you on, anyway?"

Oh, boy! The Chief was getting this all wrong. He was assuming that I was in cahoots with Skinflint. I started to explain about the pencils. It must have taken me a half hour before I could get him to calm down and listen to me. What finally convinced him was when I got him to look at my expense account. I had charged four bottles of Scotch and two bottles of Bourbon for *'entertainment.'* Woe be it to the poor shipmaster who did not entertain the Customs and Immigration ghouls in every port, foreign or domestic. What I didn't know was that Norton had been approving two bottles of cheap Rye whiskey. He only had done this after the Marine Superintendent had leaned on him pretty hard. However, when I doubled the ante to four bottles, and premium stuff at that, he rebelled. His note to me read, in part,

We have been most patient with our masters charging intoxicating beverages to their voyage expense accounts. Now, you have chosen to abuse this privilege. We therefore must, regretfully, cancel this heretofore, most generous gesture on our part. Federal law prohibits any intoxicating beverage from being brought aboard U. S. flagged vessels. Therefore, in future, if masters choose to waste their money in this fashion, reimbursement will not be honored by this office. May I wish you a belated Merry Christmas. Your humble etc., etc. T.N.

I was in some mess. If word ever got out that I killed this small, skinny goose, all the other Skippers would be after my scalp.

To end this sorry tale, I never again submitted an expense account. I bought and paid for the booze and taxis. As I look back, I suspect that this was the scheme that Skinflint had all along, especially as I was the one who branded him with his nickname.

He who loses his wealth loses little. He who loses his health loses much
He who loses his reputation loses everything.

Anon.

-55-

THE GREATEST VOYAGE OF MY CAREER
(AND IT NEVER HAPPENED)

One time I was Master of a ship that was bound for New Orleans. She was fully ladened. We were steaming down the Florida coast, inside of the Gulf Stream. It was full summer and the weather was perfect.

Sailing South inside of the Stream was very challenging to me. A rigid course had to be maintained inside of the Northern thrust of the Stream, and outside of the reefs stretching from Point Judith, in the North, all the way South to Key West.

I was like a kid with his Christmas morning toys. Constant bearings, continuous soundings on the fathometer, and very accurate steering by the quartermasters.

Navigation and Piloting had become almost an obsession with me ever since I had first assumed command. Probably because if a Skipper is blessed with a good Chief Mate, he is blessed, indeed. And I had had a succession of them so I had plenty of time to play with my toys.

Sure, the Master has all the responsibility, but a good Mate is worth his weight in diamonds. He runs the ship with all its day to day headaches. It is he who is confronted, daily, with union beefs, cargo stowage problems involving endless arguments with the Stevedore, constant squabbles with the Coast Guard on matters concerning safety, life boats, and a host of other problems involving the engine room crowd, the Steward's department, and, of course, his own deck gang. No wonder the average Mate is harassed, short tempered, always on the verge of exhaustion, but never showing it. **That** is a good Mate.

As I write these words, I reflect back to when I was Mate. Was I good one? I can't answer. Only my peers can make that judgement.

Anyway, here we were, steaming by sunny Florida, the playground of the wealthy, and I was loving every minute of it. We rounded the Keys and headed up for South West Pass, the entrance to the Mississippi River.

Supper was a treat on this ship. On all ships, the main meal of the day is served at noon, and is called dinner. Supper was usually a stale salad, cold cuts, and maybe a piece of pie. Lots of ketchup to take the curse off. Not on this vessel. The Steward did himself proud every night. Charcoal broiled steaks, or succulent lamb chops, or even prime ribs. Good fortune was smiling down upon us, and I for one, was very grateful.

324

It was just coming dark when we sighted the pilot vessel. Soon, it was, *Hard Right. Stop Engines.* The pilot scrambled up the rope ladder, carrying his little bag. As he came into the wheel house, he handed me a day old newspaper. This small courtesy was always appreciated. Then it was, *Full Ahead. Come Left Easy,* and we commenced our overnight journey up the river to New Orleans.

It was a bright, moonlit night. The pilot and I slouched comfortably against the forward windows, gossiping. I remarked that there was very little outbound traffic coming down the river. What he said took me by surprise. One of seamens' unions, the SIU, was on strike, and his orders were to anchor us off the port. That didn't sound too good. We were a SIU ship.

The next morning we swung out of the channel and dropped the anchor. As soon as we finished going through Quarantine and Immigration, I boarded a water taxi. At the boat landing I transferred to a land taxi and headed for our Agent's office. There, I got more disturbing news. There was no sign of the strike being settled. The crew was to be paid off, the boilers were to be blown down, and the ship was to lay where she was until the strike was over.

Arrangements were made for the Shipping Commissioner to come aboard that afternoon and pay off the crew. Our Boston owners telexed that just the Chief Engineer and I were to remain on the payroll, and that we were to be the ship's keepers. I didn't relish the thought of just him and me living aboard a dead ship out on that steamy, hot, muddy river. How would we eat? And what if the ship dragged anchor? That river was running at seven or eight knots, and we would have no steam to heave the anchor up. Problems, problems. Little did I know that there was an even greater surprise just around the corner.

I went to the bank and filled my brief case with cash to pay off the crew, and then headed directly for the boat landing.
The Mate met me at the head of the gangway. I gave him the bad news.

"Now, Mister, we'll delay the payoff while the Chief gets steam up. Then we will go, *Slow Ahead* and drop our second anchor. Rig up a flag signal for, **I need a towboat,** but don't hoist it. After you are all gone, I might need that signal in a hurry."

All this was accomplished by dinnertime. The Chief needed a couple of hours to shut down the engine room, and the Steward needed the same time to clean up the galley, messrooms, and saloon.

Four o'clock rolled around and the payoff commenced. I had all the crew's discharges made out. All the overtime had been figured and agreed to by the shop stewards. Everything went smoothly and without incident.

By five o'clock the crew were going down the gangway with their suit cases and sea bags. As soon as a water taxi filled, another took her place. The Mate, Steward, and I had a rather emotional scene in the saloon. They had been good and faithful shipmates, and God knows when we'd meet again.

Six o'clock found the Chief and me leaning on the boat deck railing feeling sorry for ourselves.

"Skipper, the hell with it. Let's catch a launch and go ashore and dump a few. We'll both go batty out on this pile of dead iron."

"I'm with you, Chief. Just wait until I change my shirt."

It was way after midnight. We were sitting in an air conditioned bar, still feeling sorry for ourselves.

"Captain, we will never get a launch this late at night. Besides, we would roast out on the ship. Let's we check into a hotel and be comfortable."

"Chief, you're a bloody genius. Let's go."

The next morning we both ate a huge breakfast. Somewhere along the line, we had neglected to eat any supper last night. The Chief announced that he would go to the Agent's office with me. He was going to telex our Boston office that he was quitting. He felt that he was useless, here, and wanted another berth. And that's just what he did.

I went back to the ship and spent the day wandering through the deserted passageways. It was an eerie feeling. All the familiar sounds and smells had stopped.

I sat at my desk and pondered. A few more days like this one and I'd be either be stir crazy or starve to death. *What am I going to do about eating?* I rummaged through the galley. Nothing. Same with the pantry. The Steward had done a thorough job of cleaning up. I hung around the bridge for a couple of hours, smoking cigarettes, which helped to quell my hunger. Turning in, I decided that I, too, would have a talk with Boston tomorrow.

The next morning I went ashore, as hungry as a wolf. Bacon, eggs, and grits perked me up. I set a course to the Agent's office and docked at nine, sharp. Their Manager said that I was to call the Boston office at once, very important. I could tell from his look that he knew what it was all about, but he wouldn't tell me. I plunked myself down at an empty desk and asked the switchboard girl to get me Boston. In a minute or two my old friend and mentor, the Marine Superintendent, Captain Litchfield, came booming through the receiver.

"How are you, Captain? Good trip? Cargo OK? Fine. Now listen to me and hold onto your hat. As soon as the strike is over, and your cargo fully discharged, your ship will be sold to the States Marine Line. I would ask that you stay with the ship until she is turned over. I will write you the details, later, covering such things as a joint inventory, obtaining receipts for all navigation equipment, ship's documents, etc. Will you go along with this?"

"Of course, Captain, but one question: How does the future look for me?"

"Well, now, I will be perfectly frank with you. The post war slump in ocean shipping is the direct cause of your vessel's sale. Without being complimentary, you have served this Company well. However, it could be that, shortening sail as we must, the best thing that I can do is that you might have to step back to Chief Mate again, until such time as a Master's berth becomes available. Don't give me an answer, now. Think it over, and thanks for staying on, down there. Talk to you later, my friend. "

I sat there, stunned. Here I had just lost my fine crew, all good friends. Now I was losing my ship and my job. Sure, I could step down. Sure, I could sail as Mate again, but my pride had suffered a big jolt. I was so proud of being Master. My life long ambition had been realized. I gloried in my job. It was the culmination of many hard years. *Be philosophical, swallow your pride, be practical. The economical slump was real. Face up to it. Live with it.* So I told myself. Still, it was a bitter pill that stuck in my throat and wouldn't go down. Nor could I cough it up.

I decided that as dismal as a dead ship was, I'd buy a couple of sandwiches, a thermos of coffee, and spend the night on board. Maybe I could come to terms with myself. Actually, I didn't have much choice. I had been with the same company for quite a long time, so whatever reputation I had was strictly, *In House.*

Back to the launch landing I went, loaded with enough grub to do me for the night. By God! There was a picket line parading back and forth. The white caps were all too familiar, they were SIU seamen. Sure enough, they were carrying SIU placards. I said Hi to them. They formed a solid line and wouldn't let me through.

"Hey, fellers, I'm no strikebreaker. I'm the Master of that dead ship out yonder. I'm just going out to spend the night aboard and to pick up some clean clothes. "

I might just as well have saved my breath. They wouldn't budge. I tried to reason with them.

"Listen, that ship is my home. You don't think that I'm going to get up steam and sail her away all by myself, do you?"

Fuming, I headed back to the city. From a phone booth, I got the address of the MM&P, the Masters, Mates, and Pilot's Association, of which I was a member. I knew that they had a sort of relationship with the SIU. Even though Masters weren't required to belong, I had been a member when I was a Mate, and had kept up my dues.

In I went and told my story—just wanted to go aboard, get a change of clothes, and spend the night. I pleaded, cajoled, argued, all for nothing.

"Please, just call up the SIU and tell them to let me through. God dammit, I'm no strikebreaker. What's the matter with you dummies?"

They just sat there. In a fit of rage I pulled out my MM&P card, tore it to pieces and flung it in their faces.

327

Now what to do? Too late to go to the Agent's office, and my dough was running low. I checked into a small hotel, again.

First thing the next morning I was on the sidewalk waiting for our Agent's office to open. I told my sad story to the Manager and had him hire a tow boat to take me out to the ship and wait for me while I packed my gear, which they did. I lugged my stuff off the tow boat and returned to the hotel where I struck a deal to rent the room by the week at a reduced rate. And I put it on my expense account, too.

A week or more went by. Rumors were strong that the shipowners and the SIU were close to a settlement. I sure hoped so. The days were beginning to pall. During the day I would hang around the Agent's office making a pest of myself. My evenings were spent either in the hotel bar drinking more than was my habit, or in bed reading. *The Sailing Directions,* of course. No solution to my problem came to me, and I was morose and itchy.

One morning the Agent informed me that the Marine Superintendent of States Marine would like to see me at two PM, if convenient. *Probably something about the joint inventory,* I figured. Over I went and was ushered into the Presence. He was most gracious, sending out for New Orleans coffee, to which I had become addicted.

"I guess that you want to discuss the inventory," I said.

"Well, that, too, but let's talk about you for a bit."

Very gently but cleverly, he drew my background from me. How I had started going to sea back in 1931. How I had finally got my first ticket and got out of the focsle. What ships that I had commanded. How long that I had been with my present company. I didn't mind his prying. In fact, I enjoyed it. Talking about one's self is a common failing, and I was no exception.

Then he hit me with a blockbuster.

"Your ship has been fixed to load a full cargo of cotton in Peru, consigned to Egypt via the Panama Canal, Cape Horn, and the Cape of Good Hope. I am offering you command."

I was stunned and quite unable to answer.

"Now, think it over. You don't have to give me an answer right now. However, I want to tell you a bit about this company's policy as regards our Skippers. We feel that they are one of the main keys to the success of a voyage, so we try to treat them as well as possible. You will receive a substantial increase above the Liberty ship scale. Also, we are well aware that most Masters despise paper work, and since Pursers have been done away with, we pay our Masters an extra two hundred dollars a month to compensate for all that hateful paper work. We also pay them a rather good voyage bonus for efficient ship management. And last, your quarters will be enlarged, extending out to encompass the starboard alley way and extending forward, taking the chart room and about one third of the wheel house. Think it over, Captain. We

328

would like you to come aboard."

We shook hands while I groped for the door. I walked out in an absolute daze. Never, had anything like this happened to me, and it was so flattering. My ego was inflated to bursting. My mind was a turmoil of conflicting thoughts.

I walked over to a small, shaded park and sat down on a bench to sort it all out.

First, I reviewed the tangible benefits, which were absolutely great. Then I tried to examine myself. I had always been a strong company man, and had deep loyalties. Captain Litchfield had pushed me and supported me ever since I had joined the Line. Would it be disloyal to leave him? Would I be letting him down? Stepping down to Mate would only affect my pride. With overtime, the average Mate made as much, or more than the Old Man. There was one thing, though, that overshadowed all the pros and cons—Cape Horn!

I don't know the inner thoughts of other ship masters, but all my life there lurked the hidden dream of booting a ship around Cape Stiff. It and Pentland Firth are generally accepted as two of the worst places in the world to take a ship. I already had intimate acquaintance with Pentland Firth, but Cape Horn, never. In the days of sail, it was commonplace, and many a tale has been told of those big wind ships and of their battles trying to round that desolate Cape, down there in that cold, remote part of the Oceans.

Since the advent of steam and the opening of the Panama Canal, Cape Horn had been forgotten. Why travel all those extra miles, risking life, limb, and the ship her self when you could just zip through the Canal?

Still, way in the back of my mind was the challenge of doing it. A dream never to come true, but here it was, ready for me to grasp.

Right then my mind was made up. I would take the job. Not for the extra dough and the fancy new quarters, but for a shot at Cape Stiff. It was something that I just couldn't resist.

I headed right back for States Marine and asked, again, to see the Marine Superintendent. He saw me right away. I told him that I wanted the job.

"Didn't take you long to make up your mind, Captain. What influenced you the most? The money or the new quarters? "

"Neither, Captain. It was Cape Horn."

"By God, I knew that I had you figured right. Come on. I'm buying lunch. "

So the die was cast. Now, though, those dark thoughts of disloyalty, of Captain Litchfield's steadfast support crept in to torment me. My conscience was giving me a fit, so I put off calling Boston. After all, I reasoned, I'd be on their payroll until the turnover.

With my misgivings temporarily buried, I started to walk on air. With States Marine's permission, I raided the Hydrographic Office. I bought every chart available for the Cape Horn area and the Straits of Magellan. I bought an armload for the West coast of South America, both coastal charts and detailed ones for entering any major port enroute. I bought two copies of the *Sailing Directions* for our entire voyage. These last, I hoped to have memorized before sailing day arrived.

Now I was itching to get back on board and into the chart room and start plotting courses. The strike was still on, though, so I had to be content with spreading charts all over the floor of my room. I weighted the corners down with books. God knows what the maid thought. Every night I studied the *Sailing Directions*. The more I read, the more I realized that those old clipper ships weren't exaggerating about Cape Stiff. It was no place to fool around. Down there the Southern Oceans swept completely around the globe, unimpeded by any land mass. The prevailing winds were almost always Westerly. That would be one thing in our favor. The wind should be abaft of our beam. Another thing that should be to our advantage was that we would be departing from New Orleans in the early fall, and by the time we finished loading in Peru, it would be summer down there. The seasons in the Southern Hemisphere are just the reverse of those North of the Equator.

Next, I turned to the matter of our cargo, cotton. Did it stow heavy or light? What was its Stowage Factor? Were the bales compressed? The ship had 475,000 cubic feet available for cargo. Using the Stowage Factor and the total space, the long tons that could be loaded could be ascertained. This in turn, would enable one to calculate the vessel's loaded draft. Would the ship be deep enough in the water to keep the propeller and the rudder submerged when those terrible following seas swept under our counter, down there off the Horn. And what seas they are. The highest waves in the world were roaring by Cape Horn.

My notebook was fast filling up with hundreds of facts and questions. I would check and recheck them. In spite of the fancy new office and stateroom that I would be getting, the ship was still a tired, old, underpowered Liberty ship, and God knows, or at any rate I knew, that they had their limits.

For awhile I played around with fuel oil requirements. These Libertys had three deep tanks Two in number one lower hold and one in number four. If I filled them with bunker oil, should I burn from them on the way South and then fill them with sea water, which is heavier than oil? An homogenous cargo, such as we were going to load, indicated that we should have as much weight as low in the ship as possible for stability. I decided to set this subject aside until we shipped a crew. Then the Chief Engineer and I would thrash it out. I knew that the shore staff of States Marine would be grappling with the same problem. Still, the Master takes upon himself full and sole responsibility, and I took that burden seriously. Let anything happen, anything at all, and it would be the Old Man's ass. We all knew it. That's the way ships are run. You can't say, *I was napping after having been on the bridge for three days and nights when it happened.* No way! The Old Man is **always** on watch. Part of the job.

Ho, a red letter day! I heard on the early morning news that the seamen's strike was settled. I gulped down a quick breakfast and made a bee line for the office. After consulting with the Manager, we phoned the unions and ordered six temporary A.B.s, three watertenders, and two assistant engineers. They were to report aboard at one PM and get steam up. A tow boat was ordered for three o'clock. I was told that States Marine were sending out their Chief Engineer, Chief Mate, and Second Mate. Great! Things were starting to move.

I bought a shopping bag full of sandwiches, five pounds of coffee, and headed for the boat landing. Fixed firmly under my arm was a big roll of charts, my ticket to Cape Horn.

No pickets this time, thank God. I ran up the accommodation ladder straight to the chart room with my precious charts. Then I had to run all over the ship with the Mate's big bunch of keys, unlocking all the staterooms and compartments.

Soon, the water taxi disgorged our temporary crew, including the new Chief Engineer, Chief Mate, and the Second Mate. While the black gang was firing off the boilers and raising steam, and the deck gang were laying out the mooring lines and spring wires, my new officers and I gathered in the saloon where I broke out my bag of sandwiches. We already had enough steam up to run the pantry coffee urn so the Mate charged it up. We all sat down at one of the tables and broke the ice.

I was well impressed with all three of them. They were long time career men with States Marine, and were obviously capable, dependable officers. Boy, was my luck ever holding! These three men could make life so much easier for me if they knew their job and equally important, were compatible. The latter I was determined to nurture.

"Tell you what," said I. "As soon as we get tied up, I'm springing for supper. We'll all meet at The Court of the Two Sisters, a famous New Orleans restaurant."

They accepted enthusiastically. So far so good.

There is an old saying that familiarity breeds contempt, and probably it is generally true. However, there is a fine line in the Merchant Service that is never crossed. I have had many close friends—Chief Engineers, Chief and Second Mates, Radio Operators, Stewards, that I have gone ashore with and cut up a little hell. Yet, back on board we were **always** formal. All officers were addressed as Mister except the Chief Engineer, and he was Chief. I was always Captain, but **never** Cap, as a few young, brash sailors have tried and been corrected, quick. That fine line stayed black and bold, and that's the way it should be.

The next day the winches were clattering as our cargo was hoisted out of all five hatches. A Port Captain and Port Engineer arrived from States Marine and the joint survey got under way. Everything went smoothly. Long lists were compiled and compared. So it went for two days. Only one hitch developed. Our inventory showed four thirty-eight caliber revolvers. There were only three in the safe. Someone, in the past, had swiped one.

Turnover day was drawing near. A full crew had been shipped. The galley was manned, and the ship was feeding again. Not like before, though. The cooks were Hispanic and the food reflected it. Greasy, highly spiced, chick peas daily.

My new Second Mate and I spent hours in the chart room. Interminable discussions were held about courses and distances, especially for those for transiting the Straits of Magellan.

You might think that this waterway is a straight wide passageway from the Pacific to the Atlantic. Not so. It's a bastard to traverse.

Even before getting down there we've got to steam from the Panama Canal down through sixty-three degrees of latitude. From nine degrees North to fifty-three degrees South, upwards of thirty seven hundred miles. Plus the distance from New Orleans to the Canal. And then the thousands of miles from Cape Horn to the Cape of Good Hope, at the Southern tip of Africa. Then North in the Indian Ocean to the Red sea, thence through the Suez Canal to Egypt.

Wow! This voyage is going to require some logistical planning. Where we would put in for bunkers would undoubtedly be decided by States Marine. All steamship companies had worldwide arrangements with the oil companies, so I knew that I would be advised in due course.

A strange thought intruded. Cotton from Peru to Egypt? Egypt's cotton export had been big business for years and years. How come? World trade, with all its ramifications, was beyond me, so I pushed the thought aside.

Another thought intruded, weather. It is common knowledge that the weather at Cape Horn is always bad. But what about currents through the Straits of Magellan? Did fog ever prevail, there? And if it did, were there any safe anchorages in the Straits? Did ships engage a pilot? Or were any available? And were they any good? I had a lot of studying to do and time was getting short. Better get ashore and lay in a full supply of Pilot Charts for every month for the entire route. They have always been the best source of weather information, and I put great faith in them. The Second Mate and I divided up the voyage into segments:

1. *New Orleans to the Panama Canal*
2. *The Canal to Peru*
3. *Peru to the Straits of Magellan*

332

4. *The Straits of Magellan*
5. *The Straits to the Cape of Good Hope*
6. *The Indian Ocean to the Red Sea*
7. *The Red Sea through the Suez Canal to Egypt*

This was getting bigger and bigger. And we couldn't just stick our heads in the sand like an ostrich and say, *Well, we'll just lay out courses and distances from here to the Canal, and worry about the next leg when we get there.* No way! That word **contingencies** reared up and snapped at me. A host of them had to be allowed for. What about deck stores? We should have plenty of spare tarpaulins and hatch covers. And they should be stowed where we could get at them in a hurry. Several topping mauls, several bags of hatch wedges. Oh, the hell with it. I've got a damned good Chief Mate. Dump all this kind of stuff in his lap. He will handle it, and handle it well.

Medical supplies: Speak to the Mate.

Slop Chest: That's my baby. Load her up. Plenty of cold weather gear, long johns, oilskins, cigarettes for a year. On and on it went.

This planning threatened to overwhelm me.

"Mister," I said to the Second Mate. "Lock up this damned chart room. My compliments to the Mate and the Chief. If they are free, I'd be delighted if they would be my guests for supper ashore this evening. You, too, if you are free."

High faluting talk on an old Liberty but I loved it. I always tried to observe all the niceties and protocols that have held ships together since time immemorial.

They all accepted and off we went, this time to Antoines. I've always had a weakness for French food, and Antoines was known worldwide.

We settled at a table and ordered drinks. I started the conversation.

"Gentlemen, I have a confession to make. The planning for this voyage has got me buried. We are going practically around the world, coming home via the Mediterranean, and right now, I don't know whether I'm coming or going."

The Mate cleared his throat, reached in his pocket and pulled out a thick sheaf of neatly typed papers.

"Captain, I, too, have been doing some planning. Here is my list of deck stores. By God! His list put mine to shame. He had anticipated every contingency, every emergency, and then some. I was absolutely astounded.

The Chief reached in his pocket and hauled out an even bigger stack of notes.

"Skipper, I, too, have been busy. I have had several meetings with our Port Engineer. Here are all our fuel estimates, barrels per mile, distances between bunkering ports, the amount to be loaded, and the ports where we will bunker. Again, I was flabbergasted. While I was trying to collect myself, the

333

Second Mate cleared his throat.

"Captain, I haven't got any list, but after you turned in every night, I plotted every course and distance from here to Suez. I used recommended routing, all well clear of off lying islands, reefs, and so forth. I think that you will find them quite accurate.

Well, now, I tell you, I was some touched.

"Waiter, another round. Gents, I'm ashamed of myself. My *Hands On* style of management has caught up with me. I have neglected to take advantage of the most important tool, **Good, capable people.** I am very grateful and proud to be your shipmate."

I confess, I was quite choked up.

We had a fine evening; good food, lots of shop talk, and good, congenial companionship.

The next day the Second Mate went over all his midnight work. With the exception of a few minor changes that I suggested, one in the Mozambique Channel, one or two off Madagascar, his work stood the test of my critical scrutiny. We left open the transiting of the Mozambique Channel. True, it was shorter, but was it worth it? We would have to thread our way through the Sayschelle Islands, maybe in drenching rains where the visibility would be zero. I was all for vetoing it, preferring to pass to the Eastward of Madagascar. Time enough for that decision when we were approaching the Cape of Good Hope.

At the rate we were going it would appear that we would need a truck load of charts. Every day the Second Mate came back to the ship with another armload.

The capability and competence of my three top associates took a big load off my back. In all my years at sea, I had never once sailed the Pacific. They hadn't, either, so we were all green horns. I consoled myself with the thought that good seamanship and prudence were the same on any ocean.

Every night when I turned in, my bed companion was the *Sailing Directions. Here are some of the quotes that I wrote down:*

*The passage through the Straits of Magellan is safe,
but vigilance and caution are necessary. If
the weather is thick, as is likely to be the case
for more or less protracted periods, the passage
is rendered more difficult because of incomplete
surveys, the lack of aids to navigation, the
distance between anchorages, the strong currents,
and in some cases, the narrow limit for maneuvering
of vessels.
The most dangerous winds are the violent and unpredictable squalls.*

During the strongest, which occur most often West
of Cape Froward and near the main coastline adjoining
the stormiest region at sea, the wind almost certainly
exceeds 100 knots.
In the East part of the region the WSW or SW winds blow with great
force and commonly exceed 50 knots.
The character of the tides in the Atlantic and Pacific
Oceans differ considerably. As the Straits of Magellan
forms a narrow channel linking the two oceans, a strong
tidal stream runs through the Straits, reaching a rate
of 8 knots in the narrows at springs.
Between Punta Dungeness and Primera Angostura the range
of tide is great, becoming as much as 39 feet at springs.
The Chilean Navy issues the necessary provisions regulating the
passage. They stipulate that transit of Primera
Angostura be done in daylight, under good visibility
conditions and under the supervision of a pilot.
Pilotage is obligatory for all vessels using the Straits.

The Straits are 310 miles in length. This means one overnight, maybe more. The weather and tidal currents concerned me the most. Squalls that spring up in minutes, with winds reaching 100 knots! And then changing direction without any warning. Sea fog, sleet, and blinding snow squalls. Tidal currents reaching eight knots in the narrows. Wow! A fine place to be trapped during one of those squalls.

A lot of my elation was fast leaking out. What concerned me even more than the weather and currents, was the ship herself. A beat up old Liberty with only twenty-five hundred horse power. And her high, slab sides exposed to those gales. Sea room of only two thousand yards in the narrows. I must be nuts to want to go through what was ahead of us. and then if we did make it, there was the Cape of Good Hope rearing its ugly snout 'way across the South Atlantic, waiting to pounce on us poor souls.

Writing all this, many years later, I now realize how true it is that the world belongs to our youth. At my age, now, I would no more contemplate such a voyage in such a ship than I would jump over the side.

A day or two later a sleek, well maintained British ship docked astern of us. She was an E&B ship, Ellerman-Bucknell, one of England's oldest and most prestigious Lines. I ambled over and introduced myself to her gangway watch. Said I had come to call on her Master. Moments later, his Nibs bustled out of the passageway.

"I say, jolly good of you to pop in. Come join me for a spot of gin before lunch."

335

We repaired to his very opulent suite. His Indian *'boy'* hovered over us mixing pink gins, a marvelous concoction.

"Cheers, old boy. Do have another. I'm going to."

I told him of our impending voyage and of my trepidations.

"My dear chap, if I were you, I'd be far more concerned about the Cape of Good hope than the Straits of Magellan. Do you have a copy of the Admiralty book, the *Africa Pilot?* No? Well here, take mine. I've been around that bloody Cape a few times meself, and it ain't no picnic, as you Yanks say. Go ahead, take it. It will damned well scare the bloody piss out of you."

I took it, of course, and after a fine Indian lunch, currys galore, and hot enough to make your eyes water, I took my departure.

Curling up on my settee, I opened the *Africa Pilot* to the Cape of Good Hope area. I read and read, right through supper. Oh, how right he was. This Cape was some dismal place, alright. I read of the Agulhus Current, poring down the East African coast, between it and the big island of Madagascar, attaining a velocity of three to five knots. When this flow met the terrible gales sweeping around the Cape, all the way from Antarctica, a veritable maelstrom was whipped up. Confused, sixty foot waves tumbling in every direction. Many were the ships that were overwhelmed and lost. And we were taking an old Liberty into those waters. A sobering thought.

Another thing that I learned. The Mozambique Channel **was** the way to go, notwithstanding the Agulhus Current or the Seychelles Islands.

The Second Mate and I were fast becoming experts on the Humboldt Current, a fast flowing stream of cold water pouring up the West coast of South America from the Antarctic. Rich in nutrients, it is responsible for the abundance of fish taking advantage of its bounty. For example, even though the Galapagos Islands are right on the Equator, the cold Humboldt Current sweeping by the islands creates a tremendous concentration of sea birds, all feeding on the millions of fish which are riding the current. Also, the effect of the cold water makes for a most temperate climate, there. We wanted to avoid this fast flowing current as much as possible. Bucking it would only result in excessive fuel consumption, as well as lost time.

We plotted and replotted courses and distances. We recalculated fuel consumption, and tried to figure how its loss would affect the ship's stability. Stability is expressed, nautically, by something called the Metracentric Height. which is the vertical center of gravity of the ship above its keel. The higher the MC, the less righting ability the vessel has.

This is a most important factor, especially when high seas are anticipated, and God knows, we not only anticipated we **knew** that we would encounter them down in the *Roaring Forties.*

In spite of doubts that crept into my mind, I was enjoying every minute

SECTOR 8

ESTRECHO DE MAGALLANES

PLAN.—This sector describes the Estrecho de Magallanes (Strait of Magellan) from its E entrance between Punta Dungeness and Cabo Espiritu Santo, westward to its W entrance between Cabo Victoria and Cabo Pilar, 28 miles SSE. The distance between the E and W entrances of the strait, through the various channels, is 310 miles.

Bays and anchorages are described, in the order in which they are approached, from E to W.

GENERAL REMARKS

When passing through the strait an entire change in the features of the country, and probably in the weather, will be experienced in its various parts.

From its E entrance to Cabo Porpesse, 100 miles WSW, the land is comparatively low and covered with grass, but no trees are visible.

All over this E portion of the strait the most remarkable difference takes place in the appearance of the land according to the conditions of the light in which it is seen.

In the vicinity of Cabo Porpesse the land becomes wooded and its elevation gradually increases. The forest becomes more dense and the mountains more lofty as Cabo Froward is approached. These characteristics continue as far as the E part of Paso Largo. From here, though the mountains still border the strait, the trees become smaller, until towards the W entrance of the strait the shores are bare and rocky, only the ravines showing a stunted, though dense, vegetation.

East of Cabo Froward the land is comparatively level compared to that W of the cape, where there are steep mountains, bare on the upper parts, but covered with thick moss or dense forest on the lower slopes.

The passage through Estrecho de Magallanes is safe, but vigilance and caution are necessary. The difficulties and dangers in navigating the strait in either direction are the same that are experienced in narrow channels and close harbors of the same latitude elsewhere. But if the weather is thick, as is likely to be the case for more or less protracted periods, the passage is rendered more difficult because of in-complete surveys, the lack of aids to navigation, the distance between anchorages, the lack of good anchorages, the strong currents, and in some cases the narrow limit for maneuvering of vessels.

The difference in the duration of daylight in summer and winter forms an important consideration. In December there is daylight from 0230 until 2030, while in June daylight will be limited from 0800 to 1600. Night is preferred to daylight, by some, for navigating Primera Angostura and Segunda Angostura, as the lights are more easily discernible than the beacons and other marks on land.

Paso Tortuoso is navigated by day and night by all regular trading vessels. Without local knowledge there is some risk in passing through this part of the strait owing to the strong tidal streams and the probability at any time of thick weather, either in the form of snow or rain. Anchorage should be found before nightfall, but large W-bound vessels with good radar can safely remain underway in Paso Ancho during night, to await daylight for the passage of Paso Tortuoso.

WINDS—WEATHER

Violent and unpredictable squalls are frequent all over the strait. Sustained gales are seldom encountered except in the widest entrances and passages.

In many of the countless narrow passages the wind follows the run of the passage, and has therefore, only two possible directions. It may be reversed abruptly when there has been a large shift of wind direction over the open sea.

The most dangerous winds are the violent and unpredictable squalls. The occurrence of one or more of these in succession from the same direction is no indication that the next will not be from some widely different direction. Moreover, of two possible anchorages a few miles apart, the more open may well be less subject to these squalls. These squalls depend largely, if not entirely, on the existence of strong winds or gales at sea or at a height of several thousand meters over land. As these winds strike the rugged mountains of the archipelagos they set up eddies of varying size and intensity. In a

Pub. 124

Beginning the detailed description of the Straits of Magellan in the Sailing Directions (Enroute).

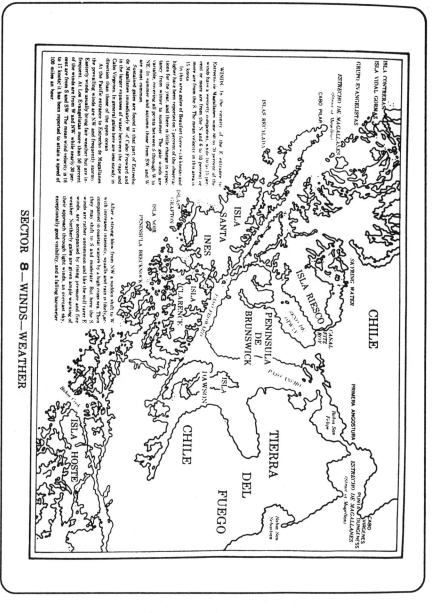

A first look at the Straits of Magellan – from the Sailing Directions for the East Coast of South America.

of this planning. Lying in my bunk at night, I felt very privileged for the chance at this voyage. Cape Horn, here we come!

The turnover of the vessel was scheduled for two days hence. The next morning I went up to our Agent's office before going to the Hydrographics office to buy yet more charts.

The Manager and I were drinking coffee and speculating on the weather, hot or hotter. His secretary came in and handed him a note.

"This is for you, Captain. You are to call Captain Litchfield as soon as possible. "

Captain Litchfield. I hadn't even thought of him for a week. Must be something about the turnover. The Manager picked up his phone and told his operator to get Boston. Handing me the phone, he said,

"That man's energy would wear down an iron man. "

The Captain's voice boomed out as usual.

"That you, Captain? Understand that turnover is for tomorrow, right? Now listen closely. I haven't got much time. I've stepped on some toes up here, and hurt some feelings, but here is what I've got for you. Command of the SS Samuel Johnston. She's laying in Philadelphia. Tomorrow night get your ass on a train for Philly and take over. All the best to you in your new command. Write me. Bye. "

Oh, my God! I dropped the receiver on the desk and stumbled out the door. That conscience of mine roared up and engulfed me.

For hours I walked the streets, not knowing nor caring where I was. My mind was in turmoil. I tried, again, to weigh the pros and cons. Captain Litchfield had once again stuck his neck out on my behalf. He had always been behind me. His good counsel and rare praise had sustained me many, many times, so why leave him and go with another company?

The answer was all too obvious—Vanity. I wanted to show off, if only to myself; to hug myself and say, *I did it. By God, I sailed her around the Horn.* Ruefully, I had to admit that vanity was a poor swap for loyalty. I stopped my blind pacing and headed for the one place I had to go, States Marine and the office of the Marine Superintendent.

I told him of my decision, and why. For awhile, he played with a pencil. Then he stood up, came around his desk and said,

"Shake. Your Captain Litchfield is one good Marine Superintendent! "

Blindly, I found the door. The thought came to me that he was pretty good, too.

The next night I was on a train for Philly. A lost dream? Maybe. I never heard of the ship, again. Did she make out OK? I like to think so. At least she had enough charts. And far more important, she had three damned good seamen, the Chief Engineer, the Chief Mate, and the Second Mate.

I did, too, hear about her, but it was many years later. I read in the newspaper that she had been towed out of the reserve fleet and sunk off Charleston, South Carolina to create a refuge for fish! An ignoble end for a rather gallant vessel. **She** went around Cape Stiff, by God!

-56-

AND MORE FANCY NAVIGATING

Some years after the War I had come ashore and gone to work for a large stevedoring firm. After a stint on the New York docks, I was fortunate enough to be dispatched to Baltimore as Manager. Baltimore was one of the company's busiest ports, and we enjoyed many excellent accounts. One of the best was HapHag-Lloyd, a post war merger of two of Germany's steamship lines, the Hamburg American Line and the North German Lloyd Line.

These HapHag vessels were arriving in Baltimore at the rate of two ships a week. Each ship had a full load of French steel, loaded at the Belgian port of Antwerp.

This was very profitable business for us. And it was going sour. Large cargoes are almost invariably consigned to many different consignees. Each lot had to loaded so that when discharged, each mark can be landed and shipped overland without containing any part of a lot consigned to another receiver. Complaints were pouring in. A had received some of company B's steel and vice-versa. We were being blamed. It was alleged that our longshoremen were paying no attention to the marks, and were throwing slings around anything and everything. We, as contracting stevedores, were paid by the ton, so we were being accused of greediness.

Throw the stuff out of the ship and the hell with sorting by mark, was our motto, or so said our critics. Cables were flying back and forth between the Line's American Agent and Germany, and from both of them to our head office in New York. Naturally, they both dumped it in my lap. It was very serious. Not only were we on the verge of losing the account; we were being billed for transhipping steel all around the country.

The more I protested that the steel was mixed up in the ship, the more nobody believed me. It got so that I was spending more time on the long distance telephone defending myself, than doing my job. They wouldn't believe me, claiming that I was trying to put the blame on the Antwerp stevedore to save my own hide. I finally reached the boiling point. Our Executive Vice President chewed me out for the umpteenth time.

"If you don't believe me, come down here to Baltimore and see for yourself. And bring that big mouthed, Mr. Neal, from the Agent's office. There's a ship due in the day after tomorrow. If the marks in that ship aren't mixed in the ship, you've got my resignation!"

Wow! Did I ever shoot my big mouth off. The die was cast, though, and down they came from New York, black Homburgs and all.

I drove them down to the ship just as the hatches were being opened. I almost had to push them up the gangway. They didn't want to get their fine suits dirty. Then, they didn't want to climb down the ladders to the lower holds.

"My job's on the line, and there is only one way that you are going to be convinced, and that is to see for yourself. Down the hatch!"

And down they went. I had Jim Kropp, our General Superintendent, with me. He explained to the hold men what we wanted. They pulled their cargo hooks out of their belts and started turning steel plates over. Thank the good Lord that watches over such as me. Every second or third plate had a different mark painted on it. The cargo was hopelessly mixed.

"Satisfied, gentlemen? Let's have a look in the other four holds."

Mr. Neal, God bless his soul, spoke up and said to my boss,

"Guess that this man of yours has been right, all along. We just wouldn't listen to him."

Turning to me he said,

"What's the solution to this mess?"

I tried to be sage and judicious, and to conceal my glee.

"Mr. Neal, somebody has got to get to that stevedore in Antwerp."

"Hmm," he says.

Turning to my boss, he made an astounding proposal.

"Let's we send this man of yours over to Antwerp and let him straighten things out, one stevedore to another. After all, they speak the same language."

I interrupted, like a dope.

"Mr. Neal, I don't speak Flemish."

"I don't mean it that way. You both speak stevedore lingo. Tell you what I'll do. In the name of HapHag, I'll authorize your expenses."

Boy, this guy was turning out to be some good friend and supporter. So it was agreed, right there on the spot. I'd go up to New York where Mr. Neal would give me a letter of introduction, and as soon as I got my passport and shots, I'd be off.

To back track a little, my wife and I lived outside of Baltimore in a quiet residential area, Dulaney Valley. In the short time that we had been there we had made some fine friends. I kept running into one in particular at weekend barbecues. He was an overseas airline pilot. He had learned of my seafaring background, and in a friendly way, was forever needling me about how old-fashioned we ship people were, and how modern the air people were. In particular, in the field of navigation. To hear him tell it, we had never changed since Columbus, while they were using all the latest gadgets. This was all in good fun, but still, the old needle was always there.

In short order, I flew up to New York. The company chauffeur, Henry, met me and drove me to a posh hotel. I was instructed to meet my boss and Mr. Neal at the Downtown Athletic Club for dinner, and that I would be departing for London the next afternoon. Henry, the driver, gave me my airline tickets and announced that he would be back at six PM to drive me downtown. Boy, talk about putting on the Ritz!

We had a fine dinner, and it was there that a lasting friendship began. Mr. Neal was an old hand in the shipping business, and there was no fooling him. Nor did I ever try in all the years that we were associated. Many times in the future, one of our hungry competitors would do their damnedest to take HapHag away from us, but thanks to Mr. Neal, they never succeeded. The shine that he took to me, and me to him, remained bright for many years.

After dinner my two big shot friends decided that I should be introduced to Manhattan's night life, so off we went with old faithful Henry at the helm. God, what a night! Sometime, long after midnight, I vaguely remember Mr. Neal playing the piano and singing at the top of his lungs. At last, I cried *'Uncle,'* and Henry drove me to my hotel. Before he left, he announced that he had strict orders to get me on the plane, so he would pick me up two hours before flight time.

The next morning, in spite of a monumental hang-over, I went down to Mr. Neal's office at the U. S. Navigation Co. There he was, bright and bushy tailed, working away at a mountain of paper work.

"Come in", he roared. "Overslept, did you?"

This guy must have a cast iron gut, I muttered to myself.

He gave me final instructions, and very wisely held back on any advice, which was flattering. He made me feel that he had the utmost confidence in me. That did more for me than all the advice in the world. A very wise man.

Back to the hotel. Old Henry was camped right in front of the door, fighting with the door man.

"No, I won't move. I'm here to drive Senator Farrar to his plane!"

Now I'm a Senator, yet!

Naturally, we made the airport with plenty of time to spare. I boarded the plane. It was a four engine, propeller driven, Boeing Strato-Cruiser. She was unique in that there were two decks. Down a flight of steps from the main cabin, was an intimate, tastefully decorated, cocktail lounge. The steward told me that she cruised at close to three hundred miles an hour.

After a short wait, we taxied out to the runway. The Captain ran up the engines, one by one. Then he slammed the throttles to *'Full Ahead,'* and off we roared.

As soon as we were airborne, and had reached cruising altitude, the no smoking and seat belt signs flashed off, and down the aisle came the Captain, greeting everyone in person. And damned if it wasn't my neighbor from

Dulaney Valley, my old needler! As soon as he saw me, he pulled up and we shook hands. Out came the old needle.

"Listen," says he. "We're heading for Gander, in Newfoundland, where we will refuel for the flight to Shannon, Ireland. As soon as we leave Gander, come on up to the cockpit and I'll show you how us **modern** navigators operate."

With a triumphant smile, he passed on down the aisle.

I must admit, needle or no, I couldn't wait to see all those wonderful electronic gadgets that took all the drudgery out of navigation. To while away the time, I slipped down to the lounge and had a couple of snorts before dinner. Our stay in Gander was brief. Gas up and away we went, heading out across the North Atlantic for Shannon.

I walked forward and knocked on the cockpit door.

"Come in," yelled the Captain.

My eyes pretty near popped out of my head. The entire dashboard was solid instruments. So was the ceiling, and both sides above the windows. Dozens of them--hundreds of them! Both pilots were lolling back smoking cigarettes.

"Don't you even have to hold onto the wheel?"

"Hell, no, she's on Auto Pilot. Just flying herself."

Ships have had automatic steering for years. We called them Iron Mikes. But planes? Way up here in the sky? Wow!

"Well, now," said I, "Where are all the fancy gadgets? I've heard that all you have to do is follow a radio beam. And that you get constant Radio Direction Finder fixes."

"Yep, we have all that equipment, but it's no good out here, over the Atlantic. We only use that stuff when flying over land, or approaching land. Step over here and I'll show you what we're doing right now."

We moved to a small chart table in back of the co-pilot.

"Here is a Great Circle chart. You will notice that we have drawn a straight line on it, connecting Gander with Shannon. Now, here is a Mercator chart of the same area. We have marked off on it, by latitude and longitude, segments from the Great Circle chart. You now see the arc of a great circle connecting Gander with Shannon. That's the route that we are following. Do you follow me so far?"

"Yes, I understand only too well because we, on ships, do exactly the same thing, using those very same charts. But how do you determine your position?"

"Why, we just use this here beauty."

He reached down and came up with a weird looking thing that resembled a science fiction death ray pistol.

"What in God's name is that?"

"It's a bubble sextant. Here, take it. You see, up here, we haven't any horizon, so we use a bubble. Take a look into the scope. See, the bubble has to be right on center. Get it?"

"I guess so."

"Good, now here are the computed altitudes of three stars, together with their azimuths. Crawl up into the coop, there, and shoot the stars. I'll mark your time."

I wriggled my way up into a little dome with a transparent roof. I tried and tried, but I just couldn't cope with that damned bubble. And the sextant itself was heavy and cumbersome. I backed down, defeated.

"No problem," says he. "I'll shoot them and you mark the time," which I did.

He would call down *'Mark,'* and I would jot down the Greenwich Civil Time. Then he would call out the sextant angle of the star, and I would write it down alongside the time of the sight. After he had shot the third star, he came down and pulled out two books.

"I don't suppose that you have seen these babies?" He waved them under my nose.

"Seen them? Why, I've been using them ever since they have been in print!"

They were the Air Almanac and H. 0. 214, my old and trusted standbys. He seemed somewhat deflated, but recovered quickly.

"OK, you work out the sights and plot them."

"Sure," I said, and promptly fell into his trap.

On a cargo ship making, at most, ten or twelve knots, we never took into consideration the distance traveled between shooting one star and the next. It was so small that it was of no consequence. But up there, whizzing along at almost three hundred miles an hour, it can be, and is, of considerable importance. This never entered my dim mind, though, and I proceeded to work out the three sights. Then I plotted them as if they had all been taken simultaneously. No good! I went over my figures again. No mistakes. My friendly tormenter was peering over my shoulder, noisily sucking his teeth.

"Where did I go wrong, Captain?"

"Well, now, you forgot that with a following wind we are doing close to three hundred miles every hour. You will notice that five minutes elapsed between the first and second sight. And six minutes elapsed between the second and third sights. This means that you have to advance your first LOP (Line of Position) by the distance flown in eleven minutes. The second LOP has to be advanced by six minutes."

Feeling as small as an ant, I did as he said, and lo and behold, there was a small, neat triangle, the center of which was our position at the time of the third sight. Speed--It was something that I found difficult to adapt. After a lifetime of eight to ten knots, three hundred knots floored me. Another thing that fooled me was the accuracy of the bubble sextant. It was not nearly as accurate as the marine sextant that we use on ships. The Captain told me that it was often off by as much as fifty miles. However, he said that it didn't seem to matter because, again, their great speed made corrections quick to make. As a matter of fact, because of that great speed, by the time you had reduced three sights to three LOP's, it was past history. You had long since flown 'way beyond the position that you had just plotted.

I must say, though, that those two pilots were careful, cautious navigators. I stayed with them for most of the night, and all during that time they were constantly fixing their position and adjusting their course.

They also used the radio for wind and weather conditions. Wind played a big part in their decisions.

Finally, towards morning the Captain said to me,

"We have to radio Shannon our ETA. You figure it out."

And again speed defeated me. I had always been in the habit of rounding off figures to the nearest whole. Tenths were unimportant. I quickly stepped off the distance remaining from our last fix, estimated the speed, and scribbled my answer.

"There you are, Captain."

He glanced at my ETA and slowly tore up my slip of paper.

"By your figures, we just passed over London!"

Speed--it had once again defeated me.

The Captain had been most gracious to me, though, and seemed quite surprised that both planes and ships found their way around the world essentially by the same methods.

Our stay at Shannon was short, and we were soon off for London where I bade my friendly Skipper so long, and boarded a plane for the short flight to Antwerp.

The Antwerp stevedore met me at passport control. We liked each other at first sight. Mr. Neal was right. We spoke the same language. On the ride into the city we chattered away like two squirrels. He let me out at my hotel where we agreed to meet the next morning down on the docks where he had a HapHag ship loading steel for Baltimore.

I stayed for over two weeks. Between the two of us we got the problem solved. All this steel was being loaded from railroad flat cars. A whole string of them would be pulled alongside the ship. We discovered that a large shipment to one consignee would occupy four or more cars, stretching abreast of three or four hatches. This meant that steel, all with one mark, would be going into three or four hatches instead of being consolidated in one. My new friend was worried. His was a small company, and HapHag his only account. If he lost it, he'd be finished. He admitted that it was all his fault. And to make matters worse, he had ignored all the cablegrams. I truly felt sorry for him. The shoe could well have been on the other foot. The truth is, all stevedores are greedy. They are paid by the ton, so the less time that they have to spend fooling around with marks, the more tonnage, and hence money, they can make. We joined forces in an elaborate cover-up. We blamed the French Railroad Company. My friend had good connections in high places. The upshot of it all, was that the railroad accepted liability and assigned a crew of dispatchers in the marshalling yards to rearrange strings of cars. Then my friend had to lay down the law to his foremen that marks would never be mixed. If one large mark went into more than one hatch, the stowage plan had to show it. It was all pretty transparent to us but it worked! We both received congratulatory cables from Mr. Neal and HapHag. Time to quit while you're ahead. I headed for the airport and London.

Talk about coincidence; When I boarded the transatlantic plane for the flight home, there was my neighbor, again! Small world!

I called my wife in Baltimore and suggested that she join me in New York for the weekend. Off we flew to Shannon. During the stopover I shot the last of my cash in the airport's gift shop for a few presents.

Right after supper we took off and headed West, this time for Goose Bay, Labrador. When it got dark, the steward passed out blankets and dimmed the cabin lights. I had a window seat on the Starboard side. A full moon started to move to the right. Slowly, it moved to our Starboard beam, then aft and out of sight. Now, the moon is a planet, and therefore not stationary, but it doesn't go whizzing around like I had just observed. We had changed course and were now headed East, back to where we had come from! The steward was asleep in the seat behind me. I woke him up and told him what I had just seen. He went flying forward to the cock pit. Strangely enough, nobody else seemed to have noticed. Back came the steward. He said that the Starboard outboard engine had conked out, and that we were returning to Shannon.

My friend made a perfect touchdown on three engines. There was a certain amount of confusion at the Airline's ticket counter when they announced that passengers would be booked on succeeding flights according to need. Immediately, every passenger had an emergency. Their mother was dying, or their father was dying, or their kids were dying. Me, like a jerk, told the truth-- that I was returning home from a business trip. Bingo! I plummeted to the bottom of the list. As a result, I got stuck in Shannon for three days. The airline gave me a little dingy den of a room and paid for my meals. Because I didn't have a visa for Ireland, Customs wouldn't let me out of the terminal. So there I stayed, practically a prisoner, while another engine was flown in from London and installed. I found out later that my wife had just about given up hope of ever seeing me again.

All's well that ends well. I finally got home, safe. My stock in the company had risen considerably. And, best of all, I got a big fat raise.

-57-

FRACTURED FRENCH

My knowledge of the French language was gleaned from the gutters of waterfront ports in France and North Africa. You might even say that I took post-graduate work in the dives of Marseilles.

French is a most difficult tongue, to say the least. Regular verbs, irregular verbs, past and future tenses; they were all beyond me. When seamen learn a foreign tongue, such as French, they care nothing for the niceties of grammar. Instead, they acquire a sort of pidgin lingo. They express everything in the present tense, thus avoiding the pitfalls of esoteric grammar. Translated, it might read something like this.

> *"Today I am going."*
> *"Tomorrow I am going."*
> *"Yesterday I am going."*

Pretty awful, but we made ourselves understood.

Two other things that we learned: In any foreign country, no matter how badly you might mangle their language, the inhabitants love you for trying. The other is peculiar to the French language. When the average American hears a French man, or more especially, a French woman speaking or singing in English, with a pronounced French accent, the sound is very pleasing to American ears. Now here is the incredible part. When an American speaks French with an American accent, the result is equally pleasing to the French listener. Surprisingly, this doesn't hold true when an Englishman speaks French with an English accent. The result is not the same. The sound is not pleasant.

All of the foregoing is by way of saying that I had learned, long before I swallowed the anchor and came ashore, that it was always the smart thing to do, to speak, or attempt to speak, a foreigner's language, no matter how badly you mangled it. I figured that this applied in business as well as ships, and I was now in business.

When I first came ashore, I was very fortunate in getting a job with a large stevedoring firm with headquarters in New York. Good fortune had smiled upon me, and I had experienced a rapid rise in the ranks. I presently held the exalted position of Operations Vice-President of the whole shooting match.

Our most prestigious and valued account was The French Line, Le

346

Compaigne General Transatlantic. Because I had played some part in acquiring the account, I had taken it upon myself to *'bird dog'* it. I made it my business to become very friendly with their North American Manager, Commandant Jean-Paul L'Eglise. We became good friends. He had been master with the French Line, so we had common interests. This was in the hey-day of the big transatlantic liners. The French Line had the Ile de France, the Liberté, the France, as well as two cargo ships a week.

The line occupied Pier 88 on the North River, the same pier where the Normandie was berthed when she caught fire, rolled over and sank, a total loss. That was during World War II. The line also occupied extensive offices in downtown Manhattan. It was from there that they conducted their far-flung freight and passenger business for the entire North American continent. Upon entering these offices, one was confronted with an enormous open area, occupied by dozens and dozens of typists, secretaries, booking clerks, and the like. They were all, without exception, French, all brought over from Paris. To my knowledge, the French Line did not employ anyone who was not French. At the end of this great open room were the glassed in offices for the executives, including Commandant Jean-Paul.

It had become my habit to visit the French Line pier several times a week in order to keep fully informed on operations. It was also my custom to call at their downtown offices one morning a week to discuss operations with the Commandant. At the conclusion of these discussions, we would take turns hosting lunch. If one of their big ships was in port, and it was the Commandant's turn to be host, we would lunch on the ship. This was some treat! These ships employed the finest chefs in all of France. Whenever the Commandant appeared, the red carpet was really rolled out. I have fond memories of those luncheons.

There was another thing that it became my habit to do. In line with my philosophy of trying to speak a foreigner's language, no matter how badly, every week on my to work I would mentally rehearse a little speech in my awful French. Then I would deliver it when I entered that big downtown office. That room full of Frenchmen and women seemed to appreciate it. As soon as I opened the door, all work would stop, and every head would turn in my direction. Strangely, the Commandant would always be standing in his doorway. Somehow, somebody was sending him a signal that I had arrived. One particular morning while I was driving to work, I commenced putting together a very special speech, and, was having difficulty. What I wanted to say in French was this:

"Today, I am very happy because it is our twenty-fifth wedding anniversary."

Let's see, now; the first part is a cinch.

AUJOURD HUI. JE SUIS TRES HEUREUX.

"Today I am very happy. So far so good. Next word, *'because.'* No problem.

PARCE-QUE.

"I'm really rolling. Next:

It is my twenty-fifth. "
"C'EST MON VINGT-CINQ. " Easy!

Hold it! I didn't have the slightest idea what the French word for *'wedding anniversary'* was. Better think this one over.
How about,

"Today I am very happy because we have twenty-five years behind us?"

A problem immediately presented itself. The French have **two** words for *'year.'* *ANS* and *ANEE.* Which to use? Damned if I knew. Better to abandon them.
How about twenty-five summers? Or winters? *WINTERS!* That's the word, *HIVER.*
Now let's see how it sounds:

"Today I am very happy because we have twenty-five winters behind us. " Perfect!

I was all set. I rehearsed it over and over until I had it down pat. As I look back, it was a miracle that I didn't run off the road and kill myself.
As was my custom, I first headed for Pier 88 where I spent a couple of hours with our pier superintendent, and then headed downtown for my weekly conference with Commandant Jean-Paul L'Eglise.
I finally found a place to park, sailed up in the elevator, and flung open the door. All work ceased. Every head turned in my direction. Jean-Paul was in his usual position. The stage was set. Enter the star. I immediately boomed out my lines:

"BON JOUR, MAIS AMIS. AUJOURD-HUI, JE SUIS TRES

HEUREUX PARCE-QUE MA FEMME ET MOI AVONS VINGT-CI-NQ L'HIVER DANS NOTRE DERRIERE."

The room erupted. It was pandemonium. Jean-Paul was frantically waving his arms at me. I bowed graciously to my audience, and joined him in his office.

He was as red as a boiled lobster and shaking with laughter.

"Captain, do you know what you just said?"

"Sure. I said that today I am very happy because it is our twentyfifth wedding anniversary."

"Not quite, Captain. What you said was,

TODAY I AM VERY HAPPY BECAUSE MY WIFE AND I HAVE TWENTY-FIVE WINTERS STUCK UP IN OUR BACKSIDES!"

And off he went, into another gale of laughter.

I was embarrassed no end, but something good came out of my performances. In a highly competitive business, not one of our hungry competitors ever once got their toes in the French Line door, and they sure tried. To add icing to the cake, they asked me to go over to Paris to discuss a new contract.

And get this: They gave my wife and me a round trip, first class, on the *Liberté*!

-58-

A KINGSPOINTER MAKES IT BIG

After I came ashore, I went to work for the John W. McGrath Corporation, the country's largest stevedoring and terminals operator. After a few years with them I wound up as the head of operations with headquarters in New York.

One of my biggest jobs was that of maintaining a large staff of superintendents. These were salaried, non-union men. They were our key to success or failure. Us so-called *'big shots'* could go out and successfully bid on a piece of new business, but if we got the account, it was the superintendents that made or broke us.

I was forever searching for new talent. This superintendent's job was a frustrating, thankless job. They worked day and night seven days a week, and most holidays. It was understood that they worked the hours that the job required. There was no extra compensation for all the extra hours, and very little satisfaction. To make matters worse, the highly unionized men that they were supervising frequently made a lot more money than they did.

I started with McGrath as an assistant superintendent, so I knew how they felt. Put yourself in their shoes for one winter night. The pier is 'way out in the wilds of Brooklyn. The temperature is hovering down close to zero. It is blowing a half gale, and snow is blowing across the exposed decks of the ship being loaded. It is three A.M. and the longshoremen are threatening to quit. This poor soul of a superintendent, who is just as cold and tired as they are, has to persuade them to finish the ship. True, his heart isn't in it, but he must try. He has promised the steamship company that their ship will be loaded by daylight. So he rants and raves. He appeals to their loyalty, a lost cause, if there ever was one. He threatens, pleads. Sometime he makes wild promises, not knowing how he will ever keep them. Most times he succeeds. The ship departs on time, and another takes her place. He falls asleep on a chair in the timekeeper's office. An hour later he is out in front of the pier for the *'shape'*. The day shift is coming in. Another day is about to start.

That is just a thumb-nail sketch of one ordinary night in the life of a stevedore superintendent. Only the very hardiest survive. They are an elite bunch of men. They are fiercely independent, very proud, and, yes, completely loyal to their company. Finding and holding such men was one of my most important jobs. It was also the most difficult. These men didn't grow on trees.

350

They were few and hard to find. I finally hit upon a scheme that just might work. I would create them!

Located on Long Island Sound is a unique Federal Academy. Its name is The United States Merchant Marine Academy. It is commonly referred to as Kings Point, the town in which it is located. It was opened at the beginning of World War II, as a two year Institute, turning out Third Mates and Third Assistant Engineers to man the mammoth ship building program that was launching thousands of merchant ships. Shortly after the War's end, the curriculum was upgraded and extended to four years. It's standards are now on a par with Annapolis. Graduates continue to graduate with a Third Mate's ticket or a Third Engineer's ticket, which is now bolstered by a BS degree. These young men come out with a firm background in ships and their operation. I had heard that some graduates, for one reason or another, did not go to sea. Jobs aboard ship were scarce. Foreign flagged vessels were driving the American flag from the seas.

I contacted the Academy and agreed to take a maximum of four graduates a year as management trainees. A few years passed. It was an unusual year when I had one Kingspointer left at the end of the year. The pace was too rough, or the pay too low. For one reason or another, they left. There was one, however, who stuck it out. His name is Jim Field. He had stuck with us like glue, and was coming along just fine. At the time of this story, we were operating piers nine, ten and eleven on the Lower North River, in New York. It was on of our busiest terminals. There, we handled two ships a week for the Alcoa Steamship Company, and two ships a week for the Venezuelan Line. We had four superintendents working there. Jim was one of the assistants working under George Lucas, the terminal superintendent. Our head offices were located at 39 Broadway, Just a short walk from piers nine, ten, and eleven. Whenever, I had to go to the office in the morning instead of a pier, it was my habit to drive into Manhattan and park at pier nine. On those days, I would invariably arrive at the pier by seven A.M. This gave me a chance to have coffee with Lucas and to talk over his problems.

One morning I pulled in as usual. George sent out for coffee, and he and I walked the piers and the two ships that were docked. Work was to start on both of them at eight. My eyes were pretty sharp in those days.

"George, I've seen all your supers except Field. Where is he?"

"Must be on one of the lighters. I just saw him a minute ago."

"Georgie, cut out the bullshit. He's not on the terminal is, he?"

George turned kind of red and admitted that Jim hadn't come in, yet. I didn't blame him. In his shoes I would have tried to cover up for a good man, too. However, it's an unwritten law on the waterfront that supervision is at the head of the pier at five minutes to eight. This is the famous 'shape.' All the longshoremen gather in a semi-circle and the hiring boss calls them in by gangs.

There is a reason besides tradition that the superintendents are there. An unscrupulous hiring boss could sneak in a few cronies who would disappear as soon as the timekeeper checked them in. So there we all stood as the hiring boss blew his whistle. In a very few minutes twelve gangs were passed through. and went to work on the two ships.

George and I were left alone sipping coffee and talking business. I happened to look across Twelfth Avenue and who do I see but Jim Field, running like a deer through the traffic. When he saw us, he skidded to a stop, a sheepish look on his face.

"And where have you been," I growled. "Helling around all night, I suppose?"

"Well, not exactly, Captain. I went to a drive-in movie last night, and over slept."

Well, score one for young Jim. At least he didn't try to lie his way out. Then I set what I thought was a clever trap.

"Tell me, Jim, what picture did you see?"

He drew himself up to the enormous height of his twenty-two years, looked way down at me and said,

"Oh, Captain, but **nobody** ever looks at the picture at a drive-in!"

Hooray for him. The younger generation is going to be alright, after all. This story has a happy ending which goes to prove that the country is in pretty good hands. This younger generation will carry on pretty successfully, as did the previous one, and all the ones before it.

A short time later, our New Orleans office reported that they had been awarded a large military contract, and they needed a good superintendent to run it. Jim Field was dispatched there and did a fine job, making a pile of money for us. Shortly after I retired, Jim was summoned back to New York, and by a series of rapid promotions, rose to be President of the entire Corporation!

-59-

"MISCELLANEOUS"

This little story isn't about ships or the sea, but it sure tickled my funny bone.

Maybe it will yours, too. After I came ashore for good, I was fortunate enough to be hired by The John W. McGrath Corporation, the country's largest Stevedoring and Terminals Operator. After a stint in New York, I was sent to Baltimore as their Manager. It was a good job. I was on my beloved ships daily, and made many friends amongst their Captains and Mates.

The Stevedoring industry is highly unionized. The controlling Union was The International Longshoremens' Association, known as the ILA. In Baltimore there were two Locals, one white, the other black. All the Stevedoring companies in the port were meticulous in splitting the work evenly between the two Locals. I soon became closely associated with the heads of both Locals. The black Local was run by two colorful characters. The President was Jefferson Davis, and the Vice-President and Business Manager was Bill Hale. I frequently met them for a drink to talk over our mutual problems and to iron out labor disputes. Jeff was a marvelous story teller, and I could listen to him for hours.

One evening after work, the three of us were sitting in a colored bar in South Baltimore. Jeff downed two big Bourbons, then announced that he would tell me a story about how bad things were during the Great Depression for him and Bill. It took him ages to tell the story because he was forever being interrupted by good-looking colored girls, vying for his attention. He had the reputation of being a stud, and I sure believed it. Here's what he told me.

One afternoon he and Bill were sitting in their little office in the Union headquarters. The subject was money, or rather the lack of it.

"Jeff," Bill said. "We've got to come up with a scheme to make a few dishonest dollars. There's no sense in even trying to shake down the steamship companies. They either have no cargoes or they are going broke, or both. We can't increase the dues. Most of our members can't pay their dues, now. Jeff, we've got to do something."

"You're absolutely right, Bill," said Jeff. "Now shut up and let me think."

He lapsed into a brown study. His face was all screwed up by the mental effort involved. Bill watched him closely. Jeff had never failed him.

Suddenly Jeff leaped up and pounded on the desk.

353

"I've got it, Bill," he shouted. "We'll shake down our own members and they'll never even know it!"

Bill looked at him in horror.

"Jeff, we can't do that. We're supposed to take care of them--protect them. No! You're crazy."

"Now you listen to me, Bill. We are going to take care of them. Besides, you remember the old expression, *Charity begins at home*, don't you?"

"But Jeff, you're talking about giving our own members a hosing."

Then greed got the best of Bill.

"Jeff, just what did you have in mind?" he whispered.

"Bill, I've just hatched the greatest scheme ever. It's a sure fire winner.   We are going to put on an oyster roast for the entire membership and their wives! Three bucks a head; all the oysters they can eat, and all the beer that they can drink. It will be a sellout! Now, let's get down to business.   How many active members do we have and how many are married?"

Bill did some fast figuring.

"Jeff, without going into the books, I figure that we have about twelve hundred members, and those that aren't married have a girl friend. Roughly, that's twenty-four hundred, total. I'd say that we could count on an attendance of two thousand. That adds up to six thousand dollars! Of course, we will have to make it mandatory that they attend. We can put up a big sign in the hiring hall saying something like:

YOU ARE A POOR UNION MEMBER IF YOU DON'T COME TO YOUR UNION'S FIRST OYSTER ROAST.

"How's that, Jeff?"

"Perfect, Bill. You take care of all those details, and I'll take care of buying the oysters and the beer. William, you can start singing, *Happy Days Are Here, Again.*

Between the two of them the final plans were made. They arranged with the high school to rent the football field for all day on a Saturday. Big signs were posted in the hiring hall, and in the windows of stores and bars. Bill was busy raking in the money. The number of tickets sold grew larger and larger. At last it exceeded the total membership times two. Then it dawned on him. The members were buying tickets for their kids and friends. The more the merrier, he thought, as he peeked into the desk drawer. It was full of crumpled dollar bills.

At last the big day arrived. Both Jeff and Bill were there early. Volunteer women were on hand to act as oyster shuckers. There was a trestle table on which sat a keg of beer. Alongside of the table was one barrel of oysters.

Promptly at ten the crowd commenced arriving. In a matter of minutes the one barrel of oysters had been consumed. So had the one keg of beer. The grumbling became louder and louder.

"Bill," Jeff said. "It's time for us to depart."

They slipped unnoticed out a side gate, and returned to the union office where they whacked up the booty and went their separate ways.

Meanwhile, back at the field a riot had erupted. About three thousand furious blacks were raising cain. The police had to be called, and with considerable difficulty dispersed the crowd.

A couple of days later the two swindlers talked by phone. They agreed to meet at an out of the way bar. As soon as they sat down, Bill commenced moaning.

"Jeff, they'll kill us for sure. They've got a petition going around to impeach us. And they have called a mass meeting of the membership for tomorrow night. We are two dead men."

"Not to worry, Bill," said Jeff. "I've got it all planned out. As the President, I'll chair the meeting. Now, here's what I want you to do. Get to the hall early and copy on the blackboard what's written on this paper. Leave everything to me. I haven't let you down yet, have I?"

They parted and went their separate ways. Bill slunk home through back alleys. He was scared to death. Once he reached the safety of home, he looked at the scrap of paper that Jeff had given him. It looked something like this:

<u>EXPENSES</u>
BEER-----------------------$8. 00
OYSTERS--------------------$12. 50
RENT, FOOTBALL FIELD-------$20. 00
MISCELLANEOUS------------$6869. 50
TOTAL EXPENSES-----------$6910. 00
TOTAL RECEIPTS---------- $6910. 00
WE BROKE EVEN, HOORAY!

Bill did exactly what Jeff had told him to do. The meeting was called for eight o'clock. At six, Bill slipped in through the back door and got the blackboard ready. Then he hid in a back room to wait for Jeff. By eight o'clock there was standing room, only. Everybody was shouting obscenities about the two skunks. Bill was actually shaking in his boots.

Promptly at five minutes to eight, Jeff slipped into the back room. He was resplendent in a tuxedo, complete with a red bow tie. Being tall and lean, he cut a striking figure.

"Are we all set, Bill?"

355

"Jeff, I'm scared. That word *miscellaneous* is going to be the death of us. Those guys out there are out for blood. Let's we just leave town."

"Bill, I told you before, you've got nothing to worry about. Not one in twenty of those guys out there can read. Let's go."

And with that, he strode confidentially onto the stage.

"Brothers, this here meeting will come to order. Brother Bill, here, will lead us in the pledge of allegiance to the flag."

Hoots and catcalls echoed through the hall. Jeff banged the gavel.

"I will have order, here. What are we, a bunch of animals? Proceed, brother Bill."

Bill stumbled through the pledge. Shouting and jeering broke out again. *Impeach 'em. Throw the two bums out. We want our money back!*

Jeff was just as cool as a cucumber. He banged the gavel, and they at last quieted down. Jeff picked up a pointer and strode over to the blackboard.

"Brothers, I call your attention to this here detailed financial statement. Look at it. Every penny is accounted for."

For a moment there was silence. Then a tall, skinny Negro, way back in the rear, rose up, and in a high pitched voice shouted,

"What's that there miscellaneous mean?"

Bill groaned.

"Oh, God, there's the one in twenty that can read. We're sunk."

Shouting broke out again.

"Yeah, answer the man!"

Jeff never blinked an eye. He banged the gavel again and shouted,

"Brother, if you don't know the meaning of miscellaneous, the chair declares you out of order! All business having been completed, the chair declares this meeting adjourned! Follow me, Bill."

Just as fast as lightening, they slipped out the back door and were gone.

To cap this story, six weeks later, Jeff was re-elected President by acclamation!

Three months later Jeff was dead, victim of a fast growing cancer! The Baltimore waterfront lost one of it's most popular and colorful characters. I was asked to be an honorary pallbearer. The funeral was held in an enormous Baptist church. It was filled to capacity. Even the balcony, which encircled three sides, was filled. Captain Bradley, the President of the Interntional was there, as was Teddy Gleason, the head of the Checkers' union, and soon to be the successor to Bradley. We were seated right behind the mourners. Jeff's wife was right in front of me, all rigged out in black, long black veil and all.

The Minister launched into a long eulogy, praising the dear departed. Right above us, in the balcony, one of Jeff's many girl friends decided to jump and end it all. We heard the screeching and yelling up above us. She had gotten up on the railing, and two or three men were trying to drag her back.

Pandemonium broke out. If she made it, she would landed right on top of Teddy and me. We beat a hasty retreat up the aisle. I decided to keep right on going, out the door. Jefferson Davis, one of a kind.

-60-

SAILOR'S LUCK

I have often mentioned what good luck fell my way before the War, during the War, and after the War. Now I should tell about two or three instances where Lady Luck was close by.

I was Chief Mate of a Liberty ship, sometime midway in the War. We had just returned from a run across the North Atlantic and were tied up to the dock, safe and sound. The fear of enemy spies reporting ships, cargoes, and destinations was rife. Therefore, a ship's destination was very hush-hush, not to be announced until the vessel had put to sea. However, we had become adept at guessing the destination by the type of cargo being loaded.

The day after we docked, a swarm of ship repair men descended upon us. They started to insulate the deck steam lines which fed the cargo winches. More of them were ripping out the walls in all the staterooms and installing insulation. They were even removing the radiators in the rooms, insulating the steam pipes. The handwriting on the wall was plain to see. We were bound for Murmansk. Murmansk, located in Russia, up around the Northern tip of Norway, above the Arctic Circle, was a fearsome place to take a ship in those days. Not only were the German submarines laying in wait, there, but Norway, which had been occupied by the Krauts, was a perfect base for their Stutka dive bombers. On top of that, the temperature of the sea water was in the thirties, so a seaman didn't live but a few minutes if his ship was sunk. Old Stalin, however, was hounding both Churchill and Roosevelt for war material, so convoy after convoy was dispatched to Murmansk, always with disastrous results. The bottom of the ocean, up there, was carpeted with ships, freighters, and their escorts.

What crew that was left on our ship took all this pretty philosophically, though. *So we're going to Murmansk. We'll get through OK.* So we thought.

The Mate's room is also his office, and a busy place it is. On those Libertys it was only as big as a large closet. My room looked as if a bomb had hit it. All the walls torn out, pipes strewn on the deck. No heat, and it was wintertime.

Now, it is a custom on all ships that whenever she is under repair, or not feeding, to be paid a *shore subsistence* allowance. Enough money to pay for meals and lodging ashore. Conditions were intolerable for me so up I went to the Port Captain's office and requested shore subsistence money. He scoffed at the idea and suggested that I sleep in the ship's hospital, a dingy stinking hole.

I got on my high horse and shot my big mouth off. *I was the Chief Officer and I'd be damned if I would stoop to bunking in the ship's hospital, blah, blah.* Things got pretty hot between us, and before I knew it, had reached the point of no return. Neither one of us would back off, and the next thing I knew, I had quit. Back to the ship I went, fuming. Packed my suit case and sea bag, grabbed my sextant from the chart room and was off for home. Me and my big mouth.

Two weeks later, the Boston Agent for the company phoned and said that all was forgiven, and that there was a ship waiting for me. Back I went, of course. As soon as I got back, the first thing I did was to catch up on the latest company gossip. God Almighty! The ship that I had walked off of had sailed with a new Mate. She was three days East of Newfoundland when a German submarine caught up with her. The Chief Mate's watch is the four to eight. At four-thirty in the afternoon she was torpedoed abreast of number three hatch, just under the bridge. The Chief Mate was out on the bridge wing. He was blown overboard and never seen again! Boy, was my luck holding. My big mouth had saved my life.

The next incident took place on April 16, 1947. I had forgotten completely, the significance of that date, until, many years later, I read in detail what had happened on that day.

Some weeks before, I had been given command of a ship laying in Boston. A few days after I reported aboard, orders were received to sail for New York. The War was over and shipping was slacking off. Arriving in New York, we bunkered and sailed for Galveston, Texas, for orders. We had a fine trip South. Good weather all the way, which was a Godsend, because we were light, not a stick of cargo in her. We came to anchor in the roadstead. The local Agent came aboard and gave us orders to proceed up the Houston Ship Channel to Texas City, there to load a full cargo of grain for Emden, Germany.

The Chief Mate put all hands to work cleaning the holds for grain. We arrived at the grain elevator and commenced loading. It doesn't take too long to load grain with four or five spouts pouring grain into the holds. This ship had carried grain on her previous trip, so all the shifting boards were in place and in good condition.

That evening the Agent came flying down the pier. Hurrying up to my room, he told me that the seamens' union were going on strike the next day. If my ship was caught in a safe harbor by a strike, she'd be tied up for the duration. If she got to sea, the strike couldn't affect us. He and I ran down the gangway and up to the office of the grain elevator superintendent. The Agent persuaded him to put more spouts aboard and increase the volume of grain pouring aboard. He agreed. About midnight all holds were full and trimmed. The feeders were full, too. The minute the spouts were swung ashore, I called for all hands, fore and aft. The Mate came piling up to the bridge, complaining bitterly.

"Captain, all the hatches are wide open and the booms swinging. We can't sail until the ship is secured for sea."

He was right, of course. No well managed ship ever leaves the dock until, *In all respects, ready for sea.* However, I wasn't about to get caught in a long strike.

"Mister, there is a tow boat alongside and the pilot is on the bridge. Pull up the gangway and let go, fore and aft. Keep all hands on deck and secure for sea. If you're not done by the time we reach the Galveston breakwater, you can finish out in the Gulf of Mexico. Let's go!"

That was midnight of the fifteenth of April, 1947.

The poor Mate worked all hands until breakfast, and then sea watches were set. Late the following day Sparks brought me a brief news flash telling of the tragic explosion that blew Texas City right off the map. That French ship that blew up was berthed right near us. Had we been there, we would have gone sky high. Nobody would have survived.

Being busy sailing around the oceans for the next several years, I never knew just how devastating that explosion was. Never knew, in fact, for over thirty years until I read about it in the Sunday paper one day.

As I look back on a career at sea, I had to have been the luckiest seaman ever to have sailed.

My log book reflected none of this.

GALVESTON FOR ORDERS. LOADED
FULL CARGO OF WHEAT FOR EMDEN,
GERMANY. DEPARTED TEXAS CITY
MIDNIGHT, APRIL 15, 1947. SHIP ON
THE GREAT CIRCLE ROUTE.

There was a lot unsaid between those brief entries.

There were a couple of more times that my luck was holding fast, although, once again, I didn't realize it at the time. They only came to light forty years later, after reading Captain Arthur Moore's outstanding book, **A Careless Word—A Needless Sinking.** From it I found out, for the first time, the American ships that got it while I was shuttling around the Mediterranean in 1943-1944. Over forty of them either mined, bombed, or torpedoed.

How many other ships and shipmates went down on my North Atlantic runs I don't know, and I guess that I don't want to know.

Another time was during the Normandy Invasion. To me it was a piece of cake, but now I find out that twelve American ships were hit during that action:

Coast Guard ship sprays remains of Texas City dock after 1947 disaster

Texas-Sized Blast

Texas City, Tex., was once virtually destroyed by explosions more powerful at ground level than the atomic blasts at Hiroshima and Nagasaki. At 9:12 a.m. on April 16, 1947, the French freighter *Grandcamp*, laden with 2500 tons of ammonium nitrate fertilizer, caught fire and exploded in a blinding wall of flames and smoke. Nearby, a steel barge was shot from the water like a toy and hurtled 100 yards inland; two light planes were obliterated in the sky. In the business district a mile away, people were hurled through doors by violent concussive drafts.

But the *Grandcamp* was only the beginning. Next, the nearby Monsanto chemical plant blew up, and soon oil refineries, tin smelters and tanks filled with chlorine gas, sulphur and nitrate were ablaze all along the 2-mile waterfront. Chunks of metal and human flesh rained everywhere. In Galveston, 10 miles away, the blasts shattered windows. Some of the explosions were audible 150 miles away and were picked up by seismographs in Denver, 1000 miles away. At 1:11 the following morning, the *Grandcamp's* sister ship, *High Flyer*, also exploded.

The final toll: 462 dead; 50 missing, 3000 injured and $55 million in property damage. "In four years of war coverage," wrote Associated Press correspondent Hal Boyle, "I have seen no concentrated devastation so utter, except Nagasaki."

Texas City, April 16, 1947

SS Louis Kassuth-Torpedoed, English Channel, 8,24,44
SS H.G. Blasdell-Torpedoed off St, Catherine's Point, 8,29,44.   *6*
killed.
SS James A. Farrell-Torpedoed off St. Catherine's
Point, 6,29,44. 4 killed.
SS John A. Trentlen-Torpedoed off St. Catherine's
Point, 6,29,44. 10 injured.
SS Lee S. Overman-Mined off Le Havre, 11.11,44
SS William L. Marey-Torpedoed by German E boat off Juno
Beach, at anchor, 8,7,44.
SS Charles Morgan-Bombed off Utah Beach, 6, 10,44, 1 killed.

At the time,I never knew of all these sinkings. Our sources of information were limited to scuttlebutt when in port, which was seldom. At sea, the gossip passed throughout the convoys by Navy signalmen on their blinker lights.

In both instances, I wonder how many British and Allied ships went down, also?

Perhaps this is a good place to explain something that might have puzzled the reader. You probably have noticed, by now, the many photos that I have included of one man, Able Seaman Moody Harrison. I guess that it was my way of depicting his epitaph. Now let me finish the awful story of his death.

He and I were friends and shipmates for several years. Shortly before the War he and I paid off the same ship, him to return to his first love, the United States Line, and me to go home to study. I never heard from him again until, years later, I read of his death in Captain Moore's marvelous book, "A Careless Word-A Needless Sinking."

Moody had shipped out on the S.S. American Leader. The time was 1942. The ship was homeward bound from Colombo, Ceylon by way of the Cape of Good Hope. She was loaded with a full cargo of rubber, coconut oil, copra, liquid latex, opium, tobacco, rugs, and other general cargo. After rounding the Cape, she put in to Capetown for bunkers, and sailed for Newport News and New York. Three days out of Capetown, on September 10, 1942, at about 7:30 PM, she was attacked and sunk by the German Raider, *MICHEL.* She carried a complement of 49 merchant crew and 9 Naval Armed Guard. Of this number, 10 crew members were killed by shell fire. The others, including Moody, were plucked from the water and made prisoners by the Germans.

The following February, they were turned over to the Japanese in Singapore. They remained prisoners in a large camp run by the Japanese for some months. Then, several hundred of them, including Australians, British, and other Allied men, and several thousand natives, were packed like sardines, in the holds of a small Japanese freighter for transport to Sumatra to work on the infamous bridge over the River Kwai. The second night out, she was torpedoed and sunk by a British submarine who knew nothing about the cargo she was carrying. It was the worst casualty in the annals of the maritime world. The Bosun on the American Leader, Stanley Gorski, survived, and told me this sad story. In total, over 6,000 souls perished when the S.S. Junyo Maru slipped beneath the waves. He told me that he was blown out of the after 'tween decks and into the sea. Moody was in the lower hold and went down with the ship.

My friend, Moody, had two vices. He was meticulously clean, and frequently took two baths a day. He was forever washing his clothes, and was the neatest man that I have ever known. His other vice was cigarettes. He went through at least two packs a day. I can just imagine what suffering he went through, deprived of soap, water, and cigarettes.

The many pictures of Moody, and my frequent anecdotes about him, are, I guess, my requiem to a good and faithful friend.

-61-

SHIPBOARD MEMORIES

Recently, a friend asked me,
"What are your best and worst memories of your years at sea?"
Well, now, let's see. I am aware of the pitfalls of nostalgia; just remember the good things. Gloss over the bad and the sad, the discouraging. As I search my memory, I am surprised that the most memorable, both good and bad, were not of big, earthshaking events. Rather, they are of small, very brief moments of either great elation or sudden dips of discouragement, fear, and rejection.

Rejection: That word rings a dim bell of an incident, small, inconsequential, but of great importance to me at the time.

Nineteen years old--a young impressionable A.B. on a ship docked in Buenos Aires. It was mid-winter and cold. One Saturday morning the Bosun assigned me the job of slushing down the foretopmast stay. This stay, or shroud, is a heavy wire cable running from the top of the foretopmast down to the bow. This job involved the rigging of a bosun's chair. It's gantline would be rove through a block at the top of the topmast. One end of the gantline would be made fast to the bridle of the chair. The other end would be run down to the deck, led around a cleat, and tended by an Ordinary Seaman. After the gantline was made fast to the chair, a large screw pin shackle was placed through the chair's bridle, and around the forestay. This was so that when the man down on deck slacked away, the chair would slide down the stay instead of falling vertically. Sounds confusing, huh? Actually, it's a simple piece of rigging.

I tied one end of the gantline around my waist and climbed up the foremast to the crosstrees; then shinnied up the wooden topmast. When I got to the top, I clamped my legs tightly around the mast and rove the gantline through the block that hung at the top of the mast. I kept pulling it through until the end reached the deck. The Ordinary, Whitey, made it fast to the bridle of the chair. Then, he hung the shackle to the side of the chair. He also tied on a bucketful of a mixture of white lead, tallow, and fish oil. Then he heaved away on the gantline, pulling the whole shebang up to me. I attached the shackle around the stay and shouted down,
"Take a round turn on the deck cleat."
When he shouted back, *All ready,* I eased myself into the chair and was ready to go to work.

363

Number one hatch was wide open, and longshoremen were discharging from it. Because of this, the forestay was vibrating like a big fiddle string, and I would soon be sailing right out over that open hatch. Today, such a foolhardy thing would never be attempted, but back in those days I guess life was cheaper. Anyways, I started to work, smearing on the slush with my bare hands, which was the way that damned Bosun insisted that it be done. That old stay had been up there ever since the ship was built, back in 1919 or 1920, and it was frayed.

All those sharp ends were making mincemeat out of my hands. I yelled down to Whitey to go up in the forepeak and get me some rags. While he was gone I looked around. I could see right over the warehouse roof. I was just about over the open hatch, and the winches pounding away made that old stay thrash around like a snake.

Whitey came back and sent me up some old pieces of sacking. It sure eased my sore hands. I yelled to slack off a couple of feet. As I coasted down, I held the sacking on the stay with both hands. Good thing I did, too, because all of a sudden the shackle pin fell half out, barely stuck by the shank. I flung one arm around the shroud, and there, I hung, the wire cutting into my arm something awful. I had committed the unforgivable. When I had first rigged up, I had forgotten to turn the shackle over so that it's bale would ride on the wire. Instead, the screw pin had been slowly unscrewing itself as I slid down the stay. I was in some mess. If I let go, I'd swing like a giant pendulum back against the steel foremast and be squashed like a bug. To make matters worse, it started to sleet and snow. I couldn't even see the deck. How I did it, God only knows, but I managed to screw the pin back in. The crook of my arm was badly lacerated. I managed, finally, to get Whitey's attention, and shouted to lower me down to the focsle head. I was soaking wet, half frozen, and limp with fright. By the time he and I got the gear stowed away, it was noon. Whitey headed for the messroom and I headed for the Mate's room to get my arm fixed up.

This all took place way back in the early thirties before the Unions, overtime, coffee time, and time off. Our Mate was a self proclaimed softy, because he had told the Bosun that whenever the ship was in Buenos Aires over a Saturday, the crew could knock off at noon, until Monday morning. That is except the night gangway watch, who worked seven nights a week as usual.

When I got midships the Saloon Mess told me that the Mate was eating dinner, and to come back at one o'clock. I went aft and ate my dinner with my right hand (I'm a lefty) because my left arm was so sore. Buckets were clattering in the wash room as the deck gang cleaned up, some to scoot ashore to have a few quick snorts, others to turn in for an afternoon snooze, so that they'd be fresh for the big night ahead. But me, I headed back midships to have the Mate fix my arm up.

"Boy, you're some mess," said he as he dumped raw iodine all over my open cuts.

"There, we'll just tie this bandage on and you're right as rain. You did finish that forestay, didn't you?"

"Well, no, Mr. Mate. I got caught up there in the snow... "

"Stop right there, Slim. I saw what happened, right from this porthole. Any A.B. worth his salt knows enough to never rig a screw pin shackle upside down. That job should have been finished before noon! Get your ass forward, rig up, and finish the job. And lower yourself. Whitey won't be with you."

And I did. Talking to my self, cursing that inhuman ape. All the way Northbound I brooded. *That cold hearted bastard.*

Many weeks later we arrived in Boston. The Shipping Commissioner came aboard, paid us, and signed us off Articles. With my discharge in my hand, I marched myself up to the Mate's room.

"What do you want, Slim?"

"I want a letter of recommendation. I quit!"

"Quit, what for? You are one of my best men."

I lamely told him of the foretopmast incident, back in B.A.

"Oh, foosh," says he. "I don't even remember it. Get your ass up to Scollay Square tonight. Those dames will make you forget anything."

And I did. Still, as I look back, I still think that I was entitled to feel a little rejected.

Contentment: Now there's a word that brings back some good memories.

Sitting out on number five hatch early in the morning. Doesn't sound earthshaking, does it? But 'way back then, it was the most welcomed, the most looked forward to, time of day.

On those old ships both the deck gang and the black gang lived aft, under the poop deck. There were two focsles, two wash rooms, and two mess rooms, divided by the steering engine room. Midships was officer country. The Bosun had his own room, all the way forward under the focsle head. The crew's mess had to carry our food back aft from the galley, located midships, just aft of the fireroom fiddley. Every morning, promptly at seven, he would arrive carrying two big enamel pots of strong black coffee. There were always three or four of us waiting with our mugs. We'd follow him into the mess room and fill up, the Bosun always first by virtue of his rank. Then, back out to sit on number five hatch. Usually, the weather was good; the sea sparkling blue, the sun low in the East, and the ship working easily. Sipping and savoring, we'd pump the Bosun for the latest scuttlebutt. Living forward, he always visited the bridge on his way aft to get his orders for the day from the Mate, and to pump him as we were now trying to do to him. He knew it, too, and made us drag it out of him. Reluctantly, he would let it slip out:

We were due at the next port Tuesday, weather permitting.

The Old Man had had words with the Chief Engineer about blowing tubes during the midnight to four A.M. watch without notifying the bridge. Soot all over the ship, which could have been avoided by the Second Mate changing course out of the wind.

This invariably made any of the black gang listening chortle with glee because, naturally, nobody likes any Chief Engineer.

We usually had time for a second mug before the usual breakfast of oatmeal, bread, and boiled mackerel. It was such a comfortable, old shoe feeling, perched on the hatch, the sun low in the East; good companionship, common interests. As I look back, that half hour on number five is stored in my memory as truly precious moments. Sounds cuckoo, I know, but you asked.

Elation: Now there's a word for you. Did I ever feel it? Bet your life I did! An inconsequential incident; nothing important about it, but it sticks in my memory. It happened this way:

World War II, was long over. We were back at our business of carrying cargos around the sea lanes of the world. This time we were again bound for Marseille. It was summertime, and perfect weather stayed with us. I was master of a freighter, and navigation was my obsession. Day after day the sun shone and the seas were slight. I was taking star sights every morning and evening, and six or eight sun lines during the day.

One morning I heard the man at the wheel say in sotto voice, to his relief,

"The Old Man's got a sextant growing out of his hand. I wonder if we are lost, or something?"

Everything was normal. I've said much worse when I was a quartermaster.

What with my snoot stuck in the Nautical Almanac day and night, it dawned on me that a most unusual event would take place later in the day. Venus, the moon, and the sun would be in position for a three way fix, which I needed like a hole in my head. With all the good weather that we had been having, I knew, within a mile or two, where we were. Right on course. Well, dammit, I'd do it anyway. Venus, being a planet, would not be visible to the naked eye during the daytime, and, like the moon, was forever straying all over the sky. I carefully precomputed the altitudes and azimuths of the moon and Venus. I enlisted the aid of the long suffering Second Mate to mark my time. Usually, I use a stop watch, but this time I was on stage and needed an audience. He had no idea what I was up to. Out I ambled onto the Starboard bridge wing. Carefully, I brought the sun down so it' slower limb just kissed the horizon.

"Mark," I called.

"Mark," answered the Second.

"Don't go away, Mister. There's more to come."

I peeked at my notes, set the sextant for the altitude of Venus, faced in her direction, and by God, there she was, right in the mirror!

"Mark."

I repeated the performance with the moon. Had to use her upper limb, though. I sauntered into the chart room.

"Here are your chronometer times, Skipper. Why three sights of the sun?"

"You'll soon see, Mister."

Quickly I reduced my three sights to three fine Lines of Position. Plotting them on the plotting sheet, I murmured,

"There you are, Mister."

"There's what, Skipper?"

"Oh, just a three way fix of the Sun, Moon, and Venus."

Showing off at it's worst, but I loved it. Still do.

Anticipation: How's that for a word? Most of us spend our lives anticipating something or other, good or bad. I'm no exception. I've been looking forward to, or dreading something all my life. Good things? As I look back, the memories are constant; little things, brief, transitory, of no importance, except to me. Here are a few of them.

Two more days steaming to a good port. Favorable exchange for the dollar. Dames known from previous trips. Food! Right at the top of the list. Not surprising when you consider the garbage that we had to choke down, on those old rust tubs. In our minds, the coming attractions took on an aura all out of proportion to reality. If we faced up to facts, they weren't so hot. A long dreary walk out of the dock area. Watered down drinks in the first joints. Rapacious whores with the heart of a snake, or snakes. Short changing waiters and bartenders. Too drunk, or tired, or both, to enjoy the food. Fools we were, but that's the way of a seaman. Most of us, though, did smarten up. We ate a good dinner, first. Then got away from the waterfront and absorbed some of the ambience of the city.

Denmark: Friends frequently ask me which country or port did I like the best. Invariably, and without hesitation, I answer, Denmark. I ask myself, why? True, it is a beautiful country. The grass is just as green as Ireland. The cities and towns are spotless. The food rivals, or surpasses, any country in the world. But other countries offer pretty much the same, so why Denmark? Why not Holland, for instance, Or Belgium, or Sweden, France? Why did I answer so quickly, so positively? Why, indeed. I pondered on this for sometime. The answer came loud and clear. The Danes really like us. They are truly friendly, not just after our dough. I sailed to Denmark many times and never got enough of the country and it's people. I've been to the big city, Copenhagen, and the small, out of the way ports like Aarhus and Korsur.

Without exception, they liked us and let us know it. Yep, it's a real pisser of a country--to me anyways. And I should know, shouldn't I?

Fear: A difficult word to define. Sometimes it gets mixed up with another word, **Elation.** Sound paradoxical?   Often one leads to the other.

Any merchant seaman who sailed during World War II, and said that he was never afraid, is either a liar or should be in a funny farm. A few of them did succumb and had breakdowns. They deserve our sympathy and more.

Me, I was one of the fortunate ones. Back and forth, we sailed across the North Atlantic. Then into the Med for the African campaign. Then Italy, and finally, the Normandy Invasion. Never had a ship shot out from under me. Never had a direct hit by a bomb. I even went to Malta, a beleaguered place if there was ever one. Fear was there, though. In the beginning, when ships were being sunk in the hundreds of thousands of tons, during the Battle of the Atlantic, I, like everyone else, was scared to death. I'm not ashamed to admit that I slept with my clothes on, night after night. My oilskins were draped over the coverlet. My life jacket was my pillow. However, as trip after trip rolled out in the wake, something that I still can't quite understand took place. The fear was still there, but it seemed to have receded into a dim corner. It was still there, but sort of subdued.

Everything became so routine. Watch on. Watch off. General Alarm! Stand down. Work to be done. Watches to stand. Weariness numbing the senses. It probably was just as well that we were so damned tired and worn out. That dark thing crouching in the corner became almost unnoticed. Almost, but it was there. Even now, if I let my mind go sort of blank, and think back, there it is. The old butterflies in the pit of the stomach are fluttering their wings again.

I put fear, Wartime fear anyway, into two categories. The first is the kind that I have just tried to describe, which is present constantly. The second kind is sort of layered onto the first kind. It comes on suddenly. The heart stopping clamor of the General Alarm bells. Big doses of adrenalin speed me up the stairways and ladders to the bridge. I'm somewhat slowed down trying to tie my life jacket straps. Concealing my heavy breathing, and trying to look unconcerned, (An utter failure. Everyone else is acting out the same charade.)

I croak,

"What's what?"

"Planes approaching," says the Naval Gunnery Officer.

His features are completely concealed by an enormous battle helmet. He busies himself talking into the sound-powered telephone hung around his neck. I can't hear what he's saying, but presumably he's exhorting his gunners to do and die for flag and country. He and I are 'way out on the Starboard side of the flying bridge.

"Here they come," somebody shouts, his voice rising to a falsetto screech. Me and Guns are the nonchalant pair; binoculars up--Nelson at

Trafalgar. Swoop! They're over and gone. Guns and I look at each other in astonishment. Without either of us knowing how, we have both moved from the outer edge of the deck, and now find ourselves with our backs pushing against the smoke stack, trying, I guess, to hide. We look away, quickly. The incident is never mentioned between us. There seems to be some shame attached to it.

The attack lasts but minutes. We steam steadily on. Now, though, the second kind of fear hits. I try to swallow. My mouth and throat are so dry that they seem paralyzed. I want to speak; say something reassuring, but I don't dare to. I'm afraid that only a squeak will come out. My legs tremble. I grip one of the funnel stays, fuss with the binoculars, manage to light a cigarette. Anything to convince anyone looking that everything is OK. That kind of fear really slams you. You recover and cover up, but boy, it packs some wallop.

Hours later at the supper table, the attack isn't mentioned. It isn't even hinted at. All of us talk too much, trying, I guess, to put it behind us. We were only kidding each other. It is, of course, uppermost in every mind. Finally, someone breaks the ice.

"Damn, I got caught in the shower. Not a stitch on."

Another hardy soul pipes up,

"I forgot to shoot my afternoon sun sight."

That's the Second Mate showing his 'devotion to duty.'

The conversation became animated; each vying with the other--how he felt--what he had been doing when the alarm rang out.

Therapy at it's best. Talking it out made those butterflies go to sleep. True, they didn't fly away, but they stopped flapping around. Stopped, that is, until the next time. And damn it to hell, there was always a next time.

Discouragement: A most common word in the life of an average man. We've all experienced it. In connection with our job, our personal life, in our relations with friends. No big deal, a common ailment. Mine were no more numerous than any other guy's, nor were they any more important. They just happened to me so I'll just set one down, here.

Almost since the beginning of the War, I had been sailing as Chief Mate, mostly with the same company. Liberty ships were sliding off the ways in the hundreds. I had had my share of them, and was heartily sick of them. One day we were laying at anchor in some Godforsaken port in North Africa, waiting for a convoy. Not too far away was a T2 tanker. These T2's were wartime built, and I had heard that they were fine ships. Fine, that is, if you didn't mind riding on top of about twelve thousand tons of high octane aviation gasoline.

Anyway, I was up on the bridge killing time after dinner. The blinker light on the tanker started winking at us.

"Flags, see what she wants."

Flags got busy. Back and forth they went.

MY COMPLIMENTS TO YOUR CHIEF MATE. COULD YOU SPARE A FEW BAGS OF FLOUR? WE HAVE RUN OUT AND THE STEWARD CAN'T BAKE BREAD.

"Flags, tell him sure. We will bring them over in the motor life boat."

I hurried down below and rousted out the Steward, who complained, bitterly, but agreed that he could spare three bags. Shortly, the Bosun, a couple of A.B.s, and I were putt putting over to the tanker. Their Chief Mate met us at the top of their pilot ladder, and invited me to come up and meet the Old Man. When I stepped into his quarters, I was struck dumb! They were palatial compared to ours. We had coffee and he thanked us for the flour. I asked the Mate if I could see his room.

"Sure, come with me."

My God, this ship was like the Waldorf Astoria compared to the cramped little coops that we lived in. I sure was envious,

It was always my habit, in convoy, to study the other ships. Libertys were all alike, but only in a superficial way. Their cargo handling gear differed. Those built on the West coast had the winches located so that one operator could handle both of them. Some, a very few, were rigged at every hatch for heavy lifts. Some, I believe, were tankers. I also began to take a closer look at a new class of vessels that were beginning to appear. They were in three classes, Cl's, C2's, and C3's. Small, medium, and large. They were fast, modern ships. Scuttlebutt had it that their quarters far surpassed what we had on the Liberties. And what's more, their pay was better.

All the way home I studied ships and fantasized about sailing on a good ship for a change. When we got back, I started asking questions. Sure enough, our company was taking on it's share of these new ships. But, and it was a big one, the senior Skippers and officers were moving up and manning them. And I was 'way down the list. The prewar officers were getting these fine ships, while I was stuck on a series of those damned Liberty ships. All this was as it should be. The senior men got the best jobs in any company. But, I rationalized, a lot of them had gotten killed or drowned, and besides, hadn't I been a good and faithful servant? I convinced myself that I deserved one of those fine ships. Buoyed up by all that fool logic, I braced the Marine Superintendent. He was a far better man than me, Gunga Din.

"Now, you've got a point, Mister. However, I want you to transfer to that Liberty laying just astern of you. Her Mate has taken sick, and she's due to make a convoy tomorrow. From the look of her cargo, I'd say that she's for a quick trip to the U.K. While you're gone, I'll see what I can do to get you on one of the C ships as soon as you get back."

Maybe he did try, and there just wasn't a slot for me. And it was a quick trip, and it was to the U.K. As soon as we docked, I hot footed it up to his holiness and tackled him, again. True, he was busy, overworked, tired, and short fused. He gave me about three minutes.

"Nothing was open. Sorry, try me next trip."

I fumed all the way back to the ship. I turned around and tramped back to his office. I couldn't get in to see him so I left word that I quit--and all over a better room! But quit I did--shifted my business to another company, and damned if I didn't get a fine Victory ship. To end this sad tale, the Mate's room on a Victory ship is just the same cramped coop as on the Libertys!

Frequently, I sit on the beach gazing, unseeing, at the horizon. Nostalgia washes over me. Again, I hear the sounds, and smell the smells of life at sea. Fresh brewed coffee in the wheel house just as dawn is breaking. The sweet, sickish smell coming from the fuel oil vent pipes as you walk by them on deck. The myriad smells from the open hatches in port, bring memories of the far places. The faint tinkle of the wheel house bell chiming the hours. And of answering on the big ship's bell when I stood bow lookout as a young A.B.

Lights are burning bright, Sir, heard from the focsle head.

And the harsh clamor of the General Alarm bells echoing through the ship. Again that song rings in memory.

> *Ah yes, my friend, those were the days.*
> *We thought they'd never end.*

But for me, end they did. As they say, I swallowed the anchor, but it remains stuck in my throat for evermore.

Memories? Yes, I've got them and treasure them.

> *A toast then...*
> *To all my former shipmates,*
> *Many of them now down in*
> *Davy Jone's Locker.*
> *When the time comes for me*
> *to cross outward bound*
> *Over the bar,*
> *I wish them fair winds*
> *and following seas.*
> *Bottoms up!*

They that go down to the sea in ships, that do business in great waters;
These see the works of the Lord, and his wonders in the deep.
                              Psalms, Verse 23

-62-

FINISHED WITH ENGINES

The time came when I had to make the most difficult decision of my life. The decision to leave the sea and come ashore.

Ever since I could read I had only one goal; to go to sea, to be a seaman. All through my childhood, that goal remained bright and steadfast, never wavering. In high school we had counselors whose job it was to steer us into a profession suitable to our talents and aptitudes. Mine was baffled. He ranted and raved and cajoled, to no avail. He said that I was wasting his time. Why, he wanted to know, was I taking a College Tech curriculum if I had no intention of going on to a technical college? My lame answer was that it was my folk's idea, not mine. And away to sea I went. Now, many years later, and with thousands and thousands of miles left behind in the wake, I came ashore.

My wife was a casualty of the War. My son, then about ten or eleven years old, was sort of cast adrift. His aunt, to whom I had entrusted him, and who devoted most of her time on his behalf, took over his charge most willingly. She and her husband had never had any children. She enrolled him in a good private school in New Hampshire. Summers, he spent at boy's camp, interspersed with vacation and holiday stints with Aunt Beulah and Uncle Walter. They were very kind to him and, I know, loved him dearly.

But to me it wasn't enough. I was experiencing severe feelings of guilt. I had left my family at the beginning of the War to the mercies of wonderful, well intentioned relatives on both sides of the family. While I was floating around in convoys, they were making do, somehow, or so I thought. Late in the War my wife suffered a personal tragedy that took not only her life but the life of our beloved little daughter, Marcia, aged three. I never knew, until months later, when I returned to these shores from yet another voyage.

Now, some years later, I had to face up to the facts. My boy had suffered, traumatically, the death of his mother and little sister. He was of an impressionable age. I had to do something. As my ship lay at Pier 25, North River, in New York, waiting for her next assignment, I tried to take stock. My boy deserved a home and family life; something that I couldn't give him while floating around the seven seas as Master of a tramp freighter. The more I pondered the more confused that I became. Finally, I decided to take things one step at a time. I would come ashore, get a job, and take it from there.

The next morning I telephoned my mentor and staunch supporter, Captain Litchfield. He was most understanding and wished me well. He also

372

sent me a letter of recommendation to The John W. McGrath Corporation, the country's largest stevedoring firm. Armed with this, I made an appointment to see Mr. John McGrath, the president. By God, he hired me on the spot!

My first assignment was as Assistant Superintendent on Pier 88, North River, the home of the French Line, the North German Lloyd Line, and the Polish Line.

It was with considerable trepidation that I reported to the superintendent, Bill Buist. The pier was bedlam, day and night. Passenger ships arriving and departing daily, plus at least two cargo ships discharging and loading.

I had rented a room from a private family 'way up the West side but could only use it one or two nights a week. Because I had no family or home, I volunteered for as much night and weekend work as I could stand. Occasionally, the French Line would let me use a stateroom on one of their ships where I could nap for a couple of hours.

The waterfront, like ships, was big on nicknames. I got one, The Thin Man, which stuck for years.

As time went by, and as I became more familiar with the work, I was sent all over the sprawling waterfront of New York, Brooklyn, Staten Island and New Jersey. Then, one day I was told to take over Pier 92, just North of Pier 88. It was bad duty. Known as New York's *hot pier,* crime was rife. My head foreman was murdered one morning. My harbormaster was found dead in an alley, a bullet through his head. Not a pleasant place to work.

It was at this time that I met the girl who was to become my wife. I had begged three days off to go home and spend Christmas with my boy. She, a head nurse at New York Hospital, was also heading home to Boston to spend the holiday with her folks. By chance we had adjoining seats on the plane. We struck up an acquaintance and had time to exchange phone numbers before the plane landed.

Back on the job, I lost no time in phoning her and we started to date. And some dates they were. I would be sent over to Jersey City to work a ship all night. She would ride the tubes with me, then turn around and ride back to the hospital. The next morning I would be back on Pier 92. Somehow, it all fell into place, and six months later we were married. Her father, a Baptist Minister, married us. We had a one week honeymoon on Cape Cod, then we two and Junior moved into an attic apartment in Bronxville. My hours were just as bad as ever, but now it all seemed worthwhile.

Three months later my big break came. The port of Baltimore was the Company's largest port, tonnage wise. The Manager, there, Captain Black, had suffered a bad nervous breakdown and was retired. I got the job. We spent six very happy years there, and made friends that we still hear from, today.

The stevedoring business never stops, day or night. The only days it stopped were Christmas, Easter and Labor Day, but I thrived on it. I was on my beloved ships, daily. I associated with their Captains, Mates, and Engineers. We spoke the same language. It was almost like being at sea. Almost, but not quite. There has never been a day since I came ashore that I haven't yearned for command again. It has been in my blood for too long. I am now over seventy, but it's still there. If the chance came, I'd pack the old sea bag, pick up my sextant and be off. Sounds like romantic drivel, I know, but the call of the sea is still loud and clear in my ears.

Frequently I sit on the beach, gazing, unseeing, at the Atlantic. Nostalgia washes over me. Again I hear the sounds and smell the smells of life at sea. Fresh brewed coffee in the wheel house, just as dawn is breaking. The sweet, sickish stink coming from the fuel tank vent pipes as you walk by them on deck. The myriad smell from open hatches in port, bringing memories of far places. The faint tinkle of the wheel house bell chiming the hours. And of answering on the big ship's bell when I had stood lookout as a young A.B. *Lights are burning bright, Sir.* And the harsh clamor of the General Alarm bells echoing throughout the ship.

Again, that song rings in memory. *Ah, yes, my friend, those were the days. We thought they'd never end.* But, for me, end they did. As they say, I swallowed the anchor. But it remains stuck in my throat for ever more.

Ships that pass in the night, and speak each other in passing, only a signal shown and a distant voice in the darkness. So on the ocean of life, we pass and speak one another. Only a look and a voice, then darkness and a silence.

Henry Wadsworth Longfellow

THE END

374

GLOSSARY

ATS-Army Transport Service. British women's army corps.

Abaft-Toward the stern of the ship.

Able Seaman(AB)-Experienced seaman who holds a certificate of proficiency. (Same as able bodied seaman.)

Aft-Toward the stern of the ship.

Alleyway-Corridor.

Athwartships-From side to side across the ship.

Azimuth-True bearing.

Ballast-Rocks, sand, gravel, sea water, etc., loaded instead of cargo to give the ship stability.

Barge-Scow. Has a flat deck, no covering.

Batten down-Cover the hatches for sea.

"Belly robber"-Derogatory title for chief steward on hungry ship.

Bilges-Bottoms of holds, running fore and aft. They collect water.

Binnacle-Cover over compass. Contains a light for steering at night.

Bitt-Cast iron post for holding mooring lines; found both on deck and on the dock.

Bitter end-End of a rope or line.

Black gang-Unlicensed members of engine room crew.

Block-Pulley.

Boom-Cargo derrick.

Bosun-Abbreviation for boatswain. Foreman of deck gang.

Bosun's chair-Rig for hauling a seaman up a mast; looks like a child's swing.

Bottoms-Another word for ships. Most commonly used by shippers and Charterers.

Bow painter-Rope attached to the bow of a life boat.

Bowditch-Famous navigation book. "The Seagoing Bible."

Bridge-Navigating area, runs "athawrtships" high on the ship.

Bridge wing-Open part of the bridge extending port and starboard from the wheel house.

Brig-Small, two masted square rigged sailing vessel.

Bristol fashion-Clean, neat, well ordered.

British Ministry of War Transport-Same as our War Shipping Administration.

Bulkhead-Steel, watertight partitions between compartments.

Bulwarks-Sides of ship extending above the deck. Usually about three feet.

Bunkers-Fuel oil. ("To bunker" is to take on fuel oil.)

Cargo runners-Wire ropes for hoisting cargo.

Cargo slings-Slings which wrap around cargo for hoisting.

Celestial Navigation-Finding ship's position by means of sun, moon, planets, and stars.

Chandler-Store that supplies ships.

Charter Party-Legal contract leasing ship.

Chief Steward-Seaman in charge of the galley and its crew.

"Chips"-Name for ship's carpenter.

Chronometer-Very accurate clock set to Greenwich time. (Greenwich, England—zero degrees Longitude.)

Clipper Ship-Fast, square-rigged sailing ship. (circa 1860-1890.)

Coaming-Raised edge of cargo hatch.

Cockleshells-Frail, small boats.

Collier-Ship which carries only coal.

Conn-To direct (a ship). Primarily a Navy expression.

Corvette-Small destroyer-type Naval escort.

Crew's Mess-Crew's dining room.

Crosstrees-Platform at the junction of the mast and the topmast. Also point at which the mast meets the topmast.

Crow's nest-Steel, barrel-shaped container fastened high on the foremast to furnish protection from the weather for the lookout.

DF-Same as RDF; Radio Direction Finder.

DWT-Dead Weight Tonnage: The maximum capacity of the ship with full cargo, stores, and crew.

Davits-Steel framework from which a lifeboat is suspended.

Davy Jones's Locker-Mythical place at the bottom of the sea where the souls of drowned sailors rest.

Deck Gang-Able Seamen, Ordinary Seaman, and Bosun.

Deck Houses-Compartments raised above the main deck.

Devil's claws-Iron hooks holding anchor while at sea.

Draft-Depth of ship in the water.

Draw- Advance on wages.

Dry Dock-Facility for ship repair. Water is pumped out after ship enters, leaving the ship's bottom available for repairs.

ETA-Estimated time of arrival.

Faking-Coiling rope in ever-widening circles. Also called flaking" or "Belgian faking."

Falls-Rope reaved through pulleys.

Fan tail-Extreme stern of ship.

Fathom-Six feet.

Fathometer-Instrument to measure water depth by sound signals.

Fiddley-Series of steel ladders extending up from fire room to deck.

Fireman-Seaman who works in boiler room. (Fire room).

"Flags"-Generic name for signal man.

Flying Fort-Four engined bomber used in WW II.

Focsle-Abbreviation for forecastle. Crew's sleeping quarters.

Foredeck- Forward deck of a ship.

Foremast-Mast nearest bow.

Frapping Line-Wrap-around rope to pull staging under the stern or bow. (Staging is planking to sit or stand on while working against the hull of the ship).

Furl-Fold.

Galley-Kitchen.

Gangway-Ladder from the ship to the dock.

Gantline-Rope, usually about 1-inch, rove through a single block.

Gib-Gibralter.

Gimbal-Device that allows a compass or other object to stay level when the ship rolls.

Glass-Barometer.

Great Circle Route-Shortest distance on a sphere.

Greenwich Civil Time (GCT)-Same as Greenwich time. Time at Greenwich, England, used as the basis for the world's standard time.

"Guns"-Generic name for gunnery officer.

Guy-Tackle to hold boom in place.

Gyrocompass-Shows true North (magnetic compass shows magnetic North.)

Halyards-Ropes used to hoist signal flags.

Hatch-Opening in the deck through which cargo is loaded.

Hatch beams-Stiffeners over hatches.

Hatch tarps-Canvas covers over cargo hatches.

Hatch wedges-Tapered pieces of wood driven against hatch tarps with a topping maul. They hold tarps in place.

Hawse pipe stoppers-Iron covers over holes that anchor chains pass through.

Hawser-Mooring line.

Heave the anchor-Hoist the anchor.

Hold-Cargo space.

Hook-The anchor.

Hove- Past tense of heave.

Hove to-Making just enough speed to keep the ship to the wind in a storm.

Jacob's ladder-Rope ladder with wooden steps.

Knot-Rate of speed. Equals one sea mile of 6,080 feet.

Lee side-The side away from the wind. (To "make a lee" is to turn the ship to provide a protected or lee, side. Usually done for an approaching small boat.)

  Lap-straked-Overlapping boards on a small boat.

Lasher-Longshoreman specializing in securing cargo.

Launch-Small, open motorboat. Also, to put a boat in the water.

Liberty ship-A cargo ship built during the World War II era, weighing 10,500 DWT tons. In all, 2700 were built.

Lifelines- Ropes stretched along the decks in rough weather to provide a safety grip.

Lighter-Covered barge.

Limey- Britisher.

Local Apparent Time-Time at the ship at any given location.

Longshoremen-Laborers who load and discharge cargo.

Lyle gun-Small cannon which shoots a line to another ship.

MM&P-Masters, Mates, and Pilots. (Union).

Mainmast-Mast next aft of foremast.

Manifest-Official list of cargo loaded on a ship.

Marlin-Tarred cord, sometimes called "small stuff."

Master- The Captain's legal title.

Mate-Deck officer. (There are Chief Mates, Second Mates, and Third Mates, each with different responsibilities.)

Mercator chart (Mercator Projection)-Type of chart with parallel meridians and increasing parallels of latitude.

Meridian-Line of longitude.

Mess-Dining room. Also applies to the seaman who serves meals.

Mess boy (man)-Dining room waiter (see Mess above.)

Midships-Command to quartermaster to place the rudder on the center line of the ship.

Milreis-Brazilian coin (see Reis).

Mister-Form of address for Mates.

Mizzenmast-Aftermost mast on a three-masted ship.

Niggar head-Revolving spool on winch, used to pull wire and rope. (Not now in good usage.)

Notice to Mariners-Corrections to charts.

Oiler-Seaman who works in the engine room, oiling main engine and auxiliaries.

Oilskins-Foul weather gear (usually overalls, jacket, and hat) Made of an oiled waterproof cloth.

"On the beach-Out of work.

Ordinary seaman-Green hand (just learning).

Pad eye- Steel eye through which a line is run.

Palm-Leather partial glove which covers the palm, serving much as a thimble, protecting the hand from the pressure of large canvas needles.

Pay off-Give the crew their wages after a voyage. Also, receiving those wages.

Pelorus-Dummy compass on the bridge wing, used to take bearings.

Pick-The anchor.

Pilot-Person licensed to guide a ship into and out of a port.

Plimsoll Mark-Design on the side of ship showing the deepest draft to which she can be loaded.

Pontoon-Steel hatch cover.

Poop deck-Raised deck over stern.

Port-Left.

Quartermaster-The seaman who steers the ship.

Quay-Dock (British term.)

RDF-Radio Direction Finder.

Ratlines-Foot ropes used to climb shrouds.

Reciprocating engine-Steam engine with pistons (usually 3).

Reef-To reduce sail area by rolling or folding part of the sail and securing it. Also, that part of the sail that is reduced by this method. Also, rocks, coral, etc. at or just beneath the water's surface.

Reeve-Thread rope through blocks (pulleys).

Reis-Brazilian money (see "milreis").

Righting ability-Ability of a ship to return to upright after rolling.

Roaring Forties-Latitude 40S. Going Southward toward Cape Horn the point at which a sailing ship changed to winter storm sails.

SIU-Seamen's International Union.

STO officer-Branch of British Ministry of War Transport.

Saloon-Officers' dining room.

Schooner-Fore and aft rigged sailing ship, usually having two masts, whose taller mainmast is nearly midships. (Can have up to seven masts).

Sextant-Hand held device for measuring the angular height of a heavenly body above the horizon.

Shackles- 15 fathom lengths of anchor chain.

Shaft tunnel- Propeller shaft covering.

Shell plating-Skin or hull of a ship.

Ship's register-Official document containing information about the ship, such as tonnage, ownership, etc. Similar to a deed.

Shoot the sun (moon, stars)-Take sights on these objects with a sextant.

Shrouds-Heavy ropes or cables supporting the masts.

Single up the lines-Release all mooring lines but two (one forward, one aft).

Skipper-Affectionate title for the Captain.

Sledge-Sledgehammer.

Slop chest-Ship's store.

Snatch block-Block (pulley) that snaps open.

Soogey-Wash paint work with a strong solution.

Sounding-Measurement of water depth.

"Sparks"- Generic name for the radio officer.

Splinter shield-Guard around a naval gun for protection.

Starboard-Right.

Stay-Same as *shrouds*. Heavy wire or rope supporting mast. Also called "forestay."

Stem winder-Ship with engines and accommodations aft.

Steering sweep-Long oar, used to steer a rowboat.

Stevedore-Boss longshoreman.

Steward-Cook.

Stokes stretcher-Wire stretcher used to transport the injured.

Stores-Supplies.

Swallow the anchor-Quit the sea and come ashore.

Taffrail-Railing around the stern.

Tail-Provide pressure by pulling on a line.

Tanker-Ship carrying oil.

"The Old Man"-The Captain. Used only behind his back.

Ticket-License. (Master's ticket, Mate's ticket, etc.)

Time ticks-Radio signals sent out over government radio. Can be heard all over the world. Consists of 59 ticks per minute; 60th tick is silent.

Topping lift-Wire tackle holding up cargo boom.

Topping maul-Sledge hammer with point on one end.

Tramp-Ship with no fixed itinerary.

Trolley line-Line rigged between two ships at sea on which objects are passed by means of a pulley from one ship to the other.

Turnbuckle-Tightening device using screw threads and a swivel.

'Tween decks-Upper compartment of a cargo hold.

Vernier-Fine adjustment screw on a sextant.

Victory ship-Improved version of the Liberty ship.

WACS-U.S. Women's Army Corp.

War Shipping Administration-Federal agency which built and allocated ships during WWII.

Watch-Duty period for seamen, consisting of four hours on, eight off. Also, the seamen on duty during a watch.

Watch partners-Two, sometimes three, seaman who stand a watch together.

Watertender-Seaman who works in the fire room.

Way-Motion or speed of a ship through the water.

Weather side-The side of a ship toward the wind.

Well deck-That part of the main deck that is forward of the poop deck and aft of the focsle head.

United States Shipping Board-Government organization which built ships during WWI.

Winch-Steam or electric engine used to hoist cargo.

Windlass-Winch used to hoist anchor.

Yard-Place where ships are built or repaired.

Zone time-Time based on Greenwich Mean Time(GMT), in which time advances or lags behind GMT for each 15 degrees of Longitude East or West of Greenwich.

ABOUT THE AUTHOR

Frank Francis Farrar started out life on dry land in Waltham, Massachusetts. He stayed right there for the early part of his life, graduating from Waltham High School at the age of sixteen. The day he graduated he put his childhood-and dry land-behind him and set sail on the *S.S. Seattle Spirit* as a Deck Boy for the grand sum of $25 a month in wages.

Gaining the post of Able Seaman, he sailed continuously until World War II broke out. He sat successfully for his Chief Mate's ticket in time to take that rank with him through the War. Just at the end of the War, he got his first command, the *S.S. Augustus P. Loring*, a Liberty ship.

Some years later, having come ashore for personal reasons, Captain Farrar went to work for the John W. McGrath Corporation, the country's largest stevedoring and terminals operator. He retired as Vice-President for Operations.

Early in his retirement, Captain Farrar owned and operated a 400 acre dairy farm, milking 80 cows with the assistance of a single hired hand. *("Nursemaid to a bunch of cows!)* He gave that up for real retirement in Melbourne Beach, Florida.

He works daily writing about the sea and ships which have been such an integral part of almost his entire life. He has published stories in *Sea History* and *Sea Classics* magazines. He has recently completed his fourth book, a novel based on recent events concerning The Panama Canal and Manuel Noriega.

Captain Farrar is a marine member of the Council of American Master Mariners. He also has the honor of being a marine member of the Boston Marine Society, the oldest such society in the world. That does not, however, mean that he is the oldest mariner in the world. He is only 77. He is, admittedly, a cat nut, having always been the one who saw to it that the ship's cats were fed. In fact, he and his wife, Dot, share living quarters with a cat. To be ecumenical, they share those quarters with a Yorkshire Terrler as well.

The author today